The God Tube

The God Tube

Uncovering the Hidden Spiritual Message in Pop Culture

JAMES LAWLER

OPEN COURT
Chicago and La Salle, Illinois

To order books from Open Court, call 1-800-815-2280 or visit our website at
www.opencourtbooks.com.

Open Court Publishing Company is a division of Carus Publishing Company.

© 2010 by Carus Publishing Company

First printing 2010

Printed and bound in the United States of America.

Library of Congress Cataloging-in-Publication Data

Lawler, James M., 1940–
The God tube: uncovering the hidden spiritual message in pop culture /James Lawler. p.
cm.
 Summary: "Explores philosophical and religious themes in popular films and television
shows"—Provided by publisher. Includes bibliographical references and index. ISBN 978-0-
8126-9648-6 (trade paper : alk. paper) 1. Religion in motion pictures. 2. Philosophy in
motion pictures. 3. Television broadcasting—Religious aspects. I. Title.
PN1995.9.R4L39 2009
791.43'682--dc22

2008049518

Contents

Introduction

We live in an age of profound, and profoundly entertaining, popular culture. Television shows such as *Buffy the Vampire Slayer* and *The Simpsons* are savvy, ironic, and smartly written, while films like the *Star Wars* saga and the *Matrix* trilogy thrill us with unheard-of special effects, complex and subtle plotlines, and moving relationships among characters. Yet beyond merely providing entertainment, these works of and for the popular imagination also contain unexpected moral and philosophical resonances. The epic fantasy of *Star Wars* returns in essence to the first century CE, imaginatively re-creating the struggle of courageous early Christians who opposed the heartlessness and injustice of the Roman Empire. Believers in freedom and equality, empowered by their connection to a benevolent, all-pervading Force, fight the tyrannical Roman Empire whose God is a dark demon of destruction. The central figure in the fantasy of George Lucas, Anakin Skywalker, is the chosen one of prophecy, a man born miraculously of a virgin, whose task is to restore a lost balance between light and darkness. In his own way, George Lucas, in the six episodes of *Star Wars*, attempts to distill the essence of religion in a way that is not far from the historical truth of early Christianity.

In this book, I argue that fantasy and other fictional worlds are becoming vehicles for a new form of religion, or rather, since the term "religion" is usually associated with institutional establishments and associated dogma, a new spirituality. Such spirituality does not require one to "believe" that the fantasy is literally true, for such literal belief destroys the very essence of fantasy. Fantasy must always remain fantasy, an empowerment of the imagination. The free flight of the imagination is not always a form of escapism from the hard and fast reality supposedly investigated by science. As in Woody Allen's *Crimes and Misdemeanors*, the creations of Hollywood in the darkened dream world of the cinema, momentarily shutting out the harsh light of a dog-eat-dog world, allow us the joy of imagining a new and just world. The creative imagination can offer new visions of moral or spiritual truths of freedom and equality, and human empowerment, against ruling powers demanding conformism to drabness, depression, and oppression. The "Agents" of the

Matrix trilogy literally seal Neo's lips when he attempts to speak his truth. Neo is another Jesus figure in contemporary fantasy. He too was prophesied, longed for, as a savior in a world seeking freedom from imperial powers. But his fundamental message, like that of the early Gnostic Christians explored in *The Da Vinci Code*, is that only people who come together in a spirit of brother- and sisterhood have the power to save themselves.

From *The Simpsons* to *The Da Vinci Code* contemporary culture is raising core, often forgotten or buried issues of the great religions and re-presenting them in new fictional forms. *The Simpsons* contrasts Lisa Simpson's radical egalitarianism of inner moral principle with the Flanders family's reliance on external religious dictums. Bart Simpson's honest devilry, which still somehow knows the difference between right and wrong, is opposed to the pharisaical Jessica Lovejoy, the minister's devious daughter. In *The Simpsons Movie*, Homer Simpson has to be dragged from his couch to church on Sunday morning. But when faced with a family and social crisis, he is guided by an Inuit Shaman woman into a spiritual experience that offers him existential and moral truth. While much has been made of *The Da Vinci Code*'s claim to a degree of factual accuracy, the keeper of hidden secrets and supposed historical truths is a grandmotherly woman who tells us, in the end, that what is important is not the factual truth, but the ideas, and the struggle between opposing ideals, that a narrow concern for factuality ultimately conceals.

In the new weirdness of contemporary culture, where religion is being subsumed and transformed, it is not necessary to leave science behind. When reason is aware of its limits, it points to other forms of consciousness as complementary for a full human life. From Plato to Kant and Hegel, a central current of Western philosophy has argued for the alliance of reason and imagination. A form of reason that rejects imagination, feeling, and the highest aspirations of moral consciousness degenerates into a self-centered utilitarianism that justifies oppressive inequality as the best of all possible worlds.

The first teacher of Socrates, the wise woman Diotema of Mantinea, says that the beginning of philosophical reason, the true opening beyond a narrow, divisive, and destructive pragmatism, requires that future philosophers first fall head over heals in love. The works of Kant and Hegel further develop the Platonic trend of philosophy in the context of modern science and democratic political thought. Through the systematic construction of his three critiques, Kant argues that science finds its proper place and limited truth only when it makes room for the ideal of a world of justice and happiness, which he calls the highest good or the kingdom of ends—echoing the kingdom of heaven on earth that is the core message of Jesus. Such a moral ideal can only be regarded as realizable—against the seemingly invincible power of the prevailing systems of inequality—when our understanding of empirical reality is transfigured through the power of imagination. Hegel called the religion of the Roman Empire the religion of expediency, whose complement is a remote God of power ruling with imperial majesty over an enslaved world. By contrast, the "consummate religion" of Christianity brings the divine back into the world as the bond of love uniting freely associating brothers and sisters. This current of Western philosophy from Plato to Hegel, whose chief ideas are presented in these chapters, ultimately provides a connected and suggestive rational underpinning to certain possibilities of a new spirituality that is explored in contemporary fantasy and fiction.

Two threads accordingly intertwine in the scheme of this book. On the one hand, the gentle reader will explore a stimulating and enjoyable series of episodes in contemporary popular culture that ingeniously translate and transform traditional ideas of religion. On the other hand, from chapter to chapter the gentle but also patient reader will build up a philosophical framework that gives rational justification and penetrating understanding for such imaginative explorations. Each chapter adds a new layer of philosophical thought to the preceding one. The first seven chapters explore, with increasing philosophical complexity, themes of spirituality within fantasy. Chapters 8 through 10 consider the images and ideas of religion directly, primarily those of Christianity. Chapter 8 examines, through the lens of Hegel's philosophy of religion, Mel Gibson's traditional portrait of Jesus as the solitary Savior. But contemporary culture tends to reject this picture for an alternative vision of salvation in which the Savior is not alone, and succeeds in his task only through the cooperation of a beloved companion.

The way is thus prepared for the final two chapters that explore Leonardo da Vinci's alternative portrait of the Jesus of the Fourth Gospel who sits at the side of his Beloved Disciple—who is, we come to see, Mary Magdalene, his sacred bride and equal partner. *The Da Vinci Code* refers this image back to currents in early Christianity that were deeply influenced by Platonic thought. The rediscovery of a suppressed and buried Gospel of Mary Magdalene points beyond the mere fact of a special relationship between Jesus and Mary to philosophical understandings rooted in Plato and carried forward in the so-called Gnostic heresy of the first centuries CE. In the end we recognize that certain currents of contemporary fantasy and fiction have implicitly given expression to a long-suppressed, philosophically rich, alternative image of Jesus. For Neo is nothing without his beloved Trinity, and Anakin Skywalker descends into hell in pursuit of his passion for Padmé. The fantasies of contemporary culture have thus prepared the way for the profound revision of the essence of religion that constitutes the powerful appeal of *The Da Vinci Code*.

1

Between Duty and Desire: Morality in *The Simpsons*

Stealing from the collection basket is really wrong! Even *I* know that.
—BART SIMPSON

Act only on that maxim through which you can at the same time will that
it should become a universal law.
—IMMANUEL KANT

The Ideal Role Model?

In a review of *Harry Potter and the Goblet of Fire* by J. K. Rowling, science fiction author Spider Robinson writes: "Okay, Harry himself is a bit
of a goody-goody . . . in fact, let's admit it: Harry is the AntiBart. But do
you *really* want your own kids to have no better role model than a
Simpson?"[1] As a role model for children, we don't have to choose
between the intrepid opponent of the forces of evil, Harry Potter, and that
bit of a hellion, Bart Simpson. There is also, for example, the role model
presented by Bart's sister, Lisa. *The Simpsons* is not reducible to any one
of its parts but comes in the totality of its perspectives. Failure to recognize the unique moral perspective of Lisa Simpson, while thinking of
morality in the form of the "goody-goody" individual, suggests a narrow
view of moral goodness.

What, then, is moral goodness? According to Immanuel Kant, a central feature of the moral point of view is a commitment to the performance of "duty." The term "duty" itself implies the presence of two

opposing forces. On the one hand, there are our spontaneous desires, feelings, and interests—including our fears and hatreds, our jealousies and insecurities. On the other hand, there is what one believes one ought to do, and the kind of person one ought to be. The term "duty" suggests that these two forces frequently come into conflict, and consequently doing what one ought to do or trying to be what one ought to be can be difficult or painful, involving sacrifices of various kinds. The word "responsibility" involves similar connotations. The responsible person *responds* to some task or requirement that comes from a source other than his normal desires, feelings, or interests. The individual who is committed to maintaining a moral point of view—the ideal moral role model—resolves to subordinate, and to sacrifice if need be, personal desires, feelings, and interests for the sake of duty. She resolves to "do the right thing," as Spike Lee calls his disturbing exploration in film of this topic, or to become the right kind of person.

The key word here is "resolves." The morally committed person has made a fundamental choice. There are two ways one can lead one's life, two general life orientations: to satisfy one's personal or individual wants, desires, needs; and to do the right thing, to do one's duty, which involves *transcending* the level of personal desire and self-interest. There is something exalted about duty, involving a sort of higher destiny that is communicated to the person who has resolved to live according to her duty.

Episodes of *The Simpsons* frequently highlight the conflict between personal desire, feelings, or interests, on the one hand, and the sense of moral duty, on the other. Each member of the Simpson family, including baby Maggie, contributes to the creation of a complex moral atmosphere, in which morality stands out in its significance as duty precisely *because* the contrary exists as well—the passionate desires, feelings, and interests of strong personalities. We will look briefly at the way these themes are played out in the characters of Homer, Bart, and Marge, before focusing on the primary instance of the dutiful moral person, in the character of Lisa. In this exposition it will become clear that the entire Simpson family, together with a cast of their Springfield friends and foes, affirms and ultimately resolves and surmounts the contradictions of duty and desire.

Homer between Moe and Flanders

Sometimes a caricature of the sense of duty underscores this conflict. Homer Simpson exhibits a great ability to rationalize his desires and interests as constituting moral duty itself, so that, sometimes at least, no difficult conflict arises for him. In "Dumbell Indemnity," Moe wants Homer to destroy Moe's automobile so that Moe can collect on his insurance policy. Homer feels intense pressure from the generally egotistical, me-first character, Moe. He is intimidated by the threat of Moe's sharp tongue and so wants to yield to his friend's insistent demand. Moe as a rule puts his own personal desires and interests first and has little or no concern for any conflicting moral duty. By contrast, Homer has a moment of doubt in which he wonders whether or not he is doing the right thing. He consults his "conscience," which takes the form of a mental picture of his wife Marge talking to him. Laughably, "Marge" tells him quite definitively: his duty consists in destroying Moe's car so that Moe can collect on the insurance. His "conscience" thereby satisfied, Homer proceeds with characteristic energy to perform the "dutiful" action.

Though in a satirical manner, the episode clearly raises the moral perspective of duty. Rather than providing a positive role model, Homer Simpson here shows us how *not* to act. We laugh at this caricature of the moral situation, but at the same time we must ask ourselves whether or not our conceptions of moral obligation are not frequently determined by a similar procedure.

Humor at the expense of Homer is no doubt one of the reasons for the great popularity of *The Simpsons*. The audience generally feels superior to Homer, but also subtly attracted to him. His mind is weak, but his heart is in the right place. He wants to do his duty, but he also wants to please his friend and is unwilling to make the sacrifice of this desire that duty, he obscurely feels, requires. In laughing at him, we are also laughing at ourselves—recognizing the common experience of having such mixed feelings. It is in fact not as easy to be superior to Homer as we first imagine. And so the superficial image of duty that Homer conveys impels the audience to make a deeper discrimination. It is in this complexity that *The Simpsons* combines popularity and art. As pop culture it draws in a wide audience. As art it provokes its audience to rise to higher levels of understanding and living.

Homer's moral dilemmas emerge in largely concrete ways, as when he must weigh his love for Marge, and his duty to her as her husband, against appealing personal pursuits such as his love for fishing. Homer truly wants to be a good father and husband, but the appeal of personal pleasures continually drives such dutiful thoughts out of his head. In "War of the Simpsons," after a particularly flagrant demonstration of Homer's thoughtlessness (after having too much to drink at a neighborhood party, Homer makes embarrassing sexual overtures to the puritanical Mrs. Flanders), Marge persuades Homer to attend a weekend marriage counseling session at Catfish Lake, led by the Reverend

Lovejoy. Although he recognizes the marital problem he has created, Homer is mainly motivated by the possibility of catching the legendary giant catfish, "General Sherman," "five hundred pounds of bottom-dwelling fury."

Homer's heart is in the right place; he truly wants to repair his relationship with Marge. But his heart is also in another place, with the giant catfish and the possible glory involved in capturing this prize. There is duty, and there is desire. When Marge is there before him, he hears the voice of duty, and feels ashamed of himself for not being a better husband to her. But when she is not there, the siren song of desire for adventure wells up within him. Surely, he thinks, he can have it both ways, and combine duty with desire.

Early on their first morning, Marge catches Homer, in full fishing regalia, trying to sneak out of their cabin. She is upset. How can he possibly think about fishing when their marriage is at stake? Sincerely ashamed once more as a result of Marge's stern face of duty, Homer renounces his plan to go fishing, and takes a walk along the lakeside instead. Seeing that someone has left a fishing pole behind, Homer conscientiously picks up the pole to return it to its owner. At that instant, General Sherman takes the bait that is attached to the line with a force that hurls Homer into a rowboat and drags him out to the middle of the lake.

Homer has not broken his pledge to Marge, and yet circumstances have so conspired that he gets to do what he wants anyway. Is there a lesson in this result? If we resolve to do our duty no matter what, should not our desires also be fulfilled? Shouldn't the universe respond to our desires as long as we remain within the bounds of duty? Isn't this the key to happiness—not doing what we want to do, but being ready to sacrifice our desires for the sake of duty, and then finding them mysteriously fulfilled?

There ensues an epic battle of will and strength between man and beast, a lonely and heroic struggle out of Ernest Hemingway's *Old Man and the Sea*. Through such evocation of classic literature, *The Simpsons* engages the higher mind of the audience, and through the appeal of popular culture and its comedy, the audience is inspired to rise to the tragic heights of great art.

Finally victorious, Homer returns to shore with great expectations of lasting fame as history's greatest fisherman, only to find a furious Marge charging him with utter selfishness. Face to face once again with the choice between selfish desire and moral duty, Homer does the right thing: he renounces fame for family and returns the gasping General

Sherman, the audience is glad to see, to his home in the watery depths. No animals have been seriously harmed in this episode. In surmounting such powerful impulses of personal desire, Homer transmutes his physical exploit into a truly great feat of moral heroism. Homer recognizes his dutiful sacrifice: "I gave up fame and breakfast for our marriage."

At the other pole from Moe is Ned Flanders, who wears his Christian uprightness and morality quite proudly on his sleeve. Flanders is also at the counseling session with his wife. In the variety of morality-related motifs in *The Simpsons*, Ned Flanders plays a special role. The Flanders family has taken their morality from religion, and follows a moral code derived from traditional religious motives. The question of religious morality is posed with characteristic humor, for, as model Christians, the Flanders should not even have marital problems. What is the problem with *their* marriage, if such a question is thinkable? It seems that Ned's wife sometimes underlines in *his* copy of the Bible!

Flanders is an important figure in the moral universe of *The Simpsons*, as he represents morality gone overboard, morality that no longer involves a conflict with personal desires and interests because Flanders no longer apparently *has* personal desires and interests. In this respect, Flanders is the opposite of Moe. For there to be a real sense of moral duty, there must be two forces, not just one: an awareness of moral duty as well strong desires for all the things that normally make a person happy. It is precisely because of the person's strong desire for happiness that doing the right thing so often takes the form of a hard duty and involves self-sacrifice.

Whereas Moe is decidedly out for himself, Flanders has no personal desires whatsoever. His life is guided from the outside, not from inner spontaneous urges and longings. In his caricature of a kind of religious morality, Flanders's life consists in following divinely commanded dictates at every moment. This point is humorously brought home in "Viva Ned Flanders," when the rather youthful looking Flanders confesses that he is actually sixty years old. The reason for his youthful appearance, Homer tells him, is that he hardly has a life of his own. Regretfully accepting this analysis, he appoints Homer as his instructor on how to live. The outcome of any scheme devised by Homer is of course disastrous, in this case involving a drunken double wedding in Las Vegas. Homer's passion for immediate personal gratification is the inverse of Flanders's moralistic failure to "get a life." Neither has much of a sense of the limits to their respective approaches to life. And both derive their morality from external sources. For Flanders, barely living this life because he is mentally occupied with the next one, this source is his Book of Rules, the voice of God outside him in the external forms and teachings of religion. For Homer, immersed in life with all its potential comforts and amusements, morality also derives from an external source, but in the personal form of the judgments, real or imagined, coming from his wife Marge.

In its subversive way, *The Simpsons* asks us to think about the nature of religion, and of the relation between religion and morality. If morality is about the conflict between duty and desire, as Kant argues, what we might call external religion actually undermines this moral perspective. External religion propounds a series of moral rules of behavior as commanded by an external deity with the power to punish us if we disobey him. On the other hand, should we follow his rules—and this God is definitely a He, not a She—we will be rewarded with eternal life. Behind its promotion of the dutiful way of life, against selfish and sinful desires, the real motivation in the heart of the faithful follower is a narrow egotism: I don't want to be punished; I want the maximum amount of happiness. Such a person, who never does wrong and follows all the rules, does so in order to reap the rewards attached to such behavior and to avoid the penalties that go along with violation. He is like the browbeaten child who acts always in fear of a punitive parent, or like the spoiled child who manipulates her parent at every step to solicit promises of rewards. The carrot-and-stick approach to life emphasizes for one the carrot and for the other the stick, and perhaps most often oscillating back and forth between these equally external motivations. Here is the deeper secret of Ned's youthful looks: because of such religion, he remains forever the obedient child with no life of his own.

Even Bart Knows That's Wrong

Bart Simpson has a lot of his father in him. His is the devil-may-care attitude of the fun-loving, trouble-seeking boy. In "Bart's Girlfriend," Bart develops a compulsive infatuation with Reverend Lovejoy's daughter Jessica. At first Bart thinks he has to convert to Sunday school piety in order to win the affections of the minister's daughter. But Jessica only becomes interested in Bart when she thinks she recognizes in him a possible partner in crime.

In the Reverend Lovejoy's daughter we see the dark side of a purely external religion. Forced to conform externally to the behavior prescribed by her father and his religion, Jessica has become an expert in disguising her real desires and in employing a religious façade to achieve them. Where morality is derived from a religious orthodoxy and reduced to external behaviors, appearances, poses, pretences, and even simulated attitudes of love and joy, inner egotism can develop unchecked. Jessica is a monster of egotism in its religious form. If Moe is a straightforward, no-nonsense egotist—capable at times of genuine fellowship, good will, and sage, practical advice for his friends and customers—Jessica is the whitened sepulcher of which Jesus spoke: "which on the outside appear beautiful, but inside they are full of dead men's bones. . . . "[2]

This episode illustrates the possibilities for *moral hypocrisy* when morality is identified with conformity to an external code of behavior. As the minister's daughter, Jessica plays the role of the "goody-goody" child for all that it is worth. She hypocritically plays on the appearances of conventional morality to secure her selfish desires. Such hypocrisy should not be so unexpected, since the religion of her father is essentially about getting one's desires satisfied and avoiding punishments by conforming to rules of behavior set by an all-powerful external authority. Such morality does not spring from an inner source within the individual herself. Jessica is an expert at presenting the external moral picture, and her father and others in the congregation are happy with her performance. Isn't this then what really matters? Implicitly, *The Simpsons* raises deeper questions about the nature of any religion that could produce such results.

Bart, who at first believes in Jessica's religious performance, can surely also play the religious hypocrite to achieve his ends. But with Bart, unlike Jessica, there are limits, a sense that enough is enough, that fun and games and a prankish joy in breaking the rules should not go too far. There are rules and there are rules. Some rules can be broken: those of the conventions of society, of external appearances that wants spiked hair tamed down to a uniform conformity. There are however important rules that shouldn't be broken, that is, the rules of a real morality. As Jessica steals from the collection basket in church, Bart does his best to oppose the theft: "Stealing from the collection basket is really wrong!" Bart tells her. "Even *I* know that." *How*, we might ask, does Bart know this? Clearly, it is not from the kind of external religion in which Jessica was raised.

When Bart gets blamed for the theft, he asks Jessica why he should protect her. She replies: "Because, if you tell, no one will believe you. Remember I'm the sweet, perfect minister's daughter, and you're just yellow trash." Jessica here evokes the conventional rules of society for which membership in one's social class is regarded as an indicator of moral goodness and badness. Jessica is a notch or two above Bart on the social scale. In the court of public opinion, the word of Bart the well-known troublemaker and associate of low-class roughnecks is no good against that of Little Miss Perfect, the Minister's Daughter. Jessica knows how society judges these matters, and uses its superficial standards to her nefarious ends. Repeatedly, *The Simpsons* challenges the conventional values of our society.

When push comes to shove, Bart knows that certain things are wrong. He does not know *how* he knows this. He does not refer to an image of his mother, or to a book of rules. He just knows this "from his heart." Morality is something internal with him, not external as it is for his father, who looks to Marge for guidance, or for Flanders, who studies his carefully underlined Bible. Because of his usual devilishness, Bart's periodic acknowledgements of duty may more effectively underline the real nature of morality than would be the case with a conventionally well-behaved child. In "Bart the Mother," Bart experiences a moving crisis of conscience when his thoughtless antics lead to the death of a mother bird. Bart decides to devote himself entirely to the raising of the parentless eggs, uncharacteristically sacrificing his usual pleasures for the sake of his demanding charges. Life has its way of turning the best of intentions, perhaps especially when grounded in emotional impulse, into the path to hell. When it turns out that the eggs contain bird-eating reptiles, banned by federal law, Bart stands by his charges. He tells his mother, "Everyone thinks they're monsters. But I raised them, and I love them! I know that's hard to understand." Marge replies with delicate irony: "Not as hard as you think."

As humor stems from the contrast between normal expectations and actuality, it is humorous to see Bart in this uncharacteristic role of the dutiful mother, giving up his normal carefree life for his shell-covered dependents. We also see a deeper Bart than usual, one capable of real regret for thoughtless deeds. He plunges into the action that such feelings inspire in him without much thought of outcome. He is capable of recognizing the evil of killing the innocent birds. He would not kill them intentionally. Even Bart knows that's wrong. And so when he sees what he has done, he tries to make recompense. We are carried along sympathetically with this turnabout for Bart, until we see even further unintended consequences. When the birds turn out to be killer lizards, the fickle morality of public opinion quickly takes sides against Bart. In the end, the plot line further thickens, fortunately for Bart. Bart's lizards decimate the pesky pigeon population of Springfield and Bart is celebrated as a town hero.

How does public opinion judge in these matters? The public is at the same time the audience, and we are taken for a ride as far as our moral judgments are concerned. At first we are pleased with Bart's healthy, boyish activism, as he concocts new adventures for himself involving BB guns and birds. Good Bart! But then the mother bird is accidentally killed. Bad Bart! Bart however takes on the mother role, tenderly caring for his defenseless eggs despite all the sacrifices motherhood demands of him. Once more Bart is in our good books. But when the birds turn out to be predators that are dangerous to a fragile ecology, and Bart still stands by them, we turn against him once again. Bad Bart! But as chance would have it, the results turn out to be good as his surrogate progeny devours Springfield's pigeon population. Who cares about pigeons that dirty up the city? Bart is a benefactor of the town.

In this sequence of events and changing moral judgments, we observe a morality based on calculation of the good and evil consequences of an action. If the results are good, the action is good. We weigh up the consequences, as these seem good or evil to us, and judge the individual's action accordingly. This way of thinking is a utilitarian morality, expressed by the notion that "the end justifies the means." The end, or result, is what counts, and whatever means lead to that end are justified accordingly. You can't make an omelet without breaking eggs.

Lisa, however, has a different way of looking at Bart's action. "I don't get it, Bart," says sister Lisa. "You got all upset when you killed one bird, but now you've killed tens of thousands, and it doesn't bother you at all." Lisa looks to the principles on which Bart has acted, and sees the contradiction between them. It's wrong to kill a bird. Fair enough. But when it's your beloved dangerous predators that are doing the killing, and you are protecting them, then you are responsible for killing thousands of birds. Where is the consistency in that? First it was bad to kill birds, but now it's OK?

Lisa exposes the problem with "Bart the mother," and with any mother who exclusively protects her children without considering the children of other mothers. Lisa looks for a universal principle, one that can be followed consistently with respect to all her actions. But Bart cannot follow her in her quest. He allows his newfound fame for killing pigeons to smother concern for whatever moral principle underlay his original actions—if it was indeed a principle at all. Bart has returned to his usual nonmoral mode and can hardly focus his mind on Lisa's ecologically relevant paradox. Lisa, on the other hand, transcends the limited morality of the mother who will do anything for the sake of her offspring. She also goes beyond a morality of consequences—the ethical stance of utilitarianism—that can shift back and forth in its evaluations as new consequences unexpectedly emerge. She evokes a different kind of morality: a morality of principle. We will come back to Lisa's morality after we look at the morality of her mother.

Marge Stands Up for Herself

Marge is characteristically submerged in her role as the conventional wife and mother without a life of her own. She becomes the focus of a high level of moral awareness when she challenges and rises above her conventional upbringing. We have duties to ourselves as well as to others, Kant insists. We have an obligation to develop the talents within us to the best of our ability. The path to independent self-development can, under certain circumstances, be a painful moral duty. It takes courage to stand up for your own personal development when social pressures and upbringing insist on service, and subservience, to others. Thus the great moral case of feminism is often put forward by Marge precisely because she is so much the traditional housewife. In the episode, "Reality Bites," borrowing from the film "Glengarry Glen Ross," Marge takes a job as a real estate agent. Her family takes her selfless services for granted, and she has had enough. She too is a person, with a right to a life of her own. Marge wants a career in which she can prove her value and abilities to herself, to her family, and to the larger society of Springfield.

As she is introduced to her colleagues in the business, we see that she is getting into a cutthroat, dog-eat-dog world. One agent venomously defends her rights to the West Side, while an older man, looking like a broken Jack Lemmon, is on the verge of complete personal demolition. Marge is unconscious of this environment at first, as she enthusiastically and proudly dons the spiffy red jacket of her company. The trouble is, Marge sincerely wants to help her customers and is prepared to sacrifice her own interests for the sake of her perceived duty. Trusting Marge, friends and neighbors defer to her opinion. Responding to that trust, Marge cannot help telling them what she actually thinks about the houses they are interested in buying. Marge is nothing if not honest with her customers—with whom she feels the ties of friendship in this tightly connected community—and as a result she doesn't make the sales that ensure her a continued place in the company. She fails to be "a closer."

Marge defends her approach to the suave manager, Lionel, by quoting the company's moral principle and slogan: "Well, like we say, 'The right house for the right person!'" Lionel replies: "Listen, it's time I let you in on a little secret, Marge. The right house is the house that's for sale. The right person is anyone." "But all I did was tell the truth!" says Marge. "Of course you did," says Lionel. "But there's the truth" (here he frowns and shakes his head negatively) "and the truth" (here he looks cheerful and shakes his head positively). A sale could be made if she would only put her product in the right light: call a tiny, cramped house "cozy," describe a ramshackle, falling-down dump "a handy-man's dream," and so forth.

Marge is unconvinced, but eventually she must face the option: either fail at her job, or do some shading of the truth. In the conflict between personal interest and moral duty, we see how, because of underlying structures of competitive social organization, she is pressured into choosing personal interest. Changing her approach, then, Marge makes a big sale while concealing from the naïvely trusting Flanders family the fact that there was a brutal murder in the house they are buying. She tries to find pleasure in the possession of Flanders's check, the sign of her success in her chosen career, the tribute to her worth as a person. But she feels guilty for what she believes is a betrayal of duty. Marge knows that it is wrong to tell a lie, that in concealing or shading the truth, she is betraying the trust placed in her by her customers. We aren't sure how Marge knows such things. That's not important as this moral truth is so obvious, both to her and to us.

We also recognize that Lionel's pretence of reconciling business and morality is insincere about the latter. At bottom, for him, is the bottom line—the sheer self-interest of *homo economicus*. But he must be careful here, because the laws and customs of the land embody some concern for the rights of the consumer, and so it is necessary to play a game with the truth. In this way, *The Simpsons* takes on fundamental questions regarding the morality of the modern capitalist economy. What principles actually govern economic life, and what principles ought to govern it?

These questions are closely tied up with what Kant calls "the highest good."[3] This tells us, Kant says, that people ought to do their duty in life and be rewarded accordingly. It's the honest people who should be closing the deals and earning the good incomes, while the dishonest ones should soon discover the error of their ways. Crime doesn't pay—or at least it shouldn't. A truly good society would be one in which such connections between duty and happy consequences are the normal case, rather than the exception to the rule. In this relationship, duty is not whatever brings about the desired consequences. That is Lionel's approach to life, and that of utilitarian morality: whatever produces the good consequences, especially for yourself or your group, is your "duty." The moral person, however, does her duty because it is her duty, whatever the consequences. And yet, it is ultimately unjust, we think, that the consequences of her doing her duty should be negative. Kant puts the relation between duty and consequences this way: we should not do our duty *because of* good consequences or rewards, or to avoid punishments. Nevertheless, rewards should *result from* the performance of duty, and punishments from its neglect or violation. In fact, however, the world we live in does not seem to support such principles of moral justice. This conflict between the requirements of morality, and the way the world actually works, is one of the major problems that moral consciousness must face. Marge unhappily runs up against such injustice.

Unwilling to achieve her reward at the expense of others, Marge's sense of duty ultimately triumphs over desire and self-interest. She decides to risk sacrificing everything she has aspired to, and goes back to her customers with the whole story about the murder that occurred in their new house. It turns out that her expectation of the Flanders's response is quite wrong. They are delighted with the excitement of living in a house with such an interesting, gruesome history. Paradoxically, in this case complete honesty would have been, from the very beginning, the best policy. After some initial fluctuation, Marge finally does her duty for the sake of duty, and still achieves her personal goals. Isn't this the way life should always work? Why should doing the right thing so often result in personal sacrifice?

Here we see the morality of the highest good in action: If you do the right thing, you ought to be rewarded. This feature of morality may seem to contradict what we said earlier about the tension and possible conflict between duty and desire. But this initial tension should only be provisional, Kant argues. Ultimately, in the long run, moral duty and personal happiness ought to be reconciled. The "highest good" and supreme moral duty is to create a world in which happiness arises out of the performance of moral duty. People who do their duty ought to be rewarded; self-centered people who pursue their goals at the expense of others ought to be punished.

Just as we are led to adopt this comfortable and consoling moral conclusion, Homer, on a parallel escapade involving a struggle over a car, crashes his automobile into the newly sold house. Emerging from the resulting rubble, Flanders turns to Marge and asks, "Do you still have that check?" Marge resignedly hands it over and he tears it up.

The lesson? Do what you ought to do whatever the consequences. Success in a career is not the most important thing in life. Marge returns to the bosom of her family amidst cheers and, at long last, respect. By her ultimate commitment to moral principle she achieves an even higher reward than a big sale—the happiness that comes from experiencing the love and respect of her family. And so we periodically catch glimpses of the "highest good," the unity of duty and happiness, in such luminous moments of the Simpson household.

Lisa Stands Up for Principle

Dutiful moral consciousness is most graphically depicted in the character of second-grader Lisa Simpson. Lisa has an acute sense of moral duty. Hers is not, however, the self-assured, institutionally based morality of Flanders, confident in the authority of his Bible and church. Hers is not an externally based morality. But neither is it the instinctive morality of her brother, closely allied as it is to unconscious feelings that somehow draw the line with him between good fun and moral goodness. Lisa's morality arises out of precocious personal reflection on the great themes of moral life: truthfulness, helping others in need, a commitment to human equality and justice. Lisa shows us how difficult it can be to live up to such principles in the face of thoughtless conventional compromises with the status quo. This conflict with conventional viewpoints points to another central characteristic of authentic morality, according to Kant. Morality is essentially inner-determined. It arises out of inner personal standards of evaluation, rather than from external social conventions or authoritative religious teachings. This is true in various ways for Bart, Marge, and Lisa. Indeed, even Homer, who looks to Marge for his moral guidance, has internal morality. He does not rely on Marge's judgment because she is a moral authority. Instead, he takes her as his voice of morality because he loves her, because she is truly his other half. But for Lisa, morality becomes fully conscious. It involves clarity and consistency in the principles by which a person lives her life.

In "Lisa the Iconoclast," Lisa discovers that the legendary and supposedly heroic founder of Springfield was actually a vicious pirate who tried to kill George Washington. Lisa receives an "F" for her essay, "Jebediah Springfield: Superfraud." Her teacher explains: "This is nothing but dead white male bashing by a P.C. thug. It's women like you who keep the rest of us from landing a husband." Lisa is merely trying to tell the truth, as she has discovered it. This is not the varnished truth of the selling profession, but objective, historical, scientific truth, to be defended as an inherent value, no matter what the consequences and no matter what the sacrifices.

Some truths about founders, however, need to be upheld *against* contemporary practices. In "Mr. Lisa Goes to Washington," Lisa discovers that a certain politician is on the payroll of private moneymakers. Lisa attempts to expose this perversion of the founding ideals of American democracy. She takes her case to Thomas Jefferson himself, who speaks to her from his monument. As usual, Lisa takes a stand for principle and suffers for it. The easier path is to go along with the crowd, not make waves, and turn a blind eye. But Lisa fights City Hall.

Committed to fulfilling her duty as determined by consistent principles, Lisa continually raises difficult questions. Is it right to eat meat, and so cause suffering and death to innocent animals? In "Lisa the Vegetarian," Lisa identifies the lamb chop on her plate with the sweet, defenseless lamb in the children's zoo. She generalizes from this experience and militantly adopts vegetarianism. In standing up for consistent principles, she again exemplifies a central aspect of Kant's moral theory, which requires that we thoughtfully examine the principles of our actions and eliminate contradictions between them. If it is wrong to harm a helpless animal in a zoo, how can it be right to condone the slaughter of an animal that is like it for our eating pleasure?

This is one way to understand Kant's formulation of his categorical imperative: "Act only on that maxim through which you can at the same time will that it should become a universal law."[4] With his categorical imperative, Kant proposes a method for checking the morality of our actions. How do we *know* whether our moral ideas are valid and true? This question introduces a second aspect of moral theory—how to decide about the rightness or wrongness of our intended actions. This is the aspect that is normally primary in the minds of most people when confronted with questions about morality. But before we can ask ourselves whether something is indeed our duty, we should first examine the experience of duty itself. In our discussion up to this point we have been concentrating on the nature of moral experience as a matter of duty. The starting point of moral theory, according to Kant, is an *experience*—the experience of duty, the experience of *having* to do something without necessarily *wanting* to do it. Once we understand that morality involves a sense of duty, we can better *understand* what our duty is. Understanding goes beyond feeling. Bart first *feels* the demands of duty before he thinks about them, and he acts on the feeling without doing too much thinking about why he does so. Bart *feels* that it is wrong to steal from the collection plate. But surely some perceived duties may be mistaken, such as Bart's alleged duty to protect his lizards when they threaten the ecosystem. Can we go by feelings alone in deciding what our duty is?

How Do We Know What Is Our Duty?

In Kant's own time, the British moral philosophers from Hutcheson to

Hume ascribed morality to a distinctive moral feeling or moral sense. Reason, Hume argues, cannot move us to action, and so, because morality *does* move us to action, it must not be based on mere reasoning. It must be a feeling of some sort. A major problem with this theory is that feelings are ordinarily regarded as effects in us of external physical causes. A theory of morality that bases morality on *such* feelings leads to determinism, and determinism is in direct contradiction to the freedom of choice that is the basis of authentic moral responsibility. And yet duty is experienced first of all as a special kind of feeling. So to be compatible with freedom of choice, it must be a feeling that arises out of an internal, not an external cause. This cause, Kant argues, is our common humanity, which is the reality behind our very ability to think. Hence when we think about what we are doing we are expressing our essence as human beings. By being consistent with the principles of our thinking we are expressing our solidarity with the humanity that is in and around us. This underlying solidarity with humanity produces a feeling within us that we experience as duty—the duty to put humanity ahead of purely private or personal desires and interests.

A second problem with the theory of moral feeling is that appeal to a brute feeling of duty provides the moral individual with no way of validating his perception of what moral duty requires. Since the subjective feeling of duty arises from within us out of the reality of our shared humanity, such feelings must ultimately conform to fundamental standards of human rationality. Moral duty is rooted in something more that mere reasoning by itself—something that makes us deeply interested in morality. This is our common or shared humanity, which can be extended to our solidarity with all sensing, feeling beings, including lambs. Reason *corroborates* this moral feeling, which actually moves us to act, with objective standards of universality and moral necessity that provide intellectual validation for our truly moral feelings. Only those feelings that can pass the tests of moral reasoning can be regarded as morally legitimate ones. Kant puts his conception of moral feeling succinctly when he writes near the conclusion of his *Groundwork for the Metaphysics of Morals*:

> The subjective impossibility of explaining the freedom of the will is identical with the impossibility of discovering and explaining an interest which man can take in the moral law. Nevertheless he does actually take an interest in it, the basis of which in us we call the moral feeling, which some have falsely assigned as the standard of our moral judgement, whereas it must rather be viewed as the subjective effect that the law exercises on the will, the objective principle of which is furnished by reason alone.[5]

Conflicting conceptions of duty spur us on to thinking about how to tell whether our perceived or felt duties are in fact real or illusory. Kant gives the following method for testing the validity of one's perceived duties: (1) Ask yourself what the "maxim" or principle of your action is. (2) Ask yourself whether you can consistently affirm this maxim as a "universal law." Can you, for example, commit yourself to the law that would be implicit in the maxim that justifies stealing? Such a maxim might be: "I should steal whenever it is to my advantage and I can get away with it." When you formulate the maxim of your action as a law, you generalize that maxim. Ask yourself in clear consciousness whether you can consistently put yourself under your maxim when you regard it as a universal law. The law would be something like: People in general should be able to steal from one another whenever it suits them, or whenever they can get away with it. But surely, even Jessica Lovejoy does not want to live under such a law. Jessica will steal from others, but she doesn't approve of people robbing *her*.

Lisa looks at the maxim of meat-eating and finds that she cannot will it as a law: Kill animals for human consumption. She can't will this law because she loves animals. From her love, she naturally wants their happiness, and to protect them. How then can she condone killing them for the pleasure, or the health, of herself and others? Sitting down at the dinner table with her lamb chops, the contradiction in her own beliefs suddenly stares her in the face: she believes in the beauty and goodness of animals *and* she also believes that it's OK to destroy and eat them. This set of beliefs is profoundly irrational, for the basic law of reason is the law of noncontradiction. Lisa concludes that she must stand up for animal rights, no matter what she suffers in the process. Lisa formulates her duties in terms of principles that she then can defend consciously, to herself and to others. She intellectualizes her morality in a way that others don't. But this doesn't mean that for her morality is *only* a matter of rationality or logical consistency. In the case of the animals, she first feels a kind of solidarity with them, and then she formulates her principle. Intellect reinforces her moral *feeling* of duty; it does not substitute for it. Thus it is necessary to distinguish clearly between the experience of duty, which comes first, and the methods by which we reflect on these experiences, in order to distinguish real from illusory duties. Once principles of morality become formulated, they play a powerful role in the life of the dutiful person.

The Morality of Tolerance

Some people regard morals as simply a matter of rationalizing actions so that they correspond to conventional moral rules. Lionel gives good examples of this kind of rationalizing that has nothing to do with serious moral reflection. But even Lisa can run into trouble on this score, as her commitment to moral principles sometimes blinds her to a deeper moral duty, as the vegetarian episode makes clear.

In fighting for her principles, Lisa ruins Homer's barbecue party. Homer is angry and Lisa feels ostracized from her family and the general community. Hasn't she done the right thing? Why then has she caused so much pain, for others and for herself? She suffers so much that she comes close to giving up on her newfound principle. The sight of sizzling hot dogs in the window of a store beckon to her to abandon vegetarianism and the sacrifices that only seem to multiply. The store, it turns out, belongs to the vegetarian Hindu storeowner, Apu. The "hot dogs" are meatless. Apu invites Lisa to his roof garden where she finds a new community with vegetarians Paul and Linda McCartney. Here, she finally feels that her ideas will be respected. And so she confidently passes judgment on the behavior of others: "When will all those fools learn that you can be perfectly healthy simply eating vegetables, fruits, grains and cheese." But the mild Apu replies, "Oh, cheese!" Lisa quickly recognizes the arrogance of her sense of moral superiority on discovering that others have other and perhaps higher or stricter standards. Some even object to taking vegetables from the earth, which they see as a violent act of tearing a living being from its rootedness in mother earth. Apu advises tolerance for the wide variety of principles and practices that different people affirm. Lisa develops a more subtle moral understanding as a result of this experience: "I guess I have been pretty hard on a lot of people. Especially my dad. Thank you guys."

What did Lisa learn from Apu and the diverse vegetarian community? It's one thing to have principles for oneself. But it's another to impose them on other people. Kant proposes a second formulation of the categorical imperative that must be integrated with the first: "Act in such a way that you always treat humanity whether in your own person or in the person of any other, never simply as a means, but always at the same time as an end."[6] If the general principle of morality is that one should be able to will the maxims of one's actions as universal laws, this implies that each individual is at the same time a universal being—connected to a universal humanity. This is true of each and every one of us by virtue of our humanity—that is, that which is universal in us. It is because of this universality within each of us that we are able to rise above the small matters of life and concern ourselves with the great ones. Lisa is concerned with the fate of the animal world, and the legitimacy of our exploitation of these beautiful beings. Each human being has this potential connectedness with the loftier demands of life, and by virtue of this fact we owe every human being the deepest respect. And so above all we should respect the humanity in every person. We should respect the fact that other persons too are acting on maxims or principles that they should in their own conscience will as universal laws. No doubt many of them are entangled in inconsistencies and contradictions, and fail to rise to the demands of consistent moral duty. But it is not our responsibility to condemn others for violating standards that we hold for ourselves. Also, given the variety of beliefs people have about the world, a variety of legitimate standards seem possible. Finally, one's own inner motivation is often dark and almost impenetrable, as Freud shows us. How then can we undertake to be the moral consciences of other people?

It is difficult enough for each of us to look to ourselves, and try to live up to those ideals that seem right to us without adopting a censorious attitude toward others. Of course, where other people use extreme acts of violence to achieve their goals, employ harmful deceptions, or break important agreements, society rightly uses the force of the law either to prevent or to punish such actions. But the legal institutions of society are primarily interested in actions, not in the intent that motivates them. It is in the inner intention of the action that its morality lies, not primarily in the outward behavior. Let each person therefore look to her conscience, reflecting on the principles of her own actions, while respecting the other person's own understanding and unique path of life. Lisa is at first adamant that it is immoral to kill and eat animals, but thinks it is OK to live off their milk and eggs, and to destroy the life of root vegetables. She learns that there are other ways of looking at these matters. The early hunting peoples, for instance, recognized the spirit of life in the animal world on which they depended for existence. When they killed the animals whose spirits they recognized as equivalent to their own, were they contradicting themselves? Or did they recognize that we are all involved in a "circle of life," celebrated so beautifully in *The Lion King*. We destroy the body of the animal, but the spirit does not die. And through ritual magic, the people participate in the renewal of life, repaying their debt and fulfilling their duty to the beings whose death gives them life. Lisa's recognition of a contradiction with the principles of her actions opens the way to deeper consideration of her responsibilities to the animal world. She is at the beginning of her path, not at the end. Her

principles will continue to evolve, become more comprehensive and sup-
ple. Recognizing her own fallibility as a moral being, how can she judge
others? Kant's second formulation of the categorical imperative enshrines
this great principle of tolerance and love of humanity, whatever faults others, including the members of her family, seem to have. Let her chide
Bart: "I don't get it, Bart. . . ." Let her express her beliefs about the principles on which to build a better life. But if she adopts an attitude of moral
superiority to other people, all she does, according to Newton's third law,
is to provoke an equal and opposed reaction. It is our respect for the
humanity in each person that creates the best context for that person to
go to a higher level himself. Kant put it this way: "Man is certainly unholy
enough, but humanity in his person must be holy to him."[7]

Lisa's Isolation

Lisa focuses attention on inescapable moral principles and makes people
uneasy with their conventional compromises. Hence she is typically isolated and suffers intensely from her isolation. She yearns for respect and
friendship. She wants to be popular and to be liked. Because she is a
Simpson she is not a goody-goody. She is not someone who finds happiness simply in doing what is acknowledged by all to be good. Like her
brother, Lisa is adventuresome, but her adventures are usually on the
moral rather than on the physical plane. Because of this, moral values
are most sharply highlighted in the Lisa episodes—positively, not negatively as in many of the Homer episodes, with principled consistency
rather than through the role-reversals of her mother.

In "The Secret War of Lisa Simpson," Lisa's moral isolation is graphically illustrated in her encounter with the military academy. Bart is being
sent to a military academy on the theory that strict military discipline will
control his wayward impulses. In Bart's very successful adaptation to the
school we see that this can hardly be the right way to restrain possible
tendencies to delinquency. "My killing teacher says I'm a natural," Bart
boasts. Such moral reflections on conventional social values frequently
shout at the viewer of *The Simpsons*. Is the objection really that there is
not enough morality in this program, or that there is too much morality—
too much of a critical perspective on our society, too much of the Lisa
Simpson outlook?

The episode focuses, however, not on Bart but on Lisa, who insists
that she be enrolled as well. Lisa is looking for the challenge that she
can't find in the dumbed-down curriculum of her school. She is also
standing up for her right as a female to equal treatment with the males.

Her introduction as the first girl in the academy involves moving all the boys out of their sleeping quarters—hardly a good way to gain the acceptance Lisa is anxious to achieve. Alone and facing a hostile male chauvinist environment, Lisa consoles herself with thoughts of Emily Dickinson. She too was lonely and yet was able to write beautiful poetry, she reflects. And then, Lisa recalls, she went crazy as a loon!

Publicly, Bart goes along with the ostracism, afraid to acknowledge his sister. Privately he apologizes: "Sorry I froze you out Lise. I, I just didn't want the guys to think I'd gone soft on the girl issue." However, Bart secretly helps Lisa train at night on "The Eliminator," a rope-crossing exercise at a vertiginous height, "with a blister factor of twelve." Ultimately, Lisa conquers the obstacle, despite shouts of "drop, drop, drop" from the boys. Bart finally stands up to the bullies, a sole but effective voice of encouragement. Even Bart knows it's wrong to abandon a sister. I doubt if such a point could be made as effectively even by Harry Potter.

Lisa's Sorrow and the Saxophone

What makes Lisa more than a goody-goody kid is the fact that she is an acutely sensitive person with a great desire for personal happiness. The conflictual nature of moral duty, with its tendency to require personal sacrifice, is accordingly represented here in all its poignancy. Hers is all the suffering that a commitment to self-determined principle creates in a precocious, sensitive child. Her deep love of life and beauty, played out against a no less profound commitment to truth and goodness, brings on the frustrations and sorrows that she expresses in the woeful, yearning sounds of the jazz saxophone. Kant holds that beauty and art bring into sensuous presence the possibilities of a higher moral life. When actual life seems to pay little or no attention to such possibilities, the doleful cry of Lisa's soul finds an outlet in the wail of a saxophone. In the character of Lisa, the comedy of *The Simpsons* does not allow us to forget a depth of tragedy.

In the episode "Moaning Lisa," Lisa has trouble going along with conventional patriotism. In a music class, instead of playing the simple notes of "My Country 'Tis of Thee," Lisa improvises a soulful jazz solo on her saxophone. "There's no crazy bee-bop in 'My Country 'Tis of Thee,'" the teacher interrupts. "But that's what my country's all about," Lisa momentously declaims. "I'm wailing out for the homeless man living out of his car, the Iowa farmer whose land has been taken away by unfeeling bureaucrats, the West Virginia coal miner, caught. . . ." "That's all well and good," says the teacher, "but, Lisa, none of those unpleasant people are going to be at the recital next week."

A letter is sent home from school, critical for a change of Lisa, not Bart: "Lisa won't play dodge ball because she is sad." The game of dodge ball seems particularly expressive of Lisa's situation. One person is singled out for attack by all the others. Lisa just allows herself to be bombarded, refusing to enter the spirit of the game by defending herself and attacking others. We should remember that this episode was made well before the onslaught of "Reality TV" with its glorification of the Darwinian struggle for survival.

The main problem is that there seems to be no one with whom Lisa can communicate the reasons that she feels are at the root of her melancholy. Bart and Homer are engrossed in ferocious video game slugfests. How can they understand her issues? Lisa tries to explain: "I'm just wondering, what's the point? Would it make any difference at all if I never existed? How can we sleep at night when there's so much suffering in the world?" Homer tries to cheer her up by bouncing her on his knees. Perhaps it's an underwear thing, he later surmises when Marge remarks on her difficult age. Homer has his heart, at least, in the right place.

Lisa's gloomy mood first begins to lift when she hears the plaintive notes of fellow saxophonist, Bleeding Gums Murphy, playing into the night on a lonely bridge in a haunting moon-illuminated cityscape. Murphy's gums bleed because he has never been to the dentist. "I have enough pain in my life," he tells her. Lisa tells about her own pain. "I can't help you with that," he says, "but we can jam together."

Lisa and Bleeding Gums jam together—"I'm so lonely, since my baby left me. . . ." And Lisa responds:

> I got this bratty brother,
> He bugs me every day,
> And this morning my own mother
> Gave my last cupcake away.
> My dad acts like
> He belongs in zoo.
> I'm the saddest kid
> In grade number two.

Marge interrupts the session and commandeers Lisa. "Nothing personal," Marge says to Bleeding Gums. "I just fear the unfamiliar."

Marge, in her persona as the conventional mother, advises Lisa to smile. That was her own mother's advice to her: "Put your happy face on," her mother tells a young Marge, "because people know how good a mom you have by the size of your smile." Lisa says she doesn't feel like smiling. Marge is firm: "Now Lisa, listen to me. This is important. I want you to smile today. It doesn't matter what you feel inside, you know. It's what shows up on the surface that counts. That's what my mother taught me. Take all your bad feelings and push them down, all the way down, past your knees until you're almost walking on them. And then you'll fit in, and boys will like you, and you'll be invited to parties, and happiness will follow."

Lisa, desperate by now for some relief, follows her mother's advice. And it works! "Hey," says one boy, "nice smile." Another tells the first boy, "What're you talking to her for? She'll only say something weird." Lisa just continues to smile. "I used to think you were some kind of braniac," says one of the boys, "but I guess you're OK." "Why don't you come over to my house," says the other boy. "You can do my homework." "OK," says Lisa quaveringly. The teacher appears and says he hopes Lisa won't have "another outburst of unbridled creativity." "No sir," Lisa answers, widely smiling.

Watching this scene, Marge recognizes the error of the traditional teaching, and sweeps Lisa away with squealing tires. "So that's where she gets it," says the teacher, revealing the deeper truth of the relation between Lisa and her mother. Marge apologizes to Lisa. "I was wrong. I take it all back. Always be yourself. You want to be sad, honey, be sad. We'll ride it out with you. And when you get finished feeling sad, we'll still be there. From now on, I'll do the smiling for both of us."

Hearing this affirmation of her own feelings, Lisa genuinely smiles for the first time. At Lisa's suggestion, the entire family goes to the club where Bleeding Gums pays homage to "one of the great little ladies of jazz" and plays Lisa's song. In the company of her happy and supportive family—including baby Maggie sucking rhythmically on her pacifier—Lisa is beaming. The moral of the story? The free, independent, dutiful individual deserves to be happy.

The Kingdom of Heaven on Earth

In this conclusion we catch a glimpse of what Kant calls "the Highest Good (the Kingdom of God),"[8] which he defines as a unity of virtue and happiness in which happiness is "in exact proportion to morality."[9] Kant's equation of "the highest good" with Jesus's term, "the kingdom of God," is an expression of Kant's idea of internally based, moral religion. Kant interprets the Gospels as promoting a *this-worldly* kingdom based on spiritual truth. As Jesus said, "The Kingdom of God is within you."[10]

In such a religion of morality, people do not do their duty for the sake of rewards, or to avoid punishment, as in the perspective of external religion. They do their duty because it is the right thing to do, whatever the consequences that befall them. But in the end, such people ought to be rewarded—not only in the sense that they feel good inside themselves for having done what their consciences require of them, but in the practical sense that their needs are satisfied and their truest desires are realized.

Kant provides a third formulation of the categorical imperative that addresses this complex system of morality and happiness. He calls the society to which morality points both "the kingdom of God" and "the kingdom of ends." Kant writes:

> In the kingdom of ends everything has either a *price* or a *dignity*. If it has a price, something else can be put in its place as an *equivalent*; if it is exalted above all price and so admits of no equivalent, then it has a *dignity*. What is relative to universal human inclinations and needs has a *market price*; what, even without presupposing a need, accords with a certain taste—that is, with satisfaction in the mere purposeless play of our mental powers—has a *fancy price*; but that which constitutes the sole condition under which anything can be an end in itself has not merely a relative value—that is, a price—but has an intrinsic value—that is, dignity.[11]

In Lionel's world of real estate, everything merely has a market price—an equivalent in terms of dollars. There is no dignity there, Marge learns. The dignity of the customer is not respected. He is a means to the end of making money. But in the ideal kingdom of ends, such relative ends, where things have a price, must be subordinated to the higher end, which is the dignity of humanity within each individual. Of course, people need money as a means for getting food, shelter, clothing, and for satisfying other basic needs. To achieve these ends, they express themselves in various ways that we define as work. They express their creativity and at the same time they contribute to the well-being of others. Ideally, they do not perform such creative activities merely for the sake of the money they get as a means to satisfying their basic human needs. Such work merely for the sake of money has no real dignity. It is a form of servitude to external needs. Marge does not work for this reason, but to show others as well as herself that she can be a creative member of society. In this we see the real dignity of labor. But how can there be any dignity when she must demean others, using them merely as means for making money? The check that she receives after what she regards as cheating others is no symbol of the dignity she wished to express. In the kingdom of ends, the kingdom of God in this world, people would be able to work for the sake of expressing their intrinsic dignity as creative human beings, and at the same time their needs would be satisfied.

In a truly just society, people who stand up for duty should also be happy. When Marge stands up for the interests of her customers in the face of pressures from the business world, or when Lisa refuses to cause suffering to animals, or when she wails on her saxophone for the exploited West Virginia coal miner, they willingly sacrifice their personal happiness for the sake of doing their duty. In a good world, the person who does her duty would be rewarded, would have her legitimate needs met, and so would be happy. This is the world as it ought to be, but unfortunately not the world as it generally operates. In a just world, the good, morally dutiful people should be rewarded, and the wicked, the narrow egotists like Lionel who are only out for themselves, would receive their deserved comeuppance.

In the moral world of the Simpson family, such moments of happiness are generally confined to the narrow circle of family and friends. When Marge returns back to the confines of her home, a failure in terms of the laws of self-interest that govern the dog-eat-dog realities of the market place, she is applauded by family and friends. She ultimately achieves the respect she originally wanted, though not in the way she had supposed. Similarly, Lisa finds her moments of happiness in the embrace of family and like-minded friends. Such moments are no doubt too few and far between, but they give the protagonists a glimpse and taste of a better world, encouraging them to keep their own kind of faith—not in an external system of rewards and punishments, but in themselves and in one another, in their true humanity.

At the basis of moral life is the freedom to choose between two radically different ways of life. Persistence in one's fundamental choice requires continually choosing between these two ways of being as our life-choice is tested through difficulties and disappointments. Freedom does not mean arbitrariness, for the life that we choose brings its own necessities. Choice of the ego essentially requires adaptation to outside forces—it is a choice to let external forces choose for us. Kant calls such a way of life "heteronomous," from the Greek word for other, *heteros*, and for law, *nomos*. The egotistical person lives according to laws made by others, or by outside forces, in the hope or expectation that adaptation to such laws will be beneficial to oneself. The choice to live according to our shared humanity, the choice of duty, also brings its necessities, its laws. But such laws are self-determining, autonomous, from the Greek word *autos*.[12]

NOTES

1. *The Globe and Mail,* July 15, 2000, D14.

2. Matthew 23:27, in The New American Standard Bible, http://www.olive-tree.com, accessed 12/18/06.

3. Immanuel Kant, *Critique of Practical Reason* (New York: Macmillan/Library of Liberal Arts, 1993), 117.

4. Immanuel Kant, *Groundwork of the Metaphysics of Morals,* trans. H.J. Paton (New York: Harper Torchbooks, 1964), 88.

5. Immanuel Kant, *Fundamental Principles of The Metaphysic of Morals,* trans. Thomas Kingsmill Abbott, http://oll.libertyfund.org/Texts/Kant0142/PracticalReason/HTMLs/0212_Pt02_Principles.html. Also see the Paton translation in Kant, *Groundwork,* 128.

6. Kant, *Groundwork,* 96.

7. Kant, *Critique of Practical Reason,* 91.

8. Kant, *Critique of Practical Reason,* 135.

9. Kant, *Critique of Practical Reason,* 117.

10. Luke 17:21, in The New King James Version, http://www.olivetree.com, accessed 12/18/06.

11. Kant, *Groundwork,* 102.

12. This chapter is an expanded and revised version of James Lawler, "The Moral World of the Simpson Family: A Kantian Perspective," published in *The Simpsons and Philosophy,* ed. William Irwin, Mark T. Conard, and Aeon J. Skoble (Chicago: Open Court, 2001), 147–59.

2

From Illusion to Reality: The Matrix of the Good Society

The Matrix is everywhere. It is all around us, even now in this very room.
—MORPHEUS

If therefore the highest good is impossible according to practical rules, then the moral law that commands that it be furthered must be fantastic, directed to imaginary ends, and consequently inherently false.
—IMMANUEL KANT

Two Theories of Illusion

In what is arguably the most powerful scene in *The Matrix*, we see endless transparent towers containing artificially cocooned, naked, and wired human bodies. This, we discover with a shock, is reality. Everything else that seemed to transpire to this point in the story, as people come and go, living their humdrum and/or frantic lives in our modern urban beehives, is appearance, dream, illusion.

From ancient times, philosophers from Plato to Buddha, from Descartes to Kant, have been asking us to consider whether our supposed real world may be hardly more than a shadow of the true reality. Perhaps the most sophisticated set of arguments to the effect that the world we see around us is a "mere appearance" is found in the work of Immanuel Kant. Kant argues that even the so-called objective properties of modern physics rest on subjective human projections. Although there is a reality that somehow plays a part in the constitution of the appearances and the phenomena of experience, this reality is not to be found in the realm of sensible appearances. The world we see and feel around us involves the projections of human consciousness. It is not the solid, independently existing reality we think it to be.

Kant reformulates the ancient doctrine of Plato in the framework of modern times and modern science. In Plato's allegory of the cave, individuals have been chained to a bench all their lives. Unknown to them, cut-out figures of objects are passed before a flame located behind them and the shadows of the figures are projected on the wall they are facing. Fixed immovably to their places, unaware of the source of light behind them, the prisoners watching these shadow projections take what they see for the true reality. In more modern times, Descartes asks us to imagine that a malicious demon has trapped us in a dream world of its own making. After all, when we are dreaming, we take what happens for reality. How do we know that we are not dreaming now in our so-called waking state?

Who is responsible for this hoax perpetrated on the human audience? In the scenarios of Plato and Descartes, the cause of the illusion comes from outside the victims of the illusion. For Kant, however, it is not some external being that creates the illusory appearances. We human beings deceive ourselves. We ourselves project outwardly the images fashioned within our own perceptual activity, and then mistakenly attribute to our projections an independent reality. By failing to recognize our ability to shape the forms of our experience, we alienate our own creative power. This abdication of creative human freedom is the fundamental generating pattern or "matrix" of the socioeconomic and political world in which most people find themselves enslaved to others.

Two Matrixes

In *The Matrix* powerful machines with artificial intelligence control most, though not all, of humanity. It might therefore seem that *The Matrix* is more Platonic or Cartesian than Kantian in its portrayal of the source of the illusion as external rather than internal. And yet the intelligences that imprison human beings in the Matrix must control their captives according to the captives' own wishes. We learn that the beings that have almost succeeded in governing humankind have had to alter their original program—the Matrix governing the nature of the seeming world—to comply with implicit human wishes. Disgusted with human imperfection, Agent Smith reveals to Morpheus, whose mind he is trying to break, that there have been two Matrixes, two different fundamental patterns and programs for governing the experiences of captive humanity: "Did you know that the first Matrix was designed to be a perfect human world? Where none suffered, where everyone would be happy. It was a disaster. No one would accept the program. Entire crops were lost." Agent Smith speculates on the reason for this anomaly: "Some believed we lacked the programming language to describe your perfect world. But I believe that, as a species, human beings define their reality through suffering and misery."

Just as contented cows create the best milk, contented humanity produces the best bio-energy, the necessary lifeblood for the intelligent machine masters. The Matrix was designed to occupy the mind while the sleeping organism performs its function as a battery for the soul-snatching machine intelligences. In an early scene, before Neo is freed from the Matrix, Switch scornfully calls him "Coppertop," for the Duracell battery whose function he unwittingly performs. Paradoxically, what turns out to fit humanity's requirements for a contented sleep is not an ideal world of happiness, but the familiar dog-eat-dog world of suffering and misery in which we, the audience, are actually living. Thus, by its veto power to choose among possible Matrixes, sleeping humanity is unconsciously and implicitly in charge of the program. Outside forces cannot imprison human beings in a world of illusory appearances without human complicity. Later, when he realizes that none of his memories of life in the Matrix was real, Neo asks, "What does that mean?" Trinity replies, "That the Matrix cannot tell you who you are."

There is a core self that persists even in the illusion of the dream. This is Descartes's fundamental starting point. Even in the dream, he asserts, it remains a self-evident truth that "I think, therefore I am." Awareness of the freedom of self-consciousness is the starting point for finding one's way out of the illusions of life that scientific philosophy seeks to penetrate and overthrow. No malicious demons, nor the power of time-honored traditions and self-interested systems of control, are powerful enough to thwart this core of truth in every human being.

Agent Smith describes the cognitive dissonance produced by the first Matrix of perfect happiness and its ironic outcome, the present world of inequality, injustice, and widespread human misery: "The perfect world was a dream that your primitive cerebrum kept trying to wake up from. Which is why the Matrix was re-designed to this: the peak of your civilization." The underlying implication of all this is that human beings themselves choose their own illusions, implicitly rejecting a certain idea of the perfect world designed for endless happiness while opting for another world, one fraught with unhappiness. Even when subject to the malicious demons and their towers of dreaming people, humanity gets what it wants.

What is the Evolutionary Purpose of Rational Beings?

But why would people want this world of suffering and misery, rather than the world of happiness of the first Matrix? This question repeats an ancient one, addressed in the Book of Genesis. In the beginning, according to Genesis, our primordial parents existed in a perfect world of uninterrupted bliss, without pain and suffering, without labor, and in a harmony with nature and nature's God. But they rejected their happiness for "the knowledge of good and evil." The outcome was a world characterized by painful labor and the hierarchical power of man over woman and a few privileged controllers over many others. The result is a world in which misery, violence, and murder are inevitable. As the Bible states explicitly and *The Matrix* restates, the world of human subservience in which we live is the choice of the human being—of the slaves themselves. In the fantasy framework of science fiction, *The Matrix* is portraying the truth that this unhappy "peak of your civilization" is the very world we, the viewers of the film, live in today. This world is not an external fact or independent reality but the result of a choice that humanity is presently making in a semiconscious, dreamlike way.

Kant asks why it is that evolving nature has produced beings with reason. If the purpose of reason had been happiness, then "nature would have hit on a very bad arrangement. . . . For all the actions [the human being] has to perform with this end in view, and the whole rule of his behaviour, would have been mapped out for him far more accurately by instinct."[1] In the original Matrix of perfect human happiness, the AI machines in charge of planning human life produced a contradiction that was bound to fail: human beings endowed with reason who are programmed like animals to do that which makes them happy. What if, considering the alternatives, rational beings decide to try something that is not really good for them? In his philosophical elucidation of the story of Adam and Eve in the Book of Genesis, Kant imagines just such a moment, when, although inclined by instinct, "that voice of God which is obeyed by all animals," to eat what is good for her, Eve decides to try a different fruit, one that is contrary to the commands of natural instinct. For "reason has this peculiarity that, aided by the imagination, it can create artificial desires which are not only unsupported by natural instinct but actually contrary to it."[2] The result may only be a stomach ache, but the experience opens up an entirely new world: it had become "impossible to return to the state of servitude (i.e., subjection to instinct) from the state of freedom, once he had tasted the latter."[3] In relation to the instinctive programs that nature has inserted in animals, reason is a fallible instrument if its primary purpose is to attain happiness. Beings with reason must therefore have another purpose than simply to find happiness.

This purpose, Kant argues, is the responsibility and sense of achievement that comes with freedom—the power for better or for worse to create our own world. To create our own world in freedom, there must be a real choice. For beings of reason with imagination, there can be no real choice of good, or creation of a good society, if there are not also apparently good reasons for a choice of evil. In contrast to instinctively oriented programs governing the animal world, human beings must have a fundamental possibility of choosing what is not good if they are to become truly responsible for their own existence. If they instinctively do what is good for them, as the animals do and as the Bible tells us was true for them in the beginning, then how could there be a real choice? Humans made a choice therefore to reject the original Matrix of creation, which was to live in a world of goodness alone as a matter of programmed instinct, in order to have the freedom to choose the good for themselves, which they can only do if they also have the freedom to choose what only seems to be good for us, but is not truly good.

We humans are endowed with a faculty of reasoning that not only often but in a systematic way confronts us with the problem of finding reality in the midst of deceptive appearances. The conflict between appearance and reality is therefore a necessary condition for human freedom and self-creation. Human beings must choose between the real and true good and the apparent or false good, and have good reasons for doing either. By leaving the paradise of good alone, by choosing the possibility of good *and* evil, humans have the choice between what is truly good and that which is only apparently good. In this way we can understand more deeply the problematic of morality that was presented in the previous chapter. The conflict between duty and desire is precisely the conflict between what is good universally and in general—that is, what is truly good—and what seems good for me as a separate individual, as an isolated ego—that is, the choice of illusory good. This alternative between morality and egotism is the fundamental condition for human freedom and responsibility and the basic choice on which morality depends.

The first choice, symbolized by the forbidden fruit in the Garden of Eden, was the choice of that which only seems good but really is not.

Propelled by this choice out of the first Matrix of instinctive or pro-grammed happiness, the next choice recounted by the Bible was the per-ception of scarcity and conflict, resulting in the choice of Cain to kill his brother Abel, whom Cain perceived to be more favored by God. Presupposed here is the choice to constitute ourselves as egos, compet-ing with one another over a world of seemingly scarce goods. This choice produces a world of illusion inasmuch as nature is as abundant as it was in the beginning, while the perceived scarcity is the result of artificial, humanly created conditions. Persistence in such an orientation is a self-fulfilling force, for it eventually reduces the abundance of the natural world to the barren bleakness of ecological ruin graphically depicted in *The Matrix*. What Morpheus calls "the desert of the real" both underlies and arises out of the illusions of the Matrix.

So, thanks to a peculiar faculty of reason connected to freedom of choice and imagination, humans have rejected the natural path of bio-logically programmed or instinctive happiness to choose a course of development that inevitably produces unhappiness. For only in this way can humans in time become truly responsible for their existence. Only by exercising the freedom to do that which is not good can they be responsible for choosing that which is really is good. From the stand-point of the ego, the choice of murder seems to be good. For as a sep-arate and naked body, the human individual is immensely vulnerable and fearful about survival in a world permeated by death. Kill rather than be killed is the seeming rationality of this world. With this framework of illusion firmly established in primary human history, the stage is set for another choice—that of the rejection of the evil will of the ego and the choice of the good will that sees past the appearance of separate bodies to the fundamental reality of human brother-and-sisterhood that persists underneath all the contrary appearances. This is the choice for respect-ing the requirements of our shared humanity over the attractions of our separate desires and interests.

We have therefore chosen to create a world of illusion, represented by the civilization of 1999 reproduced in the second Matrix, because only by freeing ourselves from such illusion, and the misery that is its inevitable consequence, is true happiness attainable. This is not the hap-piness of the original paradise or of the first Matrix, handed to humanity on a silver platter, but a happiness that results from human freedom and human endeavor. Human beings are so made, Kant argues, that we can-not really be happy unless we feel that we *deserve* to be happy. Hence happiness for human beings should be linked to freedom and responsi-bility. Only those people who realize their inner goodness (what Kant calls the good will) by performing their duties—despite the fears that stem from the apparent world that is governed by the war of egos against one another—*deserve* to be happy. Happiness therefore remains a fundamental human goal, but one that depends on a prior condition, that the happiness be truly deserved as the outcome of the choice to create a society that is good for all of humanity. The performance of duty, despite the desires and fears arising out of ego-rationality, is the path of the creation of the good society. Only in this roundabout way do human beings deserve to be happy. Until humanity makes such a choice, let us stew in our misery, for otherwise how would be ever come to see the fallacy of our ways? The universal goal and crowning duty of morality consists in creating a world based on duty, on willing what is good for all humanity, for only on this basis can humanity attain a deserved happiness. Kant calls this end purpose of human existence, in which happiness is the result of the performance of duty, the "highest good."[4]

Two Theories of Liberation

If *The Matrix* suggests two theories of enslavement to the shadows of illusion, external and internal, it also proposes two corresponding theories of liberation. Throughout the film the audience is asked to question not only whether indeed Neo is "the One," but what it means to be the One. At the beginning of the film, Choi recognizes Neo's programming power as a computer hacker who helps individuals manipulate the cybernetic systems that control their lives. As he hands Neo two thousand dollars for a computer disk, Choi says, "You're my savior, man. My own personal Jesus Christ." Choi evokes the idea of the external Savior, the God-man who will liberate human beings from the perdition they deserve as a result of their bad choices. But this kind of "liberation" is only a foreshadowing, perhaps a caricature, of true liberation.

The history of philosophy gives us two opposing interpretations of the idea of salvation. In Plato's allegory of the cave, where the source of the illusion seems to be external to the deluded human beings, the agent for the overcoming the illusion is also externalized. An already liberated individual, the philosopher, must come back into the cave to explain to its shackled inmates the nature of the illusion. In Plato's program for the ideal society, his *Republic*, an exceptional human being, a "philosopher king," is needed to guide humanity away from the shoals of misery and self-destruction and towards . . . what? The harmony and the contentment of a well-ordered existence. But in *The*

Matrix something like this idyllic world, created for humanity by their intelligent masters, has already been rejected by the dreamers within the dream world itself. In traditional Christianity, the Savior is an exceptional individual unlike others, a God-man capable of raising the dead, and, after his own death, bringing himself back to life. It is this traditional understanding of "the One" that predominates in the minds of the characters of the film until all such traditional expectations are fully overturned in the final scenes of *The Matrix*.

The other alternative, defended by Kant, is that of modern philosophical Enlightenment philosophy, the principles of which are embedded in the U.S. Constitution. The only society worth having is one in which free people rule themselves. The slaves can only be truly free if they free themselves. If freedom from shackles is handed to them without their own efforts, they will quickly fall back into servitude. In his essay, "What is Enlightenment?" Kant argues that no one can save us but we ourselves. This self-liberation of humanity is the destiny that each of us must discover for himself. In Kant's conception, Jesus is not an exceptional being who saves a helpless humanity, but the model of our own inner godlike potential to save ourselves. In this perspective, rather than claiming to be the unique Son of God, Jesus is the teacher who can show us that we are all sons (and daughters) of God. So the prayer he teaches begins, "*Our* Father." Our salvation lies in the recognition of our inherent dignity as sons and daughters of God, as godlike beings. Similarly, at the end of first *Matrix* film, Neo announces his true purpose, not as a Savior, but as a teacher of the means of human self-liberation. The tension between these two possible interpretations of the meaning of "the One" continues through the second and third parts of the *Matrix* trilogy.

Kant's conception that the perceived world is a self-imposed illusion, rather than a deception that is caused by an outside deceiver, is intimately connected with his conception that every human being has a destiny to participate in the self-liberation of humanity. Kant's systematic and comprehensive argumentation in defending these interrelated conceptions can convince the reader of their validity, and in this way strengthen ideas that are visually and dramatically presented in *The Matrix*. In this way, while the science-fiction plot line of the *Matrix* trilogy is (presumably) fictitious, the essential story remains true at a deeper level. Truth—if we understand it as the philosophers of illusion, such as Plato, Descartes, and Kant, tell it—is in fact at least as strange as fiction.

The Philosophical Implication of Copernicus's Revolution in Astronomy

In his *Critique of Pure Reason* (1781), Kant called for a revolution in philosophy "according to the hypothesis of Copernicus."[5] To achieve a Copernican revolution in philosophy means that our philosophical ideas—the general way we think about the world we live in—ought to catch up with the implications of modern science. These implications are nowhere as obvious as in the discovery of Copernicus that the sun does not revolve around the earth, *as it appears to do*, but rather the earth goes around the sun, *contrary to appearances*.

Today we smugly laugh at the naïveté and perhaps the arrogance of the older visions of the universe that placed our little blue planet (as it is seen from space) in the very center of an encircling universe. But let us give due credit to the ancient philosophers, such as Aristotle, who defended the geocentric world picture. After all, they merely formulated in general terms what we still today perceive with our own eyes. We directly *see* the sun going around the earth through the "vault" of the sky. We see the sky as a huge dome enclosing the plane of the earth that extends out from our physical bodies to the surrounding circular horizon. If we reject the ancient cosmology of Aristotle, we must accept the idea that the world as we actually perceive it is an illusion.

The geocentric view of the world is an extension of a more fundamental feature of perception—its egocentric nature. We directly see the physical world as centered on our individual physical bodies. That is the way things seem or appear to us. The world I actually perceive centers on me, on my physical self. It is the same for each of us. But a little reflection and life experience tells us that the world in itself cannot be not like this. When children take body-centered perception to be reality, we call that egocentrism. When adults persist in seeing themselves as the center of the universe, we call that egotism.

I Am the One

Naturally, spontaneously, each of us has the powerful feeling of his own uniqueness and importance. Each of us intimately feels that she is "the One." The world that we look out upon, as it actually presents itself to us, is the creation of a unique perspective. Thus Wittgenstein, reflecting on the solipsistic nature of experience, writes, "I am the world. (The microcosm.)"[6] But if each of us is a microcosm, there must also be a macrocosm—a world of worlds. The problem is how to transcend the limits of our little world to grasp this world of worlds. Little

Joey in his sand box claims the world as his—until little Suzie decides to join him and take his truck. Joey must then confront the disturbing fact that others too see the world as theirs. This contradiction is profoundly experienced as an invasion of self. Sartre evokes the solipsistic world of the peeping Tom at a keyhole, secretly observing others engaged in their private perversities, and containing them in the mastery of his view. A creaking of the floor behind him, however, jolts him from his solipsistic enjoyment: someone else is observing *him!*[7] Each of us, within our private microcosms, is the One, and each of us experiences the invasion of "the Other"—another being who lays claim, against oneself, to *really* being "the One."

There are two opposed outcomes to this experience. We can persist in taking ourselves to be the center of our own worlds, not in solipsistic solitude, which, as Sartre's example shows, is not sustainable, but against and by means of the others. In the words of Kant, we can see other human beings merely as means for the achievement of our own personal goals. This is the choice of egotism. Egotism is a central category of the moral dimension of life. Egotism consists in taking one's own individual physical existence as the primary basis of one's choices. Pragmatically, the egotist acts as though he is "the One," the center of the universe, the being for which everything has been made. The egotist attempts to will as a universal law that whatever he himself desires is right—to tell lies when this is advantageous, to take from others if he can get away with it, to harm others to advance himself. But such a law of the separate self is inherently contradictory: if it is a law, it applies to everyone. Each person can then take from the other. But that violates the principle of egotism itself. The real egotist does not want others to violate his own desires. Therefore he cannot consciously, consistently, will the principles of his actions as universal laws. And yet, as a rational human being he inevitably thinks of his goals in general or universal terms. The egotist is therefore inevitably tangled up in contradictions, which he can only escape by dulling his awareness, by becoming as unconscious as possible, by putting himself to sleep, by giving himself over to a world of self-generated illusion. But in the words of Hamlet, when we sleep, even in the sleep of death, we may still dream. And in the solipsism of the dream, Descartes convincingly argues, I nevertheless cannot help but think—and think "I." But this "I" is inescapably a universal thought, the self-awareness of each and every one of us. "I want this," implicitly translates, in the general nature of thought that is inherent in our language, into "a human being wants something." If we wish to respect our own self, the "I" as this presents itself even in our dreams, we must respect that universality of humanity that is within each of us. Thus the moral choice to act in the light of our common humanity is the only one that can be willed consistently with full consciousness.

Each individual spontaneously and naturally believes in her mysterious election as a special being, as *the* special being. Experience, however, soon teaches us that other beings have the power to limit us, to prevent us from realizing our desires. Other beings too act as if they are "the One." To solve this contradiction, ultimately it is necessary to recognize that *we*–humanity in general, all intelligent beings in the universe—are in our mutuality and oneness the true center of existence. This recognition is the "groundwork" and general perspective of the moral consciousness. The basic choice of morality is between two contradictory conceptions of reality: the sensible, perceptible world of seemingly separate, independent, and competing egos, and the intelligible or ideal world of our shared humanity. The ideal world is implicit in all the purposes of actions that are conscious and so inevitably formulated in general terms. There is seemingly good reason to accept either viewpoint, and so there is a real choice in human existence. The egotistical world is connected to the appearances of physical bodies separated from each other in space and time, and colliding with one another and interacting according to laws of external causality. On the other hand, the world seen from the standpoint of moral consciousness is a world of human unity and freedom. If the first is reality, the second must be an illusion. If we believe that the Matrix of morality is real, then the Matrix of separation and conflicting egos, which produces our own world of 1999, the peak of our civilization, must be an illusion.

To say that this world of egos is an illusion does not mean that it does not exist. Dreams too really exist; they have a reality of their own. It is to say that its existence is not absolute or natural, not inevitable or the result of the way things inevitably are. Rather, it is a choice of a way of being, but one that usually masks itself in absolutes, and evades or overlooks the fact that it is the result of a free choice. It is a free choice that hides its freedom in a deterministic frame of understanding. But because it is implicitly chosen, it is a world based on bad faith and self-deception. On the other hand, to opt for shared humanity does not mean to deny one's own individuality. But it does mean being prepared to subordinate that individuality to the laws that we ourselves proclaim and enact whenever we decide to do anything. This is the meaning and the grandeur of moral duty: living according to laws that we as human beings create for ourselves.

Choosing the Red Pill of Duty

In *The Matrix,* the moral choice for truth, freedom, and humanity is symbolized by the choice of the red pill. The red pill awakens the individual to reality; the blue pill puts one back into the sleep of self-centered illusion. Morpheus emphasizes the choice between truth or illusion: "You take the blue pill, the story ends, you wake up in your bed and believe whatever you want to believe. You take the red pill, you stay in Wonderland, and I show you how deep the rabbit hole goes. . . . Remember, all I'm offering is the truth, nothing more. . . ." Morpheus is implicitly telling Neo that in offering him truth, he is not offering him an easy life; he is not offering happiness. He is proposing the hard but noble path of moral duty, which is first of all the duty to pursue the truth.

Like Lisa in *The Simpsons,* Neo is an individual who commits himself to his duty, whatever personal sacrifices this requires of him. Duty first takes the form of knowing the truth—above all, the truth of oneself. The words of the Greek oracle, "Know thyself," adorn the kitchen wall of the Oracle of the Matrix. Neo's duty is first of all to know who he is really. Self-knowledge is not egotistical. We have duties to ourselves, and unless we fulfill them, how can we be helpful to anyone else? Ultimately, we have a duty to the humanity that exists within each of us. This humanity is an ennobling, higher reality by comparison with the self-centered desires and interests that occupy us in our endless pursuits of satisfactions in the world of sensible appearances.

In the Kantian metaphysics, the moral choice implies that we belong to two worlds—a "sensible world" whose appearances center around each one of us, and an "intelligible world" that is not directly apparent to the senses, a world of shared humanity which we hold as an ideal or goal and that we have yet to realize sufficiently in practice. In making this choice, we freely determine the fundamental Matrix or law for the world that we are in the process of creating. We have the freedom to choose between two fundamentally different laws, two Matrixes of existence. Is it the law of shared humanity, of the dignity of each human being? Or is it the lawless law of egotism—the law in which each of us says, "I am the One," while recognizing implicitly and in a dreamlike way that the Other says the same? This latter choice is indeed the choice of the knowledge of both good and evil—the good of oneself and the evil of the other. As a result of this choice for good and evil, a peculiar world is created. We create the world of the Matrix, modeled on the year 1999–the peak of modern civilization at the end of the millennium. The symbolism of this date is clear: the world to which we are accustomed is frozen in the past, in the pattern of an old, dying age. Ours is the old world based on the sense of powerlessness that each individual feels before the seemingly external forces of others. The alternative is the choice to break the spell of the old world and to realize a new Matrix: that of our shared humanity. Will humanity ever take the next step to a new millennium and New Age of authentic freedom and self-empowerment?

Choosing the Blue Pill of Slavery

Morpheus tells Neo what Neo already obscurely knows:

> You've felt it you're entire life, that there's something wrong with the world. You don't know what it is, but it's there, like a splinter in your mind, driving you mad. . . . The Matrix is everywhere. It is all around us, even now in this very room. You can see it when you look out your window or when you turn on your television. You can feel it when you go to work, when you go to church, when you pay your taxes. It is the world that has been pulled over your eyes to blind you from the truth.

"What truth?" asks Neo. Mopheus replies: "That you are a slave, Neo. Like everyone else you were born into bondage, born into a prison that you cannot smell or taste or touch. A prison for your mind. . . ."

It is true, as we have seen, that the world we see when we look out our windows is an appearance, an illusion that we take to exist independently of us but that is permeated with the egocentric standpoint of our perception. But other forces reinforce this illusion. Institutional forces of society tell us how to think about the appearances and how to regard them as the results of an unbreakable chain of causality, thereby impeding the awakening of our own free consciousness. Our old world of 1999 is governed by the culture of TV, mass media, and film, as well as by the market, by the State, and by religion—by powers that seemingly exist independently of us, and in their various ways control our thoughts and actions. But above all, the enslaving powers must imprison our thoughts, for as we think and as we believe, so we will act. The supreme paradox is that this world that controls us is empowered by us. Without our energies, without our beliefs, without our choice of the separateness of the ego, it could not exist.

The market, which is Kant's focus in his third formulation of the categorical imperative, is nothing but the result of seemingly separate individuals producing goods and exchanging them with one another. In reality, the market is the result of the combined actions of the vast majority of humanity. But since each individual perceives himself as acting separately from the others, the combined force of our common humanity exists and appears to each separate individual as an external power ruling over each of us and obliging each to adapt to *its* requirements. The market is the effect of the contradictory law of the ego that we embody in the way of life that we have implicitly, in a dreamlike way, chosen. We have *chosen* this way of life, because another way is always possible—the way of cooperation, of subordinating our separate individual goals to the requirements of our shared humanity. And yet we treat this result of our choices as an independent reality governed by independent, external, causal laws—as a deterministic force before which we are powerless. And hard experience seems to verify this power, as Neo learns when his employer confronts him with a pseudo-choice: accept the rules of this corporation, or perish.

Thus social scientists, such as Adam Smith, quite reasonably explain the laws of the economic realm as the outcome of independent mechanisms, comparable, on the human level, to the laws of Newtonian physics that appear to operate in the world of physical nature. Smith consoles his readers with the idea that the laws governing economic life operate benevolently by a kind of divine providence:

> As every individual, therefore, endeavors as much as he can both to employ his capital in the support of domestic industry, and so to direct that industry that its produce may be of the greatest value; every individual necessarily labors to render the annual revenue of the society as great as he can. He generally, indeed, neither intends to promote the public interest, nor knows how much he is promoting it. By preferring the support of domestic to that of foreign industry, he intends only his own security; and by directing that industry in such a manner as its produce may be of the greatest value, he intends only his own gain, and he is in this, as in many other cases, led by an invisible hand to promote an end which was no part of his intention. Nor is it always the worse for society that it was no part of it. By pursuing his own interest he frequently promotes that of the society more effectually than when he really intends to promote it. I have never known much good done by those who affected to trade for the public good. It is an affectation, indeed, not very common among merchants, and very few words need be employed in dissuading them from it.[8]

Who is really behind the "invisible hand" that governs the market? Is it the owners of multinational corporations? Is it the politicians who control the laws of the State? Is it the external God of religion and the powers of the church? Is it a set of alien beings, such as the AI controllers of the Matrix? No doubt, there are those who do their best

to direct the forces of this world in ways that benefit them and aug-
ment their power. But the real divinity underlying the economic
world, and the powers of market, State, and church that are linked to
it, is the combined humanity that constantly feeds into it its own
energies, beliefs, and choices. In this way human beings are the
cause of their own enslavement.

Is the Highest Good Possible?

The choice for shared humanity underlies every moral duty. To guaran-
tee its authenticity, however, we must test this choice. The person who
first chooses to awaken and live according to truth faces a crisis as this
commitment unfolds, discovering that the *realization* of this choice in
practical terms is doubtful. We have seen that the ultimate meaning of
moral choice is the duty to create "the highest good." This is a world in
which those who sacrifice their personal desires and interests out of a
sense of duty for their shared humanity finally attain the happiness they
deserve. Kant's reasoning here justifies the choice that humanity makes
in rejecting the supposedly ideal world of the first Matrix—which, in
Kant's Christian culture is represented by the original paradise or Garden
of Eden from which humanity "fell" through what has been called original sin. Original sin is traditionally understood as sinful disobedience to
an all-powerful God who sets and enforces the rules of existence, but
Kant provides an alternative perspective. No happiness that stems from
blind submission to the external laws of either nature or God is worthy
of a human being. If we are to be happy we must earn our happiness
in complete freedom. Original sin is therefore truly the original freedom
of the human being, which consists in the choice to live according to
laws we make ourselves.

What the designers of that first Matrix left out of their plan for a world
of happiness was precisely this requirement of morality—that happiness
must be earned, merited, or deserved. The highest good, which is the
goal of the freedom fighters aboard the Nebuchadnezzar, is the creation
of an altogether different kind of Matrix—a world that combines happiness with authentic freedom. The Agents of the AI designers of the original Matrix cannot comprehend the importance of freedom for human
beings, for freedom inevitably entails both imperfection and suffering. As
beings who admire the perfectly worked-out program that operates with
the sureness of instinct in the animal world, and no doubt with far less
clumsiness than is possible by nature's own trial-and-error methods, they
cannot comprehend the value of freedom. For them freedom is a mere

"anomaly," a failure to follow the perfect program. Authentic freedom requires real choice, the possibility of choosing both good and evil—the choice between duty and desire. The choice of ego-centered desire inevitably produces the suffering of the war of all against all described by Hobbes. But the choice of duty produces suffering as well, as ego-desires, promising happiness for the separate individual however ultimately harmful in the larger perspective of the totality, must be sacrificed, while the promised happiness of the moral society retreats into the realm of fantasy and faith. Hence Agent Smith is as astounded by such apparent human irrationality as he is repelled by the stink of human misery.

For people truly to deserve happiness, three conditions are necessary: (1) We must make a choice. (2) The choice must involve some sacrifice or pain, for otherwise there would be no merit in it. (3) We cannot *know* that results will reward our efforts; the reward for making the right but difficult choice is not guaranteed. The first two conditions are necessary for every moral choice involving duty. The choice to perform one's duty, by the very meaning of the term duty, involves rejecting some other course of action that one would normally prefer. Contrary to what the Stoic philosophers have argued, virtue is not its own reward. Dutiful people may be content or satisfied in their sense of having followed their conscience. But such moral contentment is not the same as happiness. If their basic needs are not met, they cannot be happy. The crew of the Nebuchadnezzar, except for Cypher, experience moral contentment—which Stoics mistakenly think is happiness. Eating the gruel served up for breakfast, Tank stoically emphasizes its health benefits. They are getting everything they need. But Mouse insists that more is required than vitamins to make him happy. The grinding and gritty life aboard the ship—even the drab and sweaty clothes on the backs of the heroes that they readily exchange for the gleam and luxury of leather when they enter the Matrix—graphically depicts the postponement and problematic character of happiness for the moral members of the crew. However, with the exception of Cypher, the undaunted crew keeps in mind the ultimately happy, and justly deserved, outcome. As Tank informs Neo, "If the war was over tomorrow, Zion's where the party would be." A free and secure society, Zion, is where the party would be—the happy ending in the future for all the pain and suffering in the present. But how certain can they be of such a happy outcome?

The third condition for deserving happiness must be emphasized here. We don't really *know* that we will be rewarded. If we did, we would not really be sacrificing anything—only postponing a lesser pleasure for a greater one. Only if the reward and happy outcome is uncertain can people finally be said to be rewarded (or punished) according to their "just deserts." In the moral perspective, one's choice to sacrifice all for the sake of the universal good should finally pay off in a world in which that universal good, involving respect for the dignity of each human being, really regulates the distribution of rewards and punishments. But the outcome of such a choice cannot be known or guaranteed in advance. Nor can the individuals who are willing to sacrifice their lives be assured that they will be able to enjoy the fruits of their efforts themselves. The deserved happiness in the end is therefore the object of *belief or faith*, not knowledge.

But this precariousness of the outcome creates a fundamental problem for morality. The happy outcome must at least be reasonably possible. If such a lofty vision turns out to be impossible, then the initial choice is also unreal. There is a moral rule that "ought implies can." There is no duty or "ought" if there is no possibility of realizing that duty—if it can't be done. We have no duty in circumstances where the realization of the supposed duty is not even possible. But if the highest good is impossible, then all of morality turns out to be a pipe dream. So Kant writes: "If therefore the highest good is impossible according to practical rules, then the moral law that commands that it be furthered must be fantastic, directed to imaginary ends, and consequently inherently false."[9]

The highest good is the keystone of all moral choices. It is like the stone placed at the top of an archway that holds the pillars underneath it together and so enables its own supporting columns to stand. Each choice to perform one's duty implies the requirement of justice—that goodness be rewarded and evil punished. If I tell the truth, I should not be punished for doing so. However, in the real world, telling the truth is often a painful duty, and whistleblowers are threatened with painful consequences for performing their obvious duty. Who can tell them that they will ultimately have their reward when there are so many cases that show the contrary? Each moral duty therefore ultimately implies an act of faith that the outcome of one's sacrifices will be a just world, the highest good. Realizing the highest good is therefore the duty of all duties.

In terms of the market, this means that those who do their duty—who are dedicated to their work, for example—should be appropriately rewarded in economic terms. From the moral point of view the market "ought" to favor the values of honesty, effort, and creativity, not luck or upbringing, or the advantages of positions of power. Rather than rewarding according to the performance of duty, the market seems to work more like a roulette wheel, with the odds in favor of the house that owns the wheel. But this is unfair. It's not just, says the morally conscious individual.

The Power of Belief

If such a just world is a pipe dream, an unrealizable utopia, then only one option is reasonable: to live one's own separate egotistical life by adapting as well as possible to the external circumstances of one's existence. The crew of the Nebuchadnezzar is striving to liberate humanity from the Matrix and assure the victory of Zion over the enemy jailors of humankind. Zion is at risk of being destroyed by the AI controllers. Because of the seemingly overwhelming power of the controllers, Cypher comes to the conclusion that the lofty goals pursued by the crew of the Nebuchadnezzar are illusory, and Morpheus is a madman, or at least a deluded dictator. Cypher's initial choice of the red pill is tested by hard experience. Thanks to Cypher, the audience comes to recognize that the initial freedom and "reality" outside the Matrix are only transitional moments in the realization of a larger freedom and a deeper ultimate reality. But for the moment, this ultimate freedom and reality exists only in the minds of those who believe in it. Cypher comes to the conclusion that the victory of Zion, the Promised Land for Morpheus, is indeed a fantastic, unrealizable goal, and all the sacrifices made in its behalf are in vain.

Using rational empirical estimates to draw practical conclusions, Cypher concludes that Morpheus's vision of freedom and reality is the ultimate illusion. While Morpheus believes in the prophecy of the Savior, the One, Cypher rationally calculates the odds that the puny forces of the Nebuchadnezzar, and Zion as a whole, can defeat the overwhelmingly powerful forces controlling the Matrix. In an early conversation with Neo, Cypher expresses his skepticism regarding Morpheus' faith-based strategy: He asks Neo, "Did he tell you why he did it? Why you're here? Jesus. What a mind job. So you're here to save the world. What do you say to something like that? A little piece of advice. You see an agent, you do what we do. Run. You run your ass off." Again, Neo is equated to Jesus. But this time, seen from Cypher's perspective, the idea of a Savior, and Neo's being one, sounds like lunacy. In his ultimate justification of his betrayal of Morpheus, Cypher exposes his own interpretation of freedom and reality. "If you would have told us the truth," he says to the unconscious body of Morpheus, "we woulda told you to shove that red pill right up your ass!" "That's not true, Cypher," Trinity argues with him, "he set us free." Cypher replies: "Free, you call this free? All I do is what he tells me to do. If I have to choose between that and the Matrix, I choose the Matrix." The freedom Cypher is looking for is merely the freedom to realize his desires. Such freedom is perfectly compatible with a fundamental determinism, as our desires are formed within us by external forces of nature, circumstance, education, and social programming. The freedom of morality supposes that whatever our natural inclinations, whatever the pressures of our circumstances and the orientation of our upbringing, we remain in control of our lives and so responsible for our decisions.

The choice for realizing the goal of the highest good, the Kingdom of Ends of our shared humanity, is represented in the Matrix by the free city of Zion. The freedom that Morpheus has in mind is not mere separation from the Matrix, but participation in a destiny or fate that has as its ultimate goal the higher liberation of humanity. This goal cannot be merely the replication "in reality" of our modern world—the "peak of civilization"—but the realization of a different, better world, a world of human perfection that combines freedom, morality, and happiness. This is the world of the New Age, the new millennium that the calendar of the Matrix's world of 1999 never reaches. Trinity's reply to Cypher is therefore inadequate, since she merely distinguishes between the illusion of existence within the virtual reality program of the Matrix and mere physical existence, which has its own illusions of egocentric perception and is governed by questionable beliefs. "The Matrix isn't real!" she says. Cypher's answer touches on a deeper truth. "I disagree, Trinity. I think the Matrix could be more real than this world. All I do is pull the plug here. But there, you have to watch Apoc die."

Which is in fact more real—the "real world" of the Nebuchadnezzar or the dream world of the Matrix? "Reality" too depends on our mind. When Neo falls from a tall building in the virtual reality simulation of the Construct, upon returning to consciousness in his physical body he finds that he is bleeding. "I thought it wasn't real," says Neo. Morpheus replies: "Your mind makes it real." "If you're killed in the Matrix, you die here?" "The body cannot live," says Morpheus, "without the mind." Like the simulated reality of the Matrix, the physical world too is governed by the mind, by our beliefs. The reality of the Nebuchadnezzar is itself premised on certain beliefs—above all the belief in the viability of the struggle to liberate humanity and to assure the security of Zion. But suppose such a lofty vision, ultimately morality's vision of the highest good, is an impossible dream? Which world is then more real? That of the Nebuchadnezzar, whose physical reality is governed by impossible beliefs, and where life is unpleasant and highly regulated? Or that of the Matrix, where illusion is recognized, by its creators at least, to be illusion, and where for Cypher there will be the sumptuous pleasure of a steak dinner? Indeed the pleasure of a good life will even appear well-earned or deserved by the famous actor that Cypher intends to become—producing the illusion of the moral good of justice. It is a great irony that Cypher's idea of reality is to become a principal participant in the manufacture of the illusory world of Hollywood cinema. In this reference, *The Matrix* proposes that we become aware of the fact that in watching this film we are ourselves participating in an illusion. But we must also ask ourselves whether in this illusory world of the film we might not be closer to reality than we are in our ordinary physical lives, subject as they are to rules laid down by powers over which we have little or no control.

The contrast between the illusory world of the Matrix and the world of ordinary physical perceptions on board the Nebuchadnezzar is therefore only the starting point for the film's exploration of the themes of illusion and reality, slavery and freedom. The initial contrast between illusion and reality, so startlingly depicted in the towers of sleeping humanity, is only the beginning, not the conclusion of the issue as to the nature of reality. This question is complicated by the fact that what is truly exciting, what captivates the audience along with Neo himself, is not life outside of the Matrix, but life within it—once its true nature is understood. Just as belief, which is possibly illusory, governs the physical world aboard the Nebuchadnezzar, so there is a captivating reality in the Matrix itself for individuals who understand the mind-based laws governing the creation of the illusion.

We can now understand why sleeping humanity persists in demanding the rat-race world of the end of the millennium. When the AI controllers offered an idyllic world in which needs are satisfied and all miseries alleviated, their subjects dimly recognized that such an illusion of happiness must *be* an illusion. For human beings who have made the choice to regard themselves as separate individuals, there can be no turning back to the idyllic world of the first perfection in paradise; there can be no turning back to the childhood of the human race immersed in nature, or to individual childhood wrapped in the arms of parental love and protection. The AI controllers are unable to return humanity to the simple state of oneness with nature that preceded the Fall, or the separation of the ego through the discovery of free choice. For the occupants in the generating towers, a world of happiness, with all desires continually satisfied, must be an illusion, for the belief in separation persists as the basic Matrix of their experience. And that belief in separation results inevitably, even dreamers recognize, in competition, struggle, and in the division between winners and losers. If happiness consists in triumphing over others, how can there not be losers as well as winners? Real, universal happiness is possible only on the basis of a radically different principle, one in which free human beings act on the basis of their true unity, not out of their apparent separation. Immersed in their life-pods, the dreamers of the Matrix inevitably think of themselves as separate individuals, as egos, and therefore find the world of 1999 with all its ordinary modern miseries only natural. They do so until they make an alternative choice, and then, like Neo in his early life in the Matrix, they begin their struggle to wake up.

The Antinomy of Practical Reason

We seek to create a perfect world of universal happiness—the ideal Matrix demanded by morality, the third Matrix of the truly good society. This perfect world has, however, certain conditions or requirements that make it incompatible with any possible world designed by alien captors for slaves in golden chains. The highest good is a world in which people are not only happy, but also worthy of being happy. Their happiness must be earned through their own free, responsible actions.

The moral quest to create the highest good is tested against the seemingly hard reality of an existing world that appears to contradict its very possibility. The moral individual tends to feel powerless against the forces of a world built on completely different principles. And so, in the face of the tremendous power generated by the Matrix of egotism, there must arise moments when the attempt to realize the ideal Matrix of morality seems utterly hopeless. Underlying such moments of despair is what Kant calls "the antinomy of practical reason." If the keystone or crowning duty of moral consciousness is the highest good, its realization must be possible. But empirical reality seems to be organized on principles that make such realization completely impossible. From the standpoint of Adam Smith's economic science, empirical reality is governed by deterministic laws of cause and effect that are the outcome of the self-interested actions of separate individuals. If such laws are an inflexible reality, then morality must be unreal. If morality is real, then the supposed iron laws of science are themselves unreal—or, as Kant has argued, laws of appearance, not reality.

Part of the solution to the antinomy of practical reason therefore consists in showing that the laws of science apply to appearance only. If the laws of science are connected to mere appearances and not reality, then morality, and its highest duty, would really be possible. If human beings are naturally separate egos in competition with one another, then the moral ideal would be an unrealizable delusion. But if such a world of competing egos, resulting in the creation of external forces ruling over them, is a choice that people make, then another choice is possible. The antinomy would then be solvable in principle. The moral goal is not in absolute contradiction to empirical reality, because the laws of that reality are the outcome of free human choices. If most people, or a significant number of them, would choose to live according to principles arising from their shared humanity, this would profoundly alter the nature of the world.

But such solutions in principle are mere theoretical consolations for the individual who is slogging it out against great and seemingly overwhelming odds. Purely theoretical possibilities based on human freedom need to be augmented by the power of belief. Morpheus and his crew are empowered to endure against the odds and to fight for the triumph of Zion not because of compelling theoretical considerations, but because they possess powerful beliefs. Referring to the standpoint of scientific knowledge, including the economic science of Adam Smith, Kant writes that "It is necessary to deny knowledge, in order to make room for faith."[10] In order to avoid despair, the individual has to have faith in the possibility of *realizing* the moral ideal as the Matrix of a fully developed world. Kant distinguishes three aspects of this faith, which he calls the postulates of morality. The postulates of moral consciousness are: freedom, God, and immortality.

The Postulate of Freedom

A certain kind of faith is necessary to sustain individuals in their struggle against apparently overwhelming odds for the self-liberation of humanity. Through adhering to the postulates or beliefs of morality, we support our efforts to follow through on our mission in life, which is to be the Ones who together can create the world of the highest good, the promised land of Zion, the kingdom of heaven on earth that was promised two thousand years ago by that earlier so-called Savior who was essentially a rabbi or teacher of human self-liberation.

Kant stresses that it is necessary to *believe* in the reality of moral experience itself. It is not possible to have scientific *knowledge* of this reality because scientific knowledge consists in explaining experience as the effect of deterministic physical, psychological, and socioeconomic laws. But the essence of moral experience is its antideterministic nature, rest-ing on the freedom of the will. Since we cannot *know* (scientifically) this freedom without reducing it to its opposite, we must have a kind of faith that our freedom to choose is something real. This faith in human freedom—despite all the deterministic laws of our sciences—is the first "postulate" or fundamental belief of moral experience.

Freedom of choice or free will is not possible in the deterministic framework of the physics of Galileo and Newton in which all motion is the effect of external forces acting upon an essentially passive object. In the seventeenth century, Hobbes said that those who know anything about the new physics will understand that free will is an impossibility, for free will supposes that some motions are not governed by external causes. This does not mean that there is no such thing as freedom in the normal sense of word, in which it means the capacity to realize one's goals without outside interference. When the dam breaks, the river becomes "free" to follow its channel. When the school bell rings, the children are "free" to go home. A "free market" economy is one in which no one tells you what job you must perform, or where you must invest your capital—if you are privileged enough to have any. But all such freedoms, involving the elimination or absence of *external* controls, are not without *internal* causes. The river necessarily flows in its channel. The children inevitably rush into the beckoning air of nature. The free worker *must* work somewhere in order to eat and pay the bills. The capitalist calculates the odds as best he can before placing his bets. None of these actions is free from causality in general.

But the postulate of free will says that human beings are free to choose, for if they were not they would not be responsible for their actions. Their actions would be the results of chains of causes stemming from environment, nature, upbringing, and societal programming. For morality to be possible, with its notions of duty and responsibility, all the forces that incline me in one direction can be held in check, as I ask the question: What is my duty? Where is my responsibility? What ought I to do? In the experience of duty, Kant says, we feel within ourselves a power, "that is, freedom and independence [of] the mechanism of nature."[11] The scientist explains everything by such mechanisms—social, psychological, or natural. As Hobbes rightly points out, this is how the scientific mind operates when it employs its causal laws to explain any kind of motion or action. But because that is the *mindset* of science, it doesn't follow that reality is actually determined by mechanical laws. The deterministic parameters of scientific explanation govern scientific *thinking* about reality, but not necessarily reality itself.

The scientific mind approaches experience by means of structured rules of explanation. Experience can never refute its a priori Matrix of interpretation, because if no cogent explanation can be found for the moment, the scientist will always continue to look for one. To admit that the cause of an event is an undetermined free will is to abandon the scientific approach. Were there some other, anticausal or noncausal feature of reality, the scientist could never see or recognize it because science knows only one kind of explanation. If there really are magicians who pull rabbits out of hats, the scientific true believer would never be convinced, supposing always that there *must be* a trick. Karl Popper has argued that a valid scientific theory must be "falsifiable." There must be possible experiences that would refute a theory if it is an empirically valid one and not an untestable "metaphysical" abstraction. But no experience can possibly falsify science itself, since in the absence of an apparent cause the scientist will always suppose a hidden one. A scientist's *belief* in such causes drives her entire enterprise. The very conception of falsifiability, in fact, is unfalsifiable. It is just another way of saying that all events must be explainable by outside causes. Thus science itself is the expression of a certain metaphysical assumption or belief about the nature of reality.

Morpheus tells Neo, while he is still connected to the Matrix, "Like everyone else you were born into bondage, born into a prison that you cannot smell or taste or touch. A prison for your mind. Unfortunately, no one can be told what the Matrix is. You have to see it for yourself." The assumption that all is governed by causal laws keeps us all prisoners, for it tells us that we ourselves are never the real causes of our own actions. It tells us that behind every apparent choice we make there is always a cause determining the direction in which we must move. How can we *know* that we are in bondage if the very rules of knowledge *presuppose* deterministic rules as the only acceptable ones? "Know thyself," in this framework, means simply, know that you are the outcome of chains of causes, and can never free yourself. But the Oracle means something quite different from such scientific knowledge—knowing oneself involves faith in the freedom to find one's own path. Neo is looking for such freedom from the controls of the Matrix. But how demonstrate that he is free when the Matrix of slavery is so all-encompassing that it includes the very rules of investigation? Hence the nature of the Matrix cannot be described in words, as Morpheus says, for the very words we use in our scientific explanations suppose the logic of determinism that keeps us prisoners of our own mind.

The scientific approach to reality, Kant concludes, is an a priori, subjective structure for organizing the data of experience. It is not an objective reflection of the nature of reality in itself. And even if it were, we could never know this since what we call knowledge simply *presupposes* causal forms of explanation. Thus causal laws are about our ways of thinking when we think scientifically, not about the structure of things in themselves. The causal laws of science are about appearances for us, not about things as they are in themselves. Things as they are in themselves are therefore scientifically unknowable. The modern sciences teach us to believe in deterministic causality. Moral experience calls on us to believe in ourselves.

The critique of a deterministic outlook leads to the conclusion that freedom of choice is theoretically possible. It is not ruled out by a scientific point of view. We can be scientists, therefore, if we understand that our science is about appearances only. Our scientific laws have pragmatic value but not metaphysical validity. But this means that reality in itself, beyond such appearances, is open to the possibility that we have the freedom to choose our own lives.

This assertion of freedom rests on faith, not knowledge. We don't know that we are free, for when we engage in the process of knowing, that is, in searching for external causes, we will never find the freedom from causality that is central to our sense of what it is to be a human being. And yet freedom is so deeply imbedded in our nature that we generally do not regard it as a belief. It seems like a certain kind of knowing, or direct intuition. With every step we take that involves some deliberation, we feel that we are free, and that we could have taken a different step in a different direction. If knowledge is what modern science defines it to be, this sense of our freedom is essentially a profound belief. It is an act of faith in ourselves. It involves a leap into the unknown and unknowable. But if such an idea that is so fundamental to our self-understanding is a matter of faith rather than knowledge, we must ask ourselves what else do we believe in such a basic way? What other beliefs do we, must we, entertain if we are to carry out a life of integrity and moral duty?

The Postulate of God

One for all and all for one. That is the slogan of truly free individuals. That is the new principle, the alternative Matrix of the Nebuchadnezzar and Zion. It is the third Matrix, which is still incomplete and mysterious, still to be fully realized. In order to see the new Matrix of the united, sharing mind of humanity through to its ultimate goal in the secure establishment and flourishing of Zion, it is necessary to believe or postulate not only that freedom exists, but that free people have the *power* to create the highest good. A second postulate is therefore necessary: the postulate that free individuals are connected on a higher plane than that of spatiotemporal appearances, share a fundamental oneness, and out of this higher reality, have the capacity to realize their fundamental unity in the world of appearances. If belief in the separation of human beings can create a world of *external* power, belief in our fundamental unity channels a power to create a radically different world. In the alternate prospect of Zion—a world based on our shared humanity and freedom—this power runs through each individual who opens up to it by pledging allegiance to the sacred flag of humanity. "Man is certainly unholy enough, but humanity in his person must be holy to him."[12]

Kant calls this second postulate, that there is a power capable of realizing the highest good or the just society, the postulate of God. In appealing to the language of religion, Kant simultaneously rejects the concept of an external deity that rules human beings with promises of rewards and threats of punishments. Belief in such a God only undermines the sense of moral duty, for instead of doing what is right because it is right, the individual is motivated by fear of punishment or desire for reward. Such an orientation only promotes egotism in the form of religion. In the traditional religious beliefs connected to the old civilization of egotism, human actions are not only controlled by media, business, and the State, but also by religion. In this religion, God is regarded as the external distributor of justice, granting happiness to those who follow his rules, and meting out punishments to the disobedient, if not in this life and on this earth, then in the afterlife.

With the almighty God of external religion, how can there be real freedom? If people are not free to be evil without facing eternal damnation, how can they be responsible for choosing what is right? In the framework of external religion, the deity commands certain actions and then punishes those who break those commands. But how can someone really be free if only one choice is permitted? If the realization of the highest good is the action of a God who enforces obedience in this way, how can the highest good be regarded as the action of human beings themselves? At first it would seem that such belief is about the power of an external God or a unique godlike Savior, and so is an admission that we ourselves, the ordinary people who need to be saved, are powerless. But for Kant, the experience of moral duty requires that *we ourselves* be capable of realizing our moral duty. Hence he says that the experience of duty is that of a power which elevates man above himself (as a part of the world of sense), a power which connects him with an order of things that only the understanding can conceive, with a world which at the same time commands the whole sensible world, and with it the empirically determinable existence of man in time, as well as the sum total of all ends (which totality alone suits such unconditional practical laws as the moral). This power is nothing but personality, that is, freedom and independence [of] the mechanism of nature. . . .[13]

It follows that the God or God-man ("the One") that we postulate should not be regarded as a separate being who perform miracles for us. Such divinity should be seen as an extension of ourselves as we transcend the limitations of physical separateness. This is what Kant calls "the divine human within us."[14] In the dynamic of *The Matrix*, there is a development from belief in an external savior to belief in our own godlike power, as united humanity, to save ourselves. This is our true inner "potential" or power. This understanding is evident in the final speech of "the One" at the conclusion of the film.

The moral duty to create the highest good is a duty for the human beings themselves. Morality is about human autonomy—about acting on the basis of laws we make ourselves and creating a world based on our own norms and choices as a united humanity. But for external religion the ordinary human individual is regarded as powerless to achieve the goals of justice in this life, on this earth. It is precisely this belief in human powerlessness that supports the Matrix of external controls. Hence as Morpheus says of the all-pervading Matrix, "You can feel it when you go to work, when you go to church, when you pay your taxes. It is the world that has been pulled over your eyes to blind you from the truth. . . . That you are a slave, Neo."

In the post-millennial religion of the New Age of Zion, however, the potential of natural and human forces is not alienated and externalized in economic or political powers, whose theological counterpart is an external, all-powerful, punitive and cajoling God. These external powers of contemporary life are epitomized in *The Matrix* by all-powerful intelligent machines who design the rules of the Matrix so as to ensure compliance to the best of their programming capacity. In the counterworld of Zion, however, the underlying, unifying power of our oneness with one another empowers each individual who opens up to it by recognizing the illusion of separate, ego-centered existence.

The shaven-headed and robed boy Potential implicitly tells Neo to put aside all categories of cause and effect when he says, "Do not try and bend the spoon. That's impossible." It's impossible because the laws of causality tell us that a physical change must be brought about by an external physical cause acting by contact. He then says, "Instead only try to realize the truth. . . . There is no spoon." That is, there are no separate objects in time and space, as this is assumed in the mechanistic outlook of a deterministic science. Once we put aside this a priori framework of scientific thought, with its laws of causality that presuppose independent objects separated from one another in time and space, "Then you'll see that it is not the spoon that bends, it is only yourself." It is the self that is the true cause—just the opposite of the mechanistic point of view. This is not an isolated self separate from other selves by the physical distances of independent bodies. That's the ego, not the true self—the ego that engenders the illusion itself. The true self is connected with all other selves in a universal humanity in which we are all "the one," or united. It is by opening to this universal humanity, with which we are all connected, that the moral person becomes the vehicle of the power behind the appearances, including the appearance of the spoon. For the spoon that we see is after all an appearance for us, a shape in experience that is produced in accord with our subjective rules of perception. If we are capable of setting aside the belief in separation from the objects that are part of our world—the world we ourselves produce—we might be able to move them by our thoughts in the same way we move our own bodies. When we move our bodies, we do not try to move something separate from us. That's impossible, and if we thought of ourselves in that way we would be incapable of moving at all. When I move my arm, I can do so because I truly believe that I am only moving *myself*. The mechanistic theory of causality is therefore refuted every time we move our bodies by a simple act of our own free will.

The "self" in this case is not the separate, isolated ego, but the higher self, in unity with the All. Godlike power will be ours if only we give up the illusion of separation. Neo must learn, not that he is *the* One—a special being apart from everyone else—but that he is one with all existence. He is, of course, "the One" who first fully understands this truth. For the mechanist, like Hobbes, the belief that the mind can move the body is an illusion, because it is contrary to the basic laws of physics.[15] Scientific thinking requires that we put aside such empowering beliefs as illusions, and adhere to the disempowering belief, so essential to the operation of the Matrix, that every movement of ours is governed by outside causes.

Fear and Trembling before the Power of Death

The third postulate of morality is the postulate of immortality. Overcoming the fear of death is essential to realizing the good and just society of Zion. By contrast, the world of the Matrix is a world governed by fear. Interpreting oneself to be a separate physical being, vulnerable to powerful physical and social forces, each individual must inevitably be afraid. The fundamental fear is fear of death, the extinction of that fragile physical existence. Fear of death presupposes that the individual fixes on his separate physical existence as the ultimate reality.

According to the belief structure of the Matrix, we can never escape from fear. In the opening sequence of the film, Neo's first step toward freedom places him vertiginously on the high ledge of his corporate tower. Then, he lets his fear govern his action rather than trust the mysterious guidance coming to him from Morpheus. The second time he confronts the fear of falling occurs in the virtual reality Construct aboard the Nebuchadnezzar. He is being initiated into the power of manipulating the illusion of the Matrix. He is discovering the exhilaration that comes from *consciously* living in the illusion. The key to uncovering one's power is to release all fear through belief in the power of his own mind. "You have to let it all go, Neo," Morpheus tells him. "Fear, doubt, and disbelief. Free your mind." Neo falls into the abyss only to discover the illusory nature of his fear. And yet, Neo in physical reality still bleeds. To Neo's questioning this, Morpheus replies enigmatically, "The body cannot live without the mind."

The meaning of this pronouncement becomes clear only with the unfolding of the logic of these ideas. Neo's initial distinction between the "reality" of life outside the Matrix, and the illusion within it, is simplistic. Those who are conscious of a reality outside the Matrix can become freer and more powerful within it. But existence within the Matrix, conversely, affects existence outside of it. Even outside the Matrix, the body is dependent on the beliefs of the mind.

The key to the realization of Neo's destiny—which is the unfolding and realization of his true self—consists in his rejection of the fear of death. Neo realizes his destiny when he chooses to give up his life for Morpheus, in accord with the prophecy of the Oracle. Rather than expound a deterministic fate, the Oracle gives him a choice: either his own life or Morpheus's life. "You're going to have to make a choice. In the one hand, you'll have Morpheus' life. And in the other hand, you'll have your own. One of you is going to die. Which one will be up to you."

The central elements in the prophecy of the Oracle can be understood through the postulates of morality. First, there is the postulate of freedom. Neo originally rejects the idea of fate because he wants to be in control of his life. He doesn't want an external power to govern his actions. He wants always to be free to choose. But fate and freedom are paradoxically interlinked. The fulfillment of Neo's fate is the outcome of his own free choice. As has been the case all along, Neo can choose differently. He could have chosen the blue pill and lived within the relative certainties of the dream life in the Matrix. The choice of the red pill, and truth, brings with it the risk of unforeseeable fears, and the enmity of the controlling powers of existence. Now the Oracle tells him that he must choose between saving himself and saving Morpheus.

Second, the prophecy of the Oracle postulates and supports the belief in a higher potential, in a power to which we all have access if we overcome our fears. In Kantian thought, we need to bolster our moral choice for the highest good with the belief in the power of its realizability—against all the appearances to the contrary. The postulate of God is the postulate that links our moral choice for the highest good to a belief in the power to realize this goal when we connect with our essential humanity, with our oneness with each other.

Turning Point: The End of Fear

The third postulate or deep belief of the moral individual is the belief in immortality. The humanity with which we are connected transcends the limited lifetime of the separate individual. Focusing on this limitation of one's separate existence naturally evokes fear. The third element of the prophecy clearly relates to death and survival. Someone must die, and someone will survive. In the world of the Matrix, where the principle of separation rules, the win-lose logic of separation is an iron law. The Oracle gives Neo this unhappy news: he is not the One, and either he or Morpheus must die.

> ORACLE: Sorry, kid. You got the gift, but it looks like you're waiting for something.
>
> NEO: What?
>
> ORACLE: Your next life, maybe. Who knows? That's the way these things go.

Of course the Oracle's prophecy is fulfilled to the letter. Neo saves Morpheus's life, loses his own, and then returns in his next life as the One. How and why this prophecy is fulfilled is the key to understanding the film.

In the process of saving Morpheus, Neo finds himself face to face with a seemingly invulnerable and all-powerful Agent. Despite their training in the Construct, which gives them tremendous powers in the

Matrix, the crew of the Nebuchadnezzar recognizes one ultimate fear-based rule: if you see an Agent, the only thing you can do is to run. This is Cypher's "realistic" advice to Neo, coupled with Cypher's debunking of any idea that Neo is the prophesied Savior. Hence, the dramatic turning point in the film occurs when Neo deliberately faces Agent Smith. He has made his choice; he will take his stand and face his death. Neo realizes this fate in complete freedom, choosing to save another person rather than preserve his own existence as a separate, vulnerable body.

Neo thereby overcomes the fundamental fear that governs the power of the Matrix both within the virtual reality world and outside of it in the so-called real world of physical bodies. The same basic rule applies to each world. If you believe that you can die, even in the world of illusion, you will really die in the physical world. The limited vitality of the physical body depends on the mind's belief in the ultimate power of death—the power of external forces and an external nature to destroy you. This is the basic rule that regulates the Matrix and extends into the physical world itself, as Cypher tellingly explains: "I think the Matrix could be more real than this world. All I do is pull the plug here. But there, you have to watch Apoc die." Your power, your reality, depends on your beliefs, and your beliefs are ultimately ruled by fear of death.

There remains only one step left in the unfolding of Neo's Fate. It is necessary to give up the belief in death. When Neo's body flatlines, Morpheus says, "It can't be." Morpheus cannot believe in Neo's death, although Neo, by all the rules of physical so-called reality, is dead. Trinity, however, goes further in defying the appearance of death. Speaking to Neo's dead body, she addresses his living spirit: "Neo, I'm not afraid anymore. The Oracle told me that I would fall in love, and that that man, the man that I loved, would be the One. So you see, you can't be dead. You can't be. Because I love you. You hear me, I love you." Thanks to Trinity's love and refusal to believe in his death, Neo comes back to life. In accordance with the words of the Oracle, Neo returns in his next life as "the One."

Immortality and Reincarnation

To fulfill one's destiny as a moral being it is necessary to give up belief in and fear of death. The postulate of immortality is necessary to the morally committed person, Kant argues, because within the limitations of one short lifetime it is impossible for the individual to perform one's ultimate duty: to bring about the advent of the highest good. We therefore inevitably project ourselves beyond this single lifetime in a kind of this-worldly immortality. The postulate of immortality is the belief in the reality of this natural projection.

The moral goal of bringing about the highest good is about our own world, not another one. Just as the postulate of freedom is about human ability in *this* world, so too must be the postulates of God and immortality. Thus, the immortality postulated by morality must be a "this-worldly" immortality. The traditional Christian doctrine of an otherworldly immortality does not adequately suit the requirements of moral consciousness. In traditional Christianity, belief in an otherworldly immortality compensates for the injustices of this world by promising justice in the next life. In practical terms, this belief reconciles the individual to injustice in the here and now and suggests he is powerless to rectify injustice with his own actions. Moreover, such belief subverts moral consciousness by offering an eternal reward for dutiful behavior: obedience to the commands of an external God will be rewarded in the afterlife. Morality is thereby reduced to a kind of spiritualistic egotism.

The main alternative to the otherworldly immortality of traditional Christianity is the "this-worldly" immortality of Hinduism and Buddhism. The Oracle's seemingly offhand reference to reincarnation, as well as the monkish robe and shaved head of the boy "Potential," suggest the Buddhist perspective. The soul or spirit of the enlightened individual or Bodhisattva, according to Mahayana Buddhism, chooses to remain on the wheel of birth and rebirth in order to facilitate the universal enlightenment of all living beings. This conception of the Bodhisattva is not that of a Savior but of a teacher who shows people how they can save themselves. In Kant's early writing, *Universal Natural History*, the immortality that expresses his cosmological perspective is one in which the individual soul is reborn over and over again as it climbs the ladder of potential human perfection.[16]

In *The Matrix*, the One who is to liberate humanity from its self-imposed imprisonment appears in three incarnations. In a first lifetime, which takes place prior to our segment of the story, he liberates a few individuals from the power-generating pods on which the AI rulers of the Matrix depend. The Oracle prophesies that this liberator will return in a new lifetime to complete his destiny—which, we begin to see, is not an externally determined one, but the choice of the individual called the One over many reincarnations to help bring about the liberation of humanity. *The Matrix* is mainly the story of the second lifetime of the One, in the persona of Neo, eminent hacker who takes the several leaps that bring him to the realization of his chosen fate. The final moments of the film give us a glimpse of the One in his third lifetime. The third lifetime fulfills the Oracle's prophecy that the One will destroy the power of the Matrix—although this occurs in unexpected ways over the subsequent films of the trilogy. Merely freeing individuals from the Matrix is an insufficient goal, one which by itself would only lead to the reproduction in physical reality of the repressive world of 1999. What then is the positive objective of the liberator's actions?

Savior or Teacher?

Liberation from the Matrix must be the creation of free human beings, not the state of beings living contented lives of happiness without freedom. Sleeping humanity rejects the unearned happiness of slaves that is the projection of their AI controllers. But how is such liberation possible under the rule and direction of a Philosopher King, or thanks to the beneficent acts of an all-powerful Savior?

Like the Christian Messiah Jesus, Neo dies and comes back to life. In the final image of the film, Neo takes on a contemporary popular culture persona as he sweeps up, up, and away, his open overcoat spreading out like Superman's cape. But Neo's final overvoice summation suggests a different interpretation: that the Savior is not an exceptional Superman, but a teacher of universal human liberation. As a teacher who shows others how to be like him, Jesus said of his follower: "The works that I do, shall he do also; and greater works than these shall he do."[17] Addressing the AI controllers, the One announces that his task of universal liberation involves the teaching of unlimited potential: "I'm going to show these people what you don't want them to see. I'm going to show them a world without you. A world without rules and controls, without borders or boundaries, a world where anything is possible."

The world without limits, where anything is possible, is a world in which, empowered by our fundamental oneness, each of us has the power to shape reality, to manipulate the Matrix of appearances and to realize the Zion of the highest good. For this good society to exist, it is necessary that egotism as a general principle of social life be overcome, that we rise to an understanding of our essential unity with one another, our common humanity. In this understanding we will find our freedom, our intrinsic connection with the godlike power to transcend the fear of death and to realize our highest ideals, "The One" may be the first superhuman being, but he is not the last.[18]

NOTES

1. Immanuel Kant, *Groundwork of the Metaphysics of Morals* (New York: Harper Torchbooks, 1964), 63.

2. Immanuel Kant, "Conjectural Beginning of Human History," in *Kant on History* (New York: Macmillan/Library of Liberal Arts, 1985), 55–56.

3. Kant, "Conjectural Beginning," 56.

4. In the *Groundwork*, Kant says that the highest good is the good will, while the complete good is the good will combined with happiness as a consequence. Later, in the *Critique of Practical Reason*, Kant uses the expression "highest good" to refer to this complete good. See Kant, *Critique of Practical Reason* (New York: Macmillan/Library of Liberal Arts, 1993), 117.

5. Immanuel Kant, *Critique of Pure Reason,* trans. Norman Kemp Smith (London: Macmillan, 1961), 22; Bxvi.

6. Wittgenstein, *Tractatus Logico-Philosophicus*, 5.63. www.kfs.org/~jonathan/witt/tlph.html. Translated from the German by C. K. Ogden. Accessed 12/18/06.

7. Jean-Paul Sartre, *Being and Nothingness* (New York: Citadel Press, 1968), 235.

8. Adam Smith, *The Wealth of Nations*, in *Great Books of the Western World*, vol. 39 (Chicago: Encyclopedia Britannica, Inc., 1952), 194.

9. Kant, *Critique of Practical Reason*, 120.

10. Immanuel Kant, *Critique of Pure Reason* (London: Macmillan & Company, 1961), 29; Bxxx.

11. Kant, *Critique of Practical Reason*, 90.

12. Kant, *Critique of Practical Reason*, 91.

13. Kant, *Critique of Practical Reason*, 90.

14. Kant, *Critique of Pure Reason*, 486; A569; B597.

15. See James Lawler, *Matter and Spirit: the Battle of Metaphysics in Modern Western Philosophy before Kant* (Rochester, NY: University of Rochester Press, 2006), 13–25.

16. Immanuel Kant, *Universal Natural History and Theory of the Heavens*, trans. Stanley L. Jaki (Scottish Academic Press, Edinburgh, 1981), 195–96. We will return to this idea in the next chapter.

17. John 14:12; The Holy Bible, Authorized (King James) Version (Chicago: Gideons International, 1961).

18. This chapter is an expanded and revised version of James Lawler, "We Are (the) One! Kant Explains How to Manipulate the Matrix, published in *The Matrix and Philosophy*, ed. William Irwin (Chicago: Open Court, 2002), 138–52.

3

The Multidimensional Universe of *Buffy the Vampire Slayer*

I was happy. Wherever I was, I was happy. At peace. I knew that every-
one I cared about was all right. I knew it. Time didn't mean anything.
Nothing had form. But I was still me, you know? And I was warm, and
I was loved, and I was finished, complete. I don't understand about the-
ology or dimensions, or any of it, really, but I think I was in heaven.
—BUFFY THE VAMPIRE SLAYER

[T]he person as belonging to the sensible world is subject to her own personality as belonging to the intelligible world. It is then not to be wondered at that the human being, as belonging to both worlds, must regard
his own nature in reference to its second and highest characteristic only
with reverence, and its laws with the highest respect.
—IMMANUEL KANT

Life Is Short

In the very first episode of *Buffy the Vampire Slayer*, "Welcome to the
Hellmouth," Buffy is standing with her Watcher, Giles, on a balcony in
the favorite Sunnydale hangout, the Bronze. Below them, young people
are pulsing to primal rhythms. Giles is aghast: "Look at them, throwing
themselves about, completely unaware of the danger that surrounds
them." Buffy replies with the wit, pathos, and directness that characterize her anguished appraisal of life: "Lucky them."

Buffy had previously been talking to Willow, her new friend at the
Sunnydale Public High School. Seemingly luckless in love and scorned

by the school's upwardly mobile fashion clique, Willow has been confessing her sense of social inadequacy: "I think boys are more interested in a girl who can talk." Willow believes Buffy belongs to the superior social set, with looks and money and guys. Buffy wants to set her straight on this score by giving Willow a soulful glimpse into her philosophy. "Well, my philosophy, do you wanna hear my philosophy?" Willow lights up: "Yeah, I do!" Buffy puts her philosophy—her basic view of life—in a nutshell: "Life is short." She pauses briefly. "Not original, I'll grant you, but it's true. You know? Why waste time being all shy and worrying about some guy, and if he's gonna laugh at you. Seize the moment, 'cause tomorrow you might be dead."

Buffy envies her seemingly happy peers, who are unaware that death lurks in every dark corner. Ignorance must be bliss, she imagines. She proposes an unoriginal philosophy of life, but for her there is ultimate originality. She is the Slayer, the only one in a generation, "one girl in all the world, a Chosen One, one born with the strength and skill to hunt the vampires. . . ." With these words, Giles exhorts Buffy to recognize her unique destiny and high responsibility. Buffy breaks in: "to stop the spread of their evil blah, blah, blah . . . I've heard it, okay?" Disturbed by her attitude, Giles reminds her of her "duty." Buffy is not moved: "I've both been there and done that, and I'm moving on."

Despite such protests in the name of ordinary life as she understands it, Buffy does assume the burden of her duty—especially when friends and loved ones and vulnerable people in general are threatened or victimized. When death strikes her schoolmates, Willow says, "I knew those guys. I go to that room every day. And when I walked in there, it . . . it wasn't our world anymore. They made it theirs. And they had fun. What are we gonna do?" Buffy knows her duty. Her fear and self-pity drop away. She answers, resolutely: "What we have to."

Moral Duty: Reverence for the Human Personality

As the Vampire Slayer, Buffy provides a powerful paradigm of moral responsibility. According to Kant, the essential feature of the moral point of view is the experience of duty. The moral person does what she has to do, what her duty requires. What duty fundamentally requires, Kant argues, is that we respect our common humanity, the fundamental essence of each individual. Kant too can put his moral philosophy in a nutshell. In his second formulation of the categorical imperative, he writes: "Now I say that man, and in general every rational being, exists as an end in himself, not merely as a means for arbitrary use by this or that will."[1]

This moral philosophy is based on the assumption that there is in each human being something that is of infinite worth and therefore requires the utmost respect—both from others as well as oneself. Significantly for our interpretation of *BtVS*, Kant extends the scope of moral respect beyond "man" or members of the human species to "every rational being"—to members of other species who are also capable of governing their lives from the standpoint of moral duty. Kant distinguishes moral rationality from instrumental rationality—intellect employed for purely pragmatic and possibly egotistical purposes. In *BtVS*, this concept of instrumental rationality is represented graphically by demonic beings whose intelligence is wholly subordinate to egotistical goals of power and pleasure, and who are altogether incapable of responding to any higher duty. It is the threat of death, Kant writes,[2] that brings to the fore the essential characteristics of morality. Aware of the infinite worth concealed in the individual, the morally committed person will sacrifice her life rather than unjustly cause the death of an innocent human person. And if the circumstances of her life make it her duty to protect others, then she will sacrifice her life to fulfill that duty.

Kant writes a kind of hymn of praise to duty in which he expresses its origins in a higher dimension than that of our ordinary human lives. Let us look at this passage on duty phrase by phrase, as a kind of philosophical poem:

> Duty! You sublime and mighty name that embraces nothing charming or insinuating, but requires submission,
>
> and yet seeks not to move the will by threatening anything that would arouse natural aversion or terror,
>
> but merely holds forth a law which of itself finds entrance into the mind,
>
> and yet gains reluctant reverence (though not always obedience),
>
> a law before which all inclinations are dumb, even though they secretly counter-work it;
>
> what origin is there worthy of you, and where is to be found the root of your noble descent which proudly rejects all kinship with the inclinations;
>
> a root to be derived from which is the indispensable condition of the only worth which human beings can give themselves?

It can be nothing less than a power which elevates the human being above herself (as a part of the world of sense),

a power which connects him with an order of things that only the understanding can conceive,

with a world which at the same time commands the whole sensible world,

and with it the empirically determinable existence of humanity in time,

as well as the sum total of all ends (which totality alone suits such unconditional practical laws as the moral).

This power is nothing but personality,

that is, freedom and independence from the mechanism of nature,

yet, regarded also as a faculty of a being who is subject to special laws, namely, pure practical laws given by one's own reason;

so that the person as belonging to the sensible world is subject to her own personality as belonging to the intelligible world.

It is then not to be wondered at that the human being, as belonging to both worlds, must regard his own nature in reference to its second and highest characteristic only with reverence, and its laws with the highest respect.

On this origin are founded many expressions which designate the worth of objects according to moral ideas.

The moral law is holy (inviolable).

The human individual is indeed unholy enough,

but she must regard humanity in her own person as holy.

In all creation everything one chooses and over which one has any power, may be used merely as means;

the human being alone, and with him every rational creature, is an end in himself.[3]

Only the existence of a higher dimension than that of ordinary physical existence makes sense of moral experience. For why would an individual sacrifice her life, or even any of her desires or interests, unless she were somehow connected to something that transcends these desires and interests, that transcends her entire "sensible" existence? This something Kant calls variously humanity, personality, or soul. He defines this higher personality as "freedom and independence from the mechanism of nature." In moral experience we directly feel the power of duty setting aside the forces of desire and interest, and all natural instincts or inclinations, whether these be for oneself or others. In the light of this moral experience, we can "postulate," rather than scientifically know, a free essence or soul that does not belong to the "world of sense" but to an "intelligible world," that is, to a world that we don't directly perceive with our five senses, but that we relate to in moral experience, and that alone makes coherent sense of this experience.

What is primary, however, is the *experience* of moral duty itself. A mere intellectual deduction of some sort of alleged duty would by itself have no power over our sensible inclinations and related goals. What comes first is the *feeling* of duty itself, and only then is there the meaningful intellectual reflection on its validity and its possible origin. Such rational reflection on the nature of duty takes two forms. The first is to validate that moral sense of duty in a particular case by establishing its accord with the fundamental laws of reason, which is what Kant calls the categorical imperative. No alleged duty can contradict the fundamental laws of reason, which includes respect for the humanity within each of us. The second level of our moral awareness involves becoming aware of the origin of duty in a higher realm or dimension than that of our common sensible experience: in a higher reality than the ordinary human world of time and space out of which arise the desires and sensible inclinations of bodily existence.

It is important to stress that it is the *experience* of duty that comes first. Buffy does not "reason out" her duty, but finds it thrust upon her as she witnesses the slaughter of innocents, and finds herself in the presence of violated humanity—the holy to which she bears witness in the face of the unholy. Giles is the expert in mere reasoning, as if logic were a power unto itself: You are a vampire slayer; and therefore, he reasons tautologically, you have the duty to slay vampires. And she replies: "blah, blah, blah." What is missing in Giles's attempt at moral argumentation is the personal experience or *feeling* of moral duty. Buffy must first find herself in the presence of a power before which all her ordinary, four-dimensional, earth-bound, midrange human goals and inclinations are set aside, or, as Kant says in the previous citation, made dumb or speechless. Only then does she experience the reverence that is called up by the sacred presence within her of duty. Kant explains that experience as due to the manifestation in ordinary life of the higher dimension of the human personality, which may first be recognized in its violation. It is not an external God that imposes commandments on human beings. It is the internal divinity of the human personality that imposes on the sensible individual or ego a duty to ignore her ordinary normal desires and cares, because she is so much more than these. The Vampire Slayer is a figure of humanity itself, for each human being has within himself a higher nature, from which stems a holy mission—to slay the darkness of living a merely sensible life, a life devoted to ego alone.

Such an explanation is in accord with Kant's distinction between appearance and reality. It is in moral experience that we come in contact with reality: the sacred inner dimension of our own being, which is not reducible to the requirements of causal laws in time and space, and before which the proper attitude is one of reverence. What is sacred, godlike in us, is our shared humanity, our fundamental unity with one another, and with all beings in the universe capable of the same self-determination that we humans, in our middle-earth positions, exercise so fitfully and falteringly.

While Kant emphasizes the need to postulate the existence of a higher, "intelligible world," the same reasoning implicitly postulates a lower world as well. In the projected lower world, sensible experience, with the instrumental intelligence that is subordinate to its demands, exists independently of all moral awareness. If moral experience points above us to higher, heavenly dimensions, it also points below—to the hell realms of vampires and demons who threaten to take over our world, and have fun in doing so.

BtVS explores the issue of pure evil, embodied in soulless beings of darkness who are able to take over the bodies of humans. There is the black humor of the vampire Spike, feeling alone and rejected by his own kind because a computer chip implanted in his brain prevents him from expressing his natural vampire nature. It is Christmas, a cold wind is blowing on a deserted street as he looks longingly into a window to see fellow vampires sitting around a warm fire enjoying the holiday—by feasting on the bodies of captured humans. Evil is goodness turned inside out, without rhyme or reason, for the bloodthirsty pleasure of doing harm.

In moral experience we tend to suppose our involvement in two opposing worlds, two dimensions of being, the purely intelligible and the purely sensible. Out of these two opposing dimensions, our intermediary, mixed human world is constructed. And the way it is constructed depends on us.

Philosopher as Vampire Slayer

In Plato's "Allegory of the Cave,"[4] the basic nature of human existence is portrayed through an imaginative fantasy involving people who live their entire lives in a dark cave. One of them somehow leaves the cave, climbs out of its darkness and up to the sunlight, and makes the momentous discovery that there is more to reality than the shadow-world that others take to be reality. *The Matrix* brings out a central feature of Plato's classic story—the contrast between illusion and reality. Ultimately, we learn that this contrast is superficial: there is illusion in the reality and reality in the illusion. It is all therefore reality in one form or another. *Buffy the Vampire Slayer* more straightforwardly presents such a multidimensional interpretation of Plato's parable. Rather than primarily contrasting illusion and reality, this seven-year-long TV series asks us to picture reality as containing different levels or dimensions. There are lower, darker dimensions of being, and higher, brighter ones. And ordinary human reality is in the middle, between various heavens and hells. It's *all* reality, but reality in this framework is multidimensional. From this point of view, the illusion consists in taking what we see with our ordinary sensibility for the *only* reality.

According to Plato, the philosopher is the person who recognizes that there is a higher dimension than that of ordinary sensible reality. The philosopher's understanding of the multidimensional structure of reality imposes a duty: to dispel the darkness shrouding and controlling the lower level of existence in order to bring its captives up to a new level of being that is closer to the light of truth. In Plato's allegory, the person who has seen the sun itself returns to the darkness of the cave to liberate the others from both their ignorance and their rigidly confined and defined, one-dimensional way of life. But the power of darkness is not easily dispelled. Just as the citizens of Athens killed their true benefactor, Socrates, the cave-dwellers kill their teacher and liberator. The performance of duty inevitably leads to a life-and-death struggle between the witness to the higher world of light and the vampirelike forces of darkness that live from their power over human minds. The viewer of *Buffy the Vampire Slayer* (*BtVS*) will readily recognize that the Vampire Slayer, because she is aware of both higher and lower dimensions, is a contemporary version of Plato's philosopher.

Kant's Multidimensional Universe

In one of his earliest works, *Universal Natural History and Theory of the Heavens*,[5] Kant reestablishes the Platonic vision of a multidimensional universe through the resources of modern science. The universe begins, Kant thinks, as an infinitely extended gaseous cloud composed of elements of widely varying densities. Through the operation of the basic Newtonian forces of attraction and repulsion, the densest elements gravitate together first to form galaxies of especially heavy material. Worlds made of finer stuff, with less gravitational pull, naturally evolve later.

The evolution of consciousness follows a parallel pattern from denser to finer, from darker to lighter. Consciousness naturally evolves in steps or stages, going from ignorance and limited practical ability to greater knowledge and skill. It is appropriate, therefore, that the very beginning of the history of spirit in the universe be situated in that very dense matter that constitutes the earliest world systems. The mental abilities found in such worlds would be of the densest and darkest kind, in psychological terms. Perhaps the inhabitants are like the demons in "The Harvest" or in "Bargaining" whose idea of fun is sheer destruction. On the scale of evolution, in which ontogeny repeats phylogeny, they are like full-grown two-year-olds in their negative stage.

We can suppose, Kant thinks, that human beings exist in the midrange of the total spectrum of possibilities. This is suggested by the fact that most of our energies are devoted to physical survival, while the higher possibilities of creative spirit are realized very seldom, sporadically, and in flashes, rather than consistently and forcefully. Human beings are *capable* of recognizing and acting on their duty, but how often do we actually overcome our lesser and lower inclinations and rise to the level that a higher duty demands of us?

Kant's early cosmology has one important difference from the cosmology we find in *BtVS*. He sees the different worlds as separated by immense temporal and spatial differences, whereas in *BtVS* the distances are reduced, the dimensions border closely on one another, and the transitions between them can be very rapid. A portal to the darkest dimensions happens to be found in the basement of Buffy's own Sunnydale High School. In his later philosophical thought, however, Kant comes closer to the hierarchical cosmology of *BtVS*, in which the contrast between higher and lower dimensions takes precedence over the temporal-spatial framework of earlier and later stages of evolution. Kant came to think that we are conditioned by our distinctly human physical and psychological makeup to subjectively *interpret* the immensity of the reality that lies beyond our possible experience *as if* it were divided by great distances, both spatial and temporal. Time and space, he later argues, are subjective frames for interpreting and organizing our sensible experience, not objectively valid features of the reality-in-itself of what we experience.

Such reality as it exists in itself may be quite different from the way we naturally think about it from our limited, midrange, human perspective. Practical moral experience, not scientific thought, gives us insight into the true nature of reality. Reality is not something that simply exists independently of us, which we then more or less accurately reflect in our perceptions and ideas. It is in part a creation of our ways of perceiving and knowing. More fundamentally, we continually create it in our practical lives as we choose between duty and desire.

Hume Wakes Kant from his Dogmatic Slumber

In his *Critique of Pure Reason*, Kant proposes this thought experiment: "Hitherto it has been assumed that all our knowledge must conform to objects. . . . We must make trial . . . whether we may not have more success in the tasks of metaphysics, if we suppose that objects must conform to our knowledge."[6] According to the old metaphysics of Aristotle, scientific thought mirrors or reflects an independent reality that we directly perceive around us. But this perspective was overthrown by the Copernican revolution in astronomy, and Galileo's similar revolution in physics. After Copernicus we can no longer accept at face value the world that we directly perceive. We directly perceive the sun going around the earth, but post-Copernican modern science claims that the opposite is really the case: the earth goes around the sun. We directly perceive ordinary bodies falling down, though some kinds of things, like fire, go upward. Aristotle concluded that earth and fire had two fundamentally different kinds of nature, each with its own natural form of motion. But according to Galileo *all* objects continue in a straight line in whatever direction they are propelled, unless or until a counterforce interacts with them to cause them to move in a different direction.

These ideas of modern science involve a fundamental revolution in the way reality is conceived. They imply that reality is not what it appears to be. Hence to attain the truth about the nature of things, it is not good enough to describe the way the world appears to our senses. There is much more to reality than meets the eye in common experience. String theory in contemporary physics claims that fundamental reality may consist of ten or eleven dimensions instead of the three dimensions of space and the fourth dimension of time that we perceive in direct experience. Such contemporary speculation validates Kant's conception that there is far more to reality than what appears in the four dimensions of ordinary experience. In this same spirit, *BtVS* expounds a universe of multiple dimensions beyond those of ordinary human-centered experience.

The Physics of Invisibility

Equipped with such Kantian cosmological metaphysics, we can think of time and space as subjective forms of knowing, not as features of reality in itself. While the constitution of ordinary humans obliges us in our sciences to represent different worlds as separated from ours by great distances, we are free to *think* and to *imagine* that in reality different densities or dimensions of the cosmic order may in fact impinge on one another in more proximate ways. Science fiction—imagination that goes beyond the limits of science without being in conflict with it—can picture for us portals into other dimensions lurking in the recesses of high school libraries.

The ordinary four-dimensional world of time and space, in which objects exist separately from one another with their own independent existence outside of our thoughts, is nothing more than the world produced by ordinary consciousness. It is an appearance, not reality. Reality as it is in itself may be quite different. Kant's metaphysics of appearance and reality therefore opens up possibilities for imaginative science fiction and realistic fantasy where the gestalt of ordinary space-time knowing is dropped or replaced with another mode of perceiving and other powers of doing, as if a being from another, more advanced, world has been born and raised in ours. Such a person, we are told, is Buffy the Vampire Slayer. With the capacity for encountering realities to which the common person is blind, the Slayer feels compelled by duty to make use of her unusual ability for the betterment of the world. At the same time, she yearns to join the standpoint of ordinary experience, the common experience of young people her age. Her duty therefore conflicts with her desires—which is what makes it *duty*, a responsibility that involves the possibility of sacrifice. In this captivating setting of the metaphysically informed drama, *Buffy the Vampire Slayer*, series creator Joss Whedon renders the possibilities of multidimensionality visible. And in this fascinating framework the perennial choice between duty and desire reappears with added power and poignancy.

Following Kant's revolutionary thought experiment, then, instead of supposing that the world as we see it is fixed and independent of our consciousness, we should recognize that we create the world of our experience out of our basic beliefs. In "Out of Mind, Out of Sight," Marcie becomes invisible after being regularly ignored by her teacher and other students. Because she mentally and emotionally sees herself as invisible, she becomes physically invisible, and begins to work gruesome revenge on those who previously ignored her. When recognition of such self-determining causality finally dawns, Xander says: "What, she turned invisible because no one noticed her?" Giles suddenly sees the light: "Of course! I've been investigating the mystical causes of invisibility when I should have looked at the quantum mechanical! Physics." Giles explains the science: "It's a rudimentary concept that reality is shaped, even created, by our perception."

According to the Copenhagen interpretation of quantum mechanics, the way the observer approaches subatomic entities shapes the form in which they appear, whether as a compact particle or a fluid wave-form. Here is a contemporary scientific validation of Kant's thought experiment that instead of regarding our thoughts as reflections of an independent world, we should think of the world of our experience as constituted in fundamental ways by our thoughts. In "Nightmares," the energy barrier between dream life and waking life collapses through a contagion of fear arising out of the unleashed psyche of an abused child. In this dreaming reality, Buffy finds herself powerless and facing the Master, a vampire: "This isn't real. You can't be free!" The Master replies: "You still don't understand, do you? I am free because you fear it. Because you fear it, the world is crumbling. Your nightmares are made flesh."

In the universe of *BtVS*, the structure and even the very existence of our world are determined by our basic choices. Fear and love are the two poles around which whole worlds are constructed. The fundamental tension between them grounds our basic choices and creates the dynamics of the evolution of our human world. These two poles of existence produce the duty of the philosopher/slayer, which is first of all to dispel the dark shadows cast by fear.

Dreams of Metaphysics

By pointing out the limits of our ordinary ways of perceiving reality, by emphasizing their subjective basis in the specific structures of human experience, Kant's philosophy awakens our imaginative and speculative thinking to the possibility of larger perspectives. If the structure of our minds, which are perhaps those of humans in the middle of the spectrum of universal possibility, imposes a four-dimensional space-time framework on common experience, critical reflection awakens us to the possibility of a richer reality transcending our species-centered limitations. In this way, imaginative fiction finds justification for its exuberant creations in Kant's critical reflection on the nature of modern science and the limitations of ordinary sense experience.

Kant remained an adherent of the old way of thinking—in which we more or less directly experience reality in itself—until he was awakened from his dogmatic slumber, as he puts it, by the arguments of David Hume. In an early work of his, Kant writes of the "Dreams of Metaphysics." If we have an inadequate or incorrect conception of reality, or metaphysics, we live mentally in a kind of dream world. Hume freed Kant from a philosophical dream world based on the idea that to attain scientific truth the mind should simply reflect the world that we perceive outside of us. But if we do that, argues Hume, we can never get the universality and necessity that characterize scientific laws. No matter how many white swans we see, we can never justifiably say that "All swans are white." All we have a right to say is that all swans that we have seen are white. This is true of all knowledge based on experience, of all "synthetic" knowledge, or knowledge involving the synthesis of subject and predicate, such as "swan" and "white."

According to Hume, only when the object is already included, by definition, in the subject, can we say that all x is y. We can be confident "a priori," or independent of any further experience, that "all bachelors are unmarried men" not because we have done a study of all bachelors, but because the term "unmarried man" is the verbal definition of bachelor. Someone who is not married is by definition a bachelor. But should we say the same about that black swan-looking creature we discover on our travels? Should we say that swans are by definition white, and so this must not be a swan? No. When investigating the nature of the external world, we are not concerned so much about our ways of defining reality as about reality as it is in itself. Scientific knowledge moves forward by breaking free from the limitations of old definitions. Hence Hume argues that we cannot know any universal and necessary truths about the world of experience. Truths by stipulation or verbal definition, whose truth we can know a priori, are called analytic truths. Hume considered all mathematical truths to be analytically true. Only such analytic truths, he holds, can be universally and necessarily true. But our synthetic knowledge about the empirical world, involving empirical or "a posteriori" discoveries, can never achieve such universality and necessity. With this argument Hume challenged the notion that modern science has discovered universal and necessary truths, and so awakened Kant from his dogmatic slumber and set the stage for what he calls his Copernican revolution in philosophy.

A *Priori* Synthetic Truths

Kant had a twofold problem to resolve. On the one hand, science, with its causal laws, seems to make morality, with its assumption of human freedom, impossible. If human actions are governed by causal laws, how can we be responsible for our actions? Hume's argument seems to give Kant a way to solve this problem. For if there are no such things as scientific laws, then they can pose no problem for morality. But Kant not only wants to defend morality; he wants to defend science as well. He does not accept the notion that such laws as Newton's first law and the law of gravity are only generalizations from a limited experience, and that we might come across new facts that disprove such laws. His Copernican revolution in philosophy allows him to solve both problems.

Consider the nature of a triangle. All triangles have three straight lines. This is an analytic truth known a priori, or independently of the study of the nature of triangles. But this "truth" is only an explanation of what we mean by the word "triangle." It is true by definition of the term that all triangles are closed two-dimensional figures composed of three straight lines. But what about the theorem of Pythagoras that in all right triangles the square of the hypotenuse is equal to the sum of the squares of the sides? Is that also an a priori, analytic truth, known by definition? Or is it a "synthetic" truth discovered in experience? People knew what triangles were for thousands of years before the discovery of the law of Pythagoras. This was a genuine discovery in the history of mathematics. Not only the physical sciences but also mathematical sciences involve discoveries regarding the nature of their respective fields, and so such discoveries are not merely analytical truths or truths by definition. But Hume's understanding of our knowledge from experience would require saying that Pythagoras's law is only an empirical or a posteriori generalization from observation of a limited number of right triangles. It is no more valid than the proposition, All swans are white. We should leave open the possibly that there might be right triangles in which Pythagoras's law does not apply. But that is clearly absurd. We are confident that Pythagoras's theorem will apply to *all* right triangles. But what is the basis of such confidence if it is neither true analytically nor through generalization from experience?

Kant answers that triangles are not externally existing things that we come across in our observations of a supposedly external reality, but objects created by human beings following certain rules of construction. We follow those same rules whether on earth or in the remotest region of the universe, and for this reason these rules apply universally and necessarily to all triangles. Pythagoras's law was a genuine discovery of the science of geometry, and not an analytic truth. But it is also not a purely empirical or a posteriori truth like that of the color of swans. We can know with universality and necessity that all right triangles conform to this law because we *actively construct* right triangles according to the same rule of construction that has as one of its necessary features, discovered through the development of geometrical science, the law of Pythagoras. Pythagoras's law is a necessary implication of the way in which right triangles are created, and therefore neither a purely analytic a priori truth, nor a purely synthetic a posteriori one. It is, Kant reasons, an "a priori synthetic" truth. The synthesis of properties that leads to the law of Pythagoras is produced a priori, through our own linking up of the basic elements of the right triangle as we create it according to a definite rule.

It follows more generally that we can know with universality and necessity all the realities that we ourselves create according to definite rules. Kant argues that we create our temporal and spatial coordinates in this way—laying down a grid on experience according to certain rules for constructing space and time. We impose other rules as we construct our own experience in a priori synthetic ways, giving us rules of causality and obliging us to consider the world as consisting of distinct objects or substances having definite properties. The world of human experience therefore has universal and necessary characteristics, such as that *all* "objects" we experience will *necessarily* be made up of various properties, exist in time and space, and follow one another according to laws of causality. But such universality and a necessity only applies "for us." We cannot insist that these *human* truths operate also in the experiences of other beings, with abilities below or above our own—beings who are operating in a different dimensional framework. The vampire Master understands this logic. "Because you fear it, the world is crumbling. Your nightmares are made flesh." We cannot say that reality in itself follows the laws that are necessary conditions for giving coherence to *our* experience.

Free Will and Determinism

Kant extends his discovery of a priori synthetic truth into the sphere of metaphysics, where we confront the perennial question as to whether all objects are governed deterministically by the law of causality, or whether there is a possibility of free will. Newton's first law is a particular formulation of this law of causality. According to Newton's first law, all material objects move in a straight line until or unless some other material object moves them in a different direction by coming into contact with them. We can see that were this true of reality, of things in themselves, we could never say that we move an arm by an act of free will, or just by willing it to move. For the law says that *all* movements of bodies are *necessarily* caused by other movements of bodies. These other movements of bodies have in turn been moved by other bodies, etc., etc. The motion of my arm cannot be due to an act of free will—that is, by an act of willing that is not caused by another force acting upon it. But according to the law of causality, of which Newton's first law is a formulation, *all* objects of experience take place in time and space and follow causal laws.

But suppose that the law of causality is a rule by which we construct our own experiences. Experience has two sources, Kant reasons: a posteriori, or from reality existing independently of us, and a priori, from our own activity. Consider the famous phenomenon of the gestalt shift. A certain figure on paper can appear in two different ways. When we first look at the figure, we see a vase. But with a shift of our attention, it appears as two faces looking at one another.

How something appears to us clearly depends, therefore, on how we look at it. The human mind is not a purely passive reflector of external facts, but imposes its own perspectives on the objects we see. We will often see what we expect to see, and miss that for which we are unprepared ahead of time. The law of causality is one of those forms of experiencing objects, Kant argues, and so wherever we are in the universe, we are able to look for causes—not because they are laws governing things in themselves, but because they are a priori ways by which we organize our experience. In our scientific "gestalt" or frame of mind, we see nothing but causal dependencies. In science we are learning about the properties of objects given to us in sensory experience, and so we implicitly adopt an attitude of quasi-passivity. This is not the pure passivity of the old Aristotelian science nor that of Humean empiricism in which a posteriori generalization from experience is the essence of science. It is a form of passivity that is already structured in advance, or a priori, by certain basic rules of organization and expectation. We cannot be purely passive, or completely open without any restriction to what is there, because if we were our experience would be a dizzying chaos of random impressions. We know ahead of time which way is up, for example. If we lose this a priori framework, we lose control of our very ability to investigate the facts. We study the behavior of distinct objects, carefully distinguished from other objects. To understand something we must first isolate it as a distinct object from its surroundings, for otherwise our thought processes would be overwhelmed by the immensity and flow of the universe. We examine these isolated objects within a structured temporal flow of events, using a watch or some other instrument for measuring time. And what we are looking for, within this space-time framework are causal laws or regularities. Thus space and time, substance and property, cause and effect, are forms of organizing our experience within the general framework or gestalt of *knowing* things.

Unknowability of Things in Themselves

It doesn't follow from this that reality in itself is spatiotemporal, discretely articulated, and subject to causal laws. These are *human* forms of knowing. Flies do not see the world the way humans do. Angelic intelligences, supposing they exist, do not have to conform to the plodding procedures of human investigation. These are *our* ways of organizing knowledge. They yield *appearances for us*, not *things as they are in themselves*.

Further evolution of science after Kant's time shows that the framework of Newtonian science is not absolute even for us. It is a limited way of organizing experience that can be superseded by more encompassing rules about space and time, interaction within fields, and so forth. By recognizing the *relative* nature of our scientific framework, Kant prepared the theoretical grounds for fundamental revolutions in science. For example, with his conception that Euclidian space and linear time are relative ways of knowing, not properties of reality in itself, Kant facilitated the development of non-Euclidian geometry, Einstein's theory of the relativity of space-time, as well as later conceptions of string theory according to which there are many more dimensions of reality than the classical four of space and time, however relativistically understood.

This does not mean that the twentieth and post-twentieth century physics has found empirical facts that refute the earlier physics. New facts are always coming in, of course. But it is not as though Einstein discovered the black swan of physics—so that Newton's physics applies to some objects but not to others. What Einstein did was to transform one general framework or paradigm for looking at *all* objects to another, more comprehensive one. The new revolutions in physics have not, however, given us knowledge of things as they are in themselves. With all the unsolved mysteries regarding the fundamental nature of things, this must be admitted. We would like to think that they have gotten us *closer* to the knowledge of things in themselves, just as Copernicus did in relation to the astronomy of Aristotle and Ptolemy. But how can we measure the distance between what we know and the reality that still remains unknown? If we had a measuring rod, perhaps the distance traveled is so minimal, and so confined to a distinctly human dimensionality, as to seem negligible in the light of higher truth. Those intelligences operating in higher dimensions may be smiling at the simplicity of our most advanced sciences, joking in their warp-speed spacecraft about the supposed absolute nature of the speed of light that we humans take as dogma.

The new developments in science simply provide new frameworks for organizing our experience, frameworks that are more adequate for certain *practical* purposes. But reality, as it exists in itself, remains a great unknown. Things in themselves are unknown, and unknowable, since our ways of knowing are *always* filtering our experiences through an a priori framework of organization and investigation. This remains the case as long as we proceed from a certain assumption or gestalt: that of the quasi-passive knower. This remains the case as long as we fail to see another side of the matter: that we ourselves are active agents in the construction of the world in which we exist. Theoretical reason has one set of expectations, but practical action raises a different perspective, yielding a quite different gestalt. And when we make the shift from theoretical explanation to practical living, we see even more clearly that reality is not something we can conceivably know. When we make that shift from theory to practice, we are no longer filtering reality according to a priori frameworks of knowledge, but we are actively creating reality itself. When we adopt the standpoint of practical activity, we inevitably see ourselves as free creators of reality itself.

With all this in mind we can see how Kant solved two problems with his one theory of a priori synthetic truths. He solved the problem that scientific determinism creates for morality. We see now that the causal framework of science with its deterministic laws is an a priori form of organizing experience, not a reflection of the way things are in themselves. So the moral perspective, with its belief in free will, is still possibly true, and in no way conflicts with the presuppositions of science. Our scientific knowledge, with its framework of causal, deterministic explanation, is about appearances, not things in themselves. Hence, it remains possible that things in themselves, which include ourselves as practical and moral beings, may be free from causal determination. In this way, the problem of the apparent conflict between science and morality is solved.

Moreover, we can understand why Hume was not entirely correct in his denial of the possibility of having genuine laws regarding objects of experience. We can defend the universality and necessity of the fundamental scientific laws inasmuch as these express our a priori modes of organizing our cognitive experience. We can say with certainty that all objects exist in time and space, not because there are no multidimensional spaces and times, or even atemporal, spatially unextended objects, but because, confined to our limited human apparatus of knowledge, we can never *know* such objects. That objects must operate on standard time and in three-dimensional space is a rule of construction for experiencing reality, and so it applies universally and necessarily *for us* because wherever we go in the universe, we always carry with us this rule for knowing things. But let us always keep in mind the fact that when we understand that something exists *for us*, we do not understand it as it is *in itself.* And so we can legitimately formulate the *idea* of other dimensions and look for the effects of those other dimensions within the four-dimensional space-time that is accessible to us.

Reality, however, must include our own activity. To make real headway toward reality as it exists in itself, it is necessary to make a gestalt switch from the standpoint of knowing to the standpoint of doing. We must move our consciousness from the quasi-passive standpoint of the receiver of information, who implicitly or unconsciously structures and transforms the inputs of experience according to a priori forms of perception and understanding, to the active subject who not only deliberately constructs a world on the basis of rules, but chooses between different kinds of worlds. Our *activity* inevitably supposes a moral dimension and a leap of freedom, even if our *science* denies such imponderables.

However, when we perform such a gestalt switch from theory to practice, let us not make the mistake of thinking that we can somehow *know* reality in itself from this practical standpoint—that we can somehow *know*, for example, that we are free. We can never know this, because as soon as we adopt the standpoint of knowing we revert to the framework of cognitive experience that includes cause-effect relationships. We shift back into the gestalt of knowing, for which any possible freedom becomes invisible. We can however *think* that we are free. We can *believe* it. Hence Kant argues that the central goal of his first *Critique* is to deny knowledge in order to make way for faith. The moral person cannot *know* that she is free, but if she is to persist in her moral frame of mind she must *postulate* the reality of freedom. Beyond knowing, with its framework of causal science, there are other cognitive activities linked with action—*thinking* about what exists beyond the horizons of knowledge, *believing* in a certain configuration of things in themselves, *postulating* objects of faith for purposes of practical life.

Contradictions of the Middle World

Human life between two worlds has a paradoxical nature. Without our sensible desires and attachments, we would not experience what we ought to do as a hard duty. The desire to enjoy the full experience of sensible life is an indispensable condition for evoking all the pathos in which the needs of the sensible ego must sometimes be sacrificed in the name of duty. Kant argues that moral experience ultimately demands that we reconcile these conflicting tendencies and create a kind of heaven on earth, the highest good, in which sensible demands are fulfilled on the basis of moral principles. We must therefore be fully embodied beings to fulfill our moral duty.

But by this very condition of morality we are constantly tempted to immerse ourselves wholly in the sensible world—to become creatures of the dark for whom the urges of a pure sensibility are the sole motivating forces. One way of escaping the conflicting demands of the earth plane, in *BtVS*, is for individuals to give up their souls and become vampires. Similar temptations of sensuous gratification and physical power take both Angel and Spike down this path. While Angel never rejoins the human species, he does achieve the status that Kant intends by "rational being" when his soul is restored to his vampire physical form. At the end of season 6, Spike too recovers his soul. Moreover, all of the Scooby Gang with the exception of Giles have relationships that put them in intimate connection with the demonic forces. Without knowledge of the dark, can we truly appreciate the light? Isn't the sun lovelier at dawn than at noonday?

In "The Initiative," the vampire Spike receives a substitute for the soul in the form of a behavior-modifying computer chip that prevents him from directly assaulting humans. In "Crush," Buffy discovers that her sister Dawn has a crush on "cool" Spike: "He's a killer, Dawn. You cannot have a crush on something that is . . . dead, and, and evil, and a vampire." She could love Angel, she says, because he has a soul. Dawn replies: "Spike has a chip. Same diff." But it is not the same. The purely instrumental technology that treats human beings as things to be used and controlled, rather than as "ends in themselves" with infinite value, cannot create a true substitute for the soul, which has the capacity for connecting to the higher dimension of existence that is implicit in the awareness of duty.

In "Anne," Buffy has once more attempted to abandon her slayer duty because of the tremendous emotional pain it has cost her. She therefore stops being "Buffy" and becomes "Anne," a waitress swallowed up in the anonymity of urban life. She discovers that the ultimate logic of this world leads not to the elusive happiness of "ordinary life," but to enslavement. Having first accepted the subordinate position of a wage-slave in a restaurant as a condition for survival, she is forced to experience to the fullest extent the inner logic of this ordinary dependence of daily life. She becomes part of a world that is completely shorn of the illusions of freedom, a denizen of an underworld system governed by fear and force. Only through following our duty, Kant says, do we acquire the true freedom that stems from our sacred personality. Otherwise, if we seek merely to satisfy our physical needs and desires, we abdicate our freedom and inevitably become slaves in a mechanistic underworld founded on our own cowardly acquiescence.

In this dark world, the higher personality is obliterated. A guard says to the prisoners: "You work, and you live. That is all. You do not complain or laugh or do anything besides work. Whatever you thought, whatever you were does not matter. You are no one now. You mean nothing." When he asks a young man his name, the young man replies, "Aaron," and is bashed to the ground. The others quickly learn the lesson, and reply, when asked their names, "No one." Buffy refuses to consent to this obliteration of her essential personality. With recovered pride and the sense of humor that always accompanies restored self-awareness, when it comes to her turn to answer the question of her identity, Buffy replies: "I am Buffy, the Vampire Slayer. And you are . . . ?"

The Power of Teamwork and Love

As a paradigm of the moral experience, Buffy is not a lone, solitary superhero. She attracts Willow and Xander who recognize through her the demands of a higher duty, and are uplifted and exhilarated by it. In "The Harvest" Buffy tells Willow and Xander: "You guys don't have to get involved." "What d'ya mean?" says Xander. "We're a team! Aren't we a team?" "Yeah!" says Willow, brightly. "You're the Slayer, and we're, like, the Slayerettes!"

Buffy could not fulfill her duty as an isolated heroine, for the world-saving tasks that confront the moral individual are too monumental to be taken on by one person alone. Entering the multidimensional universe through the portal of Buffy's courage and commitment, others too discover that they have a higher destiny and hidden abilities to fulfill that destiny. At the end of "The Harvest," the concluding episode to the first season, Willow asks, "Did we win?" Buffy replies, nonchalantly, "Well, we averted the Apocalypse. I give us points for that." Xander is trying to grasp the import of his life-changing discoveries: "One thing's for sure: nothing's ever gonna be the same."

This theme of cooperation culminates in "Primeval." In the mystical symbolism of their combined abilities, Willow is Spirit, Xander is Heart, Giles is Mind, and Buffy is Hand. Together they achieve a merging of essence (as Xander explains to Philip in "Checkpoint") that defeats Adam, the unnatural creation of purely instrumental science. The merging of souls is made possible by the mutual respect and love that conquers separation and fear. Science in the service of governmental power produces a superdemonic distortion of the forces of nature. Importantly, it is the vampire Spike who recognizes this ultimate secret weapon of the Slayer, and contracts with Adam to sow division among the Slayer's group. Egotism, fear, and separation are the natural element of the vampire.

Too Much Heaven

While the first five seasons are devoted to threats from the forces of darkness, the sixth season suggests the dangers of too much light. In "Bargaining," Xander states the facts about Buffy's death as these appear to sensible experience: "We saw her body, Will. We buried it." Willow, whose magical power taps into unseen dimensions, replies: "Her body, yeah. But her soul . . . her essence . . . I mean, that could be somewhere else. She could be trapped, in some sort of hell dimension like Angel was."

Angel's descent into a hell realm was appropriate in view of his sense of guilt and desire for atonement for his life as a vampire. But Buffy longs for a heaven in which she is freed from the burdens and contradictions of duty. "Death is your gift," says her Spirit Guide, taking the appearance of the first Slayer ("Intervention"). In "The Gift," Buffy plunges through the portal of death, simultaneously realizing her duty, and freeing herself from it. Buffy's death, motivated both by her duty as Slayer and by love of her sister Dawn, turns out to be a gift to herself. It is her portal to heaven. And heaven is simply a direct experience of her true self, her essence, her soul, unencumbered by the complexities of physical existence in the middle world of our earth. In "After Life," Buffy describes this experience: "I was happy. Wherever I was, I was happy. At peace. I knew that everyone I cared about was all right. I knew it. Time didn't mean anything. Nothing had form. But I was still me, you know? And I was warm, and I was loved, and I was finished, complete. I don't understand about theology or dimensions, or any of it, really, but I think I was in heaven."

Buffy has had a direct experience of her higher self, her true personality, the essential nature of which is to love. Her Spirit Guide (in "Intervention") had told her: "You are full of love. You love with all of your soul. It's brighter than the fire . . . blinding. That's why you pull away from it." Kant suggests that human beings are normally motivated in the first place by fear—fear of harm to one's separate physical existence, which is misperceived to be one's reality. In opposition to this tendency of fear, the essence of the individual, the true personality, the higher self, engages in universal love. It is ultimately because of this fundamental practical universality of love that we have the power of reason—that is, the power to think in universal terms.

Reason, the faculty of thinking in universals, is an expression of the essential nature of the personality, which is to engage in universal love. Reason is fundamentally an extension of this active, universal loving nature of the self or soul. But by itself, separated from the feeling of love, reason becomes an instrument of ego-centered desires and fears. It is such reason that Hume refers to when he says that "Reason is, and ought only to be, the slave of the passions, and can never pretend to any other office than to serve and obey them."[7] Such reason lacks the motivating power that is experienced in duty. In the light of the idea of Buffy's Spirit Guide, that she is really afraid of the soul itself, of the intensity of love that is her nature, Kant's conception of pure practical reason can be reformulated and deepened. The body-centered ego-consciousness, which people ordinarily identify with as their true nature, is afraid for its survival in a world of other such competing and conflicting ego-selves. But if it is afraid for its survival, it must also be afraid of the reality within itself, the sacred personality that sees other persons as other selves. For in the light of this reality, the ego loses its power and seeming solidity, which is linked to a life that is obscured by darkness and illusion. This conception of *BtVS* is similar to that of the existentialist philosophy of Jean-Paul Sartre, who also explains the self-deceptions of ordinary life by fear of one's true self. For Sartre, the essence of the true inner self, as opposed to the externally constructed ego, is freedom, freedom to choose the kind of life one will lead, and to take responsibility for one's choices as they impact on all human beings. Referring to Kant, Sartre argues that "existentialism is a humanism."[8]

In ordinary human life, where the perception of the true nature of the self penetrates with difficulty into the heavy densities of earth life, the inner nature of the self is reflected in duty. It is the obscure inkling of this higher dimension of one's own being that motivates moral duty. We experience the nature of our own authentic personalities only indirectly in moral experience—as single rays of the sun that break through a cloudy sky. The Platonic philosopher, the truly enlightened individual, experiences the sun itself. And so does Buffy when she enters the heaven of self to which death gives access. And like the Platonic philosopher, the Vampire Slayer returns to the cave of ordinary human life with its fitful and fleeting images of higher existence. She is dragged back into physical existence in response to the magical call of her companions. But her direct experience of self has been so overpowering that she now has the opposite difficulty to the one she had on first assuming her responsibility as Slayer. From being at first overly attached to ordinary life, Buffy has become too detached from it. Relative to the higher reality, earthly life, with its natural estrangement among bodies and vulnerability to darkness, now seems like a descent into hell. "Everything here is hard, and bright, and violent," she says in "After Life." "Everything I feel, everything I touch. This is Hell, just getting through the next moment, and the one after that, knowing what I've lost."

In such a context, death is no longer a threat but a promise of liberation—liberation from the burden of her duty and the contradictions of this world. For Buffy, the balance between the worlds has shifted from one in which the "sensible world" has the greatest pull, to one in which the "intelligible world," the world of the soul, has overwhelming force. We learn from these episodes that if we are called upon to realize our duty in this lifetime, it is better that we not be too intimately aware of the bliss of higher worlds. In the emotionally revelatory musical episode, "Once More, with Feeling," Buffy confesses that she has no feeling for life in this world: "Every single night, the same arrangement, I go out and fight the fight. Still I always feel this strange estrangement: Nothing here is real, nothing here is right."

In "Dead Things," Buffy reveals to Tara her fear that she has "come back wrong." In the same episode, we see Buffy once again standing on the balcony of the Bronze, looking down wistfully on the dancers below. Only this time she is not estranged from ordinary lives of blissfully ignorant teens but from her slayer companions who are practicing dance steps for Xander's and Anya's wedding. And it is not Giles at her side, urging her to realize her duty, but Spike, who whispers, "That's not your world. You belong in the shadows—with me." Paradoxically, it is only through the power of this darkness that Buffy recovers her balance. Her sexually explosive connection with the vampire Spike (they literally bring down the house in which they are making love) reignites the vital flow of physical energy that ultimately makes it possible for her to return fully to embodied existence and so to realize her duty. The shadows must draw us in when the light has become too strong. Against a traditional religious conception of life as a battle between light and dark, Buffy learns that the evolution of human existence involves a continually shifting *balance* of light and dark. To affirm the holiness of humanity in the here and now, she must battle the light as well as the dark.

It is her sense of duty—above all now to herself—that pulls Buffy once more back out of the shadows into the light of her true identity. In "As You Were," she breaks up with Spike, evoking the central commandment of morality that forbids treating oneself or others, as Kant says, as "merely as a means for arbitrary use by this or that will."[9] "I'm using you," she tells Spike, "and it's killing me." She realizes that in using Spike and letting herself be used by him, she, the Vampire Slayer, is being drawn into the darkness of the vampire.

It is her Christian, churchgoing[10] soldier lover, Riley, who reminds her of who she really is. In "A New Man," he tells Professor Walsh, meaningfully, "She is the truest soul I've ever known." In "As You Were," he tells Buffy, suggesting the dialectic of light and dark: "Wheel never stops turning, Buffy. You're up, you're down. It doesn't change what you are. And you are a hell of a woman." Buffy must continually remember her true nature. She is Buffy, the Vampire Slayer. No doubt, Riley's use of the term "hell" is not philosophically accurate. Buffy learns to live between both heavens and hells. If she takes on aspects of many dimensions, that is only as it should be.

Conquering the Inner Demon

The sixth season also shifts the focus from external battles with the demonic to internal ones. The requisite action arc involves "The Trio" of Warren, Jonathan, and Andrew as comic relief from inner struggles until their bungling leads to tragedy. While Buffy, trying to come back from the heavenly bliss of her true self, is captivated by her bouts of sexual ecstasy with Spike, Willow seeks the bliss of self-obliteration brought about by the use of dark magic. "I . . . it took me away from myself. . . .

I was out of my mind," she says in "Wrecked," as she laments the fact that she nearly caused the death of Dawn. She explains her motivation: "If you could be plain old Willow or super Willow, who would you be?" she asks Buffy. Buffy replies: "You don't need magic to be special."

In "Forever," Tara explains to Dawn, and indirectly to Willow, the ethics of magic: "Witches can't be allowed to alter the fabric of life for selfish reasons. Wiccans took an oath a long time ago to honor that." Willow's use of magic, however, is partly governed by the sense of inferiority and insecurity that she expressed to Buffy in the first episode. She does not believe that she is lovable for herself. As the Master explained to Buffy, it is fear that empowers the demonic. Afraid to lose Tara's love, Willow uses magic to hold it. When she uses magic to control the person she loves, rather than respect the fundamental freedom of the higher personality, Willow only repels Tara.

The test of Willow's true power is in defeating the inner demonic force of fear and egotism that usurps her intrinsic humanity. She must find the inner soul power that makes her truly special. At first she struggles with the pain of withdrawal from her indulgences in the power of black magic. But all such efforts cease when Tara is accidentally killed by Warren. In her rage for vengeance, Willow turns against the whole of life, against this entire middle world with all its contradictions and suffering.

In "Two to Go," Buffy tries to express her recovered love of earthly life to a profoundly disoriented Willow. Buffy will later tell Dawn ("Grave") her new insight into why she has been allowed back into this world. It wasn't because of Willow's magic, which is powerless against the death of Tara. It wasn't the duties of the Slayer, since she would have been replaced by another one. It was for the sake of Dawn herself: "Things have really sucked lately, but that's all going to change, and I want to be there when it does. I want to see my friends happy again. I want to see you grow up—the woman you're going to become. Because she's going to be beautiful. And she's going to be powerful. I got it so wrong. I don't want to protect you from the world. I want to show it to you. There's so much that I want to show you." Buffy promises a new dawn for Dawn.

But Willow will not have such an explanation, as she blames herself for all Buffy's troubles: "You're trying to sell me on the world? . . . This world? Buffy, it's me! I know you were happier when you were in the ground. The only time you were ever at peace in your whole life is when you were dead. Until Willow brought you back."

In "Grave," the world is saved from the demonic power unleashed through Willow's fear by Xander, her oldest and truest friend—Xander, the one member of the Slayer gang who has no other power than that of his heart. As Willow is about to open the gates of Hell, Xander evokes her intrinsically lovable essence: "You're Willow." "Willow" replies, "Don't call me that." She has rejected her true self, which she identifies with being a "loser" ("Two to Go"). As with Angel and Spike before her, Willow's fear and frustration with ordinary human life propel her toward egotism and darkness, which ultimately lead to the destruction of the vulnerable human world.

Xander's heart is big enough for all of this. As Willow magically cuts him to ribbons, Xander repeats, "I love you, Willow," until Willow, in tears, collapses in his arms. As Giles explains later, Xander was able to reach "the spark of humanity she had left." This "humanity" or "soul," as Kant argues, is the higher dimension of self or personality that ennobles the ordinary human individual—however unholy she becomes—and is the source of our sense of moral duty.

In the final sequence, scenes of Willow crying in Xander's arms, while the others recover from the wreckage of her demonic rampage, are accompanied by the voice of Sarah McLachlan singing the Prayer of St. Francis, which includes the words: "Where there is hatred let me sow love. Where there is injury, pardon. Where there is doubt, faith. Where there is despair, hope. Where there is darkness, light." Francis of Assisi, like his compatriot Dante, would have been comfortable with the multidimensional universe of *BtVS,* while learning from its postmodern sensibility to bless the very darkness itself, without which the light of a new dawn would not be possible.[11]

NOTES

1. Immanuel Kant, *Groundwork of the Metaphysics of Morals,* trans. H. J. Paton (New York: Harper Torchbooks, 1964), 95.

2. Immanuel Kant, *Critique of Practical Reason,* trans. Lewis White Beck (New York: Macmillan/Library of Liberal Arts, 1993), 30. See more on this in chapter 4.

3. Kant, *Critique of Practical Reason,* 90. I have slightly modified this translation to eliminate archaic forms such as thee and thou, as well as gender-biased language (e.g., putting "human being" instead of "man" and alternating gendered pronouns).

4. Plato, *Republic,* book 7; 514A–520A.

5. Immanuel Kant, *Universal Natural History and Theory of the Heavens,* trans. Stanley L. Jaki (Edinburgh: Scottish Academic Press, 1981).

6. Immanuel Kant, *Critique of Pure Reason,* trans. Norman Kemp Smith (London: Macmillan & Co. Ltd, 1961), 22; Bxvi.

7. David Hume, *A Treatise of Human Nature,* edited by L. A. Selby-Bigge (Oxford: At the Clarendon Press), II.2.3; 415

8. Jean-Paul Sartre, "Existentialism is a Humanism." Text, translated by Philip Mairet, is available at http://www.marxists.org/reference/archive/sartre/works/exist/sartre.htm. Accessed 12/20/2006.

9. Kant, *Groundwork,* 95.

10. In "Who Are You?" Buffy asks Riley how he responded so quickly to the demon takeover of a Christian church. Riley replies, "I didn't. I was just late for church."

11. This chapter is an expanded and revised version of James Lawler, "Between Heavens and Hells: The Multidimensional Universe in Kant and *Buffy the Vampire Slayer,*" published in *Buffy the Vampire Slayer and Philosophy,* edited by James B. South (Chicago: Open Court, 2003), 103–16.

4

Blinding the Eyes of Justice: Woody Allen's Tale of Crime and Punishment

It's worse than dog-eat-dog. It's dog doesn't answer other dog's phone calls.
—CLIFF

What is relative to universal human inclinations and needs has a *market price*. . . . [B]ut that which constitutes the sole condition under which anything can be an end in itself has not merely a relative value—that is, a price—but has an intrinsic value—that is, *dignity*.
—IMMANUEL KANT

Four Stories about Justice

In the Bible's classic Book of Job, the innocent, suffering Job complains against God: "Why does he look on and laugh, when the unoffending, too, must suffer? So the whole world is given up into the power of wrong-doers; he blinds the eyes of justice. He is answerable for it; who else?"[1] Woody Allen's film *Crimes and Misdemeanors* directly confronts the problem of meaning in a world in which the eyes of justice have apparently been blinded. The title of his film is based on Article 2, Section 4 of the US Constitution, which gives as grounds for the impeachment of a President the nebulous but resounding phrase, "high crimes and misdemeanors." Four central stories deftly intertwine. One is about a high and terrible crime. Judah Rosenthal, a successful eye doctor, family man, and pillar of the community, commits murder under the all-seeing eyes of God. At least that is what his religiously rigorous Jewish father had always affirmed: "I'll say it once again. The eyes of God see all. . . . There is absolutely nothing that escapes his sight. He sees the righteous and he sees the wicked. And the righteous will be rewarded. And the wicked will be punished, for eternity."

Applauded by an admiring wife, daughter, friends, and associates, Judah appears at the beginning of the film attending a banquet in honor of his philanthropic work. In the eyes of society he is happy, successful, and virtuous. In reality, underneath this glittering image, he is an adulterer, a liar, and an embezzler of his charities' funds. At least that is what his mistress, Dolores, tells him as she threatens to expose his adultery to his wife and reveal to all the world his fraudulent use for his own benefit of the charity monies entrusted to him.

Judah turns for help to his brother Jack, who has shady connections with the underworld. At first he balks at the final solution Jack proposes. "I can't believe I'm talking about a human being. She's not an insect. You don't just step on her." "I know," Jack replies. "Playing hard ball was never your game. You never like to get your hands dirty. But apparently this woman is for real, and this thing isn't just going to go away." Judah finally agrees to have Jack arrange the murder.

The second story is a tale of petty misdemeanors, jealousy, and amorous rivalry, together with the frustration of lofty moral intentions. The good guy, as he sees himself, is Cliff, who makes documentaries on some of the major issues of our time regarding homelessness, disease, poverty, injustice. His current effort is a high-minded documentary on the life and ideas of an elderly German-Jewish philosopher, Louis Levy. Cliff is trying to create a better world, a world of fundamental justice. The trouble is, few see his films and no one is interested enough to pay him decent money for them. His marriage is all but dead, and he is on the lookout for love.

The bad guy, as Cliff never tires of telling his would-be girlfriend Halley, is his brother-in-law Lester, a producer of commercially successful TV comedies. Cliff is supposed to make a favorable documentary about Lester for a TV series on "Great Minds." He owes this financially interesting opportunity, resentfully, to Lester's condescending generosity in offering his sister's husband the opportunity to make some money.

The third and fourth tales provide commentary on the first two from the higher plane of philosophical reflection. The third story is that of the existentialist philosopher and university professor Louis Levy, whose life and ideas are being recorded by Cliff in one of his idealistic documentaries. Levy, we learn, is a survivor of the Nazis' anti-Semitic persecutions that destroyed his entire family. According to Levy's existentialist philosophy, we live in a blind, uncaring universe that is completely indifferent to issues of justice and human happiness. The challenge for those who recognize the heartlessness of existence is to affirm life themselves by creating loving relationships. Levy describes the God of the Jewish culture as a projection of a society only partly able to envision the possibility of such a loving world:

> The unique thing that happened to the early Israelites was that they conceived a God that cares. He cares but he also demands at the same time that you behave morally. But here comes the paradox. What's one of the first things that that God asks? That God asks Abraham to sacrifice his only son, his beloved son to Him. In other words, in spite of millennia of efforts we have not succeeded to create a really and entirely loving image of a God. This was beyond our capacity to imagine.

The fourth tale concerns one of Judah's patients, Cliff's other brother-in-law, Rabbi Ben, a kindly and thoughtful person. At first glance, the tale of Rabbi Ben seems to reinforce the pessimistic existentialism of Levy. Ben learns from Judah that his sight is fatally compromised. This, together with the outcome of the first two stories, suggests that the universe must be indifferent to any sense of justice, since it permits the morally suspect (Lester) and outright criminal (Judah) to rise in fame and fortune and punishes the good (Cliff and Ben). But while Cliff endlessly laments the injustice of his fate, Rabbi Ben does not seem to notice this contradiction between the axioms of his faith and clear-sighted empirical appraisal of reality. Ben therefore seems blind even before he goes blind.

Two Visions of Life

As the various stories intertwine, Judah seeks the advice of his patient, Rabbi, and lifelong friend. Ben recommends that Judah confess his betrayal to his wife, Miriam, and hope for forgiveness. But Judah sees no chance that Miriam will ever forgive him for his lies and her humiliation. Ben believes there is a basic difference in their respective philosophical visions, in the way they see the world:

> It's a fundamental difference in the way we see the world. You see it as harsh and empty of values and pitiless. And I couldn't go on living if I didn't feel with all my heart a moral structure, with real meaning, and . . . forgiveness. And some kind of higher power. Otherwise there's no basis to know how to live. And I know you well enough to know there's a spark of that notion somewhere inside you too.

This basic conflict between two radically opposed visions of life is the central theme of Judah's recollection of a family dinner as he revisits the home of his youth. Vividly conjuring a scene from his past, he watches from the side as his youthful self and family members are celebrating the Jewish festival of Passover.

> *At the head of the table, his father Sol conducts prayers before eating.*

AUNT MAY, *impatiently*: Come on Sol. Get on with it. I'm hungry. . . . It's nonsense anyway. What are you putting everyone through this mumbo jumbo? Bring on the main course.

SOL: Spare us your Leninist philosophy just this once.

An argument breaks out over the fundamental nature of reality. Is there a moral structure to the universe? Is there justice—punishment for the wicked and reward for the good? If God punishes the wicked, says Aunt May, what about Hitler?

AUNT MAY: Six million Jews, and millions of others. And they got off with nothing. . . . Because might makes right. Until the Americans marched in . . . .

SOMEONE: What are you saying, May? There's no morality anywhere in the whole world?

MAY: For those who want morality there's morality. Nothing's handed down in stone.

WOMAN: Sol's kind of faith is a gift. It's like an ear for music, or the talent to draw. He believes and you can use logic on him all day long and he still believes.

SOL: Must everything be logical?

JUDAH, *intervening from the side into this vision from his past*: And if a man commits a crime, if he kills?

SOL: Then one way or another he will be punished.

AN UNCLE: If he's caught, Sol.

SOL: If he's not, that which originates in a black deed will blossom in a foul manner. . . . Whether it's the Old Testament or Shakespeare, murder will out.

AUNT MAY: And I say if he can do it, and get away with it and he chooses not to be bothered by the ethics, then he's home free.

Remember. History's written by the winners. And if the Nazis had won, future generations would understand the story of the World War Two quite differently.

SOL: Your aunt is a brilliant woman, Judah, but she's had a very unhappy life.

AN UNCLE: And if all your faith is wrong, Sol? I mean, just what if? If?

SOL: Then I'll still have a better life than all of those that doubt.

AUNT MAY: Wait a minute. Are you telling me you prefer God over the truth?

SOL: If necessary, I'll always choose God over the truth.

A WOMAN: I agree.

As the scene fades, ANOTHER WOMAN *chimes in*: I say, what goes around, comes around.

The debate between Judah's Aunt May and his father Sol offers another version of two opposing worldviews. In the materialist view of Aunt May, the universe is ultimately governed by the interaction of unconscious physical forces. This physical dynamic operates as well in human history, where the stronger force has greater impact than the weaker, and might is the basis of right, or morality. The philosopher Levy too accepts this conception of material reality, but adds that human beings are free to adopt another code than that of power, the code of love. The universe of blind matter somehow gives birth to spirit, to free, self-conscious human beings capable of loving each other and so of confronting the coldness of the play of physical forces with the warmth of a human heart.

With such a contradictory metaphysics, it is no wonder that human beings have been incapable of conceiving of a God of pure love. The harsh laws of a blind universe are inevitably reflected in humanity's conception of its God. The death of a beloved son, inconceivable from the point of view of pure love, is a common occurrence in human life, whether it results from natural causes or from human causes, as ostensibly loving fathers and mothers send their sons off to war, justifying their actions as the command of an ethical God. Abraham's readiness to sacrifice his son Isaac only sanctifies this common occurrence in ordinary life as an event in sacred history. The laws of Sol's universe are those of a morality of reward and punishment—at the hands of an exacting God

who sees and judges our every step with his merciless eye. Judah naturally interprets Ben's advice from his father's perspective of the nature of
a merciless divine justice. He can only picture an unforgiving reaction
should his actions be exposed to the light, and so he is driven to bury
them in the darkness of murder. But the moral structure of the universe
that Ben envisions is not one of reward and punishment, of inevitable
sacrifice and death to appease a wrathful God. Unlike the God of Judah's
father Sol, Ben's God does not threaten with punishment but offers the
possibility of forgiveness. Contrary to Louis Levy's pessimism, Ben's God
is indeed a God of love.

Conflicting Conclusions

The threads of all four stories come together during the final scene,
which takes place at the wedding of Ben's daughter. Judah is invited with
his family as both friend and doctor to the father of the bride. Cliff is
there with his wife Wendy, who is Ben's sister. Lester, Ben's brother,
arrives with Halley on his arm. Cliff, who is separating from Wendy,
learns that Lester and Halley are engaged and is completely crushed.
Judah finds Cliff brooding alone over a drink, and says, "You look very
deep in thought." Cliff replies, with unconscious irony, "I was plotting
the perfect murder." Knowing that Cliff is a filmmaker, Judah tells him
that he has an interesting story—his own story, as the viewer knows—
for a movie. He concludes his tale of murder:

> JUDAH: And after the awful deed is done, he finds that he is
> plagued by deep-rooted guilt, little sparks of his religious background
> which he'd rejected are suddenly stirred up. He hears his father's
> voice. He imagines that God observes his every move. Suddenly it's
> not an empty universe at all, but a just and moral one. And he's vio-
> lated it. Now he's panic-stricken. He's on the verge of a mental col-
> lapse, an inch away from confessing the whole thing to the police.
>
> Then one morning he awakens. The sun is shining, and his fam-
> ily is around him. Mysteriously the crisis is lifted. . . . As the months
> pass he finds he's not punished. In fact he prospers. The killing gets
> attributed to another person, a drifter who has a number of other
> murders to his credit. So, what the hell, one more doesn't even mat-
> ter. He's scot-free. His life is completely back to normal, back to his
> protected world of wealth and privilege.

> CLIFF: I think it would be tough to live with that. Very few guys
> could actually live with something like that on their conscience.

JUDAH, *suddenly angry and defensive*: People carry awful deeds around with them. What do you expect them to do, turn themselves in? This is reality. In reality we rationalize, we deny, or we couldn't go on living.

CLIFF: Here's what I would do. I would have him turn himself in. Because then, you see, your story assumes tragic proportions, because in the absence of a God or something he is forced to assume that responsibility himself. Then you have tragedy.

JUDAH: But that's fiction. That's movies. You've seen too many movies. I'm talking about reality. If you want a happy ending you should see a Hollywood movie.

Cliff is in fact borrowing his ending from Dostoevsky's tragic novel, *Crime and Punishment*. There, the guilt-ridden student Raskolnikov confesses to the police that he has committed a murder, although he could have escaped punishment. And Cliff does luxuriate in the harmony of morality and happiness that permeates his favorite Hollywood movies.

Judah admits that occasionally the murderer may have twinges of guilt, "But it passes. In time it all fades." Judah unwittingly expresses the ironic truth of one of Lester's supposed profundities: comedy is tragedy plus time. Today we can make jokes about the assassination of Abraham Lincoln, Lester witlessly announces. While Cliff finds Lester's philosophical pretensions ludicrous, time has in effect lessoned Judah's tragedy in his own eyes, until he can at least smile at his former guilty apprehensions of earthly or heavenly retribution. Having made his confession, in the guise of an imagined film script, he then leaves Cliff, embraces his wife, and, in the glow of apparent happiness, walks off into his protected world of wealth and privilege.

According to Kant, the highest goal of morality consists in creating a just world, or what he called "the highest good." This is a world in which happiness is "in exact proportion to morality."[2] It is a world in which those who are morally upright are happy, while those who violate moral duty in one way or another suffer as a result. Consequently, the greatest scandal for morality is that the world as we see it seems to operate on completely different principles: nonmoral and even antimoral ones. The first two stories therefore end with a lesson that appears to contradict the moral vision of the highest good. In what Judah calls "reality," it seems, a murderer prospers, while the good person, who tries to contribute to creating a just society, is left with his life in tatters.

On the second, philosophical level, this same theme at first seems to

be underscored by the abrupt suicide of Professor Levy. How could Levy
do this, after being so affirmative, after saying "yes" to life? The answer
is suggested in Cliff's documentary, where Levy explains, "But we must
always remember that when we are born we need a great deal of love
in order to persuade us to stay in life. Once we get that love it usually
lasts us. But the universe is a pretty cold place. It's we who invest it with
our feelings. And under certain conditions, we feel that the thing isn't
worth it any more." This statement provides an important perspective on
Cliff's existentialist idea that in the absence of "a God or something," the
individual ought to take responsibility for his own life. If there is no
intrinsic moral structure to existence, why should the choice of a "yes"
to life be any more valid than the choice of a "no"? Why should Levy's
choice of life and love be any more valid than Judah's choice of death
and murder? If there were no "moral structure with real meaning and forgiveness and some kind of higher power," as Rabbi Ben puts it, why
should one not simply see, behind our arbitrary projections onto the universe—our brave yeses to life—the cold face of indifference that we suppose is really there? Levy here answers that it is not enough merely to
affirm life. Life is worth living only if love sustains us. But it seems that
Levy's efforts to find love in what he believes is a profoundly loveless
universe had finally proved futile.

This message regarding the importance of love is amplified in Levy's
voiceover that provides philosophical comment to the concluding
sequence of the film. This sequence begins with Ben alone on the dance
floor, the loving father dancing with the beautiful bride, his daughter.
There follows a montage of major events in the film. The sequence concludes, at Levy's final sentence, with Ben embracing his daughter.

Levy's words are the following:

> We are all faced throughout our lives with agonizing decisions, moral
> choices. Some are on a grand scale. Most of these choices are on a lesser
> scale. But we define ourselves by the choices we have made. We are in
> fact the sum total of our choices. Events unfold so unpredictably, so
> unfairly. Human happiness does not seem to have been included in the
> design of creation. It is only we with our capacity to love that give mean-
> ing to the indifferent universe. And yet most human beings seem to have
> the ability to keep trying, and even to find joy from simple things, like
> their family, their work, and from the hope that future generations might
> understand more.

The film therefore ends with a double message. On the one hand, we
hear the voice of the atheist philosopher who underscores the injustice
of existence, where all too often the good suffer while the evil prosper.

In the moral vacuum of a cold, indifferent, essentially loveless universe, we must somehow have the strength to love and the luck to be loved. We know that this lucid philosopher, clear-eyed before what he believes to be the fundamental heartlessness of the universe, must have been loveless, for he has lost the will to live. On the other hand, what we actually see before us, as we listen to Levy's reflections, is the blind man of faith, Rabbi Ben, dancing with his daughter at her wedding, actually enfolded in love. It is Ben the believer, not the atheist Levy, who loves, is loved in return, and so is truly happy.

Perhaps then in order to find real love and happiness it is necessary to have Ben's seemingly blind faith that the universe is an inherently loving place. Aunt May, for all her clear-sightedness in looking at the injustices of life, had an unhappy life—if we can believe Sol, the man of faith, who seems to have had a happy one. Can we really trust the final picture in which we see Judah embracing his wife? Does Judah find love and happiness, as Ben surely does with his daughter? We are more likely to trust Dolores's perception of the hollowness of Judah's alleged happiness. She once said to Judah, "You're always so much more relaxed away from home. You come to life. Your whole face changes."

And when does Cliff find meaning and happiness? When, in the company of someone he loves, like his niece, Jenny, or his would-be girlfriend Halley, he leaves the glaring world of so-called reality and enters the darkened theater of the cinema, which is the cave of the creative imagination. Seemingly turning Plato's allegory of the cave inside out, Cliff willingly trades in the harsh light of the injustices of a supposed reality for the unreal images of Hollywood movies in which the moral hero always finds happiness in the end, while the dark deeds of the murderer find their foul fulfillment. But of course Plato's allegory of abandoning mere images and illusions for reality is itself an image. It is Plato's own dream of a better life. It is his script for a movie about philosophy—a tragic story of injustice in which the hero courageously overcomes darkness to rise to the light of truth, and then returns to liberate his fellows only to be killed in the process. The unhappy outcome is not utterly pessimistic, however, for the path of freedom has been cleared for others to follow. Thus it's a matter of one belief or one image in opposition to another one—an image of a higher life persuading us to see that what we consider reality is itself only an image of the real. Judah unconsciously states the paradox that so-called reality is itself an illusion: "In reality we rationalize, we deny, or we couldn't go on living."

In the compelling inventions of the morally-infused imagination, the good are ultimately rewarded with the one they love, while the wicked are exposed and deservedly punished. With the aid of Hollywood, Cliff engages in what the poet Coleridge calls the "willing suspension of disbelief." He suspends disbelief in the image before him, which provides him with the picture of a reality that indeed has a fundamentally moral structure. And as a result, for two hours of happiness he no longer believes in the reality of the unjust world to whose glaring light he eventually returns. Cliff luxuriates in going to the cinema in the daytime to shut out the aesthetic and moral ugliness this light shows him. Such moments of creative imagination provide Cliff with periodic experiences of happiness as he vicariously lives in a kind of heaven on earth. No doubt he is also happy in making his morally conscious documentaries, when he allows himself the belief, constantly renewed but never materializing in concrete evidence, that he is contributing to advancing justice and human welfare, to creating the highest good.

From Knowledge to Faith

Kant addresses the philosophical conflict between the apparent clear-sightedness of Professor Levy and the blind faith of Rabbi Ben in his preface to the *Critique of Pure Reason*, where he writes, "It is necessary to deny knowledge, in order to make room for faith."[3] This is not a completely blind faith, but a rationally defensible outlook that is based on a critique of the kind of knowledge produced by the mechanistic sciences. The critique of the pretensions of such science to give us the fundamental structure of reality makes room for the faith that is implied in the moral vision of the world.

On the one hand, natural science shows us a physical world governed by mechanical cause and effect, with no intrinsic moral structure. In social science this deterministic framework is transposed to the plane of practical life. Social science portrays individuals as motivated primarily by self-centered desires and interests or dominated by passionate drives and feelings. These motivating forces have deterministic causes in biology, education, circumstances, and social programming. For the dismal science of economics, the outcome of the actions of fundamentally self-interested individuals is the unfeeling, unloving, and indifferent economic world that obeys the laws of supply and demand, and whose requirements give rise to the physical and metaphysical enforcements of state and religious institutions. Belief in the primacy of the ego is therefore "the Matrix" of our "real world," a world in which its creators paradoxically feed the powers that rule over them.

Morality, on the other hand, involves a completely different vision—

that of the "highest good." This is a vision of a world in which people who freely choose what is right—acting with a view to their shared humanity and fulfilling their responsibilities despite the costs—ultimately find happiness. As old Sol says, this is the vision of both the Bible and Shakespeare. After emerging from his trials with a more profound understanding of the immensity of the creator, Job finds that his life has been greatly enriched. In the more secular morality of Shakespeare, criminals and fools provoke the forces that ultimately destroy them, showing that reward and punishment arise out of the very laws of life and the dynamics of our own choices and actions. But this is also the moral vision of the old Hollywood films that Cliff so loves. In the positive outcomes of classic Hollywood movies, the hero, after risking all for the good of others, finally finds love and happiness in the end. The sacrifices demanded by moral duty are therefore temporary. However, the process is uncertain, for those who act for the sake of duty do not see how the happy ending will be brought about. Nor, except in retrospect, do the villains see how they work their own downfall. Since the outcome can't be known, duty must be performed for duty's sake, not as a means to the end of happiness. There must therefore be faith, in the sense of confidence and trust, that the seeds of goodness and justice that one plants by virtue of one's dutiful actions will ultimately grow into a just world, or, conversely, that the seeds of dark deeds will blossom in a foul manner.

However comforting such a vision is for the person of faith, who is able to turn a blind eye to the contrary evidence of experience, those who stand for scientific truth and empirical evidence against the prejudices and superstitions of the ages cannot simply shut their eyes. If the so-called realistic, scientific view of the world is the correct one, Kant says, the moral vision "must be fantastic, directed to empty ends, and consequently inherently false."[4] Without the possibility of *realizing* the highest good, morality itself is a fiction. Aunt May would be right that if he has the power and can forget the ethics, the killer of millions is home free. In this framework of a cold universe of blindly acting forces, Judah tells Cliff, "You've seen too many movies. I'm talking about reality."

Kant's *Critique of Pure Reason* argues that the so-called real world, the universe that science portrays as a morally indifferent place, is not so real after all. It is only an "appearance," built up in part out of the underlying structures of the human sensibility and forms of understanding that we human beings, built no doubt differently from other intelligent inhabitants of a vast universe, employ when we seek to organize knowledge. When we pursue scientific knowledge, we inevitably employ a priori categories of strict causality and natural law. In the attempt to understand human life, the psychological, social, and economic sciences suppose that such causal laws operate through individual desires and inclinations, and if reason enters into the mix it is a self-interested, instrumental kind of rationality—working in the service of the passions and drives that determine a human life. There is nothing in the framework of these human sciences that contradicts a philosophical determinism, as our desires are governed by nature and nurture, by circumstances and the hidden and open persuaders that continually move us to act. Such determinism seems confirmed in the overriding power of economic laws. While Cliff vainly attempts to swim against the tide of such laws, Lester rides their waves to fame and fortune.

But the causal laws of the natural and social sciences reflect the structure of the human understanding and its "transcendental logic," not the nature of reality as it is in itself. "Does everything have to be logical?" Sol asks rhetorically. Kant replies that the "logical" categories of a deterministic science are in fact subjective, not objective. They express the way in which human beings, in their scientific enterprise, subjectively organize experience, not the nature of reality itself. The natural and social sciences therefore are inherently biased in the sense that the scientific approach *presupposes* determinism; it doesn't prove that the universe itself is deterministic. Beyond the "logic" of a mechanistic science, Kant argues, is a more fundamental truth, expressed in religious traditions, in the aspirations of the human heart, and in the implicit assumptions of moral consciousness. This is the deepest belief of moral consciousness: that the universe has the meaning and purpose of fostering the highest good.

A Dog-Indifferent-to-Dog World

The most advanced social science of Kant's day was Adam Smith's classic work of economic theory, *The Wealth of Nations* (1776). Smith's work, which remains to our own time one of the classic formulations of modern society, portrays socioeconomic life as the outcome of the self-interested actions of individuals. "It is not from the benevolence of the butcher, the brewer, or the baker, that we expect our dinner," Smith writes matter-of-factly, "but from their regard to their own interest."[5] But what happens to people who can't pay for their dinner? Cliff warns his niece Jenny about the purely self-interested and ugly character of the realities hiding behind the glamour and beautiful scenes constructed in Hollywood movies: "It's worse than dog-eat-dog. It's dog doesn't answer other dog's phone calls." Before Adam Smith, Hobbes had described the world of self-interested individuals as a war of all against all, that is, as a dog-eat-dog world. In the economic version of egotism advocated by Adam Smith, the situation gets even worse. Better to be eaten, Cliff implies, than to be ignored completely.

But how real is this dog-eat-dog world? Is it a hard fact of human nature to seek one's own interests over all else and thereby produce the tragic conflicts that destroy lives? Jack sees no choice in the hard ball game of life. "Apparently this woman is for real," says Jack. Judah has pleaded with her to see that she is threatening to ruin his life. But in her decision to bring Judah down she is only following his lead. His egotism is reflected in hers, and so his admitted selfishness is behind his own ruin.

But there *is* a real choice, Rabbi Ben tells him. The outcome is not fixed. There is the possibility of forgiveness, and a new and even better life. Judah, however, has no room left in his life for choice. He has locked himself together with his wife into the unforgiving structures of social life with their norms of privilege, power, and reputation, whose supposed reality is in fact a matter of rationalization, denial, and self-delusion. "How did I get in so deep?" he asks Jack. "What dream was I following?" Outside of his so-called reality is his dream world that he fit-fully creates with Dolores. But this dream brings with it real life. Love with her in their refuge by the sea revives in him a passion to live that his family and social life, imprisoned in deadening social conventions, had slowly smothered.

Jack's real world is one in which separate individuals struggle to sur-vive by any and all means necessary. The philosopher Levy tells us that "the universe is a pretty cold place. It's we who invest it with our feel-ings." But if we ought to strive to invest it with loving feelings, we more commonly invest it with our unloving ones. If our lives are the result of our choices, then the choices people make to define themselves as sep-arate, competing, mutually indifferent, and hostile egos will inevitably produce a loveless vision of the universe. The indifference that Professor Levy believes to be the harsh reality of the universe itself is only the pro-jection onto nature of our human indifference to one another.

Judah is appalled that some people murder for money. Dolores is not an insect to be stepped on, he says. But in the end his prior choices com-pel him to take that step. When money cannot buy her silence, he pays the cold-blooded killer to silence her. Here is why the universe seems such a cold place. Its coldness is not a fact of nature but the result of human choice, and a projection of our prior attitudes. The purely eco-nomic approach of competitive individualism is the result of a human decision to behave in a certain way, not a necessary requirement imposed by human nature or the causal structure of the universe. An alternative way is therefore equally valid. This is the way of morality, with its exalted vision of a just world. A way of looking at life that is not "logical" according to the norms of a dog-eat-dog world is nevertheless morally required of us.

Kant's Own Movie

To show the legitimacy of an alternative way of viewing life, Kant proposes his own story of crime and misdemeanor. The story has two parts. The first has to do with misdemeanors. Kant writes: "Suppose that someone says his lust is irresistible when the desired object and opportunity are present. Ask him whether he would not control his passion if, in front of the house where he has this opportunity, a gallows were erected on which he would be hanged immediately after gratifying his lust. We do not have to guess very long what his answer would be."[6] Judah sees himself as driven by lust and other passions, and too weak to resist them. But when Dolores threatens to destroy his carefully constructed existence, he finds it very easy to resist his passion for her. Does this mean that Judah is free from causal determinism? No. It means that there is an even greater force than sexual desire determining our actions: the love of life or self-preservation in the face of the threat of death. But in Judah's case it is not even real life that determines him, but love of an artificially constructed life based on rationalization and denial, and shackled by powerful chains of fame and fortune.

To find real freedom, Kant therefore goes on to argue, it is necessary to move to a higher level of choice. Kant continues with a tale of real crime:

> But ask him whether he thinks it would be possible for him to overcome his love of life, however great it may be, if his sovereign threatened him with the same sudden death unless he made a false deposition against an honorable man whom the ruler wished to destroy under a plausible pretext. Whether he would or not he perhaps will not venture to say; but that it would be possible for him he would certainly admit without hesitation. He judges, therefore, that he can do something because he knows that he ought, and he recognizes that he is free—a fact which, without the moral law, would have remained unknown to him.

As in Woody Allen's film, Kant's own movie script moves from a comic tale of misdemeanor to the tragedy of serious crime. Faced with the choice between saving his own life and being responsible for the death of an innocent person, the individual transcends the level of ordinary passion or desire and enters the realm of morality. Here, Kant says, he discovers the true possibility of freedom. He finds that he is able to decide to die rather than commit a crime against an innocent person. Whether or not he will actually make this decision is not the point. What is important is that he feels that he *could* make that decision. This feeling of possibility in the face of death is the experience of authentic freedom. Through moral experience of this kind, we discover our capacity to go beyond all the extrinsically determined laws of physics and biology, psychology and social science, and live or die according to laws of our own choosing.

Judah has to choose between his own life and killing an innocent person. According to Kant, this is where he should have the experience of authentic freedom. And yet Judah is intent on denying just such a possibility. He rationalizes and denies. In a dreamlike sequence Judah argues with Rabbi Ben:

> JUDAH: What choice do I have Ben? Tell me. . . . I will not be destroyed by this neurotic woman.
>
> BEN, *repeating the words of Sol*: It's a human life. You don't think God sees?
>
> JUDAH: God is a luxury I can't afford.
>
> BEN: Now you're talking like your brother Jack.
>
> JUDAH: Jack lives in the real world. You live in the kingdom of heaven. I managed to keep free of that real world but suddenly it's found me.

As in Kant's moral imperative, Rabbi Ben's God has the moral vision of love: He sees the intrinsic dignity, the humanity, of Dolores. Judah should see that too—see with God's eyes of love. Louis Levy would say that Judah is called upon to imagine a truly loving God, but like his father and his ancestors going back to Abraham, such imagination fails him. He imagines only a God of sacrifice and punishment. Like Levy himself, he rejects such a God but cannot imagine another one. Judah's rejection of love issues in murder. Levy's own failure to find love ends in suicide. Rejecting the alternative view of Rabbi Ben as the impractical fantasy of the Kingdom of God, which Kant calls the highest good, Judah locks himself into the alternative view of "reality"—the worse-than-dog-eat-dog, indifferent, loveless world of egotism and survival.

But if Kant is right, and as the characters of the film themselves acknowledge, this "real world" that Judah chooses is in fact an appearance. Judah's "real world" is a carefully crafted construct made up of denial and rationalization, of lies and crime. The "real world" is Judah's artificially protected world of wealth and privilege. He regards it as his good fortune that he is no longer bothered by a sense of guilt, but this only means that he has succeeded in burying his own deeds in a darkness where even he can no longer see them. In this sense, it is Judah, not Ben, who has truly become blind. So as not to see his own freedom, Judah has blinded the eyes of justice. Far from turning tragedy into laughter, time only allows the dark deed to blossom in a foul manner— in the rotting corpse of the truly loving life that he might have lived.

Kant's Kingdom of Heaven

In his third formulation of the categorical imperative, Kant argues against the relativism and indifference of a world centered on economic value, and for the subordination of economic life to the intrinsic dignity of each human individual. In view of his inherent "dignity (or prerogative) . . . above all the mere things of nature" there follows for the individual

> the necessity of always choosing his maxims from the point of view of himself—and every other rational being—as a maker of law (and this is why they are called persons). It is in this way that a world of rational beings (*mundus intelligibilis* [Intelligible World]) is possible as a kingdom of ends—possible, that is, through the making of their own laws by all persons as its members. Accordingly every rational being must so act as if he were through his maxims always a law-making member in the universal kingdom of ends. [7]

Kant here answers the question: How do we know what our moral duty really is? He presents three formulations for testing the validity of perceived moral duties. In the first formulation, each of us should consider whether we can formulate the maxim of our actions as the universal law of our world, of our reality. Such universality is a personal one, a universality-for-me. Its universality is in terms of one's own life. Is the principle of my action one that *I* can consistently follow in my own life— creating my life and my world on its basis? Kant proposes some basic rules stemming from such an approach. I should help other people— because I would not want to live in a world in which when I am in need no one would be there to help me. I have duties to myself, too. I should develop my own abilities and talents, because a world in which everyone tried to coast through life on the achievements of others would have no achievements to coast on. Such broadly defined or "imperfect" duties do not give us precise instructions for how to behave in particular instances—how to help others here and now, what talents to work on and how much effort to put into this. Such more specific duties arise out of highly particular circumstances and choices for which the categorical imperative provides only the broadest guidelines. The categorical imperative merely tells us that if we feel the call of duty in one circumstance or another, whether to oneself or to others, we must not adopt the antimoral rationalizations of the world of dog-indifferent-to-dog. What further norms and principles we regard as duties in our own lives must be consistent with these broad outlines. We live in an interdependent world of interacting human beings. Each of us needs the assistance of others, and each of us relies on the talents and achievements of humanity in the past. Hence we should help others and in turn contribute to the advance of humanity in our own person, even when doing so involves sacrifice.

We should therefore respect others as well as ourselves—as Kant asserts in his second formulation of the categorical imperative: treat other people as beings with ends of their own, and not merely as means to our own ends. Respecting oneself and others as free, self-determining individuals means that we respect the variety of duties that manifest in our various lives. Morality is not about establishing rules by which to judge the performances of other people. Even in one's own life it is difficult, perhaps impossible, to tell whether an action is performed for the sake of duty, or whether we are secretly motivated by the fears and ambitions of our ego-consciousness. How then can we judge others? Where behavior violates basic norms of civilized life it is right that positive laws be established for our mutual protection and to provide for maximum freedom of action for each individual. For the protection of society the crime needs to be punished, but the criminal remains a human being and should be treated accordingly. The criminal should be regarded as innocent until proven guilty, not be subject to cruel and unusual, degrading forms of punishment, and have the protection of other such civilized norms of positive law as have been promulgated in the advanced legislation of Kant's own time, such as the U.S. Constitution with its Bill of Rights and the French Declaration of the Rights of Man and the Citizen. The U.S. Constitution holds the President of the country to the highest of standards, requiring removal from office whether he be found guilty of high crimes or only misdemeanors. The fundamental principle for such an approach to the relation between morality and law is expressed by Kant where he says: "Man is indeed unholy enough, but he must regard humanity in his own person as holy." However unholy in appearance, a fundamental holiness rests in the depths of the human soul where each of us is a member of a kingdom of ends—and not an insect to be just stepped upon.

Kant calls his third formulation the most complete version of the cat-egorical imperative, one that views humanity as a totality or whole. The first formulation is the concern of the individual reflecting on his or her motivation to determine whether she is acting in a principled way. The second counsels each of us to respect the equal freedom of other per-sons to pursue their own goals as they understand them, as long as they do not interfere with the equal freedom of others. The third formulation brings these two versions together in a larger unity—which Kant calls the "kingdom of ends." To test the validity of the maxims of our actions let us ask ourselves if they are compatible with, and contribute to realizing in fact, the idea of all humanity united in a common enterprise of build-ing a truly human world.

What is this kingdom of ends? It is first of all the idea that all human beings—indeed all conscious, self-determining beings in the universe—are linked in the *mundus intelligibilis,* or intelligible world. In the sensi-ble world of space-time we are separated by physical and temporal distances. But such space-time coordinates, framing the cause-effect rela-tionships of individuals regarded as separate and competing egos, is an appearance, not reality. It rests on the a priori assumptions of mechanis-tic science, which the convoluted space-time coordinates of twentieth-century physics has long superseded. Moral consciousness, in which we feel a duty to sacrifice our lives rather than betray an innocent human being, suggests a fundamentally different relationship of human beings than that which operates on this level of appearances. It supposes an "intelligible world," a world pictured by the moral imagination, in which we are all members of a unified reality, each with absolute or infinite dig-nity, creating our individual lives as well as our common life together. No one is to be regarded as expendable or to be reduced to the status of a mere means to goals established by others. As we reflect on the moral dimension of our actions, imagining, dreaming of ourselves as belonging to such an exalted unity, let us align our intentions and actions with the idea of all of humanity legislating together with respect for the dignity of each. The overarching duty that arises out of this picture is pre-cisely the practical realization of this ideal in our actual world. The ideal of a democratic humanity governing its world together in mutual respect should be *realized* in one degree or another through the actions that each of us is intending to perform. In this way, morality must step out of the inner forum of individual consciousness and enter the outer forum of our common practices of making laws together. The ideal of a demo-cratic humanity whose existence moral consciousness postulates in a supersensible, intelligible world should be implemented by real democratic practices in the world of sensible appearances. While this common activity certainly suggests the creation of political democracies, in his elaboration of the idea of the kingdom of ends Kant first of all envisages the common economic activities that bind us all together in the increasingly global market place.

Transforming the Dog-Eat-Dog Economy

The first aspect of this third formulation of the categorical imperative relates to the nature of the subject of the law-making—self-legislating humanity as a whole. The second aspect relates to the content of the laws that are made. The idea of a self-legislating humanity carries with it a hierarchy of ends or goals for the members of this kingdom. It is this idea of a hierarchy that gives the ideal democracy the quality of a kingdom, with rulers and ruled. Each of us is both ruler and ruled, but in different respects. As rulers, we see ourselves as possessed of inherent dignity as we co-create our common world together. As ruled, we see our various actions as subordinate to and as serving that inherent dignity. The rules governing the sensible world of appearances ought to be regulated by the ideas implicit in the intelligible world of free human subjects consciously uniting to create their own world. In the world we commit ourselves to creating, there ought to be a hierarchy of goals, with some ends taking precedence over others. Kant formulates this hierarchy as follows:

> What is relative to universal human inclinations and needs has a *market price*. What, even without perceiving a need, accords with a certain taste—that is, with satisfaction with the mere purposeless play of our mental powers—has a fancy-price [*Affektionspreis*]; but that which constitutes the sole condition under which anything can be an end in itself has not merely a relative value—that is, a price—but has an intrinsic value—that is, *dignity*.[8]

What this says, in the first place, is that the combined economic activities of human beings in the market, involving the production and exchange of goods, should be subordinate to and serve the inherent dignity of human beings. Clearly an economy built on slavery does not meet this standard—for slaves work primarily for others and are treated as having no inherent dignity in themselves. But an unrestricted capitalism too fails to satisfy this criterion to the extent that the laws of the market are allowed free play without a framework in which its outcomes are consciously subordinated to the dignity of those who produce and exchange goods. In the early nineteenth century a completely unfettered free-market economy resulted in the relentless labor of a sixteen-hour six-day work week, swelling its riches like a vampire from the lifeblood of children as well as adults. But in a kingdom of ends, people who do not fit the criteria of market demands should not die of starvation, or be bereft of health care and security in old age. They should have the possibilities of education. Unfettered laissez-faire capitalism should be replaced by a mixed economy, whether this is called welfare-state capitalism or market socialism.[9] Adam Smith himself argued that unless the government introduced free public education, the spontaneously evolving division of labor, which results in mindless repetitive work, would ultimately destroy the creative capacities of labor on which the entire system rests.[10]

As an expression of the ideal of the kingdom of ends, economic activity ought to serve the goal of creating the highest good, a world in which the performance moral duty results in happiness (while failure to do so carries with it the appropriate penalties). Human happiness depends on a certain level of material well-being. The dutiful moral person achieves a certain inner *contentment* in satisfying the demands of duty, but such contentment is not happiness. A Socrates who performs his duty may justifiably feel inner moral contentment, but as he drinks the hemlock that will kill him he can hardly be regarded as a happy man. The primary purpose of the production and exchange of goods is quite simply and naturally the satisfaction of basic human needs. The morality of economic activity consists in the realization of this inherent purpose of economic life. Thus people ought to work to the best of their abilities, exercising the talents they have dutifully developed for the purpose of satisfying human needs, and as a result of this performance of duty their basic human needs ought to be satisfied. Seen in this way, the kingdom of ends with the goal of producing the highest good is essentially the expression of the intrinsic meaning or purpose of our common economic activity. For morality in general is neither more nor less than the expression of the norms inherent in human activity. The paradox of ordinary life is that people so often violate norms that are inherent in their own activities. Adam Smith expressed the systematic nature of such violation of basic norms of economic justice or "equity" when he writes:

> No society can surely be flourishing and happy, of which the far greater part of the members are poor and miserable. It is but equity, besides, that they who feed, clothe, and lodge the whole body of the people, should have such a share of the produce of their own labour as to be themselves tolerably well fed, clothed, and lodged.[11]

In his examination of the kingdom of ends (the kingdom of God on earth), Kant argues that the values attributed to the goods of economic life are inherently relative. The objects of economic activity are inherently things-for-us, not things-in-themselves. Following Adam Smith, Kant argues that these values have two aspects: utility and economic exchangeability. The goods produced by human labor have a use-value: to serve human needs. They also have an exchange-value, based on the amount of labor expended in their production. In economic terms a Bible and a bottle of whiskey have quite different utilities, for they serve different human needs, but they might have exactly the same exchange-value—$15 possibly being the price for each. What accounts for this identity of exchange value is not an identity found in their utility, but the fact that each embodies the same amount of labor—as this is worked out through the averaging tendencies of the flux of supply and demand. Human activity itself is therefore the foundation of the economic system. In the light of the ideal of the kingdom of ends, the standards or norms of economic activity ought ultimately to be in conformity with morality, and its objectives in conformity with the satisfaction of human need. Thus the realization of the kingdom of ends is the highest good: a world in which people work according to the fundamental moral norms inherent in their activities, with respect for one's own and others' dignity, and in the end have their basic human needs, those that are served by their economic activity, satisfied.

Such is the hierarchical relationship between the highest and the lowest levels of the kingdom of ends. But Kant also mentions a middle level—that of the free play of human powers. This is the realm of art and culture. In the hierarchy of the kingdom of ends, beauty and art play a mediating role between the practical affairs of economic life and the inner dignity of human beings. A world without beauty, governed only by the standard of utility and economic equivalence, is not worthy of human beings. Thus the norms of taste, the *affectionspreis* or fancy value of an object, ought to take precedence over the mere utility and exchange value of an object. The standards of beauty, taste, and culture are sensible expressions of the intrinsic dignity of free, creative individuals. Beauty, Kant writes, is "the symbol of morality."[12] In her imaginative creations the artist is capable of bringing into sensuous awareness the inner harmony of duty and desire that animates the stories of the Bible, the dramas of Shakespeare, and the classic films of Hollywood. Morality is therefore served by the creative imagination in which disbelief is suspended and the individual sitting in a darkened theater is able to enjoy a preview of the world of the highest good.

The Postulates of Morality

In his third formulation of the categorical imperative Kant gives substance to that kingdom of heaven in which Judah supposes that Ben
lives. It is founded on two pillars. One is faith, and the other is love. The
alternative that Ben holds out to Judah is the possibility of forgiveness
and mature love. But for this possibility of love, a certain kind of faith is
needed. Faith in what?

As we have seen in chapter 2, the moral vision of the highest good
requires that we make three assumptions or "postulates": freedom, God,
and immortality. The first postulate is that, contrary to the deterministic
assumptions of the natural and social sciences, human beings are fundamentally free. The deterministic assumptions of science are just that:
assumptions, frameworks for investigating reality, not inherent features of
that reality itself. This is above all true of the fundamental "matrix" of our
dog-eat-dog social experience—that we are individualistic beings separate
from one another and locked deterministically in a competitive struggle
over scarce resources. Rather than being reflections of the essential reality of human nature, such conceptions reflect a choice that human beings
have made and for the most part continue to make. It is the predominance of this choice that leads the characters in Woody Allen's film to
speak about "the real world" as one involving a life-or-death struggle
between self-centered individuals. Morality with its sense of duty, however, calls on us to rise above the level of the struggle for survival, of dog-
eating-dog, and, perhaps worse, of dog-indifferent-to-dog, which
produces a loveless world of power and privilege that stifles human creativity and love. For such morality to be meaningful, we must *believe* in
our inner power to create our own reality, and to attract the love we need.

Ultimately, there are two fundamental projections that can be represented by the famous example of a gestalt shift between a vase and two
faces. In our cognitive endeavors, there is the causal relation between
separate, independent objects. In social science, this perspective is that
of independent egos in conflict with one another. The two opposing
faces represent well this perspective (See face/vase image on page 74).
However, if we shift our perspective and make a different choice of who
we really are, this separation of egos and independent substances fades
into the background, and the unitary vase or cup comes to the fore—an
apt symbol of the shared and sharing humanity that grounds the moral
point of view.

Ultimately, Levy says, we create our own reality. Each of us is the sum
of our choices. This affirmation of freedom contradicts all that science

tells us about a mechanistic, indifferent universe, as well as about the supremacy of heartless economic laws of supply and demand. Levy implicitly rejects the deterministic picture of mechanistic science in order to affirm human freedom. But such an affirmation of human freedom, Kant shows, is an expression of moral faith. If Levy believes with Kant in freedom against the evidences of science, why does he insist on the truth of that same science regarding its conception of an indifferent, mechanistic universe? Why does he not take a further step and have faith that, despite appearances to the contrary, the universe he lives in is ultimately caring and friendly, not harsh and heartless? In other words, why does he reject the idea of the world as issuing from a loving source?

Levy supposes that the indifferent universe as presented by a mechanistic science is the fundamental truth about reality rather than a construct of our scientific approach to reality. If that construct is indeed the truth of the matter, then human beings must be products of those blind movements of chance that supposedly govern the universe. But then how could such a universe produce beings who have the capacity to choose consciously, to act purposefully, and to love? Freedom is possible only if the mechanistic universe of science is an appearance, an assumption of the scientist, not the truth of the universe as it is in itself. The universe as it is in itself, Kant argues, lies beyond the reach of our pragmatically useful sciences with their logic of indifferent and deterministic causal laws. We can however *think* about this universe in itself, and *imagine* what it must be like if it is to support our moral endeavors and the freedom these presuppose. From the perspective of morality, it is legitimate to look at the universe as a limitless field of potentiality that makes possible the realization of human projections. Rather than regard the universe as an indifferent place, we should think of it as a field of potentiality that both allows us to choose and empowers our choices. Such a universe respects and empowers a choice in which we see ourselves as competing egos, but it also sustains and supports us if we make a different choice to act as members of a fundamentally unified humanity. Belief in a universe capable of respecting and sustaining us whatever we choose, a universe that truly respects our freedom, is the essential meaning of what Kant calls the postulate of God.

To sustain the belief in the moral perspective, it is not enough to believe that we are free. It is necessary to believe that we have the power to realize our moral duty—the power to create a world based on respect for the humanity in each individual. This is not the world of dog-eat-dog, but of human unity. If such a vision of human unity is not to be dismissed as a hopeless fantasy, it is necessary to postulate the reality within

us of a godlike power to realize a truly human world. God in this perspective is not the external God of traditional religion who manipulates
humanity with threats of rewards and punishments in an afterlife, but the
ground of the possibility of the realization of moral goals by human
beings in this life. It is Rabbi Ben's God of loving forgiveness rather than
a God demanding punitive judgment and arbitrary sacrifice.

"By moral faith," Kant writes, "I mean the unconditioned trust in
divine aid, in achieving all the good that, even with our most sincere
efforts, lies beyond our power."[13] Belief in God means the belief that
where we appear to be powerless to achieve the highest good, there is
in fact a power working through our moral actions that will ultimately
prevail. The God of morality does not demand the sacrifice of human
beings, but their ultimate triumph. To persist in moral endeavor supposes
faith in a God of love who can accomplish miracles through us. The
punitive father-god of Abraham needs to be supplemented by a mother-
god of love, who sees what is in our hearts and will somehow, we trust,
work out results that correspond to what she finds there. For the moral
vision to survive the skepticism of so-called realists such as Jack, Judah,
and Lester, it is necessary to trust that out of our efforts to do what is
right, good will be accomplished. If he doesn't trust in what Ben calls the
higher power of such a loving God, if he doesn't have confidence that
the universe is somehow in sync with his highest intentions and efforts,
if he believes that his efforts for the good disappear into an empty void,
then the person who strives after the good, like Professor Levy, will
eventually give up in despair.

The third postulate of morality is the postulate of immortality. Dolores
asks Judah: "Do you agree the eyes are the windows of the soul? . . . My
mother taught me that I have a soul and it will live on after me when I
am gone. And if you look deeply into my eyes, you can see it." But Judah
sees only her body. In Dolores he might have finally seen the soulful
eyes of a deathless love looking out at him, calling him to leave his artificial, essentially unreal world of denial and rationalization. But he does-
n't notice this. With her eyes of love, she sees a transformed, truly happy
Judah: "You come to life. Your whole face changes."

In Kant's own fable of misdemeanors and high crimes, freedom
means to be able to choose between the apparent necessities of bodily
survival and respect for the infinite dignity of the human person. This
means that the human person is more than just a body, more than an
insect to be stepped on. In the end that is in fact what Judah sees in her,
the black eyes of an insect. After his trip to the dead woman's apartment,
he recounts to Jack: "I saw there, just staring up, an inert object. . . .

Behind her eyes when you looked into them, all you saw was a black void."

When Judah imagines the eyes of God, he sees the destruction of his own vision of himself. Caught up in his worse-than-dog-eat-dog world of survival, he can only imagine a God who punishes, a God who destroys. For such destruction is the negative side of morality. The moral vision of the world is incompatible with the worldview of egotism, and is its destruction. The alternative that Judah refuses to imagine is to die to this "real world." Here is the fear of the ego for its own survival in the face of the freedom and love of the personality, the soul, the individual's real self.

When Judah momentarily leaves that world behind, and lives in the eyes of Dolores's love, he finds real happiness. Then he too lives in Rabbi Ben's Kingdom of Heaven. He takes a step in the direction of real-izing the kingdom of ends. Cliff finds such moments in the movie the-ater with a loving companion. There he transports himself into a world of justice—of love and happiness for those who struggle for the good. The hero is ready to sacrifice his life, and in the end he justly finds the love he deserves. Murder on the other hand only brings murder in return—the murder of a higher life, the death of the possibility of real happiness.

When Judah kisses his wife and walks off into his carefully gilded ver-sion of happiness, we are looking at an "appearance," a staged perfor-mance, not at Judah's reality. With the aid of Kant's critique of the idea of a morally indifferent universe, an intelligent, rationally grounded faith becomes possible. Such faith enables us to see the final performance of Judah with the eyes of the Bible, of Shakespeare, and of the classic Hollywood films, and so to agree with old Sol that "that which originates in a black deed will blossom in a foul manner." There is no need to wait for a final judgment in another world to suffer the consequences of our choices. Judah's murder of his own inherent passion and love of life inevitably blossoms in the foul, loveless world of his own construction.

Hollywood Movies and the Freedom of the Imagination

Whereas *The Matrix* is a science fantasy, *Crimes and Misdemeanors* is a film about real people in the real world. Or at least that is what some of them, like Lester and Judah, want to call it. Others are not so sure about this so-called reality. Rabbi Ben lives in the kingdom of heaven, accord-ing to Judah. Cliff lives to join his niece for afternoon Hollywood movies.

Through faith, or through imagination which is the willing suspension of disbelief, such characters are transported outside of this seemingly real world, with its dog-eat-dog rules of endemic warfare. Thus the admitted fantasy of *The Matrix* becomes an essential part of this so-called realistic film. In the realistic genre of film-making according to Woody Allen, escape from such alleged reality into the alternative world or hyperworld of art plays an essential role.

Samuel Taylor Coleridge proposes for his supernatural and romantic fictions, such as "The Rime of the Ancient Mariner" and "Christabel," "a human interest and a semblance of truth sufficient to procure for these shadows of imagination that willing suspension of disbelief for the moment that constitutes poetic faith."[14] What else do we require to gain access to the Bible, Shakespeare, and Hollywood movies with happy endings for the good, dutiful heroes, but such poetic and moral faith in their possible realization? Through both religion and art we sustain moral endeavor by *imagining* the realization of the highest good in some form or other.

What happens when we watch an engaging movie? We no longer perceive our bodies; we no longer perceive our environment; we no longer judge probability or reality-test. Matter melts into spirit. We respond emotionally to the fiction as though it were real. In works of art, as well as before the beauty of nature, we suspend practical goals of utility. Temporarily, we are no longer governed by self-interest or ego. We set aside our pragmatic goals and envision something higher. Kant stresses the disinterestedness of our experiences of beauty and art, which brings its own special kind of enjoyment. We enjoy the harmony of our subjective faculties as a presentiment or anticipation of the objective harmony of sensible and intelligible worlds in the achievement of a just and happy world. Imagination links reason (higher ideas) and sensibility in a joyful harmony. We enter another realm, that "intelligible world" that Kant regards as the source of his moral kingdom. When we come out of the cave of higher reality and reenter the glare of ordinary daylight we think of our experience as "mere imagination." But while we are in it, we inevitably think of ourselves as transported into a reality that is more real than the real world.

The question is then posed to philosophical thought: which is actually more real? Isn't Judah's so-called real life actually a carefully constructed art form of its own kind? The difference is that Judah regards his struggle to survive and ultimately to kill in order "to keep up appearances" as something imposed upon him by the rules of "hardball" that finally catch up with him. Cliff at least knows that he is choosing, that he is playing, that, as a filmmaker himself, he is being creative. Hence, the Matrix of separate egos, which produces the competitive struggle of dog-eat-dog, rules Judah and others through its channeling of their own willing energy. Willing, but for the most part unconsciously willing, as they pretend there is no choice. Thus they sink into a kind of unconsciousness, sleepwalking through life in what Jean-Paul Sartre calls "bad faith." This is the attitude of those who choose their way of life, as all of us must, but at the same time pretend that they don't really choose, that their choices are imposed upon them by the unforgiving structure of a cold and harsh reality.

Ben too realizes that he is making a choice—one that he verifies daily by its effects in his own life. And one whose validity in terms of quality of life the audience is allowed to see at the end of the film. Ben indeed finds the love that makes life worth living. Blind to the real world, if that is what it is, he dances before us in his own kingdom of heaven. Morality does indeed have to be blind if it is to survive and to achieve its goals. It has to be blind to those rules of hard ball that govern the deadening logic of an ultimately unreal world. Thus, right before our eyes in the final image of the film, Ben escapes the power of the Matrix, and creates an instance of his own heavenly Zion.

Lester is willing to entertain what he supposes to be Cliff's opinion that all his Emmy awards are "bullshit." That may be true, he thinks, from some airy-fairy moralistic perspective. But for him the bottom line for testing reality is making money. Offering the possibility of making money is his idea of helping his brother-in-law. Each has made a choice. Cliff rejects the inducements of the commercial art market—art that is not subordinate to the dignity of the human being—for the sake of an art based on the more permanent values of humanity and justice. But Cliff realizes he is choosing, whereas Lester does not believe in the reality of his choice, because for him there is no real alternative to commercial success other than commercial failure. There is no higher ideal that commands his respect. There is no escape from the Matrix of egotism—although he knows that people like Cliff think there is and both despises and fears them for it.

In the end, it looks as if Lester is the winner and Cliff the loser. No kingdom of heaven for Cliff. Lester wins the woman of his choice—but for how long will he be able to hold her with his roaming eye, and how long will Halley be able to ignore his insincerity because of the charm with which he expresses it? But this is a long-term perspective for which our film has insufficient time. In the short term, clearly, Cliff is the loser, in the light of his happy Hollywood endings. But perhaps here too there is an instructive lesson for the moralist.

Earlier in the film, Cliff's wife Wendy accuses Cliff of being jealous of Lester's success. Cliff replies that he is not a jealous person—he likes her other brother, Ben. You're not jealous of him, she says with cutting insight, because he's a saint. For sure, Cliff does not want to be a saint. He does not aim at living wholeheartedly in Ben's kingdom, only at keeping it in mind as he pursues his ambitions. He cannot enter either world completely. The appeal of the moral kingdom prevents him from committing to Lester's commercial norms. But this higher attraction is not strong enough for him to resist completely the siren song of success. Hence Cliff is the Woody Allen everyman, torn in two directions, wavering endlessly between them. Here is his weakness, which is no doubt perceived by Halley. Better to join with one world, she decides, than to be split between two. Cliff has his own rewards—the love of a sister and a niece, but not yet that of a soulmate. The true moral saint, Ben, gives advice to Judah, wishing him well while realizing that the two of them operate within completely opposed belief systems. Kant does say that however unholy individuals may be humanity within them is holy. Ben respects the humanity within Judah, however unholy Judah's thoughts and deeds may be. Would that Cliff could adopt the same saintly vision towards Lester, and so free himself from the torment of his jealousies.

But then there would be Crimes without Misdemeanors. There would be tragedy without comedy. And in Woody Allen's fictional world, to which he invites us to enter through the power of his art, we are drawn into identifying with the weakness of the anti- or semi-hero rather than with the seemingly impossible feats of the superhero. In *The Matrix*, Neo forges forward despite all obstacles, and that is thrilling and exhilarating, but in the end, there is the danger that we go away thinking that all of this heroism is for someone else, not for us, weak as we tell ourselves that we are.

And that is where Woody Allen captures us, or some of us, the self-styled or apparent losers who nevertheless aspire to more than what the Matrix, the so-called real world and peak of our civilization, has to offer. If we don't go along with the system, if we wish for or imagine another reality though without complete commitment, then we are called losers. We don't have the wholeheartedness that enables us to succeed in worldly terms by going along with commercial rules in which we put little conviction, and so we fail in the terms of this world. And if we must directly confront that reality, is not the feeling of powerlessness, of weakness, the natural result? How, with such power arrayed against us, can we persist in imagining the possibility of an alternative? Can we close our eyes or blind ourselves to this reality, so as to live like Ben in the kingdom of heaven? At least we can all escape the harsh daylight for a couple of hours of cinematic satisfaction as we enjoy the dream of a just world. In the absence of an external God and the promise of heaven in the afterlife, the hero must assume responsibility for his own deeds—as Cliff relates to Judah, who quickly denounces this endorsement of human freedom as the fantasy of a Hollywood movie. By assuming our responsibility, Cliff says, the crime takes on the proportions of true tragedy. It is elevated beyond its mundane aspects into the higher realm that compelling art allows us to enter. This is the realm of an authentic morality in which we see ourselves as the creators of our own lives, living according to laws of our own making. In this intelligible realm of authentic reality, the criminal creates his own punishment, whether he does so in clear-sighted awareness, or in the blindness of bad faith.[15]

NOTES

1. Job 9:23–24, in *The Holy Bible*, trans. Ronald Knox (New York: Sheed and Ward, 1956), 458.

2. Immanuel Kant, *The Critique of Practical Reason* (New York: Macmillan/Library of Liberal Arts, 1993), 117.

3. Immanuel Kant, *Critique of Pure Reason* (London: Macmillan & Company, 1961), 29; B xxx.

4. Kant, *Critique of Practical Reason*, 120.

5. Adam Smith, *The Wealth of Nations* (New York: Modern Library, 1965), 14.

6. Kant, *Critique of Practical Reason*, 30.

7. Immanuel Kant, *Groundwork of the Metaphysics of Morals* (New York: Harper Torchbooks, 1964), 105–6.

8. Kant, *Groundwork*, 102.

9. See James Lawler, "Marx as Market Socialist," in *Market Socialism: The Debate Among Socialists*, ed. Bertell Ollman, 23–52 (New York: Routledge, 1998). See John Weber, *Socially Mixed Economies: How Social Gains Develop in Opposed Systems* (Lanham, MD: Lexington Books, 2001).

10. James Lawler, *Matter and Spirit: the Battle of Metaphysics in Modern Western Philosophy before Kant* (Rochester, N.Y.: University of Rochester Press, 2006), 299–305.

11. Smith, *The Wealth of Nations,* 79.

12. Title of section 59 of Kant's *Critique of Judgment.*

13. Immanuel Kant to J. C. Lavater, 28 April 1775, in *Philosophical Correspondence, 1759–99* (Chicago: University of Chicago Press, 1967), 81.

14. Samuel Taylor Coleridge, *Biographia Literaria* in *The Portable Coleridge*, ed. I. A. Richards, chap. 14 (New York: Penguin Books, 1950), 518.

15. This chapter is an expanded and revised version of James Lawler, "Does Morality Have to Be Blind? A Kantian Analysis of *Crimes and Misdemeanors*," published in *Woody Allen and Philosophy,* ed. Mark T. Conard and Aeon J. Skoble (Chicago: Open Court, 2004), 33–47.

5

Realizing the Highest Good: The Power of Love in the *Matrix* Trilogy

And so you see, you can't be dead. You can't be. Because I love you.
—TRINITY

For he who would proceed aright in this matter should begin in youth to visit beautiful forms; and first, if he be guided by his instructor aright, to love one such form only—out of that he should create fair thoughts.
—DIOTEMA OF MANTINEIA

Two Tests for Finding the One

The ordinary inhabitants of the Matrix have no idea that their world is an artificial one. They are like the occupants of Plato's cave, who live out their entire lives in the false belief that the shadows they see projected on the wall in front of them are reality. With some few but notable exceptions, they do not ask Descartes's question: what if the world we experience is like a dream, created by a malign intelligence to deceive us? Like most of us before being awakened from our dogmatic slumbers, they believe that the objects of their experience exist independently of them. They therefore fail to recognize the implications of Kant's Copernican revolution in philosophy—that the world of our experience is in large part a projection of our own minds.

The second film of the *Matrix* trilogy, *Reloaded*, pursues these themes of *The Matrix* with even greater deliberateness. Philosophical themes that had earlier been only suggested or intimated—and so often ignored for the compelling visuals—now directly command the attention of the audience. A lengthy and spectacular sixty-million-dollar car chase to end all car chases is a welcome interlude allowing us time to ponder the questions previously raised concerning the nature of cause and effect, freedom and destiny, love and death.

If the themes of freedom, determinism, and destiny are prominent in *Reloaded*, we also see more clearly the background texture woven from the conflicting strands of love and fear. That the *Matrix* trilogy is above all a love story is suggested from the very beginning of the series. As the film title in *The Matrix* is displayed in a rain of computer digits, we hear the intrusive voice of the navigator Cypher saying to Trinity—"You like him, don't you?" If we look carefully, we note that the opening sequence in which Trinity battles policemen and Agents takes place in a hotel named "Heart o' the City." The capital letters H, E, A, R, and T, vertically descend the height of the shabby inner city building. In a world dominated by artificial intelligence, it is still possible to find a hiding place for the heart.

Trinity is watching out for the computer programmer, Thomas A. Anderson, a denizen of the Matrix who moonlights as a computer hacker, known to his grateful clients as Neo. The company of the Nebuchadnezzar is intent on extracting Neo from the Matrix because the captain of the Nebuchadnezzar, Morpheus, believes that Neo is "the One," the individual prophesied by the Oracle to be the liberator of enslaved humanity from the Matrix. Secretly, however, Trinity's interest in Neo is more personal. Near the end of *The Matrix*, we learn that the Oracle once told her that the person she would love would indeed be "the One." While others on the Nebuchadnezzar see the test of Neo's special destiny in his unusual ability to assimilate downloaded programs of martial arts and other weapons of battle, for Trinity there is a quite different test—the test of her heart. She doesn't love him because she believes he is the One. She finally believes he is the One because she knows that she loves him.

When Neo awakens out of the dreamlike illusion of the Matrix, Morpheus greets him: "Welcome to the real world." We soon learn, however, that the distinction between reality and illusion is not as sharp as common sense would suggest. After an early training sequence in the virtual reality space called the Construct, Neo, on returning his consciousness to his body, discovers that he is bleeding. "I thought it wasn't real," he says. "Your mind makes it real," Morpheus replies. Neo: "If you're killed in the Matrix, you die here?" Morpheus: "The body cannot live without the mind." Hence Morpheus keeps insisting that Neo free his mind from all restrictive beliefs. Such beliefs continue to affect and shape reality outside of the Matrix. One of the main restrictive beliefs, apparently confirmed over and over by experience within the Matrix, is enunciated to Neo by the slimy betrayer Cypher: "You see an Agent, you do what we do. Run. Run your ass off." Thus fear of the Agents, fear of death, persists within the parameters of the Matrix even for those who understand its artificiality. So when Neo finally turns to fight Agent Smith, Morpheus, observing the events in their digital computer form, says, "He is beginning to believe." He is beginning to believe that he is indeed the One—that he has the power to destroy the Matrix and liberate its slaves. Beginning to believe in his power and destiny, he ceases to be afraid.

However, all Neo's stupendous feats of strength, speed, and agility finally fail to defeat the superior powers of the Agents. Racing to find a telephone hookup that would take his consciousness back to his body on the ship, Neo finds himself at the business end of a gun. As he is killed in the pseudo-reality of the Matrix, the computer monitor connected to his brain in the real world flatlines. The tests of strength and speed, the test of doing battle in the Matrix, seem to prove that Neo, after all, is not in fact the One. But Trinity has not been applying this test. Blaise Pascal (1623–1662) wrote, "The heart has its reasons, which reason does not know."[1] Trinity is following the test of her heart, which has reasons of which ordinary scientific-technological reason knows nothing. The Oracle prophesied that the one she loves would be the One. Trinity loves Neo. Therefore Neo must be the One. Thanks to her love, Trinity is no longer afraid of death. As it looks like all is over for both Neo and the Nebuchadnezzar, Trinity whispers over Neo's dead body: "Neo, I'm not afraid anymore. The Oracle told me that I would fall in love, and that man, the man who I loved, would be the One. And so you see, you can't be dead. You can't be. Because I love you. You hear me, I love you." She kisses Neo, and he comes back to life. The place in which Neo dies and is then resurrected to his new life as the One is that same dreary building with the word HEART prominently displayed on its marquee.

The names of the main characters in *The Matrix* each have significance. "Neo," which indicates that something new will happen despite the controls of the Matrix, is also an anagram of One. "Morpheus" is appropriately named after the god of sleep and the world of dreams. "Cypher," who betrays his crew and strives to return to comfortable oblivion back in the Matrix, wants to be the nonentity his name indicates. So then what does "Trinity" mean? I suppose that most viewers, recognizing that these other names have been chosen for their obvious meanings, are reluctant to do the same for the name "Trinity." But who is it that is capable of creating life, as Trinity does when her love restores life to Neo? In the Christian tradition, only the triune God has such power. And in God's secular ordinance the power of creating life is given to a woman in love. In Trinity, the God that is love takes flesh and creates life. Perhaps more specifically, if Neo is the representative of Jesus who embodies the Son of God, Trinity is the third person of the triune Godhead, the Holy Spirit. Hidden esoteric teachings of early Christianity reflect such a perspective—as we will see later in chapter 10.

The Oblivion of Being

Beyond the excitement of its simulated battles and the allure of its technological themes of virtual reality, the *Matrix* trilogy insinuates a subversive, critical theme regarding the very fascination with technology that draws in its audience. According to the philosopher Martin Heidegger (1889–1976), the history of the Western world is centered on the development of technology, and this focus induces what he calls the forgetfulness of being. In the course of this history, technocratic intellect has become a quasi-demonic force, creating a world of objects and a dominant mentality based on the artificial ideas of the intellect. This frame of mind blinds us to the truth of experiences that are found only outside this technological framework—such as the power and beauty of the natural world as expressed in ancient religions and early Greek philosophy, in the nature philosophy of Chinese Taoism, or in the works of certain modern poets such Hölderlin, who was a close friend of the young Hegel. In Heidegger's terms, our modern world is dominated by a technocratic Matrix that we take to be reality, but that hides from us a deeper truth about our human being.

Heidegger argues that the oblivion of being brought about by the mesmerizing spell of technological rationality has its origins in the rationalism of Plato—in Plato's disjunction between the idea, with its transcendent realm of supposedly true being, and the mere appearances that are accessible to the senses. In view of Heidegger's interpretation, we can see that Kant's own consignment of the sensible world to the status of a mere appearance, and his conception of reality as found only in an "intelligible world," is an updating of the Platonic metaphysics to accommodate the framework of modern science. In Heidegger's interpretation, Plato's allegory of the cave, which instructs us to look for ultimate reality outside of the sensory material world of immediate experience, contributes to the oblivion of being. It conceals our spontaneous awareness that there is another, more fundamental truth than that which scientific intellect attains and applies through its technology. Regarding Christianity as concentrating the minds of the faithful on a transcendent realm of heaven, and so denigrating the sensory world of earth, Heidegger concludes, "Nietzsche was right in saying that Christianity is Platonism for the people."[2] It is a paradox that Christianity, with its otherworldly perspective, contributes to the technological domination of the modern world. But the scientific-technological mentality depends precisely on the prior disenchantment of the natural world as not inherently sacred, and so as capable of being manipulated and exploited for egotistical goals. In its condemnation of the earth-centered pagan religions of Greece and Rome, an otherworldly Christianity paves the way for a purely technocratic approach to physical objects, which become looked upon, as Kant puts it, as "mere means"—or, in the language of economics, as use-values for purposes extrinsic to them, or as exchange values whose origin is quantifiable human activity.

Heidegger therefore gives us a philosophical perspective for recognizing philosophical truth in the *Matrix* trilogy, with its graphic vision of artificial intelligence (AI) machines ruling earth and humanity. Through Heidegger's philosophy we come to recognize our own world as in fact dominated by an artificial technocratic mentality that cuts off awareness of the deeper reality of human life. But what alternative does the *Matrix* trilogy offer us? In describing our sensible world as a mere appearance, in light of some transcendent reality beyond it, does not the film series ultimately reinforce the very technological demons that it seems to criticize? Does it not in fact subscribe to the Platonism, the Kantianism, and the otherworldly Christianity that, according to Heidegger, give rise to and implicitly legitimate the technocratic mentality itself? This would be the case were we to see the main struggles of the *Matrix* trilogy to consist merely in the attempt of a "good" technology, that of the One and the free human beings, to overcome an "evil" technology, that of mere machines emancipated from their proper human masters. But if this is the nature of the struggle, it is technology itself that inevitably wins. Indeed, as the Architect explains to Neo, the predictable struggle of the humans to regain mastery of the machines, to reappropriate technology once more to elusive human goals, turns out to be the very dynamic that keeps the Matrix and its technological function in place. But this is where the love story of the *Matrix* trilogy subverts a superficial understanding of its central dynamics, and at the same time reveals hidden dimensions in the philosophical underpinnings of Plato, Kant, and Christianity itself.

For Heidegger, this philosophical and religious tradition arises out of a rationalistic divorce of technocratic reason from earthy sensibility.

However, we have previously seen that Kant's kingdom of ends does not aim at a transcendent otherworld or afterlife. As the postulated reality behind the appearances, it gives rise to an emotionally powerful ideal that is meant to be realized in the here and now of *this* life. Access to this kingdom, moreover, is found first of all in the *feeling* of duty, not through some sort of detached reasoning. This is not an ordinary feeling arising out of external causes, but an inner feeling that sets aside all those external influences that appeal to the vulnerable ego. Moral reasoning is a secondary operation of testing this sense of duty through formulations of the categorical imperative. The origin of the feeling of duty as well as of reason itself is the higher reality of our shared humanity. This "intelligible world" of shared humanity gives rise to a sense of duty that contradicts the inclinations of the separate ego and the purely instrumental or technological rationality that operates in its service. Moral reason therefore involves a critique of technological reason. It is the expression of universal human connectedness, which we believe or postulate to be the source of our experiences of duty. Moral reasoning functions appropriately only as an expression and consolidation of this primary experience found in the profound feeling of respect for the holiness of our shared humanity.

Illusion of the Superhero

In arguing that morality is the expression of human autonomy, the human ability to create the laws we live by, Kant claims to be giving philosophical expression to the authentic teachings of Christianity. He thereby implicitly challenges the doctrines of a degrading external religion that relies on bribes and threats to compel obedience to a set of external rules, and that affirms human powerlessness. Neo, in his incarnation as "the One," rejects the notion that he is a savior of others, rather than a teacher who empowers individuals to save themselves. In *Reloaded*, the Kid tells Neo: "You saved me." Trying to avoid the adulation of the crowds in the beleaguered city of Zion who look upon him as their Savior, Neo replies: "You saved yourself." The Kid nevertheless persists in regarding the final salvation of Zion as the accomplishment of Neo alone, overlooking the fact that his own heroic actions, together with those of others, were an integral part of the final, happy result. The *Matrix* trilogy therefore suggests new ways of understanding both classical philosophy and the nature of religion. The relation between art and philosophy works in both directions. If philosophy can provides rational underpinnings for imaginative fiction, such art opens up new ways of looking at old ideas that have been interpreted in a one-sided manner. As we unfold the various aspects of Kant's thought in order to comprehend the complexity and depth of popular works of art, we see that it cannot be reduced to the kind of moral rationalism and metaphysical dualism that Heidegger criticizes. If the *Matrix* trilogy, aligned as we have argued with the philosophy of Kant and a Kantian interpretation of Christianity, can escape the criticisms of Heidegger, then perhaps Plato's philosophy deserves another look as well.

The *Matrix* trilogy suggests possibilities for understanding what Heidegger could possibly mean by his conception of an independent, demonic technology. How can technocratic intellect become an independent power over human minds without being embodied in intelligent entities of the type described by film? Heidegger once argued that both the United States and the Soviet Union, the two superpowers of the time, had incarnated the spirit of sheer, soulless, demonic technology that has arisen and gathered force historically over the centuries. He had hoped that his native Germany, with its superhero leader, Adolf Hitler, had retained that connection to being, to what is ultimately real, that could liberate mankind from its mind-induced shackles.[3] But this conception of salvation through the high-tech armies of Hitler's racist nationalism proved to be another illusion, an even more insidious dimension of the unfolding demonic Matrix of technocratic control.

Reloaded clearly raises the possibility that the salvation promised in the form of a superhero savior is really just another illusion, a mechanism for the perpetuation of the Matrix. According to the Architect of the Matrix, the One is not the liberator of humanity from the control of the Matrix, but a function of the program whose purpose is the preservation of the Matrix itself. When, at the end of this second film, Neo uses the power of his mind outside of the Matrix to stop the advance of the threatening sentinels, our simplistic distinction between the illusion of the Matrix and the "real world" of the Nebuchadnezzar and Zion is seriously challenged. Perhaps Neo's powers in what we thought was the real world are the expression of the fact that this real world is just another level of a vastly expanded Matrix. Is there no independent truth outside the projections and power of the technocratic mind? Is *everything* therefore illusion?

While this pessimistic perspective is prominently suggested, other strands in the film indicate a different possibility. Two paths of liberation have been proposed from the beginning. The first is to confront the technological power of the machines with the superior techniques of power, speed, and agility of the One. But in such a war of technologies, isn't it technology itself that inevitably wins? In a somber scene in *Reloaded*, the wise old councilor of the free city of Zion takes Neo on a tour of the underground machinery that supports the life of the city. We too are dependent on machines, he says. Where is there really a difference between this and the Matrix?

There is, however, another approach that sidesteps the confrontation of machines, technologies, and their mind-based powers. This is the way of the heart, Trinity's way of love. In the open sequences of *Reloaded* Neo has fully reciprocated Trinity's love. The hearts and bodies of the two lovers are entwined in passionate yet solemn embrace, as the whole city of Zion celebrates its freedom to the sensual drumbeats of love. The people have been released from their fear of the weapons of terror by the impassioned declaration of Morpheus: "This is Zion! And we are not afraid!" As the enemy advances, rather than prepare for battle, the people of Zion dance in the fires of love.

Who Was the Teacher of Socrates?

If Heidegger was himself under the mesmerizing spell of technocratic rationality, in his belief that humankind's salvation lay in the countervailing technological might of the Nazi party and its Führer, Adolf Hitler, how can we trust his interpretation of Plato? In the history of interpretations of Plato, there are two approaches, comparable to the two paths of liberation outlined in the *Matrix* trilogy: Plato as the exponent of the all-controlling forms or ideas detected by technically agile reason, and Plato as the philosopher of love.

In the allegory of the cave, Plato compares the life of the majority of human beings to that of lifelong prisoners, preoccupied solely with the shadows of reality. The philosopher is the One—the one who has been liberated from this shadow world and returns to free his fellow humans from illusion. But how is the liberation of the philosopher achieved in the first place? Is it by conquering false reasons with the technical superiority of true reasons on the battlefield of rationality—and thereby forgetting, as Heidegger would argue, that being is not something that yields to force, including the force of logic? Or is there another approach: the path of love, the way of the heart?

There is indeed a strange kind of forgetfulness in the history of Western philosophy that also persists in the historical recollections of Heidegger. In the canonical genealogy of Western philosophy, Socrates was the teacher of Plato, Plato was the teacher of Aristotle, and Aristotle was the philosopher who inspired the European Middle Ages. But who taught Socrates in the first place? Socrates himself tells us, in the *Symposium*, that his teacher was a woman, Diotema of Mantineia. Diotema taught the philosophy of the heart with its own reasons, not the philosophy of a heartless, self-aggrandizing rationality.

Philos means love and *sophos* means wisdom. The philosopher, etymologically, is a lover of wisdom. In the common understanding of the nature of philosophy, the stress is generally placed not on love but on wisdom, which then is interpreted as the transcendent idea that is only accessed by that detached, technological rationality that Heidegger says is responsible for the oblivion of being. But Diotema proposes the following curriculum for her Philosophy 101: "For he who would proceed aright in this matter should begin in youth to visit beautiful forms; and first, if he be guided by his instructor aright, to love one such form only—out of that he should create fair thoughts. . . ."[4] The first step in Diotema's philosophy is not an achievement of the mind but an affair of the heart. It is to fall deeply in love with a beautiful person. It is physical, erotic love that breaks the mental shackles that bind the individual to the darkness of the cave—a darkness that only deepens with the historical expansion in the West of purely technological rationality. Such love gives rise to the first "fair thoughts" of authentic philosophy. In recounting his allegory of the cave, Socrates says that the One, the potential philosopher, is first dragged from his position in the cave. He does not say who does the dragging. But the ascent out of the cave occurs in stages, in parallel with the ladder of love taught by Diotema. And she teaches that it is the beloved person who first introduces the light of beauty into the darkness of mind-based illusion. Enflamed by the fire of love, ordinary, self-centered reason is lost, and a new life with its fair thoughts opens to the student of love. For the person in love the world glows with a new intensity; it becomes transparent to ultimate reality.

The next, crucial step—upper-division love of wisdom leading to graduate school—is to keep on loving, to follow the path of love. When reason is linked to love, it keeps telling us not to stop at this or that person, but to recognize the beauty that potentially shines forth in every person. It reminds us that institutions too have their own beauty—if only their leaders would recognize it. It resists the temptation to close off the ultimate nature of reality with limiting beliefs. It teaches us to free our minds to see the light of beauty everywhere, and the power of darkness only in the attempt to direct our love *exclusively* to one person, one institution, one set of beliefs. In the third film of the series, *Revolutions*, Neo, whose eyes have been viciously destroyed, sees with heart-opened vision the light in the enemy machines themselves: "It's unbelievable,

Trin. Lights everywhere. Like the whole thing was built with light." Once more, as in Woody Allen's *Crimes and Misdemeanors*, it is the blind person guided by love who really sees.

As we universalize our love, discovering beauty in everyone and everything in the harmony of their multiple colors and textures, we do not have to abandon our first love. If she too is a wholehearted lover, she accompanies us on our journey—one's true soulmate who, says Aristophanes in the same *Symposium*, comes in the soul's earthly journey to those authentically devoted to the gods. True "Platonic love" is not a bland sexless sentiment but that same erotic love of one beautiful person that has been expanded to the entire universe through the heartfelt vision of the universal presence of beauty itself. Such a vision does not take us away from the sensible world, but enables us to see its true reality. Through the philosophical eyes of love, the world of matter shines with the splendor of spirit. The power of darkness, the illusory world of fear and death which has its origin in the mind-based constructions of egotism, is only dispelled by the fiery light of love.

Neo Chooses the Path of Love

In *The Matrix*, Neo has to choose between the red pill and the blue pill. Morpheus explains: "You take the blue pill, the story ends, you wake up in your bed and believe whatever you want to believe. You take the red pill, you stay in Wonderland, and I show you how deep the rabbit hole goes. . . ." But why is the path down the rabbit hole symbolized by the *red* pill? The reference to Lewis Carroll's *Alice in Wonderland* suggests another book by Lewis Carroll, *Silvie and Bruno*, in which Silvie is given the choice between a blue locket and a red one. On the blue locket are the words: "All will love Silvie." On the red locket are the words "Silvie will love all." Silvie chooses the red locket: "It's *very* nice to be loved, but it's nicer to love other people!"[5]

The choice between self-love and loving other people is given to Neo in *Reloaded* as the choice between two paths, opened up by two facing doors. As the Architect puts this choice: "The door to your right leads to the Source, and the salvation of Zion. The door to your left leads back to the Matrix, to her [Trinity] and to the end of your species." The Oracle tells Neo that he must "return to the Source." She invokes in this way the doctrine of ancient spirituality that everything that proceeds from the divine source will ultimately return to the source. In the Bhagavad-Gita, Krishna, embodying the universal divinity, declares that

> They comprehend not, the Unheavenly,
> How Souls go forth from Me; nor how they come
> Back to Me.[6]

And Lao Tzu writes in the *Tao Te Ching*:

> If you can empty your mind of all thoughts
> your heart will embrace the tranquility of peace.
> Watch the workings of all of creation,
> but contemplate their return to the source.[7]

Ultimately, Neo interprets his source to be Trinity, not a machine or a computer program, but a flesh-and-blood person. She is the godlike source of his rebirth as the One, the beloved without whom he cannot imagine his existence. The choice he faces is really a choice between mere survival, rooted in isolated existence, and his love of Trinity. The love of another person is the starting point of Diotema's ladder of universal love. Universal love is the cosmic unity of Yin and Yang, female and male, that is the true path, way, or Tao. Neo chooses the doorway of love for Trinity, which indeed turns out to be the way that leads beyond mere survival to authentic freedom and the flourishing of Zion.

Revolutions therefore distinguishes between two opposing approaches to revolution. In the repeating program that produces the larger Matrix encompassing the physical world of the Nebuchadnezzar and Zion, previous Ones, in their efforts to perpetuate a new round of senseless human existence, chose to sacrifice the beloved one to save the many. Many revolutionaries in human history, believing that the end justifies the means, were willing to sacrifice some for others, a minority for a majority. They deemed it necessary to sacrifice personal love and the well-being of loved ones for the higher cause. But such a mentality is perpetuated in the outcome—a world in which some continue to be sacrificed for others. Our beliefs are inevitably manifested in the world that we create on their basis.

The truly revolutionary approach is that of Diotema, who, like Silvie, teaches that *all* must be loved, because there is beauty in everyone and everything. The path to the free world cannot begin by abandoning your partner, your soulmate. Such hard-hearted revolutionaries, like the previous Ones, only perpetuated the cycles of war. Neo, however, follows the seemingly irrational path of love, the path of Trinity, to the very end. In *Revolutions*, Trinity must guide Neo, "the blind Messiah" as Smith calls him, to the threshold of the Machine City, where she dies. But the spirit of her love, the nature of the path she has chosen from the very beginning, lives on in him when he finally faces Mr. Smith and his endlessly expanding clone army.

The Matrix has been criticized as "a naïve fantasy of overcoming human flesh. The hero moves from being 'penetrated' and connected to others to being self-controlling and intact—even immune to bullets. . . . This fantasy suits geeky young males who yearn for autonomy and mental powers."[8] This appraisal may have been justifiable on the basis of the first film, before the love theme of the trilogy moves definitively to the foreground. The feminist criticism recognizes the seductive primacy, for some, of the masculinist path of technocratic intellect and the resulting wars of technologies. For the geeky males who were captivated by this illusory surface appearance, the emerging real theme of the *Matrix* trilogy, subverting the dominant paradigm of technocratic intellect with its climax of self-effacement, must be quite disappointing.

At the beginning of their final struggle, Smith taunts Neo for his effeminate weakness: "Why keep fighting? . . . Is it freedom or truth, perhaps peace—could it be for love? Illusions, Mr. Anderson, vagaries of perception. Temporary constructs of a feeble human intellect trying desperately to justify an existence that is without meaning or purpose. And all of them as artificial as the Matrix itself. Although, only a human mind could invent something as insipid as love." But which is the real illusion? The endless spiral of the technologies of war—represented by the infinitely expanding clone army of Mr. Smith—that is characteristic of the male-dominant societies of the past five thousand years of "civilization," or the truly revolutionary path of love on which Trinity guides Neo?

Heidegger argues that Plato separated soul from body, the ideal world from the world of sensory experience, and thereby legitimated the rule of the technocratic intellect over what must eventually become, as a result, a blighted earth. However, it was not Plato, but the Stoics, during the time of imperialist Roman rule, who radically separated soul and body, believing that the external physical world is beyond the control of the individual, and so subject to an unknowable higher will. The German philosopher G. W. F. Hegel (1770–1831) therefore called the Roman religion, in which individuals are sacrificed to the will of the gods and the Emperor, "The Religion of Expediency."[9] Here indeed we see the technological relationship of power over the earth that Heidegger criticizes. This is the true forgetfulness of being. But this is not the earth-loving teaching of the wise woman Diotema that is passed on to us through the works of Plato, if we know how to read them. Recognizing this, Hegel calls the Greek religion of the time of Plato "the Religion of Beauty."[10]

Neo puts an end to the spiral of destruction caused by the dominance of the technocratic intellect when he finally stops fighting and adopts the feminine position of allowance— allowing himself to be "penetrated" by Smith. In his realization that the war between technocratic intellects is unwinnable, Neo also follows the lead of the mother of the Matrix, the Oracle, who previously refused to fight Smith on his own terms, and allowed his attempt to penetrate and so presumably to destroy her.

Revolutions concludes with the grandmotherly Oracle complimenting the little girl named Sati, a computer program, for her breath-taking sunrise—Sati's gift of gratitude to Neo. The name Sati is the feminine form of the Sanskrit word for being. The highest ideal of the Indian philosophy called Vedanta is Sat-Chit-Ananda: Being-Consciousness-Bliss, or the blissful consciousness of being. The *Matrix* trilogy thus concludes with Heidegger's long-forgotten being in the form of a sweet girl who makes sunrises.

When Sati first meets Neo on the underground train platform, she asks him: "Are you from the Matrix?" Neo says that he *was* from the Matrix, but had to leave. Sati replies: "I had to leave my home too." For Sati there is no hierarchy, no discrimination between a real world and an artificial, illusory one. It is all reality. It is all someone's home. She is the embodiment of acceptance. She can create beauty because she sees it everywhere. In place of the pessimistic possibility that all is illusion, *Revolutions* concludes with Sati's belief that all is real, because beauty can be found, and created, everywhere. The final outcome of the *Matrix* trilogy is not the victory of the real world over the illusory one, of the humans over the machines, or vice versa, but compromise, acceptance of the differences, and so peace between all the worlds and the beginning of a reign of love. Let us not forget, Diotema teaches Socrates, that there is beauty, and so love, everywhere.

Plato's Vision of Heaven on Earth

In chapters 2 and 4 we examined in detail Kant's "postulates" as his faith-based response to the antinomy of practical reason. The postulates constitute essential beliefs that must be maintained in order to overcome the potential despair that comes to the moral individual who is conscious of the moral duty to create the just world of the highest good and yet faces seemingly overwhelming odds in the world of appearance and empirical experience. Essential to an understanding of the postulates is a critique of external religion—a religion that promotes the concept of essentially powerless people who put themselves in the hands of an external God who gives rewards in another world, in an afterlife, to those who accept suffering and misery in this one. This framework of consciousness opposes authentic human freedom or autonomy, and the goal of creating the highest good in this life.

Kant's postulates of freedom, God, and immortality do not repeat the conventional understanding of these concepts, but involve an interpretation of Christianity in the light of Platonic philosophy and the spirit of the Greek religion of beauty taught by Diotema. Heidegger endorses Nietzsche's negative appraisal of Christianity as Platonism for the masses, based on his notion that Plato disparages earth-centered vitality for an intellectualism focused on a higher world of ideas. But if Plato's conception of a higher world is based on Diotema's ladder of love, starting with passionate, physical love of one person, this appraisal of Plato's philosophy as an otherworldly intellectualism must be radically revised. And if Christianity is really connected to Plato, we must revise the interpretation of Christianity itself as an other-worldly religion. Kant in fact proposes a reinterpretation of Christianity in the light of a Platonism adapted to modern times and reconciled with modern science.

Like Plato, Kant distinguishes between a sensible world of appearances and an intelligible world of ultimate reality. The goal of this distinction, for Kant, is not to leave the sensible world behind, but to transform it from the locus of conflicting egos to the realm of the realization of the highest good. This is Kant's understanding of Jesus's teaching that the Kingdom of God is inherent within each individual. Kant simultaneously follows the journey of the Platonic philosopher who, energized by love of the beautiful, rises from the cave of sensible images, mistaken for the ultimate reality, to a realm of pure Beauty, Goodness, and Truth, that is accessible only to the highest aspirations of the human spirit. For Kant it is primarily the experience of moral duty that awakens individuals to a higher dimension than that of the survival and well-being of fortunate individuals, the winners in struggle of a dog-eat-dog world. Awareness of this higher perspective of morality is not about escaping from this world, but about transforming it in the light of this higher ideal and postulated reality.

For Plato, the One who rises out of the cave returns to the world of ordinary human experience in order to explain to fellow humans that the images they see are indeed images, not the realities they take them to be. Like Neo at the end of *The Matrix*, he wants to show the prisoners of the Matrix how to liberate themselves by recognizing the nature of illusion and reality. For this, we do not have to leave the sensory world behind, but recognize that its images reflect a higher reality that we should and can directly perceive by cultivating the higher abilities of perception of beauty and moral service to humanity, aided by an intelligence or wisdom that is inspired by love. The beautiful sunrise created by Sati at the conclusion of the *Matrix* trilogy is, in one sense, an illusion. And yet it is the ability to create illusions consciously that makes life in the Matrix something radically different from what it was for those who took their illusions for reality. There is a remarkable scene in *Revolutions,* in which the "blind Messiah" Neo sees with the eyes of spirit, his physical eyes having been gouged out, that there is an incomparably beautiful sunlight that is reflected in and shines through the apparent one, and gives it its real power. The Platonic philosopher teaches that perceiving these higher realities of the beautiful, the good, and the true, allows us to recognize their presence throughout all aspects of existence—in all individuals, in the institutions of society, and in the creations and discoveries of the arts and sciences. As a result of this higher wisdom, we do not replace a devalued sensible world with a supersensible world, but rediscover the enchantment of the sensible world after it has been devalued by egotistical interests and a rationality working to satisfy those interests.

The Platonic philosopher must realize a duty to enlighten his fellow citizens on the need to put the soul above the body, not in order to escape the bodily realm for the pure realm of the soul, but to ensure that bodily existence itself attains the highest degree of fulfillment of which it is capable. In his self-defense during his trial, Socrates puts this clearly when he says that his duty as revealed by the Oracle of the God of Light, Apollo, consists in questioning those who are authorities in the eyes of society to see if what they proclaim to know they really know in fact. So Socrates argues:

> This, I do assure you, is what my God commands, and it is my belief that no greater good has ever befallen you in this city than my service to my God. For I spend all my time going about trying to persuade you, young and old, to make your first and chief concern not for your bodies nor for your possessions, but for the highest welfare of your souls, proclaiming as I go, wealth does not bring goodness, but goodness brings wealth and every other blessing, both to the individual and to the state.
>
> Now if I corrupt the young by this message, the message would seem to be harmful, but if anyone says that my message is different from this, he is talking nonsense. And so, gentlemen, I would say, You can please yourself whether you listen to [his accuser] Anytus or not, and whether you acquit me or not. You know that I am not going to alter my conduct, not even if I have to die a hundred deaths.[11]

Socrates here does not recommend putting the soul first out of dis-approval of the body, but for the sake of bodily flourishing. He is saying that when you put bodily existence, with its attendant pursuit of private wealth and power, above everything else, the result will inevitably be harmful to a happy and flourishing human life, both for the individual and the larger society. The egotistical pursuit of wealth and power is based on the potent but illusory belief that separate bodily existence is the ultimate reality. This is the belief system of the cave, the world of illu-sion, that the philosopher, in service to the God of light and love, attempts to dispel. Those individuals who put the body first promote competition and conflict, and thereby bring about the downfall of the city. Far from teaching the youth of Athens to despise the divine, Socrates is teaching an authentic religion of moral integrity on which the flour-ishing of Athens depends.

Socrates' trial took place in 399 BC, just four years after the defeat of Athens by Sparta and its allies in the Peloponnesian War. He was put on trial as a scapegoat for Athens' loss, for he is being blamed for inciting the youth to reject the traditional religion and the authority of society that is linked to it. Those responsible for leading the disastrous war, whom Socrates had essentially exposed as imposters, were implicitly shifting the blame for defeat to Socrates himself. At his trial, Socrates turns the tables on his accusers. He is the true patriot because he teaches the youth and any who will listen to him that it is only by putting the concerns of the soul first that a united, strong, and flourishing city is possible. Souls con-cerned with beauty, goodness, and truth will be united, and a united society is the foundation of the strength, material wealth, and bodily health of the Athenian citizenry. The pursuit of egotistical goals divides and weakens the city and so brought about its defeat in the recent war.

As Neo discovers in *The Matrix*, there is a fundamental choice to make—between the primacy of the soul, on which the good of the larger social whole depends, and the good of the separate body, regarded as the battle station and fortress of the ego, which results in division and downfall. The pursuit of wealth by competing individuals paradoxically leads to poverty for the society as a whole. In the *Phaedrus*, Plato rep-resents this fundamental choice in his image of the charioteer. The soul is like a charioteer riding in a chariot driven by winged horses. While the souls of the gods experience no difficulty in guiding the horses that give them power to move through the heavens of true being, humans have to confront the antithetical nature of their steeds. There is a beautiful white horse who is noble and readily subject to the highest goal of the human will which is to follow the gods in their upward flight around the dome of the sky. The sky through which the sun courses like Apollo on his chariot of gold is a kind of veil through which it is possible to perceive the ultimate nature of reality. Plato therefore anticipates Kant in teaching that the pre-Copernican view of the sun circling the earth is an appearance, beyond which is to be found the reality of things as they are in themselves. In being empowered by such forces of light, humans share in the majesty of the gods. But humans are infected by darkness as well as light. There is also another, a dark horse, that is essentially unruly and naturally pulls in a downward direction. Within human beings therefore there is a battle between light and dark, good and evil. The charioteer must struggle hard to rein in the downward pulling steed and so master and reorient the base passions that promote a fixation on possessing material goods and dominating others.

Socrates explains that our ability to create a happy life depends on the extent to which we have made the pursuit of the virtues of the soul primary. We all implicitly strive for the highest life, represented by the life of the gods. However, those who choose a life focused on the pleasures and powers of the body naturally are attracted to one another, group together in their desire for doing battle with one another, and thereby create a worse than dog-eat-dog competitive world, a kind of hell on earth. Such a choice is the fundamental Matrix of the cave, resulting in a world that feeds on illusion:

> [T]hough all are eager to reach the heights and follow [the gods] they are not able; sucked down as they travel they trample and tread upon one another, this one striving to outstrip that. Thus confusion ensues, and conflict and grievous sweat. Whereupon, with their charioteers powerless, many are lamed, and many have their wings all broken, and for all their toiling they are balked, every one, of the full vision of being, and departing therefrom, they feed upon the food of semblance.[12]

If we choose the moral path of duty, we shall ultimately come to experiencing in this world something like the bliss of the gods: "[I]f the victory be won by the higher elements of mind guiding them into the ordered rule of the philosophical life, their days on earth will be blessed with happiness and concord, for the power of evil in the soul has been subjected, and the power of goodness liberated."[13] Central to attaining the blessing of a happy life *on earth* is the transforming and uplifting power of the love of beauty. The special nature of beauty is that it penetrates the material world and can be seen with ordinary human vision, unlike Truth, which requires the development of the higher faculty of intellect. This is why love of beauty is the real starting point of the philosophical journey. But to appreciate the full power of beauty, the eyes of the lover must be purified of all moral darkness arising from our choices in past lives and in the present one. Then, far from despising the body, the purified soul sees in the beautiful person a clear reflection of the beauty of the higher world. In a beautiful person, the morally guided lover of beauty "beholds a godlike face or bodily form that truly expresses beauty."[14] For such a person, sensible experience is not a dark and distorted image of ultimate reality, but the very presence of heaven on earth. In the presence of the beloved, the lover shudders in awe, experiencing "reverence as at the sight of a god."[15] A strange sweating and fever comes over him as a result of "the stream of beauty entering in through his eyes."[16] Long stunted and encased in a hardened shell, the wings of the soul now begin to grow again. The beloved in turn learns to trust the presence of this worshipful, respectful lover, and soon reciprocates the flow of love, receiving back from the lover the stream of love, "not realizing that his lover is as it were a mirror in which he beholds himself."[17]

Freedom, God, and immortality are intertwined in this picture: (1) freedom to choose between two opposed tendencies in life; (2) the ideal of a godlike life that consists in the harmony of all one's powers and a resulting harmony of material existence; and (3) the continuing succession and cycles of lifetimes available for realizing that godlike ideal. The nature of this immortality is graphically depicted in the *Republic*, where Socrates recounts what would today be called the near-death experience of the soldier Er. Er has apparently died, but on his funeral pyre comes back to life and tells an amazing story of the between-world life that souls lead after death. Central to that story is Er's account of the manner in which the soul's next incarnation is decided. The various lifetimes are laid out before the souls who are to reincarnate in human form. These souls draw lots to determine the order in which they get to choose their next lifetime. Such choice is intimately connected with destiny, for it is Lachesis, the daughter of Necessity, who explains to them the nature of the choice that is before them:

> Souls that live for a day, now is the beginning of another cycle of mortal generation where birth is the beacon of death. No divinity shall cast lots for you, but you shall choose your own deity. Let him to whom falls the first lot first select a life to which he shall cleave of necessity. But virtue has no master over her, and each shall have more or less of her as he honors her or does her despite. The blame is his who chooses. God is blameless.[18]

Paradoxically, the daughter of Necessity explains that all the apparent necessities of life are the outcome of a fundamental freedom. On the surface appearance of things, the individual's lot in life is the result of external circumstances and upbringing. But if we fundamentally choose our lot in life prior to our incarnation, then the necessities that we experience are those we have chosen for purposes that are only comprehensible in the light of the overall history of the soul as it progresses or regresses through many lifetimes. No external god makes such choices for us. Our choices in the between-world reflect our previous choices in other lifetimes, where we have to choose between virtue and selfishness. In our choices we are gods for ourselves. The virtues or excellencies of life, says the daughter of Necessity, are the outcome of our free choices. In a fundamental sense we choose our own destinies.

In Er's account, the famous hero Ulysses, whose adventures are told in Homer's poem, *The Odyssey,* has drawn the last straw and comes to choose last. There still remain many possible lots in life for him to select from, and after looking around for a while, Ulysses sees the outlines of a quiet, uneventful life. That, he says, is the one he would have chosen even if he had drawn the first choice. From his previous lifetime he has had adventures enough to last him for a long while. Now what he seeks is peace and quiet. We should conclude from this example that we cannot readily evaluate the attainment of virtue or nobility of the soul from the individual's actual lot in this present lifetime. Thus, when we observe a simple, unpretentious life we should remember that the secrets of the soul are deeply concealed in the external appearances, and so it is not possible to judge the nature or quality of the individual from such externals. Even an uneducated slave, as Socrates demonstrates in *The Meno,* is capable of recollecting the highest intellectual truths.

Return to the Sensible World: Beauty, Life, and History

For Kant, too, love of beauty plays a central role in the awareness of a higher human purpose. And with the experience of beauty we necessarily have to reconsider the nature of sensible experience. Kant first criticizes the "sensible world" of Euclidian space and linear time as the framework of deterministic causal analysis. As such a space-time framework is a precondition of the scientific endeavor, it describes an appearance for us, and so we are free to suppose a nonsensible or intelligible reality beyond the appearances in which freedom and morality are possible. From the standpoint of practical human activity, moral experience rests on the "intelligible world" of moral ideas and ideals, lying behind and potentially contradicting the sensible world of desires, inclinations, and related interests in material possessions and power over others. Thus the moral experience involves a conflict of light and dark, of duty and desire. However, because the moral ideal must be *realized* in the sensible world, it is necessary to return to the sensible world from the standpoint of supersensible reality that is glimpsed in moral duty. But how is it possible to realize moral truth in the sensible world if that world is fully described by the parameters of a kind of scientific knowledge that excludes morality in principle? Another kind of sensibility therefore is required as the context of moral realization. Kant follows Plato when he argues that the experience of beauty involves a form of sensibility that can be permeated with the higher perspective of morality. "Beauty," Kant argues in his third critique, "is the symbol of morality."[19]

We have already suggested this possibility in our discussion of the third formulation of the categorical imperative, with its notion of a kingdom of ends. In this kingdom of human purposes, the highest end consists in respect for the dignity of human beings, regarded as both the objects and conjoined subjects of laws we make ourselves. Awareness of laws issuing from our shared humanity inspires the emotion of reverence, for we are in the presence of that which is inherently holy. Ideally, the higher purposefulness of serving our shared humanity ought to regulate the sphere of utilitarian purposes of production and exchange—the lowest level of the hierarchy of ends. Mediating between these two levels is another set of ends—those relating to aesthetic values. The free play of conscious human powers—sensibility, intelligence, feeling, and imagination—produces those values of aesthetics and cultural creation that should take precedence over purely utilitarian and monetary values. This is the sphere of the beautiful and the sublime—in which sensibility is already in tune with the higher consciousness of morality. Hence beauty is the symbol of morality—that is, the intimation of morality in sensible experience. Kant here repeats Plato's idea that beauty is a special kind of appearance—not the "mere appearances" of subjectively projected space and time, of bodily separation and egotistical competition, but the transformed appearance here and now of the higher world of Reality, of things as they are in themselves. This is not and could not be *known*, inasmuch as scientific knowledge with its causal framework can have nothing to do with beauty—unless it be to reduce experiences of beauty to underlying causes. But in such a reductive analysis the aesthetic experience itself is lost. From the scientific standpoint a beautiful face is the result of a configuration of factors that produce a certain structure of the bones and certain pigmentation of the skin. But with such knowledge the God or Goddess who manifests before us vanishes as a figment of the unreal imagination. Kant's critique of scientific reason is therefore more than the justification of a certain kind of moral faith; it is the liberation of the imagination from the restrictions of such reductionist science.

Through his critique of scientism Kant provides theoretical grounds for faith in the possibility of the highest good. However, moral faith can only support someone for so long. Suppose that we believe that a united humanity has a providential destiny of transforming appearances and realizing the highest good, but our concrete experience is of a continually fragmenting human history, a never-ending war of all against all. How long can we maintain such a belief—for how many lifetimes are we supposed to think of ourselves as carrying on—if human history shows no sign of progress, or is even moving backwards? Let us grant that sensible experience of beauty in the natural world or the artistic works of genius give us glimpses of an interpenetration of the intelligible and sensible worlds, symbolizing and anticipating the embodiment of the highest good. But if faith can only take us so far in the face of evidence to the contrary, the beauty of the natural world seems a slight defense against the ever intensified pillaging of nature for reasons of private or public profit. How long can beauty itself sustain us if our world continues moving in the direction of the "desert of the real" of *The Matrix* in which all beauty has departed from the once beautiful earth. In such a context the works of artists are at least as likely to give expression to nihilism and despair as to provide a sense of hopefulness. Many Hollywood movies, of course, continue to be hopeful, and films such as the *Matrix* trilogy and other works of popular culture continue to perform the function of keeping the ideal of the highest good alive in our imaginations. Even the *Hitchhiker's Guide to the Galaxy*, which begins with the destruction of the earth to make room for a galactic superhighway, ends somehow, and against all the absurdist bureaucratic rationality that dominates our world, with a new and more beautiful earth.

It is therefore necessary to provide convincing evidence for hope in a better world. In the traditional external religion it is possible to continue believing against all evidence to the contrary, for such contrary evidence is simply further grounds for supporting the otherworldly standpoint of such religion. But for a religion of this world there has to be tangible evidence of forward motion. When we look at human history from the perspective of the moral ideal, Kant claims, we do indeed find such evidence. For Kant himself such evidence must have seemed palpable. The American Revolution, occurring during the writing of the *Critique of Pure Reason*, showed him that despotism could be overthrown and ordinary citizens could indeed rule themselves, as the kingdom of ends requires. And then the French Revolution, coming on the heals of the American, shows that the latter was no fluke, and progress toward the self-rule of mankind is indeed being realized in the empirical world. Even the creation of the first states, however despotic, was a big step forward, Kant thought, over the "war of all against all" that he supposed had characterized the earliest "state of nature." A larger view of history shows a clear over-all *direction* from the despotism of the early states to the democratic rule of the Greek and Roman democracies, however limited was the franchise to a minority of the population. In modern times so-called enlightened monarchies permitted thinkers like Kant a degree of freedom unimaginable in the dark Middle Ages of the divine right of kings and the power of the Church to suppress all free thought. And then the most recent flowering of the democracies in America and France shows that the moral ideals are indeed being realized one step at a time, slowly at first and then perhaps rapidly gaining force.

We are justified therefore in the supposition of the postulate of God. A divine providence appears to be working its way through the seemingly chaotic actions of human beings. In his essay, "Idea for a Universal History from a Cosmopolitan Point of View," Kant summarizes this historical evidence as grounds for confidence in the postulates of a practical faith. A "guiding thread" can be discerned in the evolutionary course of such political structures in human history "for giving a consoling view of the future."[20] A "Providence" can be discerned in which human beings, without directly intending to, are fulfilling a higher destiny—the very one to which the moral person commits herself. Morpheus puts this idea clearly in *Reloaded*: "Tonight is not an accident. There are no accidents. We have not come here by chance. I do not believe in chance when I see 3 objectives, 3 captains, 3 ships. I do not see coincidence, I see providence, I see purpose. I believe it is our fate to be here. It is our destiny. I believe this night holds for each and every one of us the very meaning of our lives."

Human history as a whole, Kant thinks, appears to have a direction and a purpose. A new way of looking at human history, as the progressive embodiment of the moral ideal, therefore seems warranted. He writes:

Such a justification of Nature—or, better, of Providence—is no unimportant reason for choosing a standpoint toward world history. For what is the good of esteeming the majesty and wisdom of Creation in the realm of brute nature and of recommending that we contemplate it, if that part of the great stage of supreme wisdom which contains the purpose of all the others—the history of mankind—must remain an unceasing reproach to it? If we are forced to turn our eyes from it in disgust, doubting that we can ever find a perfectly rational purpose in it and hoping for that only in another world?[21]

Sure, there is still a long way to go. On the international plane, the state of nature continues to operate in force, as independent nations regularly go to war against one another with no higher international power to limit the egotistical ambitions of the most powerful nations. In his essay, "Perpetual Peace," Kant therefore provides a detailed argument, based on national self-interest itself, for showing that the international rule of law must sooner or later be adopted by nations.[22]

The *Critique of Judgment* legitimizes this hopeful conception of human history by establishing the possibility of another approach to sensible experience than that of scientific knowledge. If science looks for causes of experience, morality incites us to look for purposes, to see a "teleology" or goal-orientedness in experience. Causal analysis of history gives us those narrow motivations of self-interest that by and large move the human actors to do the things that they do. But the larger picture, the over-all outcome of the combined actions of the multitude of individuals, seems to convey a higher purpose, a goal that is being realized behind the backs of individuals. If Adam Smith discerns an "invisible hand" behind the narrow goals of individual self-interest, Kant discerns a Providence whose purposes are progressively realized through the actions of the great masses of people, conscious perhaps only of their hunger and yet bringing about the downfall of despotic kings and furthering the realization of the highest good. The moral individual can therefore look at the evidence of history and see reasons for encouragement. She is not alone and powerless in her devotion to the highest duty of a human being, for humanity as a whole is lumbering, however unconsciously, in this very direction. In the *Matrix* trilogy this moral goal is represented by the peaceful compromise between humans and machines that guarantees the existence of Zion, the place where, at the end of the war, free, equal, and loving individuals have the party they justly deserve.[23]

NOTES

1. *Pascal's Pensées* (New York: E. P. Dutton & Co., Inc, 1958), 78, no. 277.

2. Martin Heidegger, *An Introduction to Metaphysics* (Garden City, NY: Doubleday Anchor Books), 90.

3. On Heidegger's assertion of the "inner truth and greatness" of Hitler's National Socialism, see Heidegger, *Introduction to Metaphysics*, 166.

4. Plato, *Symposium*, in *Great Books of the Western World*, vol. 7 (Chicago: Encyclopedia Britannica, 1952), 167; 210.

5. Lewis Carroll, *Silvie and Bruno*, chapt. 5, "The Magic Locket." Internet source: http://www.hoboes.com/html/FireBlade/Carroll/Sylvie/. Thanks to Theodore Gracyk for this reference. Ted says he got it from his son, Thelonious.

6. Bhagavad-Gita, trans. Sir Edwin Arnold, *Indian History Sourcebook*, http://www.fordham.edu/halsall/india/bhagavadgita.html, Accessed 11/29/2005.

7. Lao Tzu, *Tao Te Ching*, no. 16, http://www.wright-house.com/religions/taoism/tao-te-ching.html. Accessed 12/21/06.

8. Cynthia Freeland, "Penetrating Keanu: New Holes, but the Same Old Shit," in *The Matrix and Philosophy*, ed. William Irwin (Chicago: Open Court, 2002), 205.

9. Georg Wilhelm Friedrich Hegel, *Lectures on the Philosophy of Religion*, vol. 2, ed. Peter C. Hodgson (Berkeley: University of California Press, 1987), 498.

10. Hegel, *Lectures on the Philosophy of Religion*, vol. 2, 455.

11. Plato, *Apology*, in *The Collected Diologues* (New York: Pantheon Books, 1961), 16; 30a–b.

12 Plato, *Phaedrus*, 495; 248a–b.

13. Plato, *Phaedrus*, 501; 256a–b.

14. Plato, *Phaedrus*, 497; 251a.

15. Plato, *Phaedrus*, 497; 251a.

16. Plato, *Phaedrus*, 497; 251b.

17. Plato, *Phaedrus*, 501; 255d.

18. Plato, *Phaedrus*, 841; 617d–e.

19. Immanuel Kant, *Critique of Judgment*, no. 59, in *Great Books of the Western World*, vol. 42 (Chicago: Encyclopedia Britannica, 1952), 546.

20. Immanuel Kant, "Idea for a Universal History from a Cosmopolitan Point of View," in *On History*, trans. Lewis White Beck (New York: Macmillan Publishing Company, 1963), 25.

21. Ibid.

22. Cf., Immanuel Kant, "Perpetual Peace," in Beck, *On History*, trans. Lewis White Beck (New York: Macmillan Publishing Company, 1963), 85–135.

23. This chapter is an expanded and revised version of James Lawler, "Only Love Is Real: Heidegger, Plato, and *The Matrix Trilogy*," published in *More Matrix and Philosophy: Revolutions and Reloaded Decoded*, ed. William Irwin (Chicago: Open Court, 2005), 26–37.

6

Dialectics of the Force
in *Star Wars*

Hokey religions and ancient weapons are no match for a good blaster at your side, kid.
—HAN SOLO

Life consists rather in being the self-developing whole which dissolves its development and in this movement simply preserves itself.
—G. W. F. HEGEL

The Two Sides of the Force

Central to the unfolding plot of *Star Wars* is a question and a mystery: What is the Force? In *Star Wars Episode IV: A New Hope*, Obi-Wan Kenobi tells Luke Skywalker that his father was betrayed and murdered by Darth Vader, a Jedi Knight who "turned to evil . . . seduced by the dark side of the Force." "The Force?" asks Luke. Obi-Wan replies: "The Force is what gives the Jedi his power. It's an energy field created by all living things. It surrounds us and penetrates us. It binds the galaxy together."

All living beings create the energy field of the Force, and at the same time this energy field is essential to living beings, binding the entire galaxy—ultimately the entire cosmos—in a unified whole. The Force has both dark and light sides, but there is not a dark Force and a light Force, not evil as a separate power over against good. Such a dualistic conception of good versus evil is understandable in the context of episodes 4 through 6—the original episodes produced between

1977 and 1983—dominated by the malevolent Darth Vader. Matters become more complicated, however, when we learn that Vader is actually Luke's father. For many viewers this news only deepens a sense of repulsion for the evil servant of the dark side—a father who is the archenemy of the son. We maintain such a feeling until the last moment when Vader unexpectedly turns against his master—Darth Sidious, the Dark Lord of the Sith and Emperor of the Galaxy—and dies reconciled to his son. In the absence of the background trilogy of episodes 1 to 3—which appeared between 1999 and 2005—this ending fails to convey a sense of coherent and logical plot development. The conclusion of the original *Star Wars* trilogy appears to involve an artificial deus ex machina as a Good Darth suddenly emerges from within the Evil Darth. However, as the background story of episodes 1 to 3 unfolds, not only is the final ending fully justified, but also our understanding of the nature of the Force becomes more profound. We learn *why* there is not a dark Force and a light Force, a good opposed to an evil, but only one Force. And we understand how it is that Darth Vader, formerly known as Anakin Skywalker, is the chosen one whose destiny it is to bring the one Force into balance.

Thanks to the background story, Vader's deathbed acknowledgement of love for his son is no sentimental happy ending, but can be understood as the philosophically grounded outcome of what Georg Wilhelm Friedrich Hegel, at the conclusion of his *Phenomenology of Spirit,* calls "the Calvary of Absolute Spirit."[1] Confronting the darkness that envelops much of human life and consciousness, the One who challenges the dark forces and brings enlightenment into the open is inevitably killed, as Socrates was by the Athenians, or crucified, as was Jesus on Mount Calvary. But out of this death comes a deeper understanding and a renewed life. Hegel explains that human history consists of a series of struggles between light and dark resulting in various kinds of apparently unnatural deaths or crucifixions, temporary defeats of the light. The forces of light, the proponents of reason and enlightenment, nevertheless regroup and come back with renewed strength, with new battles taking place on new levels, in more balanced ways. This recurrent defeat of the light takes place on ever new levels, until all unnatural limitation, all splitting and antagonism of light and darkness, is finally transcended through the conscious *balancing* of interrelated opposites that characterizes dialectical reason. Such is the pathway of Spirit, a movement from a series of conflicts, wars, and revolutions involving the clash of opposing sides, to a higher stage of reconciliation or balance that opens the way to a free, enlightened, peaceful, and creative evolution for humanity. This is Hegel's philosophically probing conception of what George Lucas calls "the Force."

The Mythic Journey of the Hero

The enlarged vision of *Star Wars* from episodes 1 to 6 provides an unparalleled modern account of the archetypal journey of the hero into the nether world of darkness as a means of discovery and knowledge, of freedom and power, of love and fidelity. The Force is Lucas's distillation of religious thought and feeling throughout human history. Lucas relates that in preparing for *Star Wars* he read fifty books on the religions of the world, but of these he mentions only one, Joseph Campbell's *The Hero with a Thousand Faces*. Campbell's book details the many myths and tales of the hero's adventures as essentially a journey of self-transformation. Based on this reading, Lucas says that he "worked out a general theory for the Force, and then I played with it."[2] In his understanding of this history, and at the core of *Star Wars*, the divine is no separate deity controlling events from the outside, but the inner God-force that impels the hearts and minds of all of us as we in our relations to one another seek to fulfill our inner truth. Connecting with this Force gives the hero within each of us the insight and energy to rise to new levels of achievement and fulfillment.

Such an understanding of human destiny is clarified by the contrast between the religion of the Force and the traditional "external religions," as well as in the comparison of the religion of the Force with the secular humanist view that the primary means for achieving human goals are provided by science and technology. These oppositions of external religion, on the one hand, and science and technology, on the other, and of both to the religion of the Force, are presented in episode 4, *A New Hope*. Obi-Wan is training Luke with the aid of a robot ball that hovers in front of him, shooting laser beams as Luke, blindfolded, attempts to use the force to defend himself with his lightsaber. Han Solo is skeptical. "Hokey religions and ancient weapons are no match for a good blaster at your side, kid." Luke comments, "You don't believe in the Force, do you?" "Kid," says Han, "I've flown from one side of this galaxy to the other. I've seen a lot of strange stuff, but I've never seen anything to make me believe there's one all-powerful force controlling everything. No mystical energy field controls my destiny. It's just a lot of tricks and nonsense." In the face of this skepticism, Luke demonstrates the reality of the Force by blocking the laser attack with his eyes covered. Han calls this luck. "In my experience," says Obi-Wan, "there's no such thing as luck."

There is no doubt in the minds of the audience that the Force is something real, and that Han's reliance on empirical evidence and technological control is missing the deeper picture. But how seriously should we ourselves take the notion of such a mystical force? When we think objectively about it outside of the film, when we ask ourselves what is really real, don't we live much of our lives as Han Solo does, relying on external technologies of power and control to achieve our goals, with little or no confidence in the inner force of our own deeper consciousness? Han views the Force as a mythical all-controlling God of external religion. He rejects such religion with the skepticism of secular rational thought that promotes human self-reliance, scientific knowledge, and the power of scientifically based technologies. With his idea of the Force as an external controlling deity, Han fails to understand an alternative form of spirituality that magnifies rather than minimizes the inner Force of the human spirit. Repeating the theme of the *Matrix* trilogy, the underlying message of *Star Wars*, despite all the graphic splendor of its battles, is that the external technologies of power, without guidance from the Force that emerges out of human interconnectedness, issues in an endless cycle of destructive human warfare and disempowerment for individuals.

For conventional religious viewers who believe in such an external deity, as well as for the scientifically-minded who debunk it, the all-pervading Force as described in *Star Wars* is magic and make-believe, not something to be taken seriously outside the realm of film and fantasy. However, this real-life estimation of the Force is blind to the actual power we all experience when we yield to the appeal of the film itself. In the enchantment of the theater, as the lights around us go down and we enter the imaginative world of *Star Wars*, the magical drama of the Force with its happy Hollywood ending in the triumph and happiness of the heroes, does indeed cast its spell on us. If we fail to appreciate this real force of the fantasy itself, are we not acting like the skeptical Han Solo, dismissing in our minds as inessential and irrelevant a power that we nevertheless can feel—a power that holds us in its thrall throughout the many hours of artistic wizardry that makes up *Star Wars*? In his lightsaber training lesson, Obi-Wan tells Luke: "let go your conscious self and act on instinct . . . . Your eyes can deceive you. Don't trust them. . . . Stretch out with your feelings." It is not by empirical thinking that we grasp the real power of the Force. It is by feeling. In a world that oscillates between scientific thought regarding the sensible world and religious dogma regarding the supersensible, we are prone to dismissing our feelings as merely irrational and so as unreal. But feelings too are real, and the powerful force of the creative imagination of art and popular culture, which channels those feelings in the service of moral ideals, is undeniable.

In the pagan religions of ancient times, feelings were the domains of the gods, regarded as outside of us and inside at the same time. Thus Sophocles in *Antigone* describes the power of Aphrodite, Goddess of Love or Eros:

> Eros, undefeated in battle,
> Eros, who falls upon possessions,
> who, in the soft cheeks of a young girl,
> stays the night vigil,
> who traverses over seas
> and among pastoral dwellings,
> you none of the immortals can escape,
> none of the day-long mortals, and
> he who has you is maddened.
> You wrest the minds of even the just
> aside to injustice, to their destruction.
> You have incited this quarrel
> among blood kin.
> Desire radiant from the eyelids
> of a well-bedded bride prevails,
> companion in rule with the gods' great
> ordinances. She against whom none may battle,
> the goddess Aphrodite, plays her games.[3]

Sophocles' lines describe much of the drama of *Star Wars*, for it is a story of the power of love to bring about destruction as well as renewal. It seems to be the secret weapon of the dark side, seducing the just, such as young Jedi hopeful Anakin Skywalker, to perform acts of injustice, creating enmity between members of the same family, pitting husband against wife, father against son and daughter. If this is true, then isn't love itself an expression of the power of a superhuman force pervading our lives, drawing us into decisive and sometimes deadly actions through its connection with our feelings? Why else do the Jedi Knights warn against this dark side of the Force?

Each episode of *Star Wars* begins with the same opening lines: "A long time ago in a galaxy far, far away. . . ." We are put in mind of the classic opening formula of the fairy tale, "Once upon a time." Under the surface of a technically advanced galactic society, we are invited to enter a deeper realm of myth and magic and ancient religion. With *Star Wars* George Lucas has created a myth for our time, one that clothes in the garb of the future the ancient spirit quest of the hero. As civilizations clash over rival theologies inherited from the past, humankind is in need of an empowering belief for our time, one that provides a unifying distillation of all the religions of humankind. To appreciate the way in which *Star Wars*, with its heroic drama of the Force, responds to this need, we must first of all to let go of our conscious minds and all dependence on empirical evidence, and stretch out with our feelings and imagination. We need to let ourselves be captured by the spell of its magic.

Spirit: Hegel's Distillation of the History of Religion

Like George Lucas, Hegel attempts to distill the essence of religion in his *Lectures on the Philosophy of Religion* and other works. Religion, he argues, is distinguished from science and philosophy in being a matter of feeling and "picture thinking," rather than of rationality and conceptual thought. The object of religion may be called God or Absolute Spirit, but for the religious person such terms are labels for a peculiar object of feeling and imagination, not primarily concepts for rational inquiry. The ultimate goal of the philosophy of religion is to justify the truth of religious feeling by explaining the reality that it taps into—the all-encompassing and dynamic reality of what Hegel calls Spirit.[3] Each civilization has its own religious picture of the ultimate source of reality, the divine, the Tao, Brahman, Yahweh, the Father God, Allah, the Absolute Spirit. The distinguishing features of this picture in different societies reflect the kind of civilization each one is, and the stage of humanity's self-development that the particular civilization ultimately represents. A scientific-technological civilization that puts Matter and the creative power of Chance in place of an intentionally acting Spirit is no exception to this rule.

Hegel traces a developmental pattern in the historical succession of religious beliefs, one that produces in effect a distillation of divinity. In the succession of basic religious orientations, what one religion calls good another religion denounces as evil or darkness. But for the final distillation to appear it is necessary for the human spirit, on its heroic journey to self-fulfillment, to find the balance between these opposites.

Human history begins with the divine in nature, as human beings living off plants and animals in the wild are immersed in the natural world. For such people there is no separation between the divine and the human. Like the spirits of nature whose presence they find in dreams and evoke through vivid paintings on cave walls, human beings too wield a magical force in controlling the world around them by their wishes and in their dream fantasies. This is the childhood of humanity, Hegel says.

The mindset of the child, who willingly enters the fantasy of "once upon a time," is the general outlook of the earliest human cultures. As Yoda remarks in *Attack of the Clones*, "Truly wonderful the mind of a child." This is also the general outlook of all the ancient nature-centered cultures of the East, as exemplified in the Taoism of China, whose symbol is the unity of dark and light, yin and yang. Giving expression to this history, *Star Wars* appropriately culminates in episode 6, *Return of the Jedi*, with the battle between the monstrosities of the most advanced technological civilization and the slings and arrows of the nature people, the Ewoks. These simple people of the forest readily take the gleaming android C-3PO as a god. As a product of the advanced civilization, though, the gentleman droid lacks the power of imagination capable of accepting this worship: "It's against my programming to impersonate a deity."

In the next major stage of human history, which takes place primarily in the West, no one could mistake a physical object for a god. Human beings have developed far greater technological powers over nature, together with mighty systems of economic, social, and political power in which a small number of people have immense control over the lives of the majority. Consequently, the divine is conceived of in the image of the rulers—as a remote power radically separate from and ruling over the world. The progress of such separation between the higher realm of the gods and the lower world of nature and humans culminates in the slave empire of the ancient Romans. This slave state, which subjects all conquered peoples to an order based on the might of the Roman army, reduces everything sacred in life to an object of utility for political purposes. *Star Wars*, with its portrayal of the slide from Republic to Empire, borrows liberally from this Roman history—while suggesting parallels with our own time. Hegel calls this Roman religion the Religion of Expediency.[4]

We therefore see two opposite forms of religion in early world history. From the earliest societies and the East, there is the divine as an all-pervading natural force capable of emerging in the most unexpected objects, as in the Ewoks' vision of C-3PO as a god. From the beginnings of Western civilizations the contrary concept emerges of "an alien Being who passes judgement on the particular individual" from the inaccessible position of an "unattainable Beyond."[5] In the presence of this externalized or alienated expression of its own inner being, the "consciousness of life . . . is conscious only of its own nothingness."[6] If there is to be a distillation of the essence of religion as the core of a new myth for our time, it must reconcile and combine these two opposite conceptions of the divine. Just such a synthesis, Hegel argues, is represented by the "Consummate Religion" of Christianity with its story of a God who descends from his lofty heaven to become a human babe, who grows up with a family, enters upon his mission, and accomplishes this mission only by dying the ignominious death on Mount Calvary of a criminal nailed to a cross.[7]

What is this mission? To teach a people plunged in the darkness of a world ruled by pitiless physical force that the true God is not a menacing power ruling over us, but the deepest inner reality of each person. This reality is the Holy Spirit that is capable of binding us all together as a powerful Force capable of transforming our world. Connected to this Spirit and to one another, we are capable of wielding an irresistible Force for resisting and overcoming all inner darkness and every outer unjust form of rule. Thus, at the peak of the imperial power of Rome, intrepid bands of Christian rebels, believing that divine Force has merged with the human spirit, began the long climb from a world of Empire whose principle is that only one person is free, the Emperor, to a world whose dominant inspiration is that all should be free to rule themselves. Hegel calls this evolution from tyranny to freedom "the march of God in the world."[8] The defenders of liberty can therefore justly say, in the language of *Star Wars*, that the Force is with us. It is with *us*—a people united in the spirit of creative freedom and mutual love. For this is the nature of Spirit, according to Hegel. It is the Force that runs through us all together—especially when we are together. It is truly understood only when we overcome the darkness cast by our separation from one another, by imprisonment in our paltry egotism—only when we learn the ultimate and unconquerable power that binds us together, the power of love.

From Kant to Hegel: the Nature of Dialectical Science

We can clearly see in Hegel's vision a continuation of Kant's teleology of history. Hegel begins where Kant left off, with a perspective on the evolution of human history as containing a direction or purpose. As a postulate of moral faith in Kant's thought, God is not a separate being outside the world, rewarding and punishing in an afterlife, but an irresistible force of unfolding and development, a force of historical destiny, to which individuals may be more or less consciously connected. The moral individual who devotes herself to the goal of realizing the highest good, a community in which people rule themselves, need not feel powerless before the dark forces that appear to dominate our world. Such powerlessness is the expression of our separateness from one another, the restriction of our sense of self to the narrow confines of the ego. The sciences of our time encourage a form of thinking that emphasizes external causality and the power of a technology that is outside of the individual. But if we allow ourselves to be guided by our sense of moral duty, Kant writes, if we stretch out with the feeling that we are fundamentally connected to one another, we can sense the workings of the Force to which each of us contributes and which, as the summation of all of our lives, runs through each of us as a guiding light and connecting energy. Against a religion of fear, with punishments and rewards of an external God, morality postulates a providential universe that sustains the choices of an increasingly autonomous and united humanity.

There is this major difference between Kant's view and that of Hegel. For Kant such a conception of human history cannot truly be called knowledge. We cannot *know* the ultimate purpose or direction of human life on earth in the sense of having scientific knowledge of reality. Hegel however shows that it is indeed possible to have real knowledge of these matters. This is not scientific knowledge as this is commonly understood, but such science is a limited form of knowledge corresponding to a limited stage of human evolution. A more complete form of knowing is available to us. It is knowledge that progresses from limited forms of understanding to more complete forms through logical contradiction and practical struggles.

Hegel calls this more complete form of knowing *dialectical* science, by contrast to the *analytical* science of early modern times. While analytical knowledge emphasizes narrow units of causal interaction between separate entities, dialectical knowledge looks at the larger system of the whole in which separate segments are unified in an evolving holism of interrelated elements. Thus, for analytical science, water on the ground is the effect of a certain external cause: it rained last night. But where did the rain come from? Ultimately, it came from water on the ground, or in the seas, drawn up by the heat of the sun. Water comes from the rain, but rain comes from the water, in a process that is more circular than linear. There is a larger totality in which what is the effect, water on the ground, becomes in turn the cause in a spiraling system of interrelated events. This spiraling totality, like the Force of *Star Wars*, is a self-moving system of interrelated elements. It is not antithetical to human self-movement or freedom, and so, unlike the deterministic causal sequences characteristic of analytic science, it is able to give rise to free, purposeful human consciousness.

Hegel's dialectics is often described as a movement from thesis to antithesis to synthesis. In the case of the evolution of religion, human consciousness begins with one form of religion, which can be called the thesis: the nature religion of early humanity that continues in a more abstract form in Eastern civilizations. Consciousness then moves to the opposite polarity, in the Roman West, that of an external deity ruling over a disenchanted earth—the moment of the antithesis. Such an opposition calls for a higher, more comprehensive form of awareness, the synthesis, which is a larger vision of reality. This dialectical *Aufhebung* or "sublation" combines the preceding moments into a higher totality that removes their respective limitations while preserving the essential or core truth of each.

From Matter to Spirit: The Life Force as the Origin of Human Consciousness

In Hegel's *Phenomenology of Spirit,* the emergence of the separate ego is described after the chapter on the life of nature. In his poem "Intimations of Immortality from Recollections of Early Childhood," Hegel's contemporary, William Wordsworth, describes youth as "nature's priest." Hegel provides philosophical argumentation for such romanticism. For Hegel, the human being is indeed, and fundamentally, nature's priest, that is, nature that has become aware of itself and can appreciate itself consciously. Hegel explains the dialectical logic by which the life force of unconscious nature gives rise to human self-consciousness.

In the natural world, he argues, individuality and species universality exist in a polarity of interdependent tendencies. Individual plants and animals reproduce the species through producing other individuals of a similar kind. By this means, nature perpetuates itself as the species, which exists as a totality that is relatively separate from the individuals who produce it. The species or genus, or organic nature as a whole, maintains an immortal or supermortal life through the dissolution or death of the individuals that produce it. "Life," Hegel writes in his condensed form of expression, "consists rather in being the self-developing whole which dissolves its development and in this movement simply preserves itself."[9] In contrast to the mortal individual, the species is a kind of living universality. It is the particular *life force* that is both the product of each individual and the larger whole that unconsciously governs the life of the individual. We recognize in Hegel's account of life the definition of the Force of *Star Wars*: "It's an energy field created by all living things. It surrounds us and penetrates us. It binds the galaxy together."

What is missing from this definition are individuals who can consciously connect to the Force. The individual plant or animal does indeed connect with the species, but unconsciously—through its species instincts. At the level of its own conscious awareness, the individual organism is preoccupied with its own individual life—for example, finding food for the day, for itself and possibly for its immediate family. It is not concerned with the life of the species as a whole, even while through instinct it unconsciously or indirectly gives rise to and perpetuates that life. In moral language, the individual of a natural species is not conscious of a duty or a responsibility to the species as a whole. On the other hand, the species is itself an unconscious life force that maintains a form of existence of its own. However, in the species, life "does not exist for itself."[10] The species life force which the individuals produce exists "in itself" but it is not something "for" the individual and so also not something "for itself." The particular species, and by extension nature as a whole, exists through the individuals who serve it as a quasi-independent force. But as it lacks real individuality, it fails to appreciate its own life. In the natural world of plant and animal life, individuality and species life therefore go their relatively separate ways, in an unstable, dynamic polarity of interdependent aspects. Logically speaking, they constitute a kind of thesis and antithesis, and as such they implicitly call for their synthesis.

In this separation of narrowly conscious individuality and an unconscious, quasi-independent universality that arises out of the many individuals, the life of nature implicitly points beyond itself to a form of existence that unifies its two sides: "Life points to something other than itself, viz. to consciousness, for which Life exists as this unity, or as genus. . . ."[11] Arising out of this polarity of individuality and species life is the higher form of consciousness, human self-consciousness, in which the genus or species becomes something existing *for itself*. Through the individual human consciousness that it evolves into, the life force becomes truly aware of itself. Thus is created a being that transcends the narrow confines of its individual life through its intrinsic connection to the universality and immortality of the life force. A higher form of consciousness emerges, human self-consciousness, that is implicitly concerned with its species life as a whole. The fully self-conscious human being therefore experiences a duty to promote humanity as a whole in a conscious way. Human consciousness is intrinsically historical, connecting more or less consciously to the evolution of the human species as a whole through many forms and stages of development. Through and in such species consciousness, the individual essentially persists through multiple limited embodiments or lifetimes because the human individual is an expression of the species life itself, humanity as a whole. The self-conscious human being is the immortal life force become individualized and aware of itself. Each individual human being is therefore a unique expression of the multiple potentialities of life itself. Thus as we reflect back on the history of humankind, thanks to dialectical science, we recognize our own personal history in its broadest outlines. We identify with this history, and see our individual ontogeny in one lifetime illuminated by the phylogeny, the history, of humanity itself.

From Spirit to Matter: Involution as the Basis of Evolution

But how is it that unconscious life is able to give rise to conscious self-awareness? How can the higher forms of consciousness come out of lower forms of unconsciousness? How does something that purposefully moves itself emerge from what does not so move itself? Kant could not explain scientifically how the teleological purposefulness of human life could be seen in the natural world, which science supposes is governed by outside causality. Hence he regarded the teleological viewpoint as a projection of human purposes onto nature, even while recognizing that in the sciences of biology a teleological perspective, in which the parts are viewed as working for the good of the larger whole, is a quite natural assumption. However, he thought, if science is essentially about external causal forces, then viewing purposefulness in organic nature must be regarded as unscientific, as a projection of human purposefulness onto nature. Such projection need not be false, for reality as it is in itself is unknowable. But we cannot claim that a teleological view of nature is a matter of science. It arises out of the postulates of morality which require that the highest good be seen as realizable, and so as effectively being realized, not only in human history, but in the natural world which is an essential condition of human life.

From the perspective of Hegel's dialectical science, it is necessary to look at the circle or spiral of cause and effect at the level of the larger totality, where what is effect can be regarded in turn as cause. Human self-consciousness, as we have just seen, is the effect of the evolution of life, expressing in a new and higher form the unity of the polar sides of the life process. But this means that the higher form of the development of life, which is human self-consciousness, was somehow already implicit in the lower form of organic life itself. Human consciousness is implicit in the dialectic of organic life as the emerging synthesis of its conflicting tendencies. Similarly, life too arises out of the polarities of inorganic matter. For matter is not really inert, moved only when one inert body collides with another, as the early modern physics of external causality proposes. A better expression of the nature of matter, Hegel thought, is found in the phenomenon of magnetism, with polar forces of attraction and repulsion operating across fields of relationships. Life is capable of arising out of inorganic matter because the self-movement of life is potentially contained within the self-moving dynamics of the polarized, magnetizing, attracting and repelling forces of matter itself. But if life is potentially self-consciousness, and matter is potentially life, then self-consciousness, whose highest form as we will see is Spirit, is already present within the darkest, densest forms of matter, waiting to be awakened out of its sleep in matter through the dynamics of evolution.

On the one hand, therefore, we are investigating the dialectical processes that give birth to the highest forms of Spirit, emerging within human consciousness. But the effect is in turn also the cause. Evolution presupposes "involution." Spirit arises out of matter because it is already contained within it, and is the operating dynamic Force of the entire evolutionary process. The ultimate nature of matter, therefore, is Spirit, but a Spirit that has become the seeming opposite of itself, a light *devolving* into darkness, in order to *evolve* from it with a new appreciation of itself. Spirit must descend into matter, *become* matter, in order to return to itself. Evolution of consciousness out of matter requires that matter be already proto-conscious or implicit consciousness, already the embodiment of Spirit. Evolution presupposes "involution" or "emanation."[12]

In this way the creator does not create out of nothing, but out of herself, the divine womb or source of the universe. As we have seen in the previous chapter, in Asian thought the creation proceeds from the source and returns to the source. The neo-Platonic philosophers called this doctrine of creation "emanation." Hegel's dialectical science of creation interprets the Christian doctrine of the Trinity in just this way: the son, representing finite creation, proceeds from the father-source, becomes lost in the apparent nondivinity of the material world, and then returns to the source in the unity of the Holy Spirit. God does not impossibly create something out of nothing, for out of nothing can come nothing. The material of creation must be the God-force itself. The forces of inorganic matter from which the evolutionary process begins must therefore be the God-force in an undeveloped, enveloped, unconscious form. To repeat, it is only by supposing that the higher is already present, implicitly or potentially "involved" in the lower forms of matter, that we can explain how the higher forms are able to "evolve" from the lower.

From the Natural Consciousness
to the Unnatural Ego

Let us return to the way in which Hegel explains the emergence of human self-consciousness. We have seen what Hegel means when he says: "Life points to something other than itself, viz. to consciousness, for which Life exists as this unity, or as genus." With the emergence of the human being, the unity of life or species-being now exists as something *for* the individual consciousness. Paradoxically, self-consciousness exists only as the embodiment within the individual of the entire species. Self-consciousness is the life of the species that has become something for itself in an individual form. Instead of being immersed in the life around it as is the case on the first, animal level of consciousness, human *self*-consciousness reflects back on itself from a higher level, from a standpoint outside the physical individuality that interacts with its environment. It is its conscious connection to the human species as a whole, to humanity, that gives to the individual this higher standpoint from which to view herself. If the individual is the self-consciousness of the species, the species, humanity as a whole, has through the many individuals an intelligence and force of its own. The Force is the creation of the many individuals, as Obi-Wan says, while binding them all together.

Hegel goes on to say, "This other Life, however, for which the genus as such exists, and which is genus on its own account, viz. self-consciousness, exists in the first instance for self consciousness only as this simple essence, and has itself as pure 'I' for object."[13] Hegel thus deduces the birth of the human ego. If human consciousness is essentially the self-consciousness of life itself, and ultimately of the cosmos as a whole, such a nature and destiny is at first too much for the individual self-conscious being to grasp all at once. This new, higher type of being must become conscious of its deeper nature step by step, beginning with the simplest form of self-consciousness, the pure ego or "I" in its simplest form. In the beginning, this initial form of self-consciousness has not clearly differentiated itself from the natural standpoint of first level animal consciousness and so confuses the universality of species consciousness with the standpoint of individual, physically-embodied consciousness. This fusion of the two levels produces the ego, the "I" which is a universal that is still "meant" to be, or takes itself as, a physically distinct self. This physical self at the same time implicitly or obscurely sees itself as a universal, as the embodiment of species life as a whole, and so as the center of all-that-is. The separate ego egocentrically sees itself as the center of the universe, as "the One." Such is the

argument in Hegel's *Phenomenology*, which moves from the consciousness of life to the ego and from the ego to the life-and-death struggle
between egos. For the ego that identifies with its physical individuality
as the center of the All inevitably confronts another ego that does the
same. As there cannot be two centers of the totality, each ego struggles
to demonstrate that *It*, this physical individual, is "the One."

However, from Hegel's account in the *Philosophy of History* and the
Philosophy of Religion, as well as from later chapters of the
Phenomenology, we know that the self-consciousness of "I" presupposes
an earlier form of human consciousness in which the human being still
identifies with the natural world through a nature-consciousness or religion of nature. The very earliest form of human consciousness, which
precedes the individualistic ego, does not at first involve a recognition
that humanity constitutes something radically new. Thoroughly dependent on an independent nature, changing nothing in its environment but
a few sticks and stones, the hunter-gatherers living in kinship societies
like the Ewoks of *Star Wars* see themselves as part of the larger kinship
of life as the all-encompassing divinity of animism or the religion of
nature. This is not a complete mistake, as we have seen, for life itself is
the potential for self-consciousness, and therefore self-conscious human
beings naturally find themselves at home in the natural world. Human
self-consciousness implicitly emerges out of nature, but must work its
way out also explicitly. And so it first appears as plunged in nature, seeing itself as part of nature and nature as part of itself. This is in effect the
reason why the earliest form of consciousness is that of the religion of
nature.

As human consciousness in nature becomes self-conscious, it must
eventually gain awareness of itself as something that is new in the natural world. It seems that it must at first do so negatively, antithetically. It
cuts itself off from nature, as if fearful that by being too close to the natural world, its source would swallow up its individuality into the impersonal universality of life from which it emerged. Reflecting such an
understanding, Yoda tells Anakin in *Revenge of the Sith* (episode 3) to
accept the eventual reabsorption of himself and others into the impersonality of the Force: "Death is a natural part of life. Rejoice for those
around you who transform into the Force." But Anakin clings to his individuality, his ego, and cannot release his beloved Padmé with such
Stoical detachment.

The first distinctive form that self-consciousness takes after the initial
stage of being plunged in the animistic religion of nature, Hegel says, is
that of the pure "I" or ego. In other words, while the self-conscious indi-

vidual is essentially and implicitly the entire species or life force become conscious of itself, the self-conscious individual does not at first recognize this essential truth of its nature. It first grasps its inherent universality, its species life, on the side of its individuality, as the individualistic universal, "I," that is, as ego. The further development of human history is the process of the unfolding of this ego into antitheses and contradictions, and then the overcoming of the abstract separateness of the ego which produces these antitheses. This is the process by which the "I" recognizes itself explicitly as a species-being, as a "We." This unity of I and We is what Hegel calls "Spirit." He defines Spirit as "'I' that is 'We,' and 'We' that is 'I.'"[14]

While Hegel's *Philosophy of Religion* elaborates a primary stage of human development in the animistic religion of nature in which individuals feel one with the life force or species being that is their essence, the *Phenomenology* begins after this phase, and only later returns to it. After outlining the essential connectedness of human self-consciousness with the force of nature from which it emerges, the *Phenomenology* skips forward historically to the dialectic of the separate ego—that second phase of humanity's history that gives rise to the Unhappy Consciousness of the human individual who feels apart from nature, abandoned by God, and alienated from one another.[15] Hegel's procedure in the *Phenomenology* of beginning human history with the Western consciousness of "I," rather than with Eastern nature-consciousness, may have been pedagogically effective for his time. Hegel's audience would readily recognize the nature of the ego, for his contemporary society was one in which a certain form of the ego, the self-interested individual described by Adam Smith, is the dominant principle of social life. Only later in the *Phenomenology* does Hegel go back to the religion of nature to investigate the separation of the ego-consciousness from the preexisting nature-consciousness in which human beings have not yet appreciated their distinctness from the natural world. He examines this separation in the form it takes in Greek society, as expressed in the *Antigone* of Sophocles, with its tale of the doomed conflict between the ancient religion of nature and kinship, defended by the woman Antigone, and the new world of the separate citizen, the masculine ego, and its State, represented by the male tyrant Creon.

So in the *Phenomenology* Hegel begins his story of humanity with the ego, that seemingly self-evident form of consciousness with which we can all identify: the self-consciousness of "I." But the original, most primitive form of "I" is not the same "I" as that which dominates modern life. The latter form of "I" has already undergone a long evolution involving bloody wars and personal tragedies in which a great lesson is learned. Simply put, the lesson is that I am not the only "I," and that other people too have the right to say "I." The ego of the modern individual thus recognizes its universality by recognizing the right to exist of other egos. But this was not the earliest form of ego consciousness. For our modern ego-consciousness to evolve, it was necessary for the individual to incorporate the rights of other individuals, other "I's," into his frame of consciousness, if only implicitly at first, without full awareness of the advance that consciousness achieves in becoming tolerant of the existence of other egos.

Just as Johnny, who thinks he owns his sandbox, has had to struggle with his sense of ego-centeredness to allow Sally the right to join him, so in human history there is an "I" that does not at first tolerate the right to existence of another "I." This idea of radical intolerance seems so natural, so logical, to the understanding of modern thinkers, that Hobbes places it at the foundation of his philosophy. In the "state of nature," which if it never existed in fact seems still somehow buried within each of us, each individual sees himself as a separate "I" who will do anything to advance his own separate interests in the face of others who feel the same way. Out of this primitive form of ego-consciousness, there arises a "war of all against all," and as a result of acting on the basis of such consciousness "the life of man," Hobbes writes, is "solitary, poor, nasty, brutish and short."[16] To solve this problem of conflicting egos, Hobbes supposes that the separate individuals, each out of his own self-interest and for his own egotistical purposes, come together to create the State to enforce basic rules of coexistence. Hobbes calls this state power "the Leviathan," after the beast of the Bible that symbolizes the dark powers of existence.[17] To live longer lives, to achieve security against one another, we decide to surrender our independence and chain ourselves as slaves to this dark force of the State and its rulers that nevertheless issues from the many egos.

Hegel's *Phenomenology* shows that Hobbes has short-circuited the more detailed and complex historical process, with its many intervening stages. As well, Hobbes has imposed on this history an unnatural and unhappy conclusion in which the species being of humanity which is the essence of the individual rules over him as an alien and controlling power. In Hegel's version, the emergence of "I" does indeed give rise to a "life and death struggle" which is akin to Hobbes' war of all against all. But rather than being the natural essence of the human being, this consciousness is a narrow and limited interpretation of that essence which can only emerge or evolve into more adequate forms through the struggles to which it gives rise.

Buried within the consciousness of each individual is a primitive sense
that "I" am "the One"—that is, the only being with a right to life. In its
most primitive form, there can only be one "I." However, "I" is a word
that every individual uses to refer it herself and so is, logically speaking,
a universal. But it is "meant" to be a way of referring to a singular entity—
me, this individual standing or sitting here. Implicitly, as we have seen,
the self-consciousness of "I" is the whole species aware of itself in the
form of particular individualities, like a diamond reflecting light in a multitude of brilliant facets. But this universality must first be expressed in an
immediate or natural way as fused with the individual body from whose
standpoint the individual perceives the world. The whole world is perceived as centering on me and so is "my" world, and I first take this ego-
centered world as it appears before me to be the real world.

What then do I do when another body that I think should be centered on me adopts the same standpoint and regards the world, including me, as belonging to it? The universality of "I" in this way appears as
a multitude of separate individuals each of which thinks of itself as "the
(only) One." Such must be the case if all we have to deal with at this
stage is this primitive form of consciousness. "I" therefore first confronts
the Other "I" as an alien and hostile being. For this primitive ego there
is no possibility of reconciling the contradiction, because at this level of
consciousness there is no room within the simple consciousness of self
for another "I." The simplest way to deal with this contradiction of "I"
and "I" is for each self-centered "I" to attempt to destroy the other. If we
understand this point, we can see that Hobbes's egos who create a State
have attained a higher form of egotism, for they are aware of and capable of accepting the existence of other "I"s, while still somehow, perhaps inconsistently, giving primacy to its own "I." But this awareness
that tolerates the existence of other egos is the result of a long and
bloody history, a life-and-death struggle that gives rise to more and
more mature forms of consciousness—beginning with the world of masters and slaves that gives rise to the Roman Emperor, Dark Lord and dictator of the world.

Anakin Skywalker as the Chosen One

Anakin's mother, Shmi, tells Qui-Gon in *The Phantom Menace* (episode
1) that her gifted son was conceived without a father. "He is the chosen
one," the child of prophecy, Qui-Gon later tells the Jedi Council. The
same prophecy that foretells the growth of the dark side also tells of "the

one who will bring balance to the Force." All these echoes of Hegel's Consummate Religion of Christianity, from the prophecy of a savior to a virgin birth to a mission of liberation from darkness, set up certain natural expectations. And yet Anakin is no clone of the Christian savior as Jesus is conventionally understood. Upsetting the standard Christian paradigm, the prophesied savior of *Star Wars* becomes the archetype of modern villainy, the evil lord Darth Vader, a machine as much as a man, whose every breath sounds with menace. And yet the prophecy is fulfilled. Anakin-Vader indeed does bring balance to the Force, striking down the Emperor, and then dying in the loving embrace of his son.

Giving reason to this reversal of conventional Christianity, Hegel is sharply critical of a theology according to which Jesus is the sinless savior whose mission is to redeem a humanity sunk in darkness. He is the light, the Gospel of John says, "and the light shines in darkness, and the darkness does not comprehend it."[18] If he is the light, Hegel effectively argues, he nevertheless himself enters into the darkness. The God of the Consummate Religion leaves his throne above the world to enter the very darkness of human sin and suffering through the paradigmatic journey of the Son of God to the cross on Mount Calvary. Joining fully with humanity in its separation from God, Jesus experiences utter abandonment, crying out, "My God, my God, why have you forsaken me?"[19]

The essence of sin, Hegel argues, is the belief that one is an isolated individual, an ego separated from the All—from all other human beings and the rest of reality.[20] In his sense of abandonment Jesus too experienced such a condition of sinfulness. He plumbed the dark side of reality, and then emerged from it in a transformed body of light, demonstrating, Hegel writes, "that the human, the finite, the fragile, the weak, the negative are themselves moments of the divine, that they are within God himself, that finitude, negativity, otherness are not outside of God and do not, as otherness, hinder unity with God."[21] If we seriously accept the Christian conception of Jesus as both God and man, then the Christian religion is truly the story of the hero's journey in which the Son of God descends from his exalted heights of self-conscious divinity into the darkness of an oppressive epoch of earthly life, and by doing so is able to reconnect a world plunged in darkness with the light that is within each of us and that was never truly extinguished.

Jesus taught his followers to say the prayer that begins, "Our Father," for we are all sons and daughters of God. Every human being is therefore an expression of an aspect of divinity, an image of God. Hegel's contemporary, the English poet William Wordsworth, in his poem, "Intimations of Immortality from Recollections of Early Childhood," describes our deep-seated consciousness of this divinity within each of us:

> Our birth is but a sleep and a forgetting:
> The soul that rises with us, our life's star,
> Hath had elsewhere its setting,
> And cometh from afar:
> Not in entire forgetfulness,
> And not in utter nakedness,
> But trailing clouds of glory do we come
> From God who is our home:
> Heaven lies about us in our infancy.[22]

Wordsworth goes on to lament the fact that the emerging human ego soon separates itself from this original divinity experienced in child-hood—that is, identifies itself as a separate being in opposition to the infinite reality outside of itself. Inexplicably the shadow of darkness falls across the life of the young adult who has been "nature's priest." The estrangement of the separate ego of the adult of modern industrial-com-mercial society, the world of "getting and spending," gradually replaces the nature religion of the child, characteristic of the dawn of humanity and the East:

> Shades of the prison house begin to close
> Upon the growing boy,
> But he beholds the light, and whence it flows,
> He sees it in his joy;
> The youth, who daily farther from the east
> Must travel, still is nature's priest,
> And by the vision splendid
> Is on his way attended;
> At length the man perceives it die away,
> And fade into the light of common day.

The light of common day is the artificial light of the prison house, Plato's cave, whose inhabitants have forgotten their origin in the light and must be reminded of it by the nagging questions of the philosopher while being stirred to their depths by the energizine forces of love.[23]

NOTES

1. Georg Wilhelm Friedrich Hegel, *The Phenomenology of Spirit*, trans. A. V. Miller (Oxford: Oxford University Press, 1977), 808.

2. Laurent Bouzereau, *Star Wars: The Annotated Screenplays* (New York: Ballantine Books, 1997), 35.

3. Sophocles, *Antigone*, trans. Wm. Blake Tyrrell and Larry J. Bennett, http://www.stoa.org/diotema/anthology/ant/antistruct.htm.

4. Georg Wilhelm Friedrich Hegel, *Lectures on the Philosophy of Religion*, vol. 2, ed. by Peter C. Hodgson (Berkeley: University of California Press, 1987), 498.

5. Hegel, *Phenomenology*, 128, 131.

6. Hegel, *Phenomenology*, 127.

7. See Georg Wilhelm Friedrich Hegel, *Lectures on the Philosophy of Religion*, vol. 3, ed. Peter C. Hodgson (Berkeley: University of California Press, 1985), 61ff.

8. Georg Wilhelm Friedrich Hegel, *Elements of the Philosophy of Right*, ed. Allen W. Wood (Cambridge: Cambridge University Press, 1991), 279, para. 258.

9. Hegel, *Phenomenology*, 108.

10. Hegel, *Phenomenology*, 109.

11. Hegel, *Phenomenology*, 109.

12. Georg Wilhelm Friedrich Hegel, *Philosophy of Nature*, #252 (Oxford: the Clarendon Press, 1970), 26.

13. Hegel, *Philosophy of Nature*, 26.

14. Hegel, *Phenomenology*, 110.

15. For the "Unhappy Consciousness," see chapter 8.

16. Hobbes, *Leviathan*, 1:13; in *Great Books of the Western World,* vol. 23 (Chicago: Encyclopedia Britannica, 1952), 85.

17. Job 41:1–2, 10.

18. John 1:5.

19. Mark 15:34.

20. Hegel, *Lectures on the Philosophy of Religion*, 2:740–41.

21. Hegel, *Lectures on the Philosophy of Religion*, 3:326.

22. William Wordsworth, "Ode: Intimations of Immortality from Recollections of Early Childhood." Available at www.bartleby.com/145/ww331.html. Accessed 12/22/06.

23. This chapter is an expanded and revised version of James Lawler, "The Force Is with *US*: Hegel's Philosophy of Spirit Strikes Back at the Empire," published in *Star Wars and Philosophy*, ed. Kevin S. Decker and Jason T. Eberl (Chicago: Open Court, 2005) 144–156.

7
Turning to the Dark Side: The Problem of Evil in Plato, Kant, Hegel, and Darth Vader

I'm haunted by the kiss you should never have given me. My heart is beating, hoping that kiss will not become a scar. You are in my very soul, tormenting me. What can I do? I will do anything you ask. . . .
—ANAKIN SKYWALKER, A.K.A DARTH VADER

[In the Book of Genesis] man is represented as fallen into evil only *through seduction*, and hence as being *not basically* corrupt (even as regards his original predisposition to good) but rather as still capable of improvement, in contrast to a seducing spirit, that is, a being for whom temptation of the flesh cannot be accounted as an alleviation of guilt.
—IMMANUEL KANT

The Origin of Evil and the Dark Lords of the Sith

Instead of using philosophy to illuminate popular culture as in the previous chapter, let us here attempt to see how popular culture can shed light on philosophy. What answer do we find in *Star Wars* to the question, what is the cause of evil? What answer do we find in *The Matrix Trilogy* for humanity's captivity to alien beings, or in *Buffy the Vampire Slayer* for the onslaught of the demonic in human life? Why is the "real world" so constructed, in *Crimes and Misdemeanors*, that in order to survive Judah thinks he must kill a person he has loved? Nowhere in these works is there a clear answer to such questions, let alone an attempt to make the evils which human beings inflict on one another appear logically necessary. Thus in *Star Wars Episode III: Revenge of the Sith*, the title

162

card/crawl begins: "A long time ago in a galaxy far, far away . . . War! The Republic is crumbling under the attacks by the Separatist leader, Count Dooku. There are heroes on both sides. Evil is everywhere." Thus, we are simply informed that evil is a fact, and it is everywhere, on both sides of the struggle.

In this episode all clarity about where the light lies, and where the darkness, is obscured by a veil that casts its shadow over all. Padmé, Senator Amidala, asks in anguish: "What if the democracy we thought we were serving no longer exists, and the Republic has become the very evil we have been fighting to destroy?" She is right in her suspicions, for the head of the Republic is the Dark Lord Sidious, who is casting his cloud of confusion over the galaxy as he plays on the fears of his subjects even as he secretly provokes the divisions that motivate those fears. Who or what is this Dark Lord? Where does he come from? What motivates him? What is the source of his power to darken the minds of well-meaning individuals and even warriors of the light such as Anakin Skywalker?

According to the distillation of religion presented in *Star Wars*, the universal life force requires a balance of light and dark. But what is dark in the form of balance? For the Taoist, yin, the dark, is the passive, feminine, subjective, and emotional side of things, and light is the active, masculine, objective, and rational side. On the masculine, light side there is the detachment that comes from mental clarity. On the feminine, dark side, one is open to being moved by feeling or passion. But neither of these sides of life, by itself, is good or evil. In any individual, whether a man or a woman, both sides of the polarity are present. In the Taoist symbol of yin and yang, the dark yin contains a point of light within it, while the light yang contains a point of darkness. And both are encircled in the unity of the Tao or, we may say, the Force.

Thus the light and dark complement one another as do the male and the female in the vital creativity of the sexual union. In this perspective, dark does not mean evil. But the representatives of the dark forces in *Star Wars*, the Sith Lords, are not interested in such a balance. They want to control all and destroy the light. It is this aggressive one-sidedness that is evil. And so instead of balance there is imbalance, evil, with no rational explanation in the episodes of *Star Wars* from the nature of life itself, or the logic of development of consciousness, why this *must* be so.

The "expanded universe" of the *Star Wars* saga, however, does provide an explanation of the origin of the Dark Lords of the Sith.[1] Thousands of years before the events described in the films, some Jedi masters discovered a new way of accessing the Force—through passion, rather than through the prescribed Jedi practices of calmness of mind and emotional detachment. From this point of view, the officially recognized Jedi practices are imbalanced. According to the pioneers of the new approach of using passion to connect with the energy of the Force, the Jedi masters are too much centered on the light, rational side of the Force. The Jedi leadership, however, refused to recognize and incorporate the new practices of going to the dark side of the Force. Consequently, the rebellious dark-side Jedi found refuge among primitive peoples called the Sith, who practiced a form of nature religion. These animistic peoples recognized the godlike powers of the Dark Jedi, who became known as Lords of the Sith. The Lords of the dark side then set out to get revenge: to wage war on the light-side Jedi and establish their own power over the universe.

Whatever the Jedi Masters may think, there is no inherent evil in the discovery of the powers of passion. There is evil only in the abuse of this power to destroy and control others. Thus the choice to employ the powers of the dark side and the choice of evil per se are fundamentally distinct. The fact that they are fused in practice is due in part to the one-sidedness of the previously recognized methods of accessing the Force. If goodness and service to others, central moral features of the Jedi code, are thought to be linked exclusively to the light side's methods, then turning to the dark side becomes identified, in the minds of both sides of the issue, with condoning a license for evil, for ego-centered service to self, and power over others.

This conception of course involves a fatal mistake. The choice of evil is *motivated* by an imbalance in the earlier method for accessing the Force. But this choice is not logically *necessitated* by this. From the standpoint of purely *formal* logic, the Sith Lords could have aimed at attaining the ideal balance of dark and light sides, rather than setting out on their path of vengeance and single-minded darkness. Nevertheless, there is here a *dialectical* logic in which one limited form of understanding gives birth to its opposite and equally limited form. The two forms of limited understanding then struggle against one another because they are conditioned by one another, until a higher unity is finally recognized. The observers of this process—you and I—see that this is all a kind of misunderstanding based on mutual exaggerations. To avoid the terrible pain and suffering this entails, we would like to call out to the actors in the drama: Wait; don't you see what you are doing? However, our more enlightened perspective came into being only as a result of these struggles between more limited, earlier forms of understanding. As evolution is a movement from lower to higher forms, it is not possible to begin with the higher synthesis.

The Root of All Evil

We should pause and ask ourselves at this point: is it natural or logically necessary that the emerging human consciousness pass through a phase of murder and mayhem as a necessary step for achieving its full development? If Johnny quickly learns to accommodate Sally, because playing together is actually a nice thing to do, why did their ancestors, grownups as they were, behave like the children that our children themselves scarcely or barely are? Of course, however apparently irrational, murders and massacres are dominant features of human history, and not only in the bygone past. And so philosophers seek to give reasons for this prominent feature of human history. What is actual, says Hegel, is at the same time in some sense rational. Since murder and war, the plunder and rape of one human by another, are "actual" realities in human experience, there must be a reason for this. Hegel seeks to show that in the course of the evolution of consciousness, a stage of human self-destruction is dialectically necessary as the expression of a still immature form of ego-consciousness, and as a stimulus to further growth toward a higher goal that overcomes such disastrous limitations of humanity's full powers.

Various reasons for evil are given by philosophers. Hobbes sees darkness in the very nature of human beings: each human is by nature an egotist who will commit murder if necessary to fulfill his desires and advance his interests. The naturally egotistical humans decide to give up this freedom to murder only when they see that it does not serve them, for the war of all against all is not an environment for the flourishing of any. Recognizing this truth either consciously or instinctively, rational egotists must eventually conclude that we need the external force of the State to keep our egotistical inclinations in check. The "Leviathan" state, Hobbes argues, maintains law and order through its monopoly on the use of force and through fear of imprisonment and ultimately death.

For Hobbes "evil" is the necessary consequence of human nature. It can be mitigated only when human beings establish the controlling and frightening power of the State. To do this they must give up their original condition of freedom (which is freedom to kill if this advances one's cause) for the sake of establishing peace. Of the triumph of this philosophy in practice, one can say with Senator Padmé Amidala in *Star Wars Episode III: Revenge of the Sith*, as the Senate of the Republic hands all power over to its Chancellor for the sake of ensuring peace, "So this is how liberty dies, with thunderous applause. . . ." For Hegel, the triumph of empire is not an expression of human nature per se as it is for Hobbes, but a necessary phase in human history, a means by which the force of Spirit, the march of God in history, establishes a higher form of liberty. In contrast to Hobbes's pessimism about human nature, Hegel regards the life and death struggle as a means by which a higher Spirit emerges out of the shadows of illusion produced by an inevitable and productive phase of egotism in human history.

But surely, it would seem, God, Spirit, or the Force should not have to go to the extremes of using the mutual massacres of millions as an instrument of progress. The opening words of *Star Wars Episode III* at first seem to agree that all this warring is irrational: "Evil is everywhere." The imbalance is simply a fact. Given this fact, what the Force needs, and what it in fact produces, is a chosen one from among the light-side Jedi who by going over to the dark side gains the ability to destroy its evil master. However, if we dig into the archives of the galaxy, we find a kind of Hegelian argument. We learn about the narrow views of both the light and dark Jedi—both masters of the Force, from whom we might have expected more wisdom. And yet both are stubborn in clinging to their limited perspectives, as is the way with evolving humans when they discover some element of truth. And this is why a providential Force, the evolution of Spirit in Hegel's thought, requires the evil worked by Sith Lords to advance the cause of a better life through the eventual reconciliation and balance of the opposites. This is why the Force requires a chosen one to experience the depths and limitations of both sides in order to realize the balance that constitutes the highest good.

Kant's great predecessor, Leibniz, argues in his *Theodicy* that God necessarily chooses to create the best of all possible worlds, which consists of the greatest variety of "outflashings" of his own divine being that is compatible with the greatest possible harmony—the perfect balance of diversity and unity. The price of such balance, however, is the possibility of imbalance. For there to be true individuality, there must be freedom to choose. And with freedom there comes inevitably the *possibility* of evil—the free choice to put one's own self above all. But Leibniz assures us that all such acts of sheer willfulness are offset by advances to the larger good. Indeed, he hardly recognizes even the possibility of evil, since he holds that people always act for the good as they see it. Evil for him is simply a mistaken, limited understanding of what is actually good. There is no will to do evil for its own sake.

Leibniz deserves the scorn of his great critic Voltaire, who satirizes this philosophical blindness to evil in his novel *Candide or Optimism* (1759). An earthquake devastates the city of Lisbon in 1755, raising doubts in the minds of many about the goodness of God, and, more threateningly, of the goodness of the leaders of Church and State who

claim to speak in God's name. Consequently, a solution is found to settle the public mind: find some human scapegoats and roast them over a
slow fire. Voltaire sardonically describes the deadly perpetration of evil
by the luminaries of Church and State:

> After the earthquake, which had destroyed three-quarters of Lisbon, the
> wise men of the country had found no means more effectual for obviat-
> ing total ruin than that of giving the people a fine *auto-da-fé* ["act of faith"
> of the Inquisition]; it was decided by the university of Coimbra that the
> spectacle of a few people roasted at a slow fire, with grand ceremonies,
> is an infallible specific for preventing earthquakes. They had therefore
> seized a native of Biscay, who had been convicted of marrying a fellow
> god-parent, and two Portuguese, who in eating a fowl had rejected the
> bacon [Jews avoiding pork].[2]

The young Candide has been taught by his mentor, Dr. Pangloss—we
could translate this parody of Leibniz as Dr. Whitewash—that we live in
the best of all possible worlds. He therefore looks on this publicly sanc-
tioned celebration of evil with rose-colored philosophical spectacles: "If
this is the best of all possible worlds, I wonder what the others are like!"[3]

Kant takes seriously Voltaire's criticisms of such Pollyannaish optimism. But he also rejects the pessimism that imbues both the philosophical idea of Hobbes that human nature is naturally ego-centered and the
religious dogmas of Catholicism and Calvinism that we have inherited a
corrupted nature from the original sin of Adam and Eve.[4] The origin of
the choice of evil, like that of good, must be found in the free will of the
individual. Otherwise morality is impossible. Of course we don't *know*
this. It is, however, a necessary postulate of moral experience. If freedom
is the origin of evil in human beings, it cannot really be explained. At best
we can examine the *predisposition* of the choice of evil in a human nature
that allows for the possibility and even probability, but not inevitability,
of putting one's individual desires and interests first. Individuals can freely
choose to make self-love or ego the primary motive of their actions, but
because it is a free choice there can be no external cause of this choice
outside of the individual will. Consequently for Kant there can be no real
explanation of evil either in human nature, in preceding historical events,
such as the sin of Adam and Eve, or in some kind of logical necessity for
human evolution. All that can be said is that given the possibility of evil,
the actual choice of evil is likely to occur.

Kant gives his own philosophical interpretation of the Biblical story
of the fall: rather than follow the dictates of instinct, which determine
whether some food is good or bad for us, our first parents with their
newly emerging ability to use reason and experimentation decided to try

something that was not in the genetic palate. This was the first act of genuine human freedom.[5] For Kant, this Biblical story is an apt parable for the present freedom and responsibility of the individual, not an explanation of evil from a past act on the part of our ancestors. Every "evil" action, in which the individual chooses self-love over moral duty, must be regarded as an inexplicable, because genuinely free, fall from the innocence of the good will that is within each of us.

The Predominance of Evil in Human Experience

Thus Kant agrees with Leibniz that the possibility of evil has its origin in human freedom. But this account of how evil is possible does not explain why evil is such a preponderant feature of the human condition. Why do we regularly make such choices, and come to experience their full effect in a war of all against all, a dog-eat-dog world of competing egos? This overwhelming fact of experience tempts us to say that human nature is inherently egotistical, corrupt, or wicked. But such an explanation denies the freedom and real possibility to will the good—that is, to choose to act on the basis of duty to our shared humanity. In explaining evil human behavior from natural egotism, Hobbes is consistent in denying that human beings have freedom of choice. In denying inherent corruption or natural egotism, and in affirming human freedom, Kant nevertheless recognizes the fact of widespread, seemingly overwhelming evil in human life. He thus takes a stand between the pessimism of Hobbes and the optimism of Leibniz.

The phenomenon of widespread evil in human history gives special force to Kant's Antinomy of Practical Reason. The highest good seems at first to be a practical impossibility because of the apparently inherent egotism or fallenness of human nature. This is especially evident in the Machiavellian practices of international politics—practices which Kant says "no philosopher has yet been able to bring into agreement with morality." Consequently, "the *philosophical millennium*, which hopes for a state of perpetual peace based on a league of peoples, a world-republic, even as the *theological millennium*, which tarries for the completed moral improvement of the entire human race, is universally ridiculed as a wild fantasy."[6] Kant attempts to show, however, that the course of political evolution points in the direction of such political and theological millennia. Hegel takes up this task with his dialectical science of history as the progress of Spirit, the march of God in history.

We cannot explain the widespread fact of evil on the mere condition of the possibility of evil that is implied by freedom of the will. But if we explain widespread evil by a supposed corruption of human nature, whether natural or historically acquired, we render moral goodness and human autonomy impossible. Kant finds a solution to this dilemma in the Biblical account of the fall, which introduces an external cause of evil into the picture: the presence in human life of an evil spirit whose whole being inexplicably is bent on seducing human beings to evil. The vast extent of evil in human life is therefore not the result of a corrupted human nature but stems from an alien, inhuman source of evil that is capable of clouding human consciousness and magnifying human vulnerability and weakness. Kant concludes his discussion of evil in *Religion within the Limits of Reason Alone* with words that apply remarkably to the drama of *Star Wars*:

> [T]he rational origin of this perversion of our will whereby it makes the lower incentives supreme among its maxims . . . remains inscrutable to us. . . . This inconceivability the Bible expresses in the historical narrative as follows. It finds a place for evil at the creation of the world, yet not in man, but in a *spirit* of an originally loftier destiny. Thus is the first beginning of all evil represented as inconceivable by us (for whence came evil to that spirit?); but man is represented as fallen into evil only *through seduction*, and hence as being *not basically* corrupt (even as regards his original predisposition to good) but rather as still capable of improvement, in contrast to a seducing spirit, that is, a being for whom temptation of the flesh cannot be accounted as an alleviation of guilt. For man, therefore, who despite a corrupted heart yet possesses a good will, there remains hope of a return to the good from which he has strayed.[7]

Such a satanic spirit that wills evil for evil's sake is not motivated to choose self over others by ordinary human desires and fears, but rather by sheer pride in self and desire for power over others. Such a being is not merely weak but wicked, bent on seducing humans by means of desires and fears stemming from their weaknesses. But the fallen human beings who succumb to such evil influence maintain within themselves a basically good will that is capable of redemption—not through the heroic sacrifice on their behalf of a sinless Savior, but through their own free return to the light that continues to shine within them.

For Kant the predominance of evil in human experience is a fact that cannot or should not be explained otherwise than by *postulating* an evil spirit or spirits roaming the world. This is not religious faith in the ordinary sense, but the interpretation of ideas of a religious origin from the standpoint of autonomous moral consciousness. We are inevitably obliged to *think* about a transcendent domain of reality beyond all appearances, for we are not equipped to *know* this reality that hovers beyond the appearances of our four-dimensional space-time human experiences. The moral individual therefore chooses to adopt ideas about transcendent reality, sometimes suggested by religious teachings, in ways that support rather than undermine the moral experience.

The postulates of morality are suppositions necessary to support the moral will. In addition to freedom, God, and immortality, Kant suggests a fourth postulate—a Satanic spirit with evil intent. Given the preponderance of evil in human experience, we must choose between attributing the evil to the human will itself, or to some outside source. If we choose the former, then any hope in the possibility of the human spirit to create the moral millennium, the highest good, seems to be an unrealizable fantasy. Such pessimism would doom the just society represented in the *Matrix* trilogy by Zion and the year 2000, and in *Star Wars* by the victory of the Republic and the goal of balancing light and dark sides of the Force. If we choose to attribute the abundance of evil to the workings of an evil spirit, then our confidence in the essential goodness of the human being can still be affirmed. Such a belief or postulate makes sense of what seems to be an excessive degree of evil vastly surpassing what seems reasonable given ordinary human weaknesses and egotism. We should suppose that we have been deceived, misled, our minds clouded by a cunning dark power that has been leading us astray. As is seen in *The Matrix* as well as in *Star Wars*, we should also suppose that we have within us the inherent power to wake up from the induced slumber, or turn back from the hypnosis of the dark side, and affirm our birthright as autonomous agents in charge of our own destiny. Such a conception lies at the basis of the hero's journey of Anakin Skywalker.

For Kant, the Bible, and *Star Wars*, contrary to all purely rational understanding, there is in fact a radical imbalance in the state of the world. Darkness separates itself from light, and seeks to obliterate it altogether. The harmony of yin and yang, to which the idea of balance gives expression, cannot explain the disharmony that the Taoist sage in fact finds around him. Why this blindness to reality? Why do people create antagonism when reality is interconnection?

The Birth of Greek Tragedy

While Kant postulates the source of this evil in the malevolent intentions of an evil spirit, a fallen angel who has turned to the dark side out of sheer pride, *Star Wars* too presents evil as a given fact, with its Dark Lords inexplicably seeking power and destruction. They are no demons with the mentality of two-year-olds wrecking havoc for the fun of it, but advanced beings with a higher consciousness who nevertheless turn to evil for the pleasure of exercising their dark powers. There is, however, a back story to these beings, a legitimate complaint they might once have made against the stubbornness of the traditional Jedi practices. It is possible then that they are an instrument of the Force, which is the very essence of the human spirit, in its own evolution from lower to higher levels of balance. So for *Star Wars* there is a possible rational explanation for the evils of our world, not primarily in the existence of purely evil beings, but in the inherent dynamics of evolution. For such an internalist, rather than an externalist, explanation of evil, we have to turn from Kant to Hegel.

For Hegel, the dialectical logic of evolution requires the emergence of the ego, with the resulting separation between the human individual and the natural world, and between human being and human being. Hegel's account in his *Phenomenology* makes the evil of human self-destruction seem necessary because the self-centered ego in its earliest form is inherently incapable of accepting the existence of others on something like an equal footing. At this early point in his *Phenomenology*, Hegel does not give the full picture of human history, but rather provides an abstraction from that history which may have pedagogical validity. But the real starting point of human history is not the separate ego, the pedagogically effective starting point in the *Phenomenology*, but a form of consciousness that is still immersed in the life of nature characteristic of the early communities of kinship groups. Human beings do not begin as separate egos, but as members of kinship groups still rooted in the natural world and practicing the animistic religion of nature.

Hegel turns to this larger historical account of human origins only in the latter part of the *Phenomenology*, in the section on "Spirit," which begins with an examination of Sophocles' *Antigone*. The woman Antigone still obeys the ancient laws of kinship that require her to bury her brother Polyneices according to the traditional rites. But the male-dominated world of the State imposes its own rules. King Creon insists that Polyneices not receive the burial ritual that gains him entrance into the underworld. Polyneices has waged war against the city, killing the king, Eteocles, who is his brother, over a dispute regarding the secession. According to a prior agreement, the two brothers were to share the rule, each taking turns as king year by year. Eteocles refused the terms of this brotherly arrangement that was in harmony with the laws of kinship. So Polyneices waged a war against his brother, and the two brothers slew each other. Kinship solidarity has been abandoned by the brothers, who confront one another, not as the brothers they are by natural ties, but as separate egos, each affirming himself as "the One." Their uncle, the new king, decrees that Polyneices should be posthumously punished for treason by being denied the sacred burial rites. He thereby implicitly wages war against the old nature religion of the kinship world. The ancient Greek world is therefore split asunder, Hegel argues, with two contending principles of order, that of the dark side of ancient kinship whose protectors are women and that of the light side of modern individuality and the rule of men. The women remain devotees of the dark powers of the earth, while the men appeal for justification to the sun-god, Apollo.

But with this supposed rule of light we already find brother killing brother, agreeing with Hegel's logic of the separate ego. A one-sided, imbalanced view of what constitutes light, involving an attempt to suppress the dark forces of nature and femininity, motivates a new kind of darkness—a destructive dark side which the Greeks called the Fates or the Furies, bent on revenge for the betrayal of a larger wholeness brought about by the would-be seekers of the light.

Was this split between dark and light inevitable, a necessary outcome of the pure ego, which knows no other law than that of the separate ego? But Polyneices and Eteocles do know better. They each have the love of their sister. The old kinship community, represented by the elders who comment on the action as the chorus, is still present. There is the soothsayer, tuned into the requirements of balance or justice, who readily denounces the evil of Creon's one-sided emphasis on the new powers of the State and its reason-based laws. Concretely, then, there are other powerful factors at work than the abstract logic of the primitive ego, from which alone Hegel had previously deduced the logical necessity of the fratricidal life-and-death struggle.

Sophocles' own explanation for the spreading evil agrees more with the externalist position of Kant and the Bible, than with the internalism of Hegel's dialectics. The family of Oedipus is under a curse whose origins lie in the moral blindness of the family founder. Becoming aware of his crimes, King Oedipus puts out his eyes as a sign of the deeper darkness that has invaded his soul. And what explains this invasion is an evil issuing from the gods themselves. Ultimately, light and dark are at war on higher levels of being, and human beings must bear the brunt of this cosmic conflict. The chorus in *Antigone* sees the human tragedy played out against a larger background of superhuman evil: "When the gods shake a house, misfortune pursues the multitude of its descendants without respite. . . . [T]he evil seems to be a good to him whose mind the divinity is leading to destruction."[8] Such a view accords with Kant's view of the dark spirits of Biblical origin.

A few years after Hegel, Nietzsche, in his famous book *The Birth of Tragedy* (1871) further investigates this opposition as reflected in the religion of light and intellect, whose cult is Apollo and whose realm is the State, and the religion of darkness and passion, whose deity is the god of revelry, Dionysus, and whose sphere is the private world of the family. Nietzsche argues that we cannot really understand Plato's light-centered philosophy, with its higher forms of being that are accessed by intelligence, unless we see this Apollonian intelligence as a counterforce to the powerful presence of a passionate, Dionysian darkness. Mesmerized by the spell of Platonic intellect, later would-be followers of Plato have cut themselves off from the darkness that is the forgotten undercurrent of Plato's philosophy. Nietzsche's analysis of Greek tragedy and philosophy is later taken up by Heidegger who, as we have seen, sees the origin of our forgetfulness of being in the Platonic theory of the higher forms. We have discussed the weakness of this interpretation of Plato as solely a philosopher of dispassionate intellect. This misinterpretation overlooks Plato's account of the teaching of Diotema according to which philosophic intellect must be rooted directly in the dark-side passion of love.

Plato on the Struggle of Light and Dark

Hegel's full historical account, when compared with his explanation in the beginning of the *Phenomenology*, is in fact quite nuanced. Out of the separation seen in *Antigone* of the male from the female, of the new political organization of the State from the ancient laws of kinship, there first arises the *beautiful* world of Greek democracy. This world is beautiful, because here we see a kind of spontaneous harmony of free citizens that is still closely connected with the physicality of nature. The Athenian state is governed by the principle of sensuously beautiful individuality, expressed in Greek art with its reverence for the beautiful male body. Thus, even in the classical Greek polis, in principle split off from the darker realm of the family and kinship, there is no immediate descent into the evil of the life-and-death struggle of separate egos. But eventually these Greek male individuals who separate themselves from the kinship world of the family, and attempt to rule over the females who are still connected to it, inevitably take their individuality too far and so bring destruction on themselves. Explaining this destruction by the logic of the evolution of the ego, Hegel optimistically sees this destructive logic as a necessary but temporary process in the full emancipation of the human spirit.

Hegel therefore disagrees first with Kant and then with Plato, both of whom require an outside, nonhuman source of the evils faced by a struggling humanity. Kant roots the possibility of evil in an inexplicable free choice and then postulates a transcendent evil spirit or spirits as the source of the predominance of evil. As we have seen in the chapter on *Buffy the Vampire Slayer*, if there is a higher realm of pure spirit that is the source of duty, there should also be a lower realm of vampires, demons, and demigods who incarnate the pure wickedness that seems the only reasonable explanation for the extent to which evil so forcefully invades our middle human realm. Kant's position goes back to that of Plato, who, in his vivid image of the charioteer, represents the possibility of human evil in the dark horse of physical sensibility that pulls us downward, away from the sun of rational understanding and into the darkness of the shadow life of the cave. For Plato, like Kant, there is no inevitable choice of evil. It is up to each individual to choose which direction to take in life. But contrary to Kant, Plato refuses to explain the predominance of evil by the gods, or by godlike evil spirits. Plato rejects the explanation of classical Greek polytheism according to which the cause of evil is an evil god. Upholding the intrinsic goodness of God, Plato writes in the *Republic*, "Nor will we tolerate the saying [of Homer] that 'Zeus is dispenser alike of good and evil to mortals.' . . . nor again must we permit our youth to hear what Aeschylus says. 'A god implants the guilty cause in men / When he would utterly destroy a house.'"[9] "For the cause of evil," Plato says, "we must look for in other things and not in God."[10] We should note that Plato does not say, as he readily might have, that if we must not look for the cause of evil in God, we must see it in human beings.

Plato has his own "externalist" explanation of the fact that so many humans have taken the low road. It is not the fault of the gods, but neither is it the consequence of human choice alone. There is a larger cosmic cause of evil in the fact that the gods have withdrawn from the guidance of human life. They have done this of necessity, as the universe moves through cycles driven by the chaos of matter, which imposes inherent limitations on the extent and duration of divine guidance. The High God working with subordinate deities guides the revolutions of the earth and its various provinces as long as the primal matter out of which earth is constituted is capable of being so guided. Like a yo-yo that has been thrown out as far as possible, once the utmost reaches of the capacity for guidance are attained, the earth "begins to revolve in the contrary sense under its own impulse—for it is a living creature and has been endowed with reason by him who framed it in the beginning."[11] During the time of the forward rotation of the earth under the guidance of the gods, life is abundant and humans have no need to work. They grow up out of the earth, and reproduce as do the plants, seeding themselves and being reborn over and over. This was a time when "savagery was nowhere to be found nor preying of creature on creature, nor did war rage nor any strife whatsoever."[12]

Even during this golden age of the earth, human beings have choices to make and are responsible for making the best of the great opportunities that are available to them. Plato's spokesman, the Statesman—who like Diotema is another teacher of the young Socrates—links the pursuit of philosophy with learning from the animals. Clearly, Plato does not teach an otherworldly or higher-worldly philosophy, as Heidegger argues, but seeks wisdom in the living earth and all its creatures. The Statesman emphasizes the choice that these privileged humans had to make:

> The crucial question is—did the nurslings of Cronus [i.e., the nature-loving humans who arise directly out of the earth] make a right use of their time? They had abundance of leisure and were at an advantage in being able to converse with the animals as well as with one another. Did they use all these advantages to promote philosophical inquiry? As they associated with one another and with the animals, did they seek to learn from each several tribe of creatures whether its special faculties enabled it to apprehend some distinctive truth not available to the rest which it could bring as its contribution to swell the common treasure store of wisdom? [13]

All creatures have something to teach in this wonderful school for humanity that is the earth. The principle of universal love of beauty in all things, taught as a deep mystery by Diotema to the young Socrates, is in this period of cosmic evolution far more easily recognizable than it is in the present period of cosmic freefall.

Everything changes with the cosmic crisis that ensues when the great God must let go of the tiller of the world and allow it to reverse its direction under the inherent impulse of chaos. It now becomes more difficult for humans to converse with one another, while our links to animal intelligence are almost completely obscured. The period of the world in which we now live is one of hardship, suffering, and evils that are due to God's fated abandonment of the world to its own devices. In this downward or backward-moving stage of the cycle of time, it is above all necessary for humanity to recollect that earlier period of divine rule, which is still implicit in the beauty of physical existence, in the goodness of moral duty, and in the truths of philosophy. With such remembrance as is still possible, human beings themselves need to take charge of the affairs of the world as best they can, until such time as the divine influences can once more be directly felt and come to their aid. Without a God or something, as Cliff says in *Crimes and Misdemeanors*, human beings must take responsibility for their lives. But the *idea* of the divine, the postulate of divinity that reflects inherent features of humanity, remains a guiding light during our own unhappy period of intensified evils.

We live, Plato tells us, in an age of darkness that is making it more than difficult to experience the glory that is our natural heritage as beings whose higher nature is akin to the divine. We must therefore pit ourselves against the downward or backward course of the unwinding of the world. Contrary to Hegel's internalist logic of evolution, there is no positive outcome to this phase of the cosmic cycle. It is not caused by the naturally limited understanding of human beings in their *evolution* from lower to higher forms, for we are in a period of *devolution* from higher to lower. If in the golden age of Cronus humans are capable of misusing the advantages available to them—and Plato suggests that the old stories indicate that such abuse was widespread—in these present times of cosmic reversal humans remain essentially capable of rising above the evils with which they are afflicted. It is important to recognize that if the cause of widespread evil is not in the gods, neither is the scope of evil due to the humans themselves. Thanks to the cosmic regression, the beckoning of evil arising out of our base impulses is intensified, for the unleashed chaos of the cosmos itself is in league with these tendencies.

Synthesis of Plato, Kant, and Hegel

Who is right in this debate—Plato and Kant, who see the causes of evil both in radical human freedom and in hostile external causes that are outside of our control, or Hobbes and Hegel, who see evil as a necessary part of human existence, either as an expression of human nature or as an inevitable moment of human evolution?

Let us grant with Hegel that at some point in human evolution it is both necessary and good that the ego emerges, that the individual declares his independence of the tribe, that the light of conscious rationality separates itself from unconscious unity with the darker realm of blood relations and passionate desires. But can such dialectical evolution bear the weight of *all* the evil? In the teleology of history that both Kant and Hegel acknowledge, humanity is moving forward, whereas for Plato whatever progress we can discern pales before the earlier achievements of the golden age, and involves a struggle just to stay in place against inherently contrary tendencies of cosmic origin. But for Hegel this forward motion is impulsed by the logic of evil itself—i.e., by the logic of the separate ego—while for Kant, all moral progress over egotism is won only through an additional uphill struggle against foes of humankind who are bent on thwarting us at every point. Nevertheless, movement forward is possible, and is in fact being realized—and any golden age of perfect harmony that we find in the ancient wisdom or the Bible is a parable of a kind of natural existence that is unworthy of human beings. Thus Plato's idea that humans have to take control of their own lives should not be regarded as second-best to the rule of the gods themselves, but the true purpose of nature in creating beings with reason.

Perhaps new empirical evidence, available to the authors of popular culture, can help us answer this question of which tendency is right, the externalist or the internalist. If we are moving forward by an optimistic logic that uses evil to stimulate the good, why do we find that in the twentieth century more evil has been perpetrated than in all previous centuries? Do not the facts seem to bear out Plato's Statesman, who says that "as this cosmic era draws to its close, this disorder comes to a head."[14] Despite all progress made in the evolution of principles of self-government in history, Kant sees the continuation of the war of all against all on the international realm, and a prospect of ever-growing bloodshed as warring egotistical nations equip themselves with weaponry made ever more vicious by technological progress. Kant supposes the need to postulate dark powers of evil intent operating behind the scenes to help us comprehend how the leaders of nations can be so apparently blind to the looming devastation.

Should we then not add to Hegel's account of a rational dialectical logic of forward movement an irrational element of willful darkness that cannot be rationally explained and justified by the inner logic and needs of human life? As the ego emerges out of the kinship societies of ancient history, an irrational darkness mysteriously descends on these separate individuals, obscuring their feeling of kinship with one another so thoroughly that they come to regard their fellow humans, no less than their mother the earth, as enemies and prey.

In reading Hegel, therefore, we should incorporate the perspective of Kant, with supplementation from Plato. Kant clearly faces the fact of evil as a predominant feature of human history that seems at first to render hopeless all aspiration toward a world federation of peaceful peoples and the even more exalted goal of the highest good. However, morality requires a framework of belief that leaves room for hope. We must lift ourselves up by our own bootstraps by adopting beliefs that allow us, like Rabbi Ben, to turn a blind eye to all the blindness, to become a blind seer—as Oedipus attempted to do and as Sophocles represents the soothsayer Tiresias—or even a "blind Messiah," like Neo guided by his soulmate Trinity. Let us then postulate that the deepest fault is not in a corrupt human nature, or in a necessity of human evolution, but in something like a falling back of the universe itself, as Plato's *Statesman* claims, or in invading hostile powers—fallen angels who rebel against God and the good. It seems necessary to add, in the spirit of Plato, that the divine appears unable or unwilling to stop this cosmic vandalism—at least for now.

Popular culture, reflecting on the horrors of the twentieth century that continue unabated in the twenty-first, provides vivid pictures of the evils that stubbornly confront the warriors of the light. In the *Matrix* trilogy, inhuman forces have taken over the human world. In *Buffy*, the subterranean worlds give rise to demons, vampires, and demigods bent on absolute power. In *Star Wars* there is the history of great beings of power, the Sith Lords, who in their unfathomable choice of evil are bent on Empire. Evil is thus presented as a fact whose origin is outside ordinary human beings per se, although there is within the human being a possibility of evil and a proneness to its seductive force. But at the same time, hope is possible because goodness is inherent in the human will, which has the power to overcome the seductive attractions and confusions arising from the darkest depths of the dark side. Despite these seeming infections from other worlds and dimensions, heroic individuals continue to hold to the light and to seek balance. Near the end of Episode 3, Yoda says of the twin babes secretly born of the union of Padmé and Anakin: "Save them, we must. They are our last hope." Thus *Revenge of the Sith* is followed by episode 4, *A New Hope*.

But even if *Star Wars*, along with Plato and Kant, is right in its evocation of a higher origin to the darkness that shrouds the history of humankind, a logic of hope can still be discerned in these shadows. Hegel dialectically strengthens Kant's teleology of human evolution which gives reason for hope. Where Kant sees scientifically unexplainable facts of progression from despotism to liberty, Hegel illuminates these stages with a dialectical logic of evolution through the struggle of opposites. Moderating Hegel's rationalism with Kant's critique of reason, we might say that the logic is not a necessary one, for it requires free choice to be sustained. Nor is this logic the only force in operation, for perhaps it is the case that irrational outside forces seek to cloud all our rationality. An Hegelian logic of evolution is nevertheless a real force for advance, adding to the arsenal of the Kantian postulates by strengthening their core meaning with a new understanding. Hegel's evolutionary spiral replaces

Plato's repetitious cycles. In the complex distillation of such ideas in *Star Wars*, as the reversal of the world motion reaches its outer limit and the evil draws to a head, in *Revenge of the Sith*, its very concentration becomes an impetus to a great awakening and creative action. The living earth herself mobilizes once more for renewal, while the humans who have relearned the dialectical science of the gods can now actively combine with them in reversing the evil's course toward chaos.

Master and Slave

With this enlarged perspective in mind, we can return to Hegel's presentation of the life-and-death struggle to see where its logic leads. In the abstract dialectic of the *Phenomenology*, each "I" attempts to rid itself of a competing "I" in order to assure itself of what it believes to be the truth—namely, that "*I* really am the One." Because the "I" is implicitly a universal, a multitude of egos would struggle against one another endlessly unless some of these egos surrender, and, in fear of annihilation, say to the stronger opponent, "Yes, you *are* the One." Out of this surrender of the weak to the strong, emerges the world of masters and slaves. A more subtle dialectic then begins between the masters and the slaves. For if the subservience of the slave seems to prove to the master that he is indeed "the One," such servitude creates an implicit dependence of the masters on the slaves. In the end, the slaves do all the work, while the masters fatten themselves in indolence. *Star Wars* epitomizes this outcome of the master-slave dialectic in its portrayal of the monstrously obese slave-master, Jabba the Hutt.

While the masters inevitably deteriorate in the lap of luxury, the slaves achieve great skills in their work of transforming nature through their own intelligent labor. In some form or other the slaves must eventually recognize that they, not the masters, are in touch with reality and are the real powers of creative transformation. We the observers of this historical drama clearly see this. We also see that with their combined power the slaves are capable of ending a state of subservience that is less and less justifiable by any real abilities on the part of the masters. To achieve such unity, the slaves must overcome the false separation of the ego. They must recognize that their power lies in unity with each other. This potential power is the Force of Spirit—an I that is a We and a We that is an I. In surrendering to the masters for the sake of survival they have already given up the infantile ego's one-sided conception of itself. This makes them open to a new kind of community. However, the next step in the evolution stops short of the ultimate goal, the recognition of their connection to one another as Spirit. To fully understand this next step, we must also see what is taking place on the master side of the dialectic.

While the masters are implicitly undermined from the side of the slaves by their own apparent success, what about the continued struggle within the master class itself? The logic of the life-and-death struggle may be mitigated by the emergence of a world of masters and slaves, but the competition between egos among the masters continues until finally everyone is subservient to the one emperor—the Dark Lord of the ego that is the deepest potential and ultimate aspiration within every separate ego. Only one person can be *the* One, and so the logic of the separate ego culminates in the concentration of power in the hands of one person, the emperor. Since even the so-called masters in the Roman Empire discover their powerlessness, they too become open to a new conception of life.

The immediate outcome of these developments, according to Hegel, comes in the form of the emergence of the Stoic philosophy. Among the most prominent Stoic philosophers, one, Epictetus, was a slave and another, Marcus Aurelius, was a Roman emperor. Stoicism is a philosophy that rises above the master-slave opposition by holding that we are all potential masters through mind and thought, and all slaves through emotion and body. The slaves must rise above the emotion of fear that has moved them to capitulate to the masters. The masters must rise above servitude to bodily needs and pleasures to which dependence on slaves has brought them. It is in such a framework that we can understand the emergence of Stoic philosophy at the time of the Roman Empire.

The Stoic sage preaches the independence of the mind in relation to the body. As the master is in the process of twisting his leg, the slave Epictetus calmly tells him: if you twist it any further it will break. The master continues to twist and only succeeds in proving Epictetus right. Instead of proving his power over his slave, he only shows his stupidity as Epictetus smiles through the pain of a broken leg with superior knowledge that tells the master, I told you so. In this way, through the power of the dispassionate, detached mind, the Stoic slave rises above the brute force of his master.

The Stoic sage preaches detachment from emotional involvement in the surrounding world in order to free himself from all external sources of control. Epictetus advises: "If you kiss your child, or your wife, say that you only kiss things which are human, and thus you will not be disturbed if either of them dies."[15] The Stoic recommends detachment from emotional involvement with things and people by siding with a higher Force in the belief that whatever inscrutable plan the divine power has orchestrated for humanity, there must be good in it. "Nothing happens by accident," Qui-Gon tells Shmi as he decides that Anakin is the child of prophecy, the chosen one of the Force. But the Skeptic delights in refuting such beliefs as infantile by pointing to the empirical testimony of hard realities. There is no all-powerful Force that masters the universe. There is only one's own cunning, and the power of a good blaster, says the rebel Han Solo.

Faust and the Dark Side of Love

We the observers of this dialectic can see where it is all going and what underlies the various steps of the evolution of consciousness. Reality, we learn early on in this history, is ultimately "Spirit." Our deeper nature is not to be an "I" separate from other "I"s by the confines and distances of our material bodies. Wherever there is one such separate "I" there are others, and each of these egos must struggle against the others. Where every "I" asserts itself against every other "I," there is murder and mayhem—that perilous life of humankind described by philosopher Thomas Hobbes as "solitary, poor, nasty, brutish and short."[16] The Stoic steps beyond this egotism by recognizing the unity of mankind, but only at the level of intellect since such unity is achieved by renouncing attachment to the realm of the body and its emotional ties. Hence this limited step forward toward Spirit remains one-sided and so suffers negative consequences of its own. The life of the mind detached from the body is empty of empirical content and so readily embarrassed by the skeptical empiricist. In the next chapter we will explore the emergence of the Unhappy Consciousness that, according to Hegel, stems from this collision of Stoicism and Skepticism.

But even an intellect enriched by empirical content remains emotionally impoverished. A life of detached mental activity eventually reveals itself to be deprived of emotional vitality. A longing for a richer connection to life eventually arises. By contrast to abstract intellectualism, the "I" that is "We," or Spirit, reveals its deeper vitality in the experience of *love*. The true meaning of the sacred journey of the hero, exemplified in the life and death of the Christ figure, is infinite or unconditioned love.[17] This is the lofty goal of the "Calvary of Absolute Spirit." But the goal or endpoint requires an unavoidable path of crucifixion, without which it remains a purely intellectual concept. Without the path of personal discovery and suffering that teaches compassion on the emotional plane, love is an intellectualized compassion. Often "Platonic love" is represented as a detached relationship in which the pain of personal passion has been short-circuited by a premature intellectualism. However, as Diotima teaches Socrates in Plato's *Symposium*, the path to infinite love begins with the passionate, erotic love of one person.[18]

A crucial moment in the historical as well as intellectual, emotional, and spiritual journey of mankind, described in the *Phenomenology of Spirit*, is occupied by a pivotal work of popular culture of Hegel's own time, Goethe's tragic poem *Faust*. As Hegel interprets this, the one-sidedness of the life of the intellect that characterizes the modern age of science gives rise to a romantic longing for a lost vitality. In Goethe's story, the aged intellectual Faust falls in love with the young maid Gretchen. Salvation from too much light from the side of the male intellect comes from the magnetic attraction of the dark side of a woman's love. This polarization of intellect and love implies limitation on both sides, for it takes place at a time when women are still excluded from the life of the mind and the public world. But instead of glorying in masculine power over the old kinship order, as Creon does in *Antigone*, the weary Faust finds himself choked by the dust that covers ancient manuscripts in which he vainly seeks the secret of life. Human consciousness is fundamentally or implicitly consciousness of life, but in the course of its evolution the Western world has abandoned the vital connection to nature of kinship and Eastern societies for the path of the ego and the disconnected intellect. Out of the life-and-death struggle of the abstract ego and the master-slave dialectic to which it leads, there arises the limited Stoic response to egotism, which seeks a unity of mankind through purely intellectual universality. At first this development appears to be a triumph over the tyranny of empirical power, but it merely abstracts from the tangible world of fear and trembling, leaving intact the ego-based world of wealth and power that it disparages. The achievement of the Stoic eventually reveals its hollowness, and gives rise to a yearning for a deeper connectedness.

The fulfillment of this yearning for love is made possible by Faust's bargain with the devil—to give up his soul in exchange for a return to youthful vitality and the intense experience of life that can only be found through a passionate love of a beautiful being. In the diabolic shadow of such a limited dialectic, Faust believes that to go over to the dark side of love he must give up his soul to the evildoer, the devil Mephistopheles, who entices him on with apparent truths that only mask deeper lies. As the chorus of *Antigone* declames, "the evil seems to be a good to him whose mind the divinity is leading to destruction."[19]

This is indeed where the power of love seems to lead if we start from the Stoic consciousness that has left nature and vital feeling behind—to the very loss of one's soul. If the soul is identified with detached mental clarity and this is linked with service to the good, then the emotional attachment of love appears to require the loss of the soul and surrender to evil. Evil is in fact worked by this Faustian love that takes place in secret and in separation from the community to which Gretchen belongs. She has a love child that is illicit in the eyes of her community and so she murders the child to maintain the secret. She is found out, and is condemned to death. But Faust is ultimately at fault because he ignores the fact that Gretchen is not a detached ego, like himself, but, as a soul-sister of Antigone, she is a woman embedded in a community.

Through his love for Gretchen Faust implicitly feels the pull of authentic Spirit. But because he has not fully transcended the confines of the separate ego, because he envisages the light of truth from the narrow standpoint of a puritanical Stoic morality of detachment, the power of love and the life it enkindles appear to arise out of Satanic darkness. Desperate for a love that is forbidden to the Stoic intellect, Faust becomes the willing instrument of the evil one. Such a love inevitably brings death to Gretchen as well as threatens to plunge the immortal soul of the lover into eternal darkness. Nevertheless, humanity in the person of Faust learns that the way forward toward vitality and wholeness is to abandon Stoic detachment for a passionate love in which body and soul are totally at stake. In this way, Hegel fully incorporates and dialectically sublates the dark forces of the Evil One, in the form of Goethe's Mephistopheles, in a rational development that stimulates the progress of humanity. In this "Calvary of Absolute Spirit" there is no surplus of evil that points to supernatural and extrarational interference in humanity's self-unfolding. For Hegel, Mephistopheles is not a real spirit of evil intent preying on human weakness, but only a symbol of humanity's still-limited evolutionary state.

A Love that Conquers Death

Hegel helps us appreciate a central problem with the Stoic philosophy of the Jedi masters. Their ideal of detachment from emotional involvement with others seeks to forestall the descent into the darkness of a Faustian love, but in doing so they leave no room for the higher vitality that only comes through deeply personal connections with particular individuals. The one-sidedness of Jedi Stoicism originally provoked the dark Jedi into rebellion and evil. It is this unnatural Stoic detachment that seems to leave a lovelorn and confused Anakin no alternative, and so precipitates his Faustian bargain with the Dark Lord.

In a debate within the Jedi Council in *Episode I: The Phantom Menace*, Jedi master Qui-Gon defends the boy Anakin's candidacy for Jedi knighthood, despite his age. Anakin has spent the first nine years of his life living alone with his mother, has naturally become attached to her, and is therefore disqualified to become a Jedi knight. Yoda explains to Anakin why his attachment to his mother is dangerous for a Jedi warrior: "Afraid to lose her, I think." "What's that got to do with anything," Anakin protests. "Everything," Yoda tells him. "Fear is the path to the dark side. Fear leads to anger. Anger leads to hate. Hate leads to suffering." Qui-Gon disagrees with the negative assessment of Anakin. He tells the Jedi Council, "Finding him was the will of the Force. I have no doubt of that." Indeed, for the devotee of the Force, as Qui-Gon says to Anakin's mother Shmi earlier in this episode, "Nothing happens by accident." Only the mysterious power and intelligence of the Force could explain the series of events that led from the leaking hyperdrive of the Naboo spacecraft to an emergency stop on an obscure planet, and then to the discovery of the slave boy Anakin with his remarkable abilities. As skeptical here as Han Solo, the Jedi Council would rather put this all down to accident, for accepting Anakin means confronting their own deepest fears. If it is possible to be seduced by the dark side, it must also be possible to be overly attached to the light—and overly fearful of the dark. The Stoic Jedi masters too are afraid—afraid of real human love, afraid of connection with the other person, afraid of the loss of self-control that comes to the "I" of passionate love which, ultimately, is at the same time a "We."

Padmé asks the grown-up Anakin in *Attack of the Clones*: "Are you allowed to love? I thought that was forbidden for a Jedi." Anakin replies: "Attachment is forbidden. Possession is forbidden. Compassion, which I would define as unconditional love, is central to a Jedi's life. So you might say we are encouraged to love." Anakin wants a personal love but his Jedi education acknowledges only a detached compassion and so he plays on the meaning of love. For surely, in the sense that Padmé means, love is indeed forbidden to a Jedi. The goal of universal compassion, without possession and being-possessed, can be the outcome of a lengthy dialectical process that begins in passionate attachment, a ladder of love such as Diotema explains to Socrates. Or else it is a short-circuited, abstracted, intellectualized form of love, a misnamed "Platonic love" such as the Stoics recommend.

There is a partial truth to Yoda's argument. Attachment and possession are forbidden because such connections to particular things and people lead to fear for them and fear of losing them. And fear, developing into anger and hatred, does in fact lead to acts of evil, and, more importantly, to seduction by the dark powers that exacerbate our misdeeds and enthrall us to themselves. Therefore it seems that the love of the Jedi master must be a detached love—if it can indeed be called love with its willingness to sacrifice friends and loved ones for the perceived higher good. Anakin rejects this detached love of the Stoic sage, as does Luke in *The Empire Strikes Back* when he spurns Yoda's declaration that his training is more important than the life of Han and Leia. Giving an ironic twist to the deeper unity of the light with the dark, the Emperor echoes Yoda's counsel in *Return of the Jedi* (episode 6), when the Dark Lord tells Luke that his love for his friends is his great weakness. The Jedi masters fear what the Sith Lord despises, the power over the intellectualized ego wielded by human love. We recall that in the climactic battle of *The Matrix Revolutions*, Agent Smith, with characteristic disgust, similarly tells Neo that "only a human mind could invent something as insipid as love."

Anakin's eventual declaration of love in episode 2, *Attack of the Clones*, in the most sexually seductive scene in the whole of *Star Wars*, is worthy of Shakespeare: "I'm haunted by the kiss you should never have given me. My heart is beating, hoping that kiss will not become a scar. You are in my very soul, tormenting me. What can I do? I will do anything you ask. . . ." Such passionate, tormented love indeed leads Anakin to the dark side. As Yoda feared in rejecting the nine-year-old Jedi candidate, Anakin kills indiscriminately out of rage against his mother's murder. From the beginning of their relationship, Anakin and Padmé sense that their secret love, cut off from the light through pretense, lies, and betrayal, will ruin them. The potentially harmonious darkness of love motivates Anakin's turn to the dark side of pure evil as a result of a distorting context in which passionate love is forbidden to the spiritual master and allowed only within the confines of the conventional power structures.

However, it is not love itself that ruins Anakin, but insufficient trust in the power of love. The Dark Lords who have turned to evil recommend all the passions but love. Fear, anger, hatred—these are the powerful emotions that will unleash the dark side of the Force. But these emotions are closely linked with power and control over others, implying the egoic choice of evil. But what about love? It too is a passion, the deepest passion of all. And so it issues from the dark side of the Force. But it is a passion that intrinsically wants life, not death, freedom of the other, not control and servitude.

When in *Revenge of the Sith* Anakin becomes convinced that Padmé will die, his love drives him to try to save her. But the mind manipulations of the Emperor blind him to the power of love itself. It is the intensity of hatred, not the full force of love, that the Dark Lord seeks to cultivate. Neither the Jedi nor the Sith acknowledge the force of love itself to give life. And so it is understandable why Anakin fails to follow through on the path of love to which Padmé urges him.

PADMÉ: Anakin, all I want is your love.

ANAKIN: Love won't save you, Padmé. Only my new powers can do that.

PADMÉ: At what cost? You are a good person. Don't do this.

Anakin understands that the fulfillment of love requires that he overcome death. He cannot accept Yoda's Stoic advice in the face of death: "Death is a natural part of life. Rejoice for those around you who transform into the Force. Mourn them, do not. Miss them, do not. Attachment leads to jealousy. The shadow of greed, that is. . . . Train yourself to let go of everything you fear to lose." Against such impersonal dissolution of the personality in the Force, Darth Sidious offers Anakin the seductive promise of overcoming death while retaining personal consciousness, of attaining eternal youth for himself and Padmé. The Dark Lord's promise tempts Anakin, like Faust, to make his deal with the Devil.

Ultimately, however, it is not Darth Sidious who holds the secret of immortality, but the Jedi master Qui-Gon. Qui-Gon has gone into the Force, and yet, contrary to the dissolution of personal consciousness that Yoda supposes, Qui-Gon has preserved his individuality. It is therefore not necessary for the lover to resign himself to the dissolution of the beloved. In spirit form Qui-Gon explains this higher possibility to Yoda in *Revenge of the Sith*: "When I became one with the Force I made a great discovery. With my training, you will be able to merge with the Force at will. Your physical self will fade away, but you will still retain your consciousness. You will become more powerful than any Sith." Yoda comments meaningfully, "Eternal consciousness." Qui-Gon elaborates: "The ability to defy oblivion can be achieved, but only for oneself. It was accomplished by a Shaman of the Whills. It is a state acquired through compassion, not greed."

Star Wars thus does not only postulate, in the manner of Kant, a belief in personal immortality as a condition for perseverance in the cause of the good. It explains how to achieve that immortality. As both Plato and Hegel argue, connection with the eternity of Spirit implies immortality for the individual who recognizes this connection. Such a recognition requires purification from all transitory forms of consciousness—the path of the evolution of consciousness which Hegel calls the Calvary of Absolute Spirit. All one-sided forms of attachment must be overcome, not by circumventing them in a short-circuited Stoic intellectualism but by passing through them and undergoing painful crucifixion to limited forms of existence on the way to achieving a higher balance.

Qui-Gon continues to recommend the detachment of "compassion" as a means of achieving this goal, but this can't be the kind of detached compassion that was taught him by his Jedi teachers. Qui-Gon has gone beyond the Stoic detachment that implies dissolution of the individual personality in the universality of the Force. The source of this new form of compassion is said to be a Shaman of the Whills. Shamans are the spirit masters of the nature people, like the Ewoks or the Sith. This reference to another nature people, the Whills, suggests that the path toward the fulfillment of spiritual connection involves reconnection with nature. There is here an implicit reference to the dark side of the Force, but in the spirit of a love which, as Diotema teaches, climbs a ladder from one person to all of reality. Or, as the Statesman argues, wholeness and meaning are found in the ways of animal life. Such compassion is not achieved by denial of nature and by avoiding personal attachment, but by following the dialectic of evolution through all the forms of life, combining nature religion and the religion of the ego in a single harmonious balance of darkness and light.

According to Qui-Gon one can only achieve immortality for oneself—contrary to Anakin's plan to achieve immortality for Padmé. But she does not need a male savior to find her own way to higher awareness. A new prospect for love comes to fulfillment in the final scene of episode 6, which shows the immortal spirits of Anakin, Yoda, and Obi-Wan forming a circle of love around their beloved Luke. In the new understanding, it is no longer necessary to give up one's loved ones to the impersonal immortality of the Force. No one can make another person immortal; no one can be the savior of another. Each person must attain immortality for himself or herself through the unfolding of love into universal compassion. As Aristophanes maintains in Plato's *Symposium*, soulmate lovers can join one another in the common quest for an eternity of love. This is the path of love of wisdom, *philos-sophos*, that Diotema teaches young Socrates. At the end of episode 6, Luke does not stand alone. He has not had to detach himself from his loved ones by consigning them to the impersonality of the Force. His loved ones remain with him, shimmering in the light alongside him.

With such an understanding of the background story, we finally come to appreciate why Luke recognizes the good in his father. It is because Anakin does not fear to go where love takes him, both when his love of Padmé takes him into the darkness and when his love of Luke brings him back again. Anakin in turn recognizes in Luke the true child of his long-forgotten love. Like Neo in the *Matrix* trilogy, Luke in the end refuses to fight. He relies wholly on the Force. That is to say, he relies completely on the power of love and thereby reconnects with his father. Anakin reawakens within the black shell of Darth Vader to his destiny, and strikes down the evil Emperor, the Dark Lord of the Sith. We can now fully understand that his destiny, subtly and richly orchestrated by the will of the Force and the magic of George Lucas's art, has all along been to love. By loving in a way that is truly unconditional, without fear of the darkness into which his love leads him, he fulfills his destiny, destroys the Emperor, and so brings balance to the Force.

I expect that a future special comprehensive edition of the *Star Wars* saga will at last fully integrate the back story with the original episodes. All that is necessary to give visual completion to our philosophical understanding is one additional figure in the final scene of the episode 6. Standing behind Anakin, previously restored to his youthful self through the magic of computer-aided composition, will be Padmé herself, in spirit-pervaded luminosity, Anakin's beloved companion and teacher in the art of love.

NOTES

1. See Wikipedia's article on the Sith: http://en.wikipedia.org/wiki/Sith. This expanded universe is the officially approved universe of books that add to the *Star Wars* universe without contradicting the central mythology of the films.

2. Voltaire, *Candide and Other Writings* (New York: Barnes and Noble, 1995), 15.

3. Voltaire, *Candide*, 16.

4. In his examination of the theories of the origin of evil, Kant says, "the most inept is that which describes it as descending to us as an *inheritance* from our first parents." Immanuel Kant, *Religion within the Limits of Reason Alone* (New York: Harper Torchbook, 1960), 35.

5. Kant, "Conjectural Beginning of Human History," in *Kant on History* (New York: Macmillan, 1985), 56.

6. Kant, *Religion*, 29–30.

7. Kant, *Religion*, 38–39.

8. Sophocles, *Antigone*, lines 595, 622–24. Cited by Paul Ricoeur in *The*

Symbolism of Evil (Boston: Beacon Press, 1967), 226.

9. Plato, *Republic*, in *Plato: The Collected Dialogues* (New York: Pantheon Books, 1961), 626–27; 379e–380a.

10. Plato, *Republic*, 626; 379c.

11. Plato, *Statesman*, in *Plato: The Collected Dialogues*, 1034; 269c.

12. Plato, *Statesman*, 1037; 271e.

13. Plato, *Statesman*, 1037–38; 272b–c.

14. Plato, *Statesman*, 1039; 273c.

15. Epictetus, *Enchiridion*, #3. Available at http://classics.mit.edu/Epictetus/epicench.html.

16. Thomas Hobbes, *Leviathan*, part 1, chapter 14, in *Great Books of the Western World*, vol. 23 (Chicago: Encyclopedia Britannica, Inc., 1952), 85.

17. Georg Wilhelm Friedrich Hegel, *Lectures on the Philosophy of Religion*, vol. 3, ed. Peter C. Hodgson (Berkeley: University of California Press, 1985),125.

18. Plato, *Symposium*, in *Great Books of the Western World*, vol. 7 (Chicago: Encyclopedia Britannica, 1952), 167, 210.

19. Lines 595, 622–24. Cited by Paul Ricoeur in *The Symbolism of Evil* (Boston: Beacon Press, 1967), 226.

8

Faith with Reason: Mel Gibson's *The Passion of the Christ*

He was oppressed and he was afflicted, yet he opened not his mouth; like a lamb that is led to the slaughter. . . .
—ISAIAH 53:7

"God himself is dead," it says in a Lutheran hymn, expressing an awareness that the human, the finite, the fragile, the weak, the negative are themselves moments of the divine. . . .
—G. W. F. HEGEL

The Pessimistic Alternative

Justice requires that the good be rewarded and the wicked punished. But at the same time, achieving reward or avoiding punishment cannot be the motive for performing acts of goodness without undermining the essential, inner nature of morality itself. The good person does her duty for the sake of duty, not for the sake of a reward or to avoid a punishment. The prospect of reward is generally uncertain, while in the moment the sacrifice of some present pleasure or interest is required by the pressing requirements of moral duty. And yet the larger goal of moral endeavor is to create a world in which the good are rewarded and the wicked punished. Is this goal, which Kant called the highest good, a realizable ideal or a hopeless and impossible fantasy? According to old Sol, in Woody Allen's *Crimes and Misdemeanors*, both the Bible and Shakespeare affirm the moral nature of our world, in which crime is ultimately punished and good people do indeed live happy lives. This is the also the vision of Hollywood movies such as the *Matrix* trilogy and *Star Wars*, as well as popular TV series such as *The Simpsons* and *Buffy the Vampire Slayer*.

But against these optimistic visions of the ultimate triumph of human goodness over evil, there is a profoundly pessimistic strain in the history of philosophy, as in the philosophy of Hobbes, according to which human beings are so entrenched in egotistical evil that only the external force of a fear-inspiring State can prevent them from demolishing one another. Hobbes's philosophy was a secularized expression and parallel formulation of his understanding of the Christian religion. For Christianity, as Hobbes understood it, only the God-man, Jesus Christ, by sacrificing himself on the cross, could save humanity from its entrenched sinfulness. Such is also the central idea of Mel Gibson's very popular film *The Passion of the Christ*. In this film, which vividly expresses a certain orthodox Christian theology, evil has so triumphed over mankind that only a superhuman being, a God-man, can free humanity from the clutches of the Evil One, and raise it from the depths to which it has sunk. We have seen that the *Matrix* trilogy poses the question of the Savior through the actions of "the One." Is "the One" a Savior who liberates humanity from its shackles, or a Teacher who shows people how to liberate themselves? All the while providing parallels with the Christian model, the *Matrix* trilogy take a clear position against the conception of the external Savior who liberates mankind from its imprisonment by evil powers through his superhuman abilities and ultimate self-sacrifice. This is the very type of Savior that Mel Gibson presents Jesus to have been. This conception of the external Savior presupposes a certain logic of justice rooted in the Hebrew Bible, the Old Testament of the Christians.

The Trials of Job

The book of Job presents a Biblical theory of justice that has much philosophical nuance and depth. Satan, whose name comes from the Hebrew word for "adversary," appears before the throne of God announcing humanity's widespread dereliction of God's laws. Evil is everywhere. But there is still one good man, God replies, his faithful servant Job. One good man is enough in God's eyes to justify humankind as a whole. Satan, however, has a response: for his faithful adherence to God's commands, Job is richly rewarded with family and flocks. Let me afflict him with sorrow and suffering, and then watch him recant his so-called morality. Paradoxically, it is Satan who here affirms the purity of morality by arguing that a performance of moral or religious duty that is motivated by rewards and punishments is not true morality. God agrees with this assessment and allows Satan to put Job's morality to the test by depriving him of his wealth, his family, and eventually his health. His friends, finding him so sorely struck down with loss and illness, are appalled. What have you done to bring such misery upon yourself? Your sins must have been great indeed, they charge. But Job protests his innocence before the all-seeing eyes of God:

> And this was a man that had bound his eyes over by covenant; never should even his fancy dwell upon the thought of a maid! Well I knew that God Almighty in high heaven would have neither part nor lot with me else; ruin for the sinner his doom is, disinheritance for the wrong-doer. . . . When I gazed on the sun in all its splendour, on the moon in her royal progress, did these things steal my heart away, so that mouth kissed hand in adoration? That were great wrong done, to deny the God who is higher than all.[1]

Job is faithful above all to the code of monotheism that condemns pagan worship of the splendors of creation and affirms sexual purity in the face of the rites of spring that were practiced by the neighboring polytheistic agricultural peoples. "Have wiles of woman entangled my heart; did I lie in wait under my neighbor's window?" (Job 31:9). He is also a fair dealer when it comes to commercial exchanges: "Walk I by crooked ways, run I eagerly after false dealing, he can weigh my offence with true scales; let God himself bear witness to my innocence!" (Job 31:5–6). The scales of justice, borrowed from the trader's craft, are perfectly balanced in Job's eyes. Why then does he suffer? For Job there are only two possibilities: either he has committed wrong, or God himself must be unjust. Having rejected the first of these options, he bitterly concludes that the second must be the case: "Why does he look on and laugh, when the unoffending, too, must suffer? So the whole world is given up into the power of wrong-doers; he blinds the eyes of justice. He is answerable for it; who else?" (Job 9:23–24). We previously considered this passage at the beginning of our chapter on Woody Allen's multileveled examination of justice in *Crimes and Misdemeanors*.

It is important to note that Job's conception of justice is thoroughly worldly. There is no question of an otherworldly reward. Job does not look forward to better things in an afterlife, for this earthly life is the only one for him:

> Bethink thee, Lord, it is but a breath, this life of mine, and I shall look on this fair world but once; when that is done, men will see me no more, and thou as nothing. Like a cloud dislimned in passing, man goes to his

grave never to return, never again the home-coming, never shall tidings of him reach the haunts he knew. And should I utter no word? (Job 7:7–11)

There is of course another possibility—Professor Levy's atheistic philosophy according to which "the universe is a pretty cold place." If there is supposed to be only one God who is both good and just, as the monotheistic religions affirm, then the suffering of the innocent is argument against the very existence of God. Such a position is unthinkable to Job. Like old Sol, you can use logic on him all day long and he will still believe in the existence of God. But Job has enough logic that he cannot turn a blind eye to the suffering of innocent people when he knows they are innocent. And he knows that he himself is an innocent man. He therefore takes an even harsher view of the universe than Professor Levy. It is worse than a cold place; it is the playground of an evil God.

Having heard this withering denunciation, God then, with great display of power, joins Job in verbal combat:

Then, from the midst of a whirlwind, the Lord gave Job his answer: Here is one that must ever be clouding the truth of things with words ill considered! Strip, then, and enter the lists; it is my turn to ask questions now, thine to answer them. From what vantage point wast thou watching, when I laid the foundations of the earth? Tell me, whence comes this sure knowledge of thine? Tell me, since thou art so wise, was it thou or I designed earth's plan, measuring it out with the line? How came its base to stand so firm; who laid its corner-stone? To me, that day, all the morning stars sang together, all the powers of heaven uttered their joyful praise. Was it thou or I shut in the sea behind bars? No sooner had it broken forth from the womb than I dressed it in swaddling-clothes of dark mist, set it within bounds of my own choosing, made fast with bolt and bar; Thus far thou shalt come, said I, and no further; here let thy swelling waves spend their force. (Job 38:1–11)

Thus is Job chastened. Who is he to match wits with the Creator of the universe? How should he measure God's ways with his own puny scales of justice—the God whose power is greater than the mighty seas and whose mercy is shown in the very steadiness of the earth under our feet? "I have spoken as fools speak," Job finally confesses, "of things far beyond my ken" (Job 42:3). With this admission of the transcendence of God and the mysteriousness of God's ways, Job successfully passes the test to which he has been put. He is rewarded with twice what he lost, lives on to one hundred and forty years, and dies the beloved patriarch of a great family of his descendents. The justice of God, elevated beyond a simplistic theory of crime and punishment, has thus been demonstrated in the case of the good man Job who nevertheless suffers. Morality too has been vindicated. We must do what is right, remaining confident of the ultimate triumph of justice, despite short-term evidences that would seem to contradict such an outcome. Suffering is thus a trial that proves the mettle of one's goodness, while justice is shown in the end with the deserved happiness of the moral hero.

The Suffering Servant of Isaiah

There is one glaring flaw in this argument. What should be said of the innocent servant of God who suffers unto death? What if the good person dies in the midst of his trial without any reward in sight? Isaiah describes the suffering servant of God:

> Despised and rejected of men;
> A man of sorrows, and acquainted with grief . . .
> he was despised, and we esteemed him not. . . . .
> We did esteem him stricken, smitten by God, and afflicted.[2]

So did the "friends" of Job look on him as stricken by God, but justly so, they thought, because of Job's own transgressions against divine law. In this case, however, the afflicted man is indeed afflicted by God, but not for his own sins. He is stricken down for the offenses of others. And as a result, a sinful people finds salvation:

> But he was wounded for our transgressions;
> He was crushed for our iniquities;
> Upon him was the chastisement that brought us peace,
> And with his stripes we are healed.
> All we like sheep have gone astray;
> We have turned every one to his own way;
> And the Lord has laid on him the iniquity of us all. (Isaiah 5–6)

The writer is referring to the sufferings of the prophets, such as was Isaiah himself. They protest against the injustices of kings and tyrants, as well as of the abuse of man by man, and suffer the consequences of their honesty and forthrightness with their own death. They willingly accept both suffering and death as the inevitable price they must pay for confronting powerful rulers who benefit from a world of inequality and so are afraid of their teachings regarding human equality, love, and forgiveness. There is no real difference here from the case of Socrates, who is sentenced to death for boldly challenging the authorities of his own time.

There is in this passage implicit reference to traditional Jewish rites of atonement. On the day of atonement (Yom Kippur) as described in the book of Leviticus, one bull and two young goats are selected to be sacrificed, the bull to be a burnt offering, one of the scapegoats to be slaughtered, the other sent out to the desert. Regarding the latter, Aaron the high priest "must put both hands on its head, confessing all the sins and transgressions and faults Israel has committed, and laying the guilt of them on its head. And there will be a man standing ready to take it into the desert for him; so the goat will carry away all their sins into a land uninhabited, set at large in the desert."[3] The sins of the people are thereby symbolically placed on the innocent scapegoat and, with appropriate ritual and repentant feeling, the sins are atoned through such acts. Whether at one time this ritual was understood magically as itself performing the saving sacrament of atonement, it came generally to be understood as an external symbol for an inner act of repentance. God does not really need the slaughtered animal. He wants the minds and hearts of human beings, where the true turning from evil must take place.

Isaiah evokes this symbolism by describing the suffering prophet in the role of the scapegoat—the innocent lamb of God who is led to the slaughter:

> He was oppressed and he was afflicted,
> Yet he opened not his mouth;
> Like a lamb that is led to the slaughter. . . .
> He was cut off out of the land of the living,
> Stricken for the transgression of my people. . . .
> There was no deceit in his mouth.
> Yet it was the will of the Lord to crush him;
> He has put him to grief. (Isaiah 53: 7–9)

It is God's will for a just world that the prophet upholds, as he upbraids the people for their waywardness, their oblivion of fundamental truths of human kinship. For this protest he must inevitably suffer the consequences brought upon him by vengeful and frightened people.

Ultimately, however, he will be justly rewarded for his efforts. But how is that possible in the context of Jewish this-worldliness? Murdered for his protest against an unjust society, he has no chance of living on like Job for one hundred and forty years and dying in the bosom of a great and loving family. How could otherworldly bliss for himself mean anything to the prophet who strives for justice in *this* world? The book of Isaiah therefore pictures the spirit of the deceased prophet looking down on earth and enjoying the triumph of his cause—the victory of his followers in creating a just and loving world, the final happiness of Zion, the Kingdom of God on earth:

He shall see the travail of his soul, and shall be satisfied;
by his knowledge shall my righteous servant justify many;
for he shall bear their iniquities.
Therefore will I divide him a portion with the greater,
and he shall divide the spoil with the strong;
because he hath poured out his soul unto death . . .
and he bare the sin of many,
and made intercession for the transgressors. (Isaiah 53:11–12)

It would have been with such an understanding that the prophet John the Baptist, himself about to be slain for telling truth to power, points out his successor Jesus to his disciples, saying "Behold! The Lamb of God who takes away the sins of the world."[4]

There is nothing in these understandings to suggest that the suffering servant literally pays for the sins committed by others through his own suffering. He points out the sins committed by his fellows, as well as by the rulers they blindly uphold, and for this he suffers the inevitable consequences of telling the truth. He does his duty and suffers for it, as is the way of things in a world governed largely by egotism. By his teaching and example, he calls the people back from their betrayal of moral truth, and leads them to the creation of a more just society. His spirit lives on to rejoice in the spectacle of the triumph of the cause he inspired.

Leading the Lamb to the Slaughter

However, a radically different interpretation, following the doctrine of the Council of Nicea (325 CE), takes literally the metaphor of the scapegoat, and sees Jesus, the unique Son of God, of the same divine substance as the Father, taking on his shoulders the sins of mankind and suffering all the punishment that is due to a sinful humanity. Later Christians, identifying the suffering servant of the book of Isaiah with Jesus, would interpret these passages literally: God's justice demands punishment for sin. But mankind is so given over to evil that were the evil justly punished mankind as a whole would be eternally doomed. God therefore spares the sinners by sending his own son to bear on his shoulders the weight of sin, and suffer the punishment himself. Through faith in this act of redemption, humanity then has access to divine forgiveness.

Looking back on the history of the Jewish people, the philosopher Levy in *Crimes and Misdemeanors* laments the story of the Bible in which God demands that Abraham sacrifice his beloved son Isaac. This shows, Levy concludes, that we have been unable to imagine a truly loving God. But according to the interpretation of the Nicene Creed, the God of Christianity is willing to sacrifice his own son to the harsh requirements of his own merciless justice. As a Jew, Woody Allen discretely confines his indictment to his own religious tradition.

According to the orthodox Christian theology of the Nicene Creed, then, God the Father sent his only begotten son into the world to atone for the sins of mankind. For God is a just God, and justice demands punishment for sin. But God is also merciful, loving. So instead of punishing humanity for its sinfulness, as we deserve, he sent a substitute, an innocent sinless being, his own son, to be punished on our behalf. Thus the demand for justice is satisfied, and God's loving mercy for humanity is simultaneously expressed. For this logic of atonement, the more innocent the victim, the greater is the sacrifice, and so the more sins are expiated. It follows that the harsher and more barbaric and brutal the punishment actually inflicted, the greater is the benefit in terms of the economics of salvation, where sin is bought back and redeemed at the price it demands.

How appropriate then, as the religious imagination soars on the wings of this bloodthirsty rationality, to suppose the most sadistic forms of violent torture inflicted by the most degraded specimens of human sinfulness! And so in *The Passion of the Christ* Mel Gibson does not spare his audience one drop of blood, one sliver of flesh, in his unflinching portrait of God's love for humanity. As if the punishment described in the Gospels were not enough, we see Jesus brutalized from the moment of his arrest and then plummeting over a bridge until his chains violently break his fall. As if the scourging of Jesus with ordinary whips were not enough, Mel Gibson adds razor blades to the humanly impossible torture. Not only is Jesus nailed to the cross, but the heavy cross falls so that now flesh-rending nails instead of gentler chains break his fall.

In exemplifying this theology, *The Passion of the Christ* draws a stunning portrait of the darkest side of the human soul. It depicts all the depravity, the malice, and the meaningless of what the religious imagination of a certain cast understands by sin. So we see a sinister Satan lurking behind scenes in which Goodness Himself is systematically, unequivocally, thoroughly, and completely desecrated and destroyed. As the sun is covered by black storm clouds at the moment of Christ's death, evil triumphs over good, darkness shuts out the light. Or so it seems.

And yet it was all for nothing. Satan's efforts were counterproductive, so that in the end we see him screaming uncontrollably in a fit of fury and frustration. The insane frenzy of punishment produces the opposite of what was intended. Jesus rises from the dead, whole in the flesh once again, except for a stigmatized body to remind his followers that what took place was not a dream. If the film, in its exhaustive depiction of the passion of the Christ, leaves little to the imagination, its final scene is a brilliant stroke of understatement. The solitary Savior sets out from his tomb with an uncanny expression of purposeful endeavor. The propitiation has been accomplished. He must now announce the achievement to his followers, so that they can bring the Good News to humankind: The sinner is no longer mired in his sin as long as he recognizes the means of his salvation, the terrible price that has been paid as his ransom from the maggoty stench of Satan's maw. Each drop of blood that was shed, which seemed only to deepen the pit of wickedness which humanity digs for itself, fills the chalice of communion with the Savior for whomever will drink of it. Although wholly sunk in unworthiness, the sinner who washes his sins in the blood of the lamb is raised to the highest heaven.

Hegel on the Death of God

In 1789, the German philosopher Georg Wilhelm Friedrich Hegel (1770–1831) entered the Protestant Seminary at Tübingen University in the German state of Württemberg with the goal of becoming a pastor or perhaps a theologian of the Lutheran Church. Under the powerful influence of the French Revolution, he and his friends and fellow seminarians, Johann Hölderlin (1770–1843) and Friedrich Schelling (1775–1854), became fervently caught up in the revolutionary movements for liberating Germany from despotic government in alliance with a corrupt Church interested primarily in sanctifying the privileges of wealth and power. In his ongoing effort to comprehend the historical events of his time, Hegel sought the roots of this corruption in a distortion of the real teachings of Christianity, which he understood as truly manifested in the principles of liberty, equality, and brother-and-sisterhood that inspired the French Revolution. Although Hegel abandoned his initial plan of becoming a pastor for the career of a university professor, he continued throughout his life to deepen his goal of reconciling Christianity with revolutionary French Enlightenment ideals of a community founded on freedom and equality, and fully in accord with the higher requirements of dialectical rationality.

Central to this goal was the critique of feudal and medieval ideas of hierarchical political systems and their alliance with hierarchically organized religion. Hegel understood the theological revolution of Martin Luther (1483–1546) to be a radical critique of an external Savior and of the institution of religion as an indispensable mediator between God and a fallen, sinful humanity. The fundamental theological justification of this hierarchical religion is the notion of the radical separation of Creator and creature, of God and humanity. To overcome this separation, a God-man is required to mediate between God and fallen humanity. And when that Savior returns to Heaven after enacting the saving sacrifice of his flesh and blood, the Church takes his place on earth as the indispensable means of salvation from the threat of eternal damnation. The theology of atonement thus underpins the hierarchical power of the priesthood over the laity, with all the potentiality for abuse that this implies. The greatest abuse, for Hegel, is the abuse of human intelligence itself.

It is not the degradation but the exaltation of the human spirit, expressed in Luther's conception of the priesthood of the laity, that is for Hegel the deep meaning of Christianity. Christianity rejects the notion of an unattainable deity and the separation of God and humanity in its astounding portrait of God becoming a human being and dying the wretched death of a criminal on the cross. In his *Lectures on the Philosophy of Religion* (1827), Hegel reflects on the Christian doctrine of "the death of God": "'God himself is dead,' it says in a Lutheran hymn, expressing an awareness that the human, the finite, the fragile, the weak, the negative are themselves moments of the divine, that they are within God himself, that finitude, negativity, otherness are not outside of God and do not, as otherness, hinder unity with God."[5] Hegel calls the Christian vision of the death of God "a monstrous, fearful picture [*Vorstellung*], which brings before the imagination the deepest abyss of cleavage."[6] The cleavage or separation of God and humanity culminates in Jesus's cry from the cross: "My God, my God, why have you forsaken me?" (Mark 15:34; Matthew 27:46). While suggesting the monstrous, fearful picture presented by *The Passion of the Christ*, Hegel develops an alternative interpretation to the traditional theology of the atonement.

According to Hegel, the central teaching of Christianity is that Jesus is both God and man, both human and divine. He emphasizes Jesus's statement in the Fourth Gospel: "I and the Father are one" (John 10:30).[7] The death of Jesus must therefore be the death of God. But instead of separating Jesus as the divine God-man from the rest of humanity, as the orthodox theology of atonement maintains, this doctrine serves instead to elevate humanity as a whole from its false conception of separation from God to the same oneness proclaimed by Jesus. Accused of blasphemy in asserting his oneness with God, Jesus replies, according to the Fourth Gospel: "Is it not written in your law, 'I said, you are gods?'"[8] The holy Scripture itself, Jesus here replies to his critics, calls even the corrupted leaders of the people "gods." He who believes in Jesus, that is, he who understands and puts into practice what he teaches, knows that he too is one with the Father.

In an interview for *Hollywood Jesus News*, Mel Gibson affirms both the theology of atonement and the death of God: "There is no greater hero story than this one, about the greatest love one can have, which is to lay down one's life for someone. The Passion is the biggest adventure story of all time. I think it's the biggest love-story of all time; God becoming man and men killing God. If that's not action, nothing is. . . . Christ paid the price for all our sins."[9]

But what can it possibly mean to say that God died on the cross? We have outlined two conceptions of the death of Jesus. There is the theology of atonement which informs *The Passion of the Christ* according to which the sacrifice of the unique Son of God redeems a sinful humanity. And there is Hegel's quite different conception that if the man Jesus is truly God, then humanity itself, the human species to which Jesus belongs, must be fundamentally one with God. The crucifixion of Jesus then epitomizes the depth of darkness to which a human being can fall, and consequently, humanity, despite and within all the negativity we are capable of experiencing, constitutes a "moment . . . within God himself."

Kierkegaard's Leap of Faith

Hegel's alternative conception of Christianity is based on his distinctive theory of the relation between faith and reason. Contrasting Hegel's conception of the relation of reason and faith with that of the Hegel's later critic, Søren Kierkegaard (1813–55), will help clarify Hegel's position.

For most ordinary Christians, focusing on these images of the suffering, death, and resurrection of the Son of God, the core teaching of Christianity is an unfathomable mystery. How the infinite God can be at the same time a finite human being baffles ordinary rationality. Instead of trying to comprehend the mystery, the pious Christian normally attempts to feel its meaning, to experience it awe-inspiring power. Like Luke in *Star Wars,* she puts aside her ordinary rationality with its either/or logic and attempts to feel something that is evoked by this paradoxical idea that the finite human can be one with the infinite divine.

Kierkegaard seems at first to support this essentially nonrational, emotional nature of ordinary religious piety. However, he does so in the context of attacking a theology which represents Christianity as a doctrine that is addressed primarily to the rational intellect. Against such a theology, Kierkegaard maintains that belief in the unity of divine and human in Jesus requires a surpassing of all logic and all reason, a leap of faith. The radical replacement of reason by faith, Kierkegaard argues, is the very heart of religion. Reason separates and compartmentalizes according to a logic of "either-or." There is either God or man—there cannot be both. Here is God—the infinite, the all-powerful, the absolute—and here is the human—the finite, the impotent, the negative. Logic formulates the matter clearly: there is A and not-A, the divine and the nondivine, that is, the wretched human, the almost-nothing by comparison with the everything of God. But Christianity teaches that, in Christ, A is indeed identical with non-A. In this core Christian doctrine, therefore, the fundamental law of reason, the law of noncontradiction, is flagrantly violated. To be a Christian, then, logic must be utterly transcended by a leap of faith.

Kierkegaard sees himself as the gadfly of the contemporary "Christendom" of his time, in both its practical aspects and in its theological doctrine. In practice, there is nothing in the comfortable lifestyles of the churchmen of his time to suggest the sacrificial path of worldly renunciation found in the example of Jesus himself. The theology in vogue in Kierkegaard's Denmark, heavily influenced by Hegel, was similarly complacent, giving the impression that there is nothing in Christianity that a rational individual could not accept. Kierkegaard pitted himself especially against this "Hegelian" understanding. Do Christians who hear the words of their faith recognize how thoroughly they contradict the rationality that guides them in everyday life? Such rationality may guide us in the sphere of moral obligations, as Kant argues. But religious faith requires that we leap beyond logic and the universal laws of reason, including the laws of morality. Religious faith instead is about the unutterably singular—the meeting with God where no general rule can guide us. When God tells Abraham to sacrifice his son Isaac, Abraham does not flinch from undertaking what in the eyes of morality is the most despicable act of murder, that of one's own beloved son. When this story is intoned from the pulpit on a Sunday, how many who hear the words really listen to what is being said, and so become fully aware of the intellectual scandal that is posed by their faith?

The philosopher Levy, we can add, clearly recognizes this scandal, and chooses reason instead of such a scandalous faith. He therefore rejects the very notion of a God who could command such a foul deed. Mitigating the scandal, of course, is the fact that this God does not oblige Abraham to carry out the murder. Bringing the knife to his son's throat is enough to prove his faith. Abraham passes the test, and the audience to this story is relieved with the happy ending. In Thomas Mann's *Joseph and his Brothers*, the favored son Joseph comes across his distraught father, Jacob, and asks him why he is so sorrowful. Jacob replies that he has been thinking about the great story of his grandfather Abraham and his father Isaac. He doesn't believe that his faith is as strong as that of Abraham, he sighs. If God were to command him now to kill Joseph, he doesn't think he could do it. Joseph consoles his unhappy father. Don't worry, father, I'm sure you could, he replies tenderly, if disconcertingly for the reader.

Isn't it an even greater scandal to all reason and morality, Kierkegaard asks, for God to sacrifice His own Son—and this time with no scapegoat available as a substitute, no earthly reward forthcoming as the result of passing such a test of faith, as was the case in the Old Testament story. And so the question, Who killed Christ? has only one answer: God Himself, the Father who sent his only Son to the slaughterhouse. The fact that God knows that his divine Son is immortal does not to lessen the sacrifice, the pain, the negativity, the real death, for the Son is also, incomprehensibly, a fully human being.

Hegel on the Relation between Faith and Reason

Although Kierkegaard directed much of his exposition of the nature of religion against Hegel's earlier thought, it is debatable which of the two philosophers was more ready to emphasize the idea that the central teachings of Christianity are a stumbling block to ordinary rationality. When Hegel says that the death of Jesus equals the death of God, and, perhaps slyly, cites a Lutheran hymn as evidence of the theological orthodoxy of this assertion, he recognizes that ordinary rationality must find such a notion incomprehensible. But for Hegel there is no leap of faith into the abyss of intellectual blackness, or blinding light—the two are equivalent. For Hegel, the images proposed by Christianity contain profound truths that the rational human mind, on its own level, is capable of appreciating and comprehending. Such rationality does not, however, *replace* the distinctly religious level of feeling and imagination, as Kierkegaard supposed, based on the writings of the Danish theologians he criticized. The philosophical understanding of Christianity that Hegel proposes parallels and complements, but does not substitute for, the proper domain of religion, which appeals to a different level of consciousness. To grasp in conceptual terms the truth that Christian religion presents at the level of feeling and imagination, it is indeed necessary to go beyond ordinary logic and the metaphysics of reality that is closely linked to such logic. But beyond this ordinary logic of what Hegel calls "the abstract understanding," there is a higher form of reason linked to a more flexible, more real and living logic—the dialectical logic of the movement of forms of human existence that both contradict and yet logically require one another.

The Christian religion—indeed all religion—takes us beyond ordinary logic, the logic that regulates the operations of the empirical sciences and related technologies. So science and religion seem inevitably to be in conflict. Theologians and scientists may find some common ground in considering such matters as whether or not God created the universe in the Big Bang. But what can the scientist say to the Christian teaching that this same God who could produce a universe became an individual human being and died on a cross to redeem sinful humanity? Surely Hegel and Kierkegaard are right in focusing on the unintelligibility of this notion for the ordinary logical mind.

And yet, in our scientific age the thinking mind becomes ever more insistent on its own right to explore all aspects of consciousness and human experience. This requirement of reason opens up the possibility of a fundamental misunderstanding of the nature of religious consciousness in the supposition that religious teachings are directed to the intellect, rather than being addressed to feeling and imagination. Science nevertheless poses a legitimate demand to find intelligibility even in areas of experience where nonrational forms of consciousness predominate. So there can be a philosophy of art without supposing that art is something essentially rational. And there can be a philosophy of religion, without attempting to replace religion with reason.

Traditionally, the problem of the relation between faith and reason has been solved by drawing a line somewhere and saying, up to this point we have the sphere of reason, and beyond this we have truths that are made accessible to us only by revelation. But if you can't make any sense of these teachings of revelation, what does it mean to believe in them? If you don't really know *what it means* to say that God has become human and dies the death of a criminal, how can you accept this incomprehensible idea on faith? If someone whom you regard as reliable tells you that he has seen flying saucers, you understand what he means by this and so you can decide whether or not to accept what he says as a revelation for you. But if the revelation involves a logical contradiction, implying that A and not-A are one and the same, what can it mean to accept this on faith? This is what Christian doctrine appears to be saying in affirming the oneness of God and humanity, of the divine and the non-divine, in the person of Jesus. Kierkegaard holds that this is in fact the very point of Christianity. By presenting us with the rationally unintelligible contradiction of A and not-A, it provides a springboard beyond reason into the arms of a transforming, reason-obliterating life of faith. Kierkegaard gives expression to a Christian tradition going back to Tertullian, who, in combat with the pagan rationalistic philosophers as well as Gnostic Christians, exulted in the very unintelligibility of Christian doctrine: *Credo quia absurdum.* I must believe in it, because this is something that is absurd for purely rational understanding.

Hegel agrees that religion is not something rational. It operates through images or "picture thinking" rather than through concepts. Its main appeal is not to the intellect but to the emotions. The faithful Christian *feels* the infinity of God—the melting of the finite into the infinite, of the individual personality into the All—and projects this feeling into the images portrayed visibly and tangibly by religion. So religious devotion is expressed in such practices as meditating on the Stations of the Cross where the believer reenacts for himself the dissolution of the finite personality by emotionally identifying with the images of the suffering and death of Jesus. It is in such a frame of mind that the ordinary believing Christian approaches *The Passion of the Christ.* In this amalgam of feeling and imagination there are no logical or conceptual difficulties to be surmounted—contrary to what Kierkegaard requires for authentic religion. The religious person does not raise logical problems because she does not think rationally about her faith in the first place, but engages in a radically different form of consciousness—primarily that of feeling. The human being is not merely a rational being, but also a being of feeling as well as of imagination. We do not demand a rational formulation of the lines of a poem, and neither should we do so of religion. To do either is to destroy the integrity of these distinctive forms of awareness.

For Hegel ordinary religious faith does not need the mental gymnastics recommended by Kierkegaard: beginning with reason, becoming aware of the contradictions involved, and then using the contradiction as a springboard to faith. Ordinary religious belief is a radically different form of consciousness from that of mental or rational thought. In the religious consciousness, feeling is connected with thinking in images—not in the concepts of the rational mind. For most believers the doctrines of theology are labels for images that engender feeling, not concepts to be reflected upon by the rational mind. There is therefore a basic misunderstanding of religious consciousness in Kierkegaard's idea that the individual must first consider the teachings of religion from a logical perspective in order to leap beyond logic to a reason-shattering religious consciousness.

As Hegel says above, Christianity first presents a monstrous "picture" [*Vorstellung*] of the death of God. Religious consciousness operates through images or "picture thinking" rather than through concepts. Its main appeal is not to the intellect but to the emotions. The faithful Christian *feels* the infinity of God, and thereby emotionally enacts the melting of the finite into the infinite, of the individual personality into the All. The images of religion both foster and reflect such feeling. Similarly, through imagination and feeling, the Christian believer who attends a showing of *The Passion of the Christ* relives for himself the dissolution of the finite personality into the infinity of the divine by identifying with the images of the suffering and death of Jesus. Perhaps above all the film's depiction of the *Mater Dolorosa*, the sorrowing mother of Jesus, invites us to identify with the suffering Jesus through a mother's love, so anxious to avoid any harm to her child, yet compelled to accompany him helplessly on this gruesome journey. All the egotistical concerns of the separate personality dissolve in a mother's love that knows no limits. This is not a matter of doctrine about the separation of God and man and the need for a Savior, but a feeling, an experience—the experience of oneness with infinite motherly love which Christianity tells us is the real meaning of God.

Reflective consciousness balks at the theoretical interpretation of this picture given by the doctrine of atonement. What kind of mother would send her own son to such a death? As a work of art, Mel Gibson's film invites us to *identify* with Jesus as the good son of his loving mother, a talented carpenter who is proud of his work, a man who sees through a hierarchical society's hypocritical condemnation of the prostitute to the beautiful soul of Mary Magdalene and thereby recognizes her own real worth. Above all we identify with Jesus as a being of flesh and blood like ourselves, and so we cringe with every flailing stroke of the whip. But the theology of atonement puts Jesus on a pedestal and deifies him in a realm utterly apart from us, the audience. This theoretical *understanding* implicitly obstructs our identification with the action hero Jesus that the film wants us to *feel* and conflicts with the requirements of both art and religion.

Blaise Pascal (1623–1662), the first Christian apologist of the dawn of modern science, said, "The heart has its reasons, which reason does not know."[11] Pascal contrasts the emotional sphere of the heart with the mental sphere of reason and at the same time points to another kind of rationality that is intrinsically connected to the feelings of the heart. Hegel attempts to develop just such a heartfelt form of rationality through his conception of dialectical reason that explores the multiform phenomena of consciousness. Dialectical reason is capable of taking us into spheres of consciousness that are off limits to ordinary rationality with its logic of either A or not-A. Hegel's *Phenomenology of Spirit* takes us into spheres of consciousness where contradictions are rife yet meaningful, transformative impulses to growth from limited to more comprehensive perspectives.

On the Separation of Creator and Creation

From the point of view of ordinary logic, the unity of God and not-God is not comprehensible, to be sure. But so, argues Hegel, is their separation. If there is a created world outside of God, then God cannot be infinite. If there is something that is not-God—the finite, limited world of mortal creatures—then God too must be a finite being who is *other than* what is not Him—other than, for example, a finite human being condemned to die.[11]

A God outside of the world may be very large, very powerful, far more than the world he creates, but he remains one distinct finite being along side all the rest. This is how the ancient polytheists pictured their gods—bigger, more powerful than the humans they lord over, but otherwise finite beings just as we are. To say that there is only one such overlord does not change the substance of the matter. But this view rejects the commonly held Christian notion that God is *infinite*. If God is infinite, the unbounded totality of all that is, there can be nothing outside of God. The orthodox theologian who insists on the separation of God and the world, and so the need for a external mediator and a caste of priests to save us, fails to go beyond the level of ancient polytheism with its powerful but finite divinities, and fails to rise to the level of authentic Christianity. If God is truly infinite then everything that exists must be within God. If there is something outside God, then God cannot truly be infinite, but simply one being alongside others. But if God is infinite, it follows that "the human, the finite, the fragile, the weak, the negative, are themselves moments of the divine."[12]

The Christian teaching that God has become a human being is intimately linked to the doctrine that God is infinite. The separation of Creator and creature is a projection of the narrow vantage point of the separate ego. This was understood by the great Christian mystic and theologian, Meister Eckhart (ca. 1260–1328). Hegel cites with approval the teaching of this Christian mystic: "The eye with which God sees me is the eye with which I see him: my eye and his eye are the same." This is not the God of Job, nor that of old Sol in "Crimes and Misdemeanor," the lofty deity who sees all our deeds from above and beyond the world. Hegel cites Eckhart's rejection of the separation of God and the human being: "If God did not exist nor would I; if I did not exist nor would he."[13]

The same fundamentally Christian idea of the unity of God and humanity is at the foundation of modern Western philosophy. If Descartes begins with "I think," he goes on to show that all thinking takes place in the light of the idea of God, which is the ideal of perfection to which we humans inevitably aspire in theoretical science and practical life. Jean-Paul Sartre follows this Cartesian idea when he argues, "God, the value and supreme end of transcendence, represents the permanent limit in terms of which man makes known to himself what he is. To be man means to reach towards being God. Or if you prefer, man fundamentally is the desire to be God."[14] To understand what "God" means, we must understand what a human being is. In chapter 6, we saw that for Hegel the human being is initially the universal life force become conscious of itself in self-conscious individual human beings. In the full development of human consciousness this life force is realized as the Holy Spirit of the loving community, an I that is a We and a We that is an I.

The Unhappy Consciousness

For his consistent affirmation of the Christian doctrine that God and humanity are one, Meister Eckhart was condemned by the Church as a heretic. The theology of atonement insists on the radical separation of God and humanity, with the one exception being the God-man, Jesus. But how can God and humanity be radically separate if even one human being can be God? Such would-be orthodox theology is not content with enunciating images for the devotional expression of feeling, but claims the status of conceptual thought for its representations. Consequently, this conceptual theology inevitably falls within the evolution of contradictory forms of consciousness explored in Hegel's *Phenomenology*. Specifically, the theology of atonement occupies the place in the evolution of consciousness that Hegel calls "The Unhappy Consciousness." The theologians of Kierkegaard's Denmark made the mistake of confusing religious and philosophical levels of consciousness, and so fell afoul of Kierkegaard's own dialectical deconstructions and reconstructions. But because he mistakenly took his socially complacent and rationalistic theologians for Hegelians, Kierkegaard failed to understand Hegel's own dialectical phenomenology as a unity-in-opposition of understanding and emotion.

The Unhappy Consciousness is a moment or stage in the evolution of the master-slave dialectic that arises in Hegel's *Phenomenology* out of the standpoint of the separate ego. We have seen in the previous chapter that the ego inevitably confronts other egos in a life-and-death struggle. Out of fear of death, the losers in this struggle submit to the winners, and so the standpoint of the ego gives rise to a society of masters and slaves, of dominators and dominated, or rulers and ruled.[15] It is in the context of the Roman slave empire that early Christianity affirms the moral supremacy of the slave over the master. It is the slave, by really transforming nature through his intelligent labor, Hegel argues, who ultimately triumphs over the master—reduced to passivity and indolence, as well as unmitigated brutality. Hegel supports this reversal of the master morality by Christianity.

Hegel's dialectic of master and slave anticipates Friedrich Nietzsche's (1844–1900) notion that Christianity is an expression of "slave morality." But for Hegel, if Jesus appeals to the slave with his blessings for the outcasts, the prostitutes, the disfigured, and the despised of contemporary Jewish society, he transforms the spirit of abasement with his teaching that humility of the ego is a necessary step for recognizing that beyond narrow ego-consciousness the human being is essentially divine, the dwelling place of the Kingdom of God. The death of Jesus represents the death of all that is finite and vulnerable in human existence and the demonstration, through his resurrection, that human beings are truly one with Infinite Being. What dies on the cross on Mount Calvary is both God and humanity: God as the transcendent Creator, separate from his creations, and the separate human individual, a finite, fragile, negative being. Resurrected from this twofold negation is the unity of God and human being as the universal truth of the unlimited power and fulfillment of the loving human community, which Jesus called the Kingdom of God on earth. The true meaning of the Church therefore is not that of a hierarchical power over the laity, but the loving community that implicitly embraces all of humanity. In this way, the ideas of the French revolution find their roots in an egalitarian Christianity of universal human brother- and sisterhood.

But before attaining this kingdom, the human being as a finite, separate individual must recognize the nullity of the separate ego, and so descend to the depths of the Unhappy Consciousness. For this consciousness, God is an unreachable Beyond, and the human being is less than nothing, a mere worm, lower than the beasts in fact for being truly bestial, like the human-looking brutes in *The Passion of the Christ* who laugh as they flay the helpless flesh of Jesus. What is the real meaning of sin, Hegel asks, if not the separation of the self as a finite ego from all the rest of reality, from Infinite Being. Such separation or "cleavage" produces the knowledge of good and evil, the world of duality and separation.[16] Prior its descent to this unhappy position, the finite, separate ego boasts of its truth and power as the center of the universe, its lord and master. We have seen that a *world* of such egos unleashes what the philosopher Hobbes calls "a war of all against all" and what Hegel calls "the life-and-death struggle." The world of separate egos is a reign of murder in which each ego attempts to triumph over every other ego. Inevitably some egos do triumph over others, producing the world of masters and slaves. This world is epitomized by the Roman slave empire, into which was born the babe of Bethlehem.

The ultimate truth implicit in the master-slave dialectic is the illusory nature of the separate ego. The slave, both because of her abasement before the master and the achievement of her creative work, is much closer to this truth than the master, who glories in his separate individuality with all the displays of pomp and circumstance that the spoils of conquest and the creative efforts of his slaves can produce. The pathetic weakness of the master, in contrast to the dignity of the slave, is seen in the contrast that *The Passion of the Christ* draws between the dithering Roman governor, Pontius Pilate, and the simple yet courageous Simon of Cyrene. Simon is a kind of Everyman, naturally reluctant to be dragooned into an awful job with no pay and no glory, but soon siding with the oppressed Jesus. Hang in there, friend, he tells Jesus; it will all be over soon.

The slave mentality nevertheless has some devices for avoiding the lesson of the essential nullity of the separate and separating ego consciousness. Stoic philosophy teaches that true freedom is freedom of thought and such freedom is attainable even for the individual in shackles. But Skeptical philosophy, which dialectically follows on the heals of Stoicism in the *Phenomenology*, undermines the pretenses of such abstract rationality, showing that to every would-be universal truth affirmed by the Stoic an opposite truth is just as convincingly defensible. The Stoic calmly accepts the fact that the physical being of the slave has been reduced to a state of impotence, but glories in the superiority of the mind. For the Stoic, mere bodily existence, whether in chains or on the throne, is insignificant, for true freedom is only available to the mind. However, through the attacks of a relentless Skepticism, the mind of the Stoic too is revealed as empty of any concrete truth. Because the Stoic abstracts from the concrete world of the struggle of masters and slaves, his truths are purely formal ones: do what you have to do. If you are a slave, be a (good) slave. If you are a master, be a (good) master. For the Skeptic such alleged truths are mere tautologies and so empty of any real meaning. As this Skeptical consciousness penetrates the Stoic defenses, the truth that seemed to be within the grasp of Stoic consciousness recedes into "an unattainable beyond."[17] The Stoic had argued that the mind is everything and the body nothing. But with the discovery that the vaunted achievements of purely mental existence are an illusion, there is nothing left to contemplate but the bodily existence that he has previously reduced to insignificance. Thus the deflated consciousness that has passed through Stoicism and Skepticism is left to contemplate the essential nothingness of both body and soul.

Jesus as Sinful Human Being

This anguish over the nothingness of the separate ego, the Unhappy Consciousness, is vividly depicted in *The Passion of the Christ*, both in Jesus's agonized plea in the Garden of Gethsemane that he be spared the coming trial, and more completely in his despairing cry from the cross: "My God, my God, why have you forsaken me?" Here we are furthest from the conception of a deified Jesus who is radically different from ordinary humanity. How is this completely human anguish compatible with the doctrine of the God-man, separate from the rest of us? Another artist, inspired by another conception of Christianity, would linger over this moment as Hegel does in his lectures, in which Jesus plumbs the depths of human despair. Hegel's interpretation radically departs from the theology of atonement. Jesus saves sinners only by being one of them.

In plumbing the depths of the radical separateness of the finite ego, Jesus embodied human sinfulness to its fullest extent. The deep spiritual meaning of the atonement is at-one-ment: the at-oneness or reconciliation of the human and the divine through the death of the separate self. It is not that Jesus, as a separate deified individual, takes on the sins of others and sacrifices himself for them, but that he himself fully embodies human sinfulness, that is, human finitude and separation, to the extent of dying the infamous death of a criminal on the cross. In the context of Roman civilization Jesus was indeed a criminal for his teaching of the oneness of God and humanity, profoundly contradicting the hierarchical authority of the Roman slave-state with its religion of the unique god-man, the Emperor. And yet despite this teaching, and his continued *intellectual* awareness of his essential oneness with God, Jesus *felt* to the depths of his soul the separation of the finite, fallen, ego-based human consciousness. One who does not know of his oneness with God can never truly experience the paradox and pain of abandonment: of feeling separate from the being one nevertheless is. Hence, it was *his own* sinfulness that was "expiated" through his death.[18]

Jesus is not a scapegoat for others; he did not expiate the sins of others. He suffered the price exacted by the ego-consciousness of humanity through his own embodiment of this consciousness. In taking human sinfulness to its final stage of self-conscious despair, he showed the Way and the Truth for each of us. He who taught about the implicit or essential unity of the human being and the divine fully embodied the finite, the fragile, the negative character of the separate ego unto its death. In the anguish of his abandonment on the cross, Jesus both comprehended and transcended the Unhappy Consciousness of the separate ego and so initiated a new stage in which human consciousness grasps its true nature. Having taken the all-too-human form of ego consciousness to its logical conclusion in an ignominious death, he died to death itself, and so rose from this death in the transformed existence of Spirit. In the final scene of *The Passion of the Christ*, this Spirit is identified with Jesus as a solitary Savior. For Hegel, however, the resurrected Spirit is primarily that of the revolutionary new human community that has overcome the Unhappy Consciousness.

The resurrection of Jesus brings out the full meaning of his death. The death of God is at the same time the death of death, for Spirit is precisely that inner bond within each human being that unites with others and so survives the death of the finite separate self. Hegel defines Spirit [*Geist*] as the overcoming of the separate ego: "'I' that is 'We,' and 'We' that is 'I.'" The "I" that confronts all the separate "I"s in a life-and-death struggle must die to this separation to rise to the level of Spirit. This full meaning of the human Spirit as the overcoming of the separation of the ego and the Unhappy Consciousness to which it leads is the goal of the *Phenomenology*, a goal that is *implicitly* realized in the religious experience of the Christian who identifies, in the form of feeling, with the death of Jesus.

The Calvary of Absolute Spirit

The remainder of Hegel's *Phenomenology* consists in bringing this implicit state of transformed consciousness into an adequate conceptual form by overcoming all remaining limited understandings and forms of experience. The following chapters of the *Phenomenology* explore these developments. We have seen how Goethe's *Faust* occupies one moment in this process, the moment in which an abstract intellectualism confronts its emptiness and yearns for the vital force of emotional love. At the conclusion of the *Phenomenology*, Hegel calls the preceding stages of consciousness the "Calvary of Absolute Spirit."[19] In this formulation, Hegel declares that the *Phenomenology* as a whole, with its successive stages of the evolution of limited forms of human consciousness driven by contradiction, constitutes the full unfolding of the meaning of the crucifixion of Jesus.

By placing the burden of universal human self-transformation exclusively on the shoulders of the separate God-man Jesus, the theology of atonement remains fixated at the stage of the Unhappy Consciousness. In holding that the individual must affirm his own essential nothingness before an almighty Beyond, and so requires a mediator to save him, this theology ultimately fixes the sinner in his sin and establishes him as incapable of real redemption. No one can perform the transformation of consciousness that saves us from the nullity of the isolated ego for anyone else. Jesus doesn't save us; we, following Jesus's lead, save ourselves. So the *Matrix* trilogy argues, as the Kid tells Neo, "You saved me." And Neo, rejecting the role of the superman savior in which he has been cast, replies, "You saved yourself." Against the superficial theology of atonement, the teachings of Jesus present at the level of feeling and picture-thinking or in parables what conceptual philosophy shows to be the fundamental meaning of the human spirit. In this way reason is not replaced by or cancelled by faith, but faith finds its counterpart in a rational understanding that complements, elucidates, and justifies the religious evocation of feeling. Enlightenment philosophy, achieving its mature form in dialectical reasoning through the philosophy of Hegel, demonstrates that the history of humanity is the crucifixion and resurrection of Absolute Spirit.

The Passion of the Christ concludes with the resurrected Jesus setting out to announce his message. But what is this message; what is the Good News? That humans are abject sinners incapable of saving themselves and yet happily find themselves saved by Jesus? Or that the human spirit is indeed indestructible, and that we must all reach beyond our own separate ego-identification, like the two Marys and Simon, and recognize the reflection of divinity in each human being? *The Passion of the Christ,* insofar as it embodies the theology of separation, wants to perpetuate the radical human abasement of the Unhappy Consciousness, but in its fidelity to the Gospel account, which includes heroes and heroines as well as villains, it implicitly challenges this theology.

Hegel's own treatment of the passion of the Christ does not end with the death and resurrection of Jesus, but continues with the story of the new human community founded on the recognition of the Holy Spirit as an I that is a We and a We that is an I. This is the Kingdom of Heaven, which Jesus likens to a mustard seed.[20] It cannot therefore be an other-worldly realm of rewards and punishments. It starts as the tiniest of seeds in the hearts of individuals who recognize the holiness of humanity in one another. It naturally multiplies and spreads until it makes the earth a welcome abode for all of humanity. Hegel stresses the words of Jesus that he must go away, or die, so that the Comforter, the Holy Spirit, can descend on his followers.[21] Otherwise they would be tempted to turn the individual Jesus into a separate deity, and establish separatist communities of believers depending on whether or not they accept this new god—instead of recognizing the divine where it belongs, in themselves as human beings, bound together in spirit, in love. Jesus therefore really has to die, to leave the scene, Hegel says, for his teachings to be truly understood. For his teaching is not about himself as a special being, but about what is special in all of us.

Just as it is not necessary for us today to repeat all the illusion and suffering of slave society in concrete forms to grasp the lessons of this history, so we do not have to be nailed to a cross to die to the separate ego. The historical Jesus dramatically performed this exemplary act in the flesh. But each human being must repeat this death in the recognition of his or her own consciousness, and so be reborn in the awareness of our oneness with universal Spirit, that is, of the oneness of the individual with all humanity, and ultimately with All That Is, the Infinite Reality. The kingdom of God on earth is present here and now for those who understand the meaning of the evolution of human experience. This, Hegel brilliantly shows, is the deep meaning of Christianity.

For Jesus, we are all, like him, sons and daughters of God. And so the one prayer that he taught begins with the words, "Our Father." As in Jesus's parable of the prodigal son, as separate human egos we get lost in the worldly pursuit of riotous living, until we are reduced to a state of despair.[22] In chapter 6 we have seen how Spirit is "involved" already in matter so that matter can "evolve" into Spirit. Such a conceptual understanding is presented emotionally in the picture-language of the Christian religion. As in the parable of the Prodigal Son, the Father God allows his Son, the expression of himself in ordinary human ego-consciousness, to go into the world to have experiences of limitedness, want and conflict, anguish and despair. For only by overcoming the illusory state of nondivinity, can the divine essence of each individual be fully appreciated. And so, we human beings live our lives of noisy or quiet desperation in our various forms of isolation from the Infinity of Being. The Father, personifying in an emotionally laden picture the starting point of the dialectic logic of Spirit, knows that such a life leads inevitably to the crucifixion of the ego, but gives Himself, in the form of the Son, in the form of ego-centered human life, to this experience. The inevitable abandonment, impoverishment, and spiritual death to which this experience leads is not the end of the story, however. The Son, abandoning the abandonment, returns to the Father in the unity of the Holy Spirit, reborn in the experience of his inalienable truth as a being inseparable from all other beings, one with the All, an I that is a We and a We that is an I. In this way Hegel explains the philosophical essence of the Christian doctrine of the Trinity, which is also the theoretical meaning for philosophical consciousness of the Passion of the Christ.[23]

Jesus says that whatever we do to the least of his brothers and sisters we do to him, for there is no separation between Jesus and the most wretched human being.[24] It is Hegel's thought, not the theology of atonement, that gives full meaning to the words of Jesus: "He who believes in me, the works that I do he will do also; and greater works than these. . . ."[25]

In today's world of global economic unification, doctrines that promote religious exclusivity, like the theology of atonement, exacerbate the dangers of violence and the threats of war. According to Hegel, the God that rules over an unworthy humanity from a lofty heaven is the reflection of a human world of masters and slaves, rulers and ruled. The God of Christianity instead is one with the wretched of the earth, dying the death of a criminal, so that even the lowliest human beings can discover that the kingdom of heaven is within them, but only when they are willing to join together across separating political and religious borders to create a world that is worthy of us. Is it not written in the Scriptures, Jesus said to his critics, that you are gods?[26]

NOTES

1. Job 31:1–7, 31:26–29. In Ronald Knox's translation, *The Holy Bible* (New York: Sheed and Ward, 1956). Subsequent references to the book of Job are to this edition unless otherwise noted.

2. Isaiah 53:3–4, King James Version. Subsequent references to the book of Isaiah are to the King James Version.

3. Leviticus 16:20–22 (Knox translation).

4. John 1:29 (New King James Version).

5. Georg Wilhelm Friedrich Hegel, *Lectures on the Philosophy of Religion*, ed.

Peter C. Hodgson (Berkeley, CA: University of California Press, 1985), 3:326.

6. Hegel, *Lectures on the Philosophy of Religion*, 3:125.

7. Hegel, *Lectures on the Philosophy of Religion*, 3:121.

8. John 10:34; see Psalms 82:6.

9. David Bruce, ed., "Mel Gibson Interview," April 23, 2003, http://www.hollywoodjesus.com/newsletter053.htm (accessed 11/22/2005).

10. Blaise Pascal, *Pascal's Pensées,* no. 277 (New York: E. P. Dutton & Co., Inc, 1958), 78.

11. Georg Wilhelm Friedrich Hegel, *The Logic of Hegel* (Oxford: Oxford University Press, 1968), paragraph 95,176–77.

12. Hegel, *Lectures on the Philosophy of Religion*, 3:326.

13. Hegel, *Lectures on the Philosophy of Religion,* 1:347–48.

14. Jean-Paul Sartre, *Being and Nothingness*, Hazel E. Barnes translator (New York: Washington Square Press, 1992), 724.

15. Georg Wilhelm Friedrich Hegel, *The Phenomenology of Spirit*, trans. A. V. Miller (Oxford: Oxford University Press, 1977), 111–19.

16. Hegel, *Lectures on the Philosophy of Religion*, 2:740–41.

17. Hegel, *Phenomenology of Spirit*, 131.

18. Hegel, *Lectures on the Philosophy of Religion*, 3:128–29.

19. Hegel, *Phenomenology of Spirit*, 808.

20. Mark 4:31, Matthew 13:31, Luke 13:19.

21. Hegel, *Lectures on the Philosophy of Religion*, 3:222; John 16:7.

22. Luke 15:11–32.

23. Hegel, *Lectures on the Philosophy of Religion*, 3:327–28.

24. Matthew 25:40.

25. John 14:12 (New American Standard Bible).

26. This chapter is an expanded and revised version of James Lawler, "God and Man Separated No More: Hegel Overcomes the Unhappy Consciousness of Gibson's Christianity," published in *Mel Gibson's Passion and Philosophy: The Cross, the Questions, the Controversy,* ed. Jorge J. E. Gracia (Chicago: Open court, 2004), 62–76.

9

The Real Secret of
The Da Vinci Code

And Jesus said to her, Mary.
—THE FOURTH GOSPEL 20:16

Bring some of the fish you have caught, Jesus said to them; and Simon Peter, going on board, hauled in the net to land. It was loaded with great fish, a hundred and fifty three of them. . . .
—THE FOURTH GOSPEL 21:10–11

Two Faces or . . . the Holy Grail?

The great success of Dan Brown's *The Da Vinci Code* cannot be explained by stylistic brilliance or even by the intrigue and excitement of a fast-paced mystery-adventure. Its appeal stems mainly from its ideas, raised in the course of a plot that provides scaffolding for their compelling, page-turning exposition. As the narrative unfolds, cryptic messages are uncovered and complex codes concealing hidden truths are deciphered. As uncovered clues accumulate, traditional Western theology, philosophy, and sociology are deconstructed in view of an ultimate secret unveiled toward the end: that Jesus had a wife, who was none other than the great harlot of the gospels, Mary Magdalene.

Through the twists and turns of the adventure, we learn about a sacred love that establishes a bloodline connected to the quest of the Holy Grail. According to the novel, this secret truth has inspired its great guardians and transmitters—including such illustrious and influential figures as Andrea Botticelli, Leonardo da Vinci, Isaac Newton, Victor Hugo, and Jean Cocteau. Prominent artists and scientists were Grand Masters of a secret society, the Priory of Sion, which has as its mission the guardianship of ancient documents that would substantiate this truth.

Much of the controversy surrounding *The Da Vinci Code* stems from its claim to rest on "Fact." Page 1, headed "Fact," lists the following as facts: (1) the existence of the Priory of Sion, (2) the reality of Opus Dei, a specially protected "prelature" of the Catholic Church, with "reports" of its practices of brainwashing and corporal mortification, as well as (3) "all descriptions of artwork, architecture, documents and secret rituals in this novel." In the novel itself, certain claims of factuality drive the plot as people are presumably murdered in attempts to prevent the publication of hidden documents guarded by the Priory. While agents claiming to protect founding beliefs of the Catholic Church are suspected of seeking to destroy the challenging evidence, the guardians of the Grail are believed to be committed to revealing the truth at the right time—at the turning of the millennium, at the End of Days, and the dawn of the New Age. But the millennium has come and gone, and the Priory guardians have not done their alleged duty. No doubt this failure is due to blackmail by the dark powers of ignorance ensconced in the Church. At least, this is the motivating supposition of the genial archvillain of the story, Leigh Teabing, who will do whatever it takes to make the Truth known.

It is indeed a fact that throughout Western history there have been secret societies to which illustrious figures belonged—societies formed for the pursuit of forbidden wisdom and the promotion of practices that implicitly or explicitly challenge reigning ideas and the powers that benefit from them. The existence of the latter necessitates the existence of the former. For example, scholars today are publishing the once-secret writings of Isaac Newton. Physics was practically a sideline for Newton in comparison with his explorations of such occult matters as the identity of the Whore of Babylon in the book of Revelation. Newton held anti-Trinitarian views at a time in England when such beliefs could be punished by death. Like the supposed members of the Priory of Sion, Newton shared his dangerously unorthodox ideas with an inner circle of friends, and in his published writings he deliberately left clues to his real beliefs for those who could read between the lines, or under the layers.[1]

In a two-thousand-year history that has been and continues to be dominated by institutions of power and privilege, alternative thinking and countervailing practices have inevitably been driven underground and into secrecy. Based on the supposed evidence of the *Dossiers Secrets*, *The Da Vinci Code* claims that Newton was a leader in the Grail story, and indeed, considering the indubitable facts contained in the once-hidden documents published by "The Newton Project," if there was such an organization, he certainly *could* have been its leader.

But the real secret and truth, we finally discover at the end of the novel, is not to be found in hidden documents. The Priory of Sion is committed *never* to reveal its secrets, according to the grandmotherly protector, Marie Chauvel. "The End of Days is a legend of paranoid minds," she says: "It is the mystery and wonderment that serve our souls, not the Grail itself. The beauty of the Grail lies in her ethereal nature. . . . For some, the Grail is a chalice that will bring them everlasting life. For others, it is the quest for lost documents and secret history. And for most, I suspect the Holy Grail is simply a grand idea . . . a glorious unattainable treasure that somehow, even in today's world of chaos, inspires us."[2] What really counts, therefore, is not the Fact, but the Idea—a glorious Ideal.

But surely, Robert Langdon objects, if the documents are kept hidden, "the story of Mary Magdalene will be lost forever." Marie Chauvel replies: "Will it? Look around you. Her story is being told in art, music, and books. More so every day. The pendulum is swinging. We are starting to sense the dangers of our history . . . and of our destructive paths. We are beginning to sense the need to restore the sacred feminine."[3] The secret truth is thus far from secret. As an idea and ideal, the pursuit of the Grail has deeply impacted Western culture through its inspiration of chivalric romance, the Arthurian political ideals of Camelot, and other underlying currents of a history that, on the surface, privileges male power and hierarchical control in social life, in political institutions, and in religion.

Evidence of sorts there clearly is. There is the evidence of . . . the *Mona Lisa*'s mysterious smile! What hides behind that smile? Perhaps it is her knowledge of the secret of the Grail, confided to her by the painter himself. But more convincingly for us, we can see with our own eyes the clearly feminine features of the figure at the right hand of Jesus in Da Vinci's "Last Supper." Dan Brown invites his readers to see this important evidence for ourselves. This is not evidence that Mary Magdalene was in fact the spouse of Jesus. But at least it shows, or seems to show, that Da Vinci, one of the iconic figures of Western history, so revered the one he believed to be Jesus' beloved that he hid her portrait in open view for all who have eyes to see. To see this evidence, all one needs is an idea, and in its light to perform a gestalt switch. Before we are told of this idea, we saw only a pious portrait of a group of important men, all too familiar to us from innumerable portraits of men in power. And lo and behold, thanks to the idea, we now see a woman, right in center view, joined below the waist to the Son of God. As in the classic example of the gestalt switch, where at first we see the outlines of two faces, and then, suddenly, by a change of focus, a cup appears. Or is it *the* cup? Is it the Grail itself?

So it's really all about ideas, not things, documents, or facts. The popularity of *The Da Vinci Code* is the result of the tantalizing attraction of a simple but revolutionary idea with the power of overthrowing a two-thousand-year paradigm of the solitary, heroic, ascetical, and intellectual masculine identity. Instead we now see a sacred couple, male and female, bound together through the fires of love. Of course there is nothing unusual about bringing the long-hidden mysteries of sexual love into the open in post-twentieth-century culture. What is new in recent popular culture is the connecting of sexual love with metaphysical truth. The Christ figure in the *Matrix* trilogy, Neo, is nothing without his Trinity. The Christ figure in *Star Wars*, Anakin, is transformed through his passion for Padmé. And now, thanks to *The Da Vinci Code*, we learn that these figures of popular culture may in fact reflect the hidden truth of Christ himself.

Quest for the Meaning of the Grail

What does "holy grail" mean anyway? What is a "grail"? This word is a mystery all in itself. As Robert Langdon explains to Sophie Neveau, the original form was the French word, "Sangraal" which evolved into "Sangreal" and divided into two as "San Greal." Ninety pages later, after a number of other cryptic messages have been deciphered, we are prepared to look at this word again, but, thanks to a gestalt shift, with a different focus. Instead of "San Greal" or Holy Grail, we suddenly see the words "Sang Real"—which the French-speaking Sophie recognizes immediately as meaning royal blood—"sang" for blood and "real" for royal. A new idea shines forth: the Holy Grail actually stands for royal blood.[4] And the blood in question is not the blood of Christ collected by Joseph of Arimathea in the cup that was used at the Last Supper. This is the surface legend for popular consumption in a repressive world that has made the actual truth unthinkable. The real truth, the reader is informed, is the royal bloodline established by the marital union of Jesus and Mary Magdalene through their child and later descendents. Evidence of this bloodline is purportedly contained in documents discovered in Jerusalem in the eleventh century and used to blackmail the Church into giving immense power to the Priory of Sion and its military wing, the Knights Templar. How else explain the sudden, mysterious rise to enormous wealth and power of the Knights Templar after an initial sojourn of a small number of unimportant adventurists in Jerusalem?

These documents, we eventually learn from Marie Chauvel, are to be kept secret forever, because what matters is the quest in the name of a revolutionary idea and not the discovery of any facts that underlie this quest. Moreover, it doesn't matter what's in the documents, because the idea they verify has its own force of self-revelation. What after all would be achieved by demonstrating that ancient sources believed in the marriage of Jesus and Mary Magdalene? This would not establish the *truth* of their belief. It's a matter of choice, Leigh Teabing says: "The Sangreal documents simply tell the *other* side of the Christ story. In the end, which side of the story you believe becomes a matter of faith and personal exploration. . . ."[5]

The deeper question therefore has to do with ideas. What is the significance or meaning of such a possible marriage? Why should it upset two-thousand-year-old dogmas of hierarchical rule? In answer to this question, *The Da Vinci Code* in fact proposes two apparently contradictory answers: (1) The marriage of Jesus and Mary would show that Jesus was, after all, merely a man, not the Son of God, the second person in the Trinity—contrary to the tenets of the Nicene Creed and Christian orthodoxy. (2) It would provide legitimacy to the concept of the sacred feminine.

According to Teabing, up to the Council of Nicea, called by the Emperor Constantine in 325: "Jesus was viewed by His followers as a mortal prophet . . . a great and powerful man, but a *man* nevertheless. . . . By officially endorsing Jesus as the Son of God, Constantine turned Jesus into a deity who existed beyond the scope of the human world, an entity whose power was unchallengeable. This not only precluded further pagan challenges to Christianity, but now the followers of Christ were able to redeem themselves *only* via the established sacred channel—the Roman Catholic Church. . . ."[6] On the other hand, Robert Langdon tells us: "Knights who claimed to be 'searching for the chalice' were speaking in code as a way to protect themselves from a Church that had subjugated women, banished the goddess, burned nonbelievers, and forbidden the pagan reverence for the sacred feminine."[7] But the first idea undermines the second. Only if Jesus is God can his wife be Goddess. If Jesus was only a human being, a man with ordinary male needs and desires, who naturally took a wife as would have been expected of him in the Jewish milieu of his time, how would knowing this elevate the status of women? It is therefore not so obvious what the discovery of Mary Magdalene's relation to Jesus would actually mean. Beyond the quest of the Grail as the idea of a royal marriage and bloodline is the deeper quest, and question, of the *meaning* of this royal bloodline of Jesus and Mary. Why should power and privilege bend at the idea that the alleged harlot of the gospels is really the bride of Christ?

The Jews of the time of Jesus were looking for a Messiah, a Chosen One of God who would overthrow the Roman occupation and reestablish an independent kingdom. A King must have his Queen, because there must be heirs—above all male heirs. But such a perspective hardly challenges the generally subordinate position of women in the history of monarchy and patriarchy. Other than being an argument today for reactionary European monarchists, what is the significance of the royal bloodline of Christ for the revaluation of femininity and the rediscovery of the sacred feminine?

Peter, the "rock" on which Jesus established his Church and the first bishop of Rome, was a married man. This fact of the gospels has not deterred the Catholic Church from insisting on celibacy for the priesthood and confining the priesthood to men. In Mark's gospel, Peter's family is mentioned because Peter's mother-in-law was ill. And so, "Jesus went and took hold of her hand, and raised her to her feet. The fever left her and she attended to their needs."[8] We suppose there is a wife and children, but we don't learn anything about them because they didn't count for the purposes of the narrative. Moreover, the one woman who matters in this narrative, because she is healed by Jesus, quickly assumes a subservient role. If the main role of women is to serve the needs of the men, what would it matter to the tradition of male supremacy if not only the first Bishop of Rome, the first Pope, but Jesus himself was served by his wife? All that it would establish is that men have . . . certain needs. If it were the case that Jesus too had such needs, this might argue against a certain conception of his divinity, but how would it elevate the role of the woman who served those needs?

Mary Magdalene as Teacher

The Da Vinci Code accordingly adds a second argument for the subversive character of Mary Magdalene. Not only is she the wife of Christ, but it is really she, not Peter, who was appointed by Jesus to establish his Church. This, together with the nondivinity of Christ, is established by the rediscovery of ancient documents that had been suppressed by the early Church, Leigh Teabing tells us, citing telling passages from recently discovered documents, the Gospel of Philip and the Gospel of Mary Magdalene. Teabing cites the Gospel of Philip: "And the companion of the Saviour is Mary Magdalene. Christ loved her more than all the disciples and used to kiss her often on her mouth. The rest of the disciples were offended by it and expressed disapproval. They said to him, 'Why do you love her more than all of us?'"[9]

This is indeed the deeper question that *The Da Vinci Code* implicitly raises. Why did Jesus love Mary? Was it for the usual reasons that men love women, and husbands their wives? Leah Teabing claims that the Gospel of Mary Magdalene proclaims Mary as the primary teacher of Christianity, placing her over Peter. In this gospel, the risen Jesus gives four disciples—Peter, Peter's brother Andrew, Mary Magdalene, and Levi—some teachings and then takes his final departure from them. Distraught and seeking words of comfort, Peter asks Mary to talk to them about Jesus: "Sister, we know that the Savior loved you more than all other women. Tell us the words of the Savior that you remember, the things which you know that we don't because we haven't heard them."[10] Mary complies, but the results are unexpected. Instead of providing homely information that might be expected of a woman who shared private spousal moments with a man, Mary says, "I will teach you about what is hidden from you." She then provides a complex metaphysical teaching that has heads spinning. Andrew finds this teaching quite strange and Peter all but accuses Mary of making the whole thing up, bringing Mary to tears. He cannot believe that serious teaching could come from a mere woman. Levi then comes to Mary's defense: "Now I see you contending against the woman like the Adversaries. For if the Savior made her worthy, who are you then for your part to reject her? Assuredly the Savior's knowledge of her is completely reliable. That is why he loved her more than us."[11] Levi here goes beyond Peter in claiming that Jesus not only loved Mary more than other women, but more than the male disciples as well. She may be a woman, but Jesus is more than an ordinary man, and so is capable of making even a woman worthy—elevating her to the status of an authentic teacher. The disciples should therefore listen to what she has to teach.

Thus once-buried documents that have actually been revealed to the public in recent times clearly establish the fact that in at least some of the early Christian communities the status of Mary Magdalene as the beloved and companion of Jesus was not in dispute. What was disputed was whether this special relationship went beyond that of an ordinary female companion or wife. The issue was whether Mary in particular, and women in general, had something of their own to say, teachings that they received either directly from Jesus, as in the case of Mary, or from visions or other sources of inspiration. In the Gospel of Mary, Mary relates a vision she had, and then recounts her discussion of this vision with Jesus. The teachings of other visionary women are in this way implicitly defended. More than being a mere female companion or wife, Mary was herself a teacher of deep truths, of special knowledge or "gnosis." Implicit in the Gospel of Mary is therefore a division between levels of teachings—the well-known public teachings of Jesus and special teachings which Jesus gave only to those whom he regarded as capable of understanding, in the first place to Mary Magdalene. In the Gospel of Philip, when Jesus is asked why he loves Mary above the others, he replies, cryptically, "If a blind man and one who sees are both in the dark, they do not differ from each other. When the light comes, then the one who sees will see the light, and the one who is blind will remain in the dark."[12] Unlike some of the others, Mary can see the light.

If Mary is placed above Peter, as Leigh Teabing claims in *The Da Vinci Code*, it is no wonder that the institutional Church, founded on the primacy of Peter and establishing a patriarchal hierarchy, attempted to destroy documents such as the Gospel of Mary and the Gospel of Philip. The place of women in the Christian churches was a contentious issue debated in the first half of the second century. The pseudo-epistle of Paul of 1 Timothy, in which the author declares that "I permit no woman to teach or to have authority over men," was probably written at this time. Thomas Cahill writes,

> First Timothy belongs to the period of the patriarchalization of the Christian churches, when bishops began to emerge as the only legitimate leaders and, surveying the disorder (or, more simply, lack of uniformity) they saw before them, endeavored to put all the 'excessive' enthusiasms of the Pauline churches back into the box. Paul is actually the New Testament's ultimate democrat; and it is a pathetic irony that the first person in history to exclude consciously all social grades, isms, and biases from his thinking, believing that nothing—not birth, nor ethnicity, nor religion, nor economic status, nor class, nor gender—makes anyone any better than anyone else, should so often be made to stand at the bar accused of the opposite of what he believed so passionately.[13]

The polemical meaning of the Gospel of Mary consists in rejecting any such law that establishes fundamental differences between men and women. That Peter is singled out for criticism does not necessarily mean that a canonical or official church is being rejected in the name of an alternative vision. At the time it was probably composed, in the early second century, there was as yet no clearly recognized "canon" of truth. Another two hundred years of evolution took place before the final subordination of women, and the destruction of texts such as the Gospel of Mary. *The Da Vinci Code* evokes the hostility of Peter toward Mary to explain Da Vinci's portrait of Peter in the "Last Supper," with his hand menacingly drawn across the neck of Mary Magdalene.[14] But the savagery of this gesture in Da Vinci's painting reflects the perspective of a later history. At the time of the Gospel of Mary, the figure of Peter had not yet come to evoke repellant sentiments of the power and privilege of mitered bishops and papal palaces.

On Gnosticism and Orthodoxy

As *The Da Vinci Code* plausibly argues, the establishment of male hierarchy in the Church, together with a certain conception of orthodoxy, became firmly cemented by the Council of Nicea in 325 AD. Elaine Pagels devotes much of her book, *Beyond Belief: The Secret Gospel of Thomas*, to examining some main steps in the historical process culminating in the enormous privileges that were granted by the Roman Emperor Constantine to the orthodox Roman Catholic Church, ruled by male popes, bishops, and priests.[15] Soon after the Council, documents holding what had become officially banned heretical views, such as the Gospel of Mary, were everywhere destroyed, except for those that were carefully hidden. Some fifty-two of these were discovered over fifteen hundred years later near the village of Nag Hammadi in Egypt in 1945.

What the newly discovered documents clearly demonstrate is the historical falsity of a core idea of Christian orthodoxy: that Jesus handed down a recognized set of beliefs to twelve male apostles, who then faithfully taught these beliefs in the various parts of the world to which they were assigned. The texts reveal an early Christian pluralism without a definite rule of authority and an established set of beliefs. As the Gospel of Mary and other "Gnostic" texts demonstrate, for many Christians, what was central to Christianity was not a set of beliefs, doctrines, or dogmas, but an inner experience giving rise to a transformative knowledge or gnosis. Pagels estimates that at the end of the second century, when a certain conception of dogmatic orthodoxy began to be vigilantly entrenched against supposed heretics, perhaps half of the Christians of the time had some such Gnostic orientation as is proposed in the Gospel of Mary.[16]

What later historians have described as Gnosticism, under the misconception of the existence of a well-defined orthodoxy, was primarily the idea of going beyond the nominal acceptance of certain beliefs, centered on the death and resurrection of Jesus, and participation in ritual practices, such as baptism and the communion meal. It is the idea that there is a deeper level of understanding that goes "beyond belief" (the title of Pagels's book) and involves the experiential transformation of personality—that is, the discovery of the true self, the image of God that is in communion with divinity. For these "gnostics," or seekers after transformative spiritual knowledge, what matters are not primarily beliefs regarding the meaning of certain historical facts but the life-altering knowledge or gnosis that is at the heart of such beliefs.

In general, then, for this Gnostic orientation, the Christian beliefs regarding Jesus are not about a special individual set apart from ordinary humanity whose sacrificial death is necessary to salvation—the standard conception of "atonement" that was established as orthodox dogma at the Council of Nicea. Instead, we must understand the inner meaning of these beliefs at the level of real knowledge or philosophical truth. The beliefs, understood rightly, are indicative of the potentiality of spiritual transformation that lies within each one of us. As the Gospel of Philip puts it, as a result of the process of spiritual transformation that begins with faith and ends with gnosis, one is "no longer a Christian, but a Christ."[17] Jesus here is certainly more than a mere mortal human. But so potentially is every human being. To become a true human being or "Son of Man"—which the Gospel of Mary claims is the secret teaching of Jesus—we must liberate ourselves from the ordinary slavery that most of us mistake for a human life.

Was Mary the Bride of Christ?

Does the Gospel of Mary demonstrate that Mary was the wife of Jesus? The documents cited above claim that Jesus loved her more than others. She was his "companion" and he often kissed her.[18] But this is not their main thrust. What matters in these documents is not the banal fact, which is not considered remarkable, but the spiritual or Gnostic meaning of Jesus's special love of Mary. The somewhat prurient modern interest in establishing the mere fact of Jesus's marriage did not seem to have been of interest to the writers of the time.

In her scholarly and densely argued book on the Gospel of Mary, Karen King devotes just one very cautious paragraph to this question:

> It is true that from early on [since the discovery of the Nag Hammadi texts] the possibility had existed that Mary Magdalene might emerge from the speculative fray as Jesus' wife and lover. The Gospel of Philip said that Jesus used to kiss her often, and in the Gospel of Mary Peter affirmed that Jesus loved her more than other women. The third-century church father Hippolytus also used erotic imagery to allegorize the *Song of Songs* into an intimate relationship of the Church to Christ by treating Mary of Magdala as the Church-bride and Jesus as the Savior-Bridegroom. Of

course, the rise of celibacy to a position of central importance in determining Christian authority structures put an official damper on these
kinds of speculations. Still, the notion of an erotic relationship between
Jesus and Mary Magdalene has surfaced at odd moments throughout
Western history and is still capable of arousing a good deal of public ire.[19]

In a footnote, written without knowledge of *The Da Vinci Code*, the
author mentions *Jesus Christ Superstar* and the dream sequence in Martin
Scorsese's film *The Last Temptation of Christ*. King omits mention of Walt
Disney, whose films, *Snow White*, *Cinderella*, and *Sleeping Beauty*,
according to *The Da Vinci Code*, "dealt with the incarceration of the
sacred feminine."[20] In Disney's *The Little Mermaid* Ariel's underwater
home prominently contains Georges de la Tour's seventeenth-century
painting, "The Penitent Magdalene."[21] King criticizes Scorsese's film, and
by implication the novel by Kazantzakis on which it is based, for its suggestion that female sexuality is the great temptation for men. The controversy surrounding this film nevertheless shows how any portrayal of
Jesus as a fully sexual person runs afoul of deeply embedded belief. Is
this because, as *The Da Vinci Code* suggests, and even approves, it contradicts the doctrine that Jesus is, as the Nicene Creed puts it, "of one
substance" with God the Father? If so, how does this diminishment of
Jesus facilitate the promotion of the sacred feminine?

The Gospel of Mary does more than affirm that, as Peter willingly
admits, Jesus loved Mary more than other women—perhaps in the sense
that any man presumably loves his own wife more than other women.
It moves beyond this common assumption of all the characters in the
account and asks, in the spirit of Gnostic understanding, what is the
deeper meaning of this relationship? Peter takes for granted that Jesus has
a special relation with Mary, but does not expect this to have any special *spiritual* or, let us say, *philosophical* significance, any relevance to
understanding the teachings of Jesus. The Gospel of Mary is all the more
convincing evidence that Mary was indeed the wife of Jesus, in the ordinary understanding of this relationship, in that it accords no particular
significance to such a merely "worldly" relationship. Just as Peter's having a wife is of no particular significance to the Gospel of Mark, so in the
Gospel of Mary Jesus's having a husbandlike relationship to Mary is of
no particular significance to Peter, other than as an occasion for comforting anecdotal information. Men have needs. They eat, they sleep, and
they have sexual needs. This document therefore confirms the argument
of *The Da Vinci Code* that in the Jewish context of the time, a man of
Jesus's age would have been expected to marry, and his marriage would

not have been especially remarked upon. What would have needed explanation and comment would have been Jesus's bachelorhood.[22]

The reason for the respect and the authority accorded to Mary among some early Christians was therefore not because she was seen as the wife of Jesus, but because, as a result of the special nature of her love-relation to Jesus, she was regarded as a teacher and spiritual leader in her own right. Jesus's love for Mary went beyond the confines of the ordinary love of a man for a woman. Levi intimates this deeper level of Jesus's love when he says that "he knew her completely and loved her steadfastly"—unlike the sporadic and incomplete love characteristic of men in general for their wives. Levi recognizes that the love of Jesus for Mary was an unusual kind of love—unusual in relation to the ordinary model of male-female relationships of the time, limited to fulfilling certain basic needs in which men require the service of women. The Savior sees in Mary something that goes beyond what the ordinary man sees in a woman. His love for her is therefore a unique, a new kind of love.

Does the Gospel of Mary then replace the authority of Peter with that of Mary Magdalene? Peter's fallibility is many times referred to in the canonical gospels, above all his three-times denial of Jesus which is reported in the Fourth Gospel. (The term Fourth Gospel is used here instead of the common name, Gospel of John, for reasons that will become clear soon. The charitable reader will excuse a little mystery here of our own making.) But he always has the humility and love of Jesus to acknowledge his faults and rise above them. In the Fourth Gospel, Peter has the opportunity to tell the resurrected Jesus three times of his love for him, and so make amends for his earlier betrayal. Thus the legend is plausible that when he came to be crucified in his turn, Peter, feeling unworthy to die as his Master did, insisted that his cross be inverted. If such a pattern of denial and then reversal is presumed for the missing pages of the Gospel of Mary, Peter would correct his initial error in doubting Mary's teaching, recognize the veracity of her message, and not make rules that go beyond the Savior's teaching—such rules as that women cannot be teachers in their own right. There is no reason to think that the Gospel of Mary argues, as Leigh Teabing thinks, that Mary supplants Peter in his practical role as the organizational leader selected by Jesus. It does however clearly assert Mary's position as a source of wisdom and a teacher in her own right—and so the right of other women as well. But in the consolidated authority structure of the later Roman Church empowered by the Emperor Constantine this alone would be enough to ensure the suppression of this teaching.

Sinners and Marys in the Canonical Gospels

Mary's special status proved strong enough to survive the suppression, persecution, and denigration of the "Gnostic" Christians who followed Mary and taught subversive doctrines of special knowledge or gnosis as well as of the possibility of women teachers. Some reflection of Mary's special status is expressed in the title given to her in ancient times and reaffirmed by the Catholic Church, as "Apostle to the Apostles." Such recognition is primarily the result of the unique position of Mary Magdalene in the Fourth Gospel, where she is the first to see the resurrected Jesus, who tells her to bring the news of his resurrection to the disciples. She is therefore the apostle who is sent by Jesus to the other apostles. The distraught Mary has found the tomb empty and runs to tell Peter and "that other disciple, whom Jesus loved" (John 20:2). These two verify that she is right. But Mary stays on, and is rewarded by encountering Jesus, whom she first mistakes for the gardener. She recognizes Jesus when he calls to her, "Mary." This story is told only in the Fourth Gospel, which was the last to be written of the four canonical gospels. In the three other, so-called Synoptic Gospels, one angel or two angels announce to a number of women, including Mary Magdalene, that Jesus has risen. Mark and Mathew, but not Luke, then have Jesus meet first with Mary Magdalene. But in the Fourth Gospel it is only Mary who is present at the tomb, and Jesus appears directly to her alone. Here is a cryptic puzzle put to us by the gospels. Why this striking difference between the earlier stories and the one told in the Fourth Gospel?

Who then is Mary Magdalene, that she has such a special position in relation to Jesus as to be the first to whom he announces the glorious news of victory over death, and then the one who brings this good news to the others? Mary's prominence has clearly been diminished in subsequent ecclesiastical history and church doctrine. Traditionally she is identified primarily as a repentant prostitute. Karen King, like the fictional authority Leigh Teabing in *The Da Vinci Code*, argues that the identification of Mary as a prostitute is an invention of the later Church, beginning with Gregory the Great in the sixth century, seeking to devalue Mary's influence for independent women and Christians. The account in the Fourth Gospel of the threatened stoning of the woman caught in adultery, as well as another account in the Gospel of Luke of a woman described as a sinner from the city who anoints Jesus's feet with precious oil, have traditionally been associated with Mary Magdalene. But neither account actually names the woman, and so they provide no clear textual evidence for the "accusation" that Mary was a reformed prostitute. Hence, Karen

King argues that from being an apostle in her own right as well as possibly the bride of Christ, Mary has been demoted by a textually unfounded Church construction to being only a repentant sinner.[23]

Mel Gibson's film *The Passion of the Christ* follows tradition in identifying Mary Magdalene with the woman about to be stoned for adultery. Jesus saves her with the words to her accusers, "Whichever of you is free from sin shall cast the first stone at her" (John 8:7). In Gibson's portrait, Mary is indeed the repentant sinner who loves Jesus. However, she is not selected for special attention on the part of Jesus himself. The film's ending, with the resurrected Jesus alone in his crypt, is not found in the gospels. Gibson's film omits the authentic gospel account of the first appearance of Jesus after his death. This moving scene of the Fourth Gospel does not show Jesus as the solitary Savior, but depicts him standing alongside the distraught Magdalene, who is weeping beside his tomb, and addressing her, tenderly, "Mary."

But why not *both* prostitute and bride? The idea that Jesus chose a prostitute for his bride is far more subversive than any traditional form of marriage with a virgin bride. The true spouse and partner of Pericles was the prostitute Aspasia, who became a powerful woman in ancient Greece. Where male supremacy reduces most women to domestic slavery, prostitution is the sole avenue for independence for many women. The Bible itself has a precedent that would not be lost on the followers of Jesus. Tamara, who is twice foiled in her attempts as a legitimate wife to bear a child to the sons of Judah, uses prostitution to get a child by Judah himself, and so have her offspring enter the sacred bloodline of the promised Messiah. When her father-in-law, who is also the father of the child in her womb, is about to have her burned alive for her unseemly condition, she hands him his own ring, which Judah unknowingly had previously given to her as payment for her sexual services.[24] The cunning part-time prostitute Tamara is accordingly mentioned in the genealogy of Jesus at the beginning of the Gospel of Matthew.

The reluctance of the canonical gospel accounts to clarify the identities of variously described Marys and sinners itself requires some explanation. In addition to Mary Magdalene, there is the Mary who lives in the village of Bethany with her brother Lazarus and sister Martha. This is the one place in the gospels that Jesus can really call home.[25] In the Fourth Gospel, this Mary is described as the woman who anoints Jesus with ointment and wipes his feet with her hair (John 11:2)—as does the unnamed "sinner" in the Gospel of Luke. As the Fourth Gospel tells it, the episode takes place at a feast for Lazarus, whom Jesus has recently raised from the dead.

This most striking of all the miracles of Jesus occurs as a result of the intercession of "Mary of Bethany." When Jesus arrives outside Bethany, Mary's sister Martha comes to meet him, for Mary is staying at the house with the mourners. Jesus has been calmly discussing the death of Lazarus in connection with the possibility of resurrection, which Martha interprets as coming only "when the last day comes." Jesus then sends Martha to get Mary. When Mary comes to him in tears, Jesus is for the first time visibly moved, and soon he himself is also in tears. Mary is not willing to wait until the end of time for the resurrection of her brother. Jesus orders the tomb to be opened, despite Martha's protest that the body, four days dead, would be putrid. According to the Fourth Gospel, the miracle of Lazarus was the chief event that precipitated Jesus's death, for news spread quickly and the Jewish authorities became fearful that Jesus's popularity would provoke Roman anger.

During the celebration party for Lazarus's return in the home of "Simon the leper," Mary pours precious ointment over the feet of Jesus, and wipes them with her hair. Judas Iscariot is astounded at the extravagance of this gesture, for the pure spikenard ointment was worth three hundred pieces of silver. Mary of Bethany is clearly a very wealthy woman. The same story of the woman with the ointment is told in the gospels of Matthew and Mark, though in these accounts neither the woman nor her accuser is identified.[26] In these two accounts the event is said to take place in the home of "Simon the leper" in Bethany. In all three gospels, Jesus justifies the expense by alluding to the ointment for his burial. But in the Fourth Gospel, the Mary who comes to the tomb with precious ointment to salve the brutalized body of Jesus, and finds instead the resurrected Jesus, is clearly identified as Mary Magdalene. Is it not obvious that the Mary who is here called "the Magdalene" is the same Mary who lives in Bethany, the sister of Martha and Lazarus?

As mentioned previously, the same story of the woman with the ointment is told also in Luke, but there the event takes place in the home of "Simon the Pharisee," not "Simon the leper," and the woman is described mysteriously as "a sinful woman in the city." What is a wealthy "sinner" doing in the home of a Pharisee, and at the table no less? Unless she is Jesus's companion! For the reader of all three gospel accounts with a certain idea in mind, Mary of Bethany is readily seen to be Mary Magdalene, as well as a former sinner, or prostitute.

In the gospels Jesus is frequently accused of eating with "tax collectors and sinners." Just before Luke's story of the lavish gesture of "the sinner in the city," Jesus complains of the hypocrisy of those who accuse him: "When John came, he would neither eat nor drink, and you say, he is possessed. When the Son of Man came, he ate and drank with you, and of him you say, Here is a glutton; he loves wine; he is a friend of publicans [tax collectors] and sinners" (Luke 7:33–34). Jesus makes a similar comparison between John the Baptist and himself in the Gospel of Matthew: "John came among you following all due observance, but could win no belief from you; the publicans believed him, and the harlots, but even when you saw that, you would not relent, and believe him" (Matthew 21:32). Here Jesus clearly says that some of John the Baptist's followers, like his own, were tax collectors—despised by Jews for their service on behalf of the Roman occupiers—and prostitutes.

Levi is mentioned as a tax collector among Jesus's followers. Mark mentions that Levi had a big party for Jesus at which there were many tax collectors and sinners (Mark 2:145). Tax collectors and harlots follow Jesus. Levi is mentioned as a tax collector. But who among Jesus's followers could have been a harlot? A pattern begins to emerge: tax collector and harlot: Levi and . . . ? Of course, we suddenly see, Levi and *Mary*—the two who truly understand the message of Jesus in the banished and buried Gospel of Mary. Hence the radical message of the teaching and practice of Jesus: it is the excluded, the despised, the downtrodden of Jewish society who best grasp the Good News that true humanity does not stem from one's physical make-up, possessions, and the estimation of society and the law regarding one's occupation— whether as a tax collector for the Romans or as vender of a few moments of earthly bliss for men.

The Gospel of Luke shows Jesus at the home of Simon the Pharisee with a "sinful woman in the city" who "brought a pot of ointment with her, and took her place behind him at his feet, weeping; then she began washing his feet with her tears, and drying them with her hair, kissing his feet, and anointing them with the ointment" (Luke 7:37–38). Simon, the Pharisee in whose home this scene takes place, complains that if Jesus is the prophet he is said to be he ought to know what kind of woman this is. Jesus replies:

> Dost thou see this woman? I came into thy house, and thou gavest me no water for my feet; she has washed my feet with her tears, and wiped them with her hair. Thou gavest me no kiss of greeting; she has never ceased to kiss my feet since I entered; thou didst not pour oil on my head; she has anointed my feet, and with ointment. And so, I tell thee, if great sins have been forgiven her, she has also greatly loved. He loves little who has little forgiven him. (Luke 7:44–47)

Immediately following this account, Luke writes:

Then followed a time in which he went on journeying from one city or village to another, preaching and spreading the good news of God's kingdom. With him were the twelve apostles, and certain women, whom he had freed from evil spirits and from sicknesses, Mary who is called Magdalen, who had seven devils cast out of her, and Joanna, the wife of Chusa, Herod's steward, and Susanna, and many others, who ministered to him with the means they had. (Luke 8:1–2)

Thus the first name that follows the account of "the sinful woman in the city" is that of Mary Magdalene. Luke describes Mary Magdalene as one of the wealthy women who provides financial support for the spreading of the good news of the kingdom of God. One of these women at least must be that harlot that Jesus associates with and that everyone is complaining about, and whom he apparently invited to the dinner at the home of Simon the Pharisee. Luke seems barely able to refrain from explicitly making the connection between the sinner in the city and Mary Magdalene. Luke does not connect Mary Magdalene with Mary of Bethany. But we who also read the account of the Fourth Gospel naturally want to identify Mary of Bethany, who pours precious ointment over Jesus at the party for her brother Lazarus in the home of Simon the Leper, with the sinful woman of the city in the Gospel of Luke who pours expensive ointment over Jesus at the home of the Simon the Pharisee. And we also see that Mary of Bethany in the Fourth Gospel, like Mary Magdalene in the Gospel of Luke, is a wealthy woman who is supporting the cause. How many women can there be who can afford such extravagance, and display lavish gestures, in the home of someone named Simon no less? If they are different women, why doesn't Luke also mention Mary of Bethany as one of the wealthy women who is supporting Jesus's teaching, as she surely must have been if, as the Fourth Gospel recounts, she could afford to pour three hundred silver pieces' worth of precious oils over him? It doesn't take the genius of Robert Langdon to connect the dots: Simon the Pharisee in the Gospel of Luke is that same Simon the Leper in the Fourth Gospel who housed the party for Mary's brother Lazarus. And seeing this we now understand how a "sinner" could be present at the home of the pious Pharisee: it was her own party!

Is it any wonder that ordinary readers from the earliest times, no less perspicacious than a sixth-century Pope, have put two and two together and connected Mary Magdalene with the "sinner," whose wealthy and high-placed clients once paid great sums for her beauty, and who now so extravagantly and unabashedly loves Jesus alone? And what about the unnamed "woman who had been found committing adultery" (John

8:1–11), related in the Fourth Gospel? Here again, Jesus accuses the critics of hypocrisy: whoever is without sin, let him cast the first stone. Jesus then exhorts the rescued woman to begin a new life. The Gospel of Luke depicts Jesus with a woman who was once a sinner, but who loves much because, as Rabbi Ben says in *Crimes and Misdemeanors*, she has found forgiveness and the possibility of a new life. Luke then explicitly identifies Mary Magdalene as a woman whom Jesus had previously saved from the dark powers of seven devils. The Gospel of Mary as we will see in the next chapter, gives full intelligibility to this obscure statement. As a result of these subtle harmonies, one of the extent manuscripts of the New Testament appropriately places the "floating text" of the woman caught in adultery in the Gospel of Luke. The story finally settles, even more appropriately as will become clear, in the Fourth Gospel.[27]

The Gospel Code

But why is there no direct identification of Mary of Bethany with the sinner of the city, the woman taken in adultery, and Mary Magdalene? If they are all the same person, wouldn't the gospel writers tell us that? Why would they create these separate identifications? And why is there no chapter in the gospels that pauses to put all these items together and marvel at the remarkable relation of Jesus and Mary? Why do the gospel writers, nearly two thousand years before Dan Brown, collectively create a theological mystery story, "the gospel code," for fascinated readers to puzzle over?

Once the gospel code is deciphered thanks to a certain key idea, we can see that each writer of the canonical gospels is at pains to hide the secret of Mary Magdalene. The reason cannot have been to hide the marriage of Jesus, as if this would have been something shameful for a Jewish Rabbi of the time, and particularly one who was regarded as the promised Messiah. Later Christian disparagement of marriage for priests and saints would not have applied to the Jewish culture of the gospels. It is not Jesus's marital status that is the problem, but the specific identity of the one whom he married. Jesus's marriage is not mentioned, not because the gospel writers had a problem with his being married, but because mention of marriage would require identifying the woman whom he married. We can understand the reluctance of the gospel writers in identifying the woman who is so close to Jesus as a former prostitute. In calling attention to Mary's erstwhile profession they run the risk of demeaning Jesus, as they think he should be understood. They run the risk—no doubt even more disturbing—of demeaning themselves, followers of the man they call the Messiah, the Savior, the Son of God, who nevertheless, inexplicably, married a woman whose prior occupation was for them the cause of deepest embarrassment and confusion. In acknowledging and, more importantly, in probing the meaning of the prominence Jesus accords her, they open unappetizing and indigestible cans of worms for themselves. A fine line must therefore be walked between too much belittlement and too close attention. In trying to find a happy medium, they implicitly show their failure to grasp the revolutionary meeting of the extremes that is at the heart of Jesus's own teaching—that she who is last shall be first.[28] Thus far from being a demeaning invention of Pope Gregory, the identification of Mary Magdalene as a prostitute is in fact the key both to revealing the mystery of her ambiguous presence in the gospels, as well as for grasping the deepest significance of the life and teaching of Jesus. Of course, without these added meanings, her identification *solely* as a repentant prostitute is indeed demeaning.

Perhaps this ambiguity and mystery is what appealed most of all to Irenaeus some one hundred years after the Fourth Gospel was written as he came to identify the Christian canon of only four gospels. He excluded whatever writings were too open, too forthright, too categorical in their depiction of the position of Mary. Whereas the canonical gospels unproblematically speak of Mary's love for Jesus, a serious problem arises for a resurrected patriarchy when certain gospels put the spotlight on Jesus's love of Mary. The four canonical writers are in agreement that Mary must be mentioned, but in a way that conceals her true reality. But the gentile physician Luke, working with Paul in his mission to the non-Jews, does not coordinate his account with that of Matthew and Mark, who do not identify the woman with the ointment, either as a sinner or as Mary Magdalene. They do, however, place the event in Bethany, at the home of Simon the Leper and during an event involving many disciples of Jesus. The accusation of extravagance, in these accounts, is by anonymous disciples. But the Fourth Gospel, written last of all, finally fills in some of the blanks in Matthew and Mark by identifying this woman as Mary of Bethany, though not directly as Mary Magdalene. Moreover, the one who accuses her of extravagance is identified as the notorious traitor, Judas. While the Fourth Gospel does not describe Mary as a sinner, the wonderful account of the woman taken in adultery draws special attention to itself by mysteriously floating throughout the extant texts, not appearing in the earliest manuscripts, coming at the very end of another, before finally settling at the beginning of the eighth chapter of the Fourth Gospel. Surely this story was a hot potato for the various editors who for some reason found it difficult to handle.

When the different accounts are put together we see that Luke has clearly identified Mary of Bethany's generous gesture toward Jesus with that of a mere "sinner in the city," the hostess of a glorious occasion transformed into a repentant prostitute. Luke's antipathy to the legend of Mary, whom he probably never met in person, comes out in his account of the resurrection, where, as in the account of his leader Paul, Peter gets the best part and Mary, still for him the "sinful woman," is an unimportant bystander.[29] But despite his efforts to the contrary, Luke gives unconscious testimony to the centrality of the relation between Mary and Jesus when at the very end of his gospel he describes Jesus's final departure, when he is "carried up to heaven," as taking place in Bethany (Luke 24:50–51).

Why Did Judas Betray Jesus?

It was not only a certain Pharisee named Simon who had trouble with Mary. Mary is too prominent, too powerful, too poignant a figure in Jesus's life for the gospel writers to ignore her. But for the male disciples, who regularly fail to grasp Jesus's meaning, she was just too puzzling a question for them to seriously pursue.

Andrew Lloyd Webber's rock opera *Jesus Christ Superstar* insightfully identifies the sinful woman in the home of Simon the Pharisee in the Gospel of Luke, the Mary of Bethany celebrating Lazarus's resurrection in the home of Simon the Leper in the Fourth Gospel, together with the woman who is caught in adultery, as none other than Mary Magdalene. Here a problem is solved that arises when we connect these two accounts of the woman who pours expensive ointment over Jesus. If we suppose that Mary, who no doubt is spending lavishly, is the co-hostess of the celebration for her brother, it is quite unlikely that Simon the host, a man who may have been a Pharisee who was cured by Jesus of leprosy, would have criticized Mary for being a prostitute. But Luke is trying to avoid giving away the true identity of the sinful woman, and so it seems that he puts the criticism of Mary's prostitution as well as of Jesus's association with her in the mouth of a secondary character, introduced and dismissed as a representative of the despised Jewish Pharisees. But if the event actually takes place in Bethany, with Mary as a central figure, who there would attack Mary? It is Judas, according to the Fourth Gospel, who complains about the extravagance, which, the author says, is because he was the treasurer of the group and a thief. In the Lloyd Webber version, with lyrics by Tim Rice, it is therefore Judas who both blames Mary for wasting three hundred silver pieces in her anointment of Jesus as well as criticizes Jesus for his association with this woman who was a prostitute. In making such a juxtaposition of texts we see another cryptic linkage of Jesus and Mary. Judas is the traitor in the camp of Jesus; and he is also the only Apostle in the four canonical gospels who explicitly criticizes Mary.

With the addition of one more clue, this connection leads to a startling insight into the cause of Judas's betrayal. While the Gospel of Luke has an anonymous Simon the Pharisee upbraid Jesus over the unsavory occupation of the woman sitting at his feet, the Fourth Gospel tells us it that this critic of Mary was actually the traitor Judas. Has Luke then deliberately lied to hide the evidence? But the main rule of an authentic mystery story is that the story teller tells no lies, but cleverly misleads the incautious reader while leaving clues to the actual truth. The Fourth Gospel tells us several times that Judas Iscariot (from the town of Kerioth) is the son of . . . *Simon*. Judas's name is Judas (bar) Simon. Luke is therefore using Judas's family name, his patronymic. So Luke is effectively saying: This (Judas) Simon, this hypocritical Pharisee who really wants to betray Jesus, dares to belittle him in front of everyone. And when the Fourth Gospel has Judas speak out so bluntly against Mary, we see that he has a certain right. The prostitute Mary is not only degrading his own (or his father's) house by her presence, but has the gall to take it over to celebrate the resurrection of her brother.

The pieces of the puzzle fit together perfectly. When he sees Mary pouring expensive oils over Jesus, Judas, who is in charge of the group's treasury, can't bear to see such waste, such foolishness. He quite reasonably complains: How many poor could be helped with the price of these oils—worth three hundred pieces of silver! In response to the complaint of Judas, Jesus defends Mary, not him. You can always help the poor, Jesus says, but I won't be with you for much longer. Mary's anointment, says Jesus, foreshadows his immanent death, for the dead body must be anointed. Judas is jealous, angry, and afraid. On being publicly rebuffed by Jesus, he finally gives in to all his building resentment, thinking, we must suppose: Here he is letting this slut not only tell me how to do my job but take over my own house. Judas storms out, seeking revenge and justice. With mounting enthusiasm among the people over reports of the raising of Lazarus, and growing hostility of the authorities, a crisis is clearly looming. Thanks to Mary's interference in wheedling Jesus into a premature display of his power, the whole Jewish establishment is up in arms. And yet with this dangerous turn of events, instead of calling for an uprising Jesus calmly talks about his funeral arrangements. Judas boils with righteous indignation against the cause of all this turmoil: that upstart whore, Mary. So Judas decides: Jesus is doing everything he can to ruin the mission. He is listening to a woman rather than fighting for the kingdom he keeps talking about. Damn her! Who is the real traitor? If he really is the Messiah, I must force his hand.

The Beloved Disciple

Both the Gospel of Mary and the Gospel of Philip, heretical texts banished by the later Christian orthodoxy, describe Mary as the beloved of Jesus. But this designation is explicitly contradicted by the canonical Fourth Gospel, which describes its author, clearly identified as a man, as the beloved disciple of Jesus. The Fourth Gospel concludes by saying, "Peter turned, and saw the disciple whom Jesus loved following him; the same who leaned back on his breast at supper, and asked, Who is it that is to betray thee? . . . It is the same disciple that bears witness of all this and has written the story of it; and we know well that his witness is truthful." (John 21:20, 24). Strangely, the name of the beloved disciple is nowhere given in this very Gospel of which "he" is the acknowledged author. A tradition stemming from Irenaeus at the end of the second century identifies the beloved disciple and author of the Fourth Gospel with the apostle John son of Zebedee. Irenaeus relates that he heard this information from Bishop Polycarp when he was a child. Many contemporary scholars, who do not consider the memories of a child an adequate basis for ascribing this authorship, regard the author of the Fourth Gospel as unknown. If Polycarp definitely knew the identity of the author of the Fourth Gospel, why did he entrust this important information only to a child?

How is it possible that early Christian documents, including the texts discovered in the deserts of Egypt, appear to postulate two different beloved disciples? In the Nag Hammadi texts, buried during the persecutions of heretics after the Council of Nicea, this person is clearly identified as Mary Magdalene. However, in the Fourth Gospel, the beloved disciple is not named. Why is the identity of the beloved disciple kept a secret in this work? Simple economy of reasoning suggests that the same reason for banishing the so-called Gnostic texts were at work in the reediting of the Fourth Gospel: not only the fact that its author is a woman, but the immense difficulty in identifying the beloved disciple of Jesus as the former prostitute Mary Magdalene.

Raymond K. Jusino argues that the beloved disciple and author of the Fourth Gospel is none other than Mary Magdalene. Jusino finds a general framework for his argument in the work of the American Catholic biblical scholar, Raymond E. Brown.[30] Brown, who at one time thought that the Fourth Gospel was written by John son of Zebedee, later decided that evidence for this belief based on late-second-century testimony reflected the institutional consolidation and simplification of Christian doctrine in the early church.[31] Brown distinguishes three phases in the development of the community of the beloved disciple that produced the Fourth Gospel: (1) An early phase, from 50–80 CE, in which a community originally led by the beloved disciple coalesces around the teachings contained in the original oral or written version of their gospel. (2) Between 80–90 CE a split develops in the community as a result of growing divergences between its beliefs and those of others, both Jews and Christians, who were consolidating their institutionalized frameworks and reining in an earlier pluralism of beliefs and practices. Brown calls the two groups the Secessionists and the Apostolics. (3) Between 90–100 CE the adherents of the Apostolic trend join with the mainstream of Christians, producing the final version of the text. The other group persists with their distinctive beliefs and practices.[32]

As to how there might be two groups coincidently claiming different persons as the beloved disciple, Brown argues that the followers of Mary Magdalene attempted to refute the prior notion of the Fourth Gospel that the beloved disciple was a man.[33] But it is the Fourth Gospel, not the Gospel of Mary, that explicitly opposes Mary to the beloved disciple, as if trying to make the point that this disciple is *not* Mary, as others have previously claimed. In the Fourth Gospel the beloved disciple is twice clearly identified as *not* being Mary Magdalene. After so much mystery surrounding the identity of Mary Magdalene, these two passages provide a very clear identity, but in the negative: Mary is *not* the beloved disciple of Jesus. As for the identity of the beloved disciple, we learn two things: he is a man, and he is *not* this woman, Mary Magdalene. And that is all we are told, in two different scenes, about the identity of the beloved disciple.

In the scene in which Jesus first appears to Mary after his resurrection, Mary runs to get Peter and another individual who is strangely unnamed but clearly identified as a man and Jesus's beloved disciple. This tells the reader that although Jesus does first appear to Mary, she is *not* the beloved disciple as this appearance might at first imply. For some reason Jesus does not first come to the beloved disciple, who is definitely a man—which is all the text can say for him. This suggests that these passages of the Fourth Gospel were written to refute a prior idea that the beloved disciple is Mary.

According to Jusino, moreover, the Fourth Gospel was originally popular among the Gnostic Christians, those who produced the Gospel of
Mary, before it was adopted by the orthodox Christians as the gospel of
a male disciple. The original text of the Fourth Gospel, he argues, clearly
identified Mary Magdalene as its author. However, as growing institutional forces made it more and more difficult to adhere to radical
Christian egalitarianism, it became increasingly embarrassing to identify
the founder of this group as a woman. The group accordingly split into
two tendencies, with one continuing to defend the original identification
of Mary as the beloved disciple (Brown's Secessionists) while the other,
seeking acceptance with a coalescing Christian mainstream, modified
their text to make it appear that their founder was a man, and not Mary
Magdalene (Brown's Apostolics). In some cases this was just a matter of
changing the gender of pronouns, while suppressing any identification
of a certain disciple, who goes unnamed in the new version, with Mary
Magdalene. In other instances, such as the famous account of Jesus's
appearance to Mary, a more elaborate alteration was required.

As a result of these alterations, a mystery is created for no apparent
reason. There is an important disciple, who is the beloved of Jesus, yet
whose name cannot be mentioned. A mysteriously unnamed but important male disciple appears in many places in the Fourth Gospel. In some
cases it was necessary to engage in more drastic alterations of an earlier
text to distinguish this disciple from Mary Magdalene. As a tradition had
been firmly established among the general body of Christians that Mary
Magdalene was at the foot of the cross and was also the first to meet with
Jesus after the crucifixion, suppression of such matters would have been
too obviously a distortion. The editor therefore adopted the device of
introducing a male disciple into the narrative alongside Mary Magdalene,
and transferring the designation of beloved disciple from her to him.
However as we will see, these modifications introduced clumsy phrasing
into the final document which on close inspection suggests deliberate
alterations. With no clear substitute candidate in view who would be
acceptable to Christians who had some already settled understandings,
the Apostolics from the community of the beloved disciple had to leave
their founder unnamed, while maintaining that person's special relation
to Jesus as the one whom he loved. The other group, Brown's so-called
Secessionists, continued the tradition of the original text, and of later
texts, especially the recently discovered Gospel of Mary, which
unashamedly identify the beloved of Jesus as Mary Magdalene.

For contemporary readers of the once buried, forbidden texts a clear
candidate for authorship of the Fourth Gospel, which should be called

the Gospel of the Beloved Disciple, jumps into sharp focus. She is that very same beloved disciple mentioned in the Gnostic gospels, as well as the first person to whom Jesus appears after his death and so the "Apostle of the Apostles," Mary Magdalene. How, after all, could there be two very different beloved disciples? And if there were, why is the identity of one of them not named? The Fourth Gospel in fact gives us names not mentioned elsewhere. In the first place, it is the only gospel that tells us that Jesus especially loved certain persons, and identifies those persons by name: Mary of Bethany, her sister Martha, and her brother Lazarus (John 11:5). It tells us quite clearly who betrays Mary, or tries to betray her, thereby linking Mary and Jesus through the common enmity of Judas. It is only the Fourth Gospel, moreover, that describes a complex scene including Jesus's very personal meeting with Mary at the tomb. As the Synoptic gospels merely claim that angels met with a group of women including Mary, it would have been relatively easy, contrary to Jusino, to suppress this passage without a lot of suspicion, and stay with the vaguer account. But the editor could not go that far in betraying the singularity of his precious document. He must describe the beloved disciple as a man, and not Mary Magdalene, to gain entrance for his group with a consolidating apostolic, male-dominated church. And yet he cannot resist telling us that Jesus appeared first of all to Mary Magdalene, and not, strangely enough, to this alleged beloved male disciple. The mystery of the different gospel accounts of the events at the tomb is easily solved if we recognize that, while the other gospels continued their game of hiding the truth about Mary, in the Fourth Gospel, Mary was writing of her own experience.

Thanks to our idea of the identification of Mary with the beloved disciple and author of the Fourth Gospel, the conspiracy against Mary assumes ever larger proportions. Seven times in the Fourth Gospel there is mention of a mysterious disciple of Jesus, sometimes called the beloved disciple, but sometimes simply mentioned without any identification, despite playing a prominent role. Mention of an unnamed disciple goes back to the very beginning of Jesus's ministry. As recounted in the Fourth Gospel, the first disciples to follow Jesus were two followers of John the Baptist. John has identified Jesus as the one for whom he has been prophesying: "Behold! The Lamb of God who takes away the sins of the world." John has seen the Spirit descending on Jesus in the form of a dove and recognizes that while he, John, baptizes with water, the man who will come after him will baptize with the Holy Spirit. On the next day, John points Jesus out to two of his own disciples, saying, "Look, this is the Lamb of God." The two followers of John then approach Jesus, ask him where he lives, and spend the rest of the day together with him. One of the two is Andrew, the brother of Peter, who quickly brings Peter into the group. Two other early disciples are then identified, Philip and Nathanael, but the other one of the first two who was there from the very beginning mysteriously goes unnamed (John 1:29–45). According to the Fourth Gospel (and only there) John was at this time preaching in Bethany! (John 1:28). Thus Jesus's public teaching career both begins and ends in Bethany, home of Mary Magdalene.

The first use of the designation of beloved disciple occurs at the Last Supper: "Jesus had one disciple, whom he loved, who was now sitting with his head against Jesus' breast . . ." (John 13:23). When Jesus announces that one of them will betray him, Peter has to ask this disciple to ask Jesus which one of them Jesus means. Da Vinci portrays this scene with the beloved disciple sitting at the right hand of Jesus, leaning away from Jesus toward Peter, and Peter leaning forward with a menacing gesture that cuts across the beloved's neck.

Peter is similarly with an unnamed disciple after the arrest of Jesus. When Jesus is taken away by temple guards, Peter and another unnamed disciple follow them to the high priest's court. The unnamed disciple must be a prominent person because he or she is well known to the high priest, and as a result gains access to the courtyard. (John of Zebedee, whom Jesus nicknamed, together with John's brother James, "the sons of thunder," was a simple fisherman.) This important disciple then enables Peter too to enter. This mysterious other disciple is clearly a well-connected individual, known even to the doorkeeper to be an associate of Jesus. Even the common doorkeeper knows the name of the unnamed disciple, although he doesn't know who Peter is, for he has to ask Peter if he is another of the companions of Jesus. We, the readers, are the only ones kept in the dark here. In contrast to his bold associate, whose relation to Jesus is well-known and readily acknowledged, Peter immediately denies any relation to Jesus, and pretends to be only warming himself by a fire. What then follows is the interrogation of Jesus by the high priest.

We next meet the beloved disciple in two complicated and verbally confusing scenes: at the foot of the cross, and then at the tomb of Jesus. In each of these passages Mary Magdalene is explicitly mentioned *alongside* the beloved disciple, who is clearly identified as a man. The text in each case gives evidence of inconsistencies that show the hand of an editor working with an earlier manuscript. In the first case, we read: "and meanwhile his mother, and his mother's sister, and Mary Magdalen, had taken their stand beside the cross of Jesus. And Jesus, seeing his mother there, and the disciple too whom he loved, standing by. . . ." Three indi-

viduals are first mentioned at the foot of the cross, three women, all
clearly identified. Next to Jesus's mother is the one whom he loved—
clearly, the reader who pauses at this point must think, that is Mary
Magdalene. This passage is strikingly similar to that of the Gnostic Gospel
of Philip, which identifies the same three women and singles out Mary
Magdalene as Jesus's beloved: "There were three who always walked
with the lord: Mary his mother and her sister and Magdalene, the one
who was called his companion."[34]

Disrupting this harmony of references, suddenly a fourth, mysteriously unnamed person, a male, precipitates into the scene: ". . . [Jesus]
said to his mother, Woman, this is thy son. Then he said to the disciple,
This is thy mother. And from that hour the disciple took her into his own
keeping" (John 19:25–27). Three persons are first mentioned at the foot
of the cross, but when Jesus speaks he addresses a fourth person. The
beloved disciple is *not* Mary, we are told, but a man whose name is for
some mysterious reason withheld. Moreover, Jesus must awkwardly
adopt this beloved man into his family by declaring him to be the son of
his Mother Mary. Of course if he is speaking to Mary Magdalene, and if
the fourth individual is interjected by a later editor to hide this fact, the
reference to her as the daughter of his mother is quite natural, for indeed
she is his mother's daughter by marriage.

First Apostle and Fastest Runner

The beloved disciple appears next after the resurrection when Jesus
appears first of all to Mary (see John 20:1–17). But before he does so there
is an interesting footrace. Mary goes to the tomb and finds it empty. She
then runs, presumably some distance, to find Peter "and that other disciple, whom Jesus loved," to tell them the startling news. Peter and the
beloved disciple, another man, then race back to the tomb "running side
by side, but the other disciple outran Peter, and reached the tomb first."
The unnamed beloved disciple looks into the tomb, sees the discarded
linen cloths there, lets Peter enter first, and then follows. The two men
then leave the tomb, "but Mary stood without before the tomb, weeping."
The narration has missed a logical step. How did Mary get back to the
tomb after running to find the two male disciples? The thematic continuity of the passage is broken. Mary is the first runner, setting the impassioned pace for the entire scene. But she vanishes in the following
sequence only to reappear as if teleported into the next. In her place is
the beloved disciple, an unnamed man, who runs alongside Peter. The
beloved disciple is, like Mary in the first place, a good runner, for "he"

outruns Peter. Mary is not mentioned on the return footrace, and yet at the end of this flurry of running we find her somehow back at the tomb.

Everything would be clear and coherent if the text had said that it was Mary who both ran to find Peter and than ran back with Peter, outrunning him, but then, in deference to his leadership position, allowing him to enter the tomb first. The subsequent scene would then follow without a misstep. Peter goes away wondering who took the body, while Mary remains behind, clearly the more shaken of the two and the one who is the more attached to the scene. As if rewarding her patience and persistence, Jesus then appears to Mary, who recognizes him when he calls her by name, "Mary." Mary passionately embraces Jesus, but he warns her away: "Do not cling to me thus; I have not yet gone up to my Father's side."

Here would be a perfect love story, complete with the contest of loyalty, faith, and love between Peter and Mary that we find in the suppressed texts. The very same contest can be read throughout the Fourth Gospel too were it not for the failure to identify a mysterious but important disciple, and the awkward introduction of an unnamed third party as the beloved disciple. It is Mary, along with Andrew, and *not* Peter, who is Jesus's first disciple. At the Last Supper, the beloved disciple passes on crucial information to Peter directly from Jesus. After the apprehension of Jesus, this person boldly precedes Peter into the courtyard of the High Priest as a well-known disciple of Jesus, but Peter denies any knowledge of the Master. Finally, the resurrected Jesus appears first of all to Mary, and *not* to Peter. And to put icing on the cake, she, if we read the text with the symmetry it deserves, can even beat Peter in a footrace. The contest with Peter is also prominent in the conclusion of the Gospel, as we will soon see. It seems more than a little strange that in the extant text, Jesus does not first reveal himself to "the disciple whom he loved"—who plays a very feeble role for a person with such a designation—but instead to this problematic woman Mary. It would indeed be strange, were she not indeed his beloved disciple.

The next appearance of the beloved disciple occurs on the seashore after a night of fruitless fishing. Jesus is standing on the shore, and tells the fishermen off shore to cast their nets one more time. They follow the instructions and bring in a big haul. The exact number of the fish they catch is carefully stated—exactly one hundred and fifty three. Despite this new miracle of the fishes, Peter does not recognize Jesus until the "disciple whom Jesus loved" tells him: "It is the Lord" (John 21:7). Whereupon Peter, with characteristic energy, leaps out of the boat to wade to Jesus. "The other disciples" follow in their boat with the catch—

that is, disciples other than Peter and the beloved disciple. This special disciple is not on the boat, but already on shore. The picture comes into sharp focus: the beloved disciple is waiting with the other women for the men to return from their work. Of course she naturally recognizes Jesus first, for he is standing right next to her.

Finally, the resurrected Jesus is speaking to Peter and asks him, three times, whether he loves him. Peter, who had denied knowing Jesus three times, here cancels out his previous betrayal by affirming his love three times. Jesus tells Peter, "Feed my sheep." He then prophesies Peter's death, arms spread out and led against his will. After hearing of his own death, Peter notices the beloved disciple coming behind them and asks, "And what of this man, Lord?" Jesus replies, "If it is my will that he should wait till I come, what is that to thee? Do thou follow me."

Different deaths are allotted to these two principle leaders, and rivals, of the early Christians. Peter will be savagely crucified by the Romans, but Mary will have a happier fate. Previously her embrace of Jesus at the tomb had to be postponed because he was not yet going to the Father. In this final scene, she is promised that postponed embrace. She will not die in the savage manner of Peter, but will be taken away by Jesus himself. The gospel concludes with words clearly interjected after the death of the beloved disciple. But perhaps in the last sentence we can hear the original text, the first-person sentiment of the woman who knew Jesus intimately, his beloved and companion, who had so much more to say:

> That is why the story went out among the brethren that this disciple ["the disciple whom Jesus loved"] was not to die. But Jesus did not say, He is not to die; he said, if it is my will that he should wait till I come, what is that to thee? It is the same disciple that bears witness of all this and has written the story of it; and we know well that his witness is truthful. There is much else besides that Jesus did; and if all of it were put into writing, I do not think the world itself would contain the books which would have to be written. (John 21:23–25)

One Hundred and Fifty-Three Fishes

Did someone actually count the number of fish hauled up under the instructions of Jesus? It is not impossible, given the extraordinary nature of the circumstances. But even then the number itself must have some special significance for it to be worthy of mention. Or else, because the number has a special significance it was inserted at some point in the evolution of the text to convey a cryptic message. But what message? Here again we find that the gospel text contains a secret code, but this time it is one that is deliberately constructed for those who understand how numbers can have meaning. The most famous example of such meaningful, mysterious numbers in the canonical texts is the number 666. Revelation 13:18 gives the reader this puzzle to solve: "Here is room for discernment; let the reader, if he has the skill, cast up the sum of the figures in the beast's name, after our human fashion, and the number will be six hundred and sixty-six."

The study of the hidden meaning of words through the numerical significance of the letters of the alphabet is called "gematria" from the Greek word "geomatria." Gematria is therefore a kind of sacred metrics of words and phrases. The letters of the Hebrew and Greek alphabets corresponded to numbers. So "alpha" is 1, "beta" is 2, "iota" is 10, "kappa" is 20, "rho" is 100, "sigma" is 200, and so forth. As the gospel texts were first written in Greek, the numeric associations of words would come naturally to the educated writer and reader. Understanding the gematria of the words can clarify certain puzzles, including, for example, the name "Jesus" itself. In the Aramaic language of the time spoken by Jesus, he was called "Yeshua," a name that would naturally have come into English as "Joshua." So why is the founder of Christianity called "Jesus" and not "Joshua"? The Greek "Iesous" (Ιησουσ) is not the most natural transliteration of "Yeshua" or "Jeshua." But the Greek letters of "Iesous" add up to a striking number: 888. Three 8s is the triple power of 8. According to Margaret Starbird this number would have had great significance for the early Christian community which saw itself as representing a new age. The age of the Old Testament or covenant with God was frequently represented by 7. The seventh day, for example, is the day of rest, when God rested from the creation, the day of the Jewish Sabbath. The number eight therefore signifies following day, and the *New* Testament.[35]

Some numbers reflect an initial mathematical significance. The number 666, the number of the beast, is the number of "the magic square of the sun." This is the square composed of six numbers across and six down, in which the numbers from one to thirty-six are arranged in such a way that the sums of the numbers in each row and column, as well as diagonally, add up to 111, while the sum of the entire box is 666.[36] According to Margaret Starbird, the sun is the symbol of masculinity and male power in isolation from female balance. It is "yang" without "yin," and so the number of tyranny. The number of the feminine principle is 1080, which is the measure of the radius of the moon, as well as the gematria of terms such as "the Holy Spirit" (το αγιον πνευμα) and its anagram, "the Earth Spirit" (το γαιον πνευμα).[37]

In one of his parables to explain the kingdom of God, which contains the essence of his teaching, Jesus uses a peculiar metaphor, comparing his kingdom "To a mustard seed; when this is sown in the earth, no seed on earth is so little; but, once sown, it shoots up and grows taller than any garden herb, putting out great branches, so that all the birds can come and settle under its shade" (Mark 4:30–31). The kingdom of God is no otherworldly heaven—for how could the afterlife be compared to a mustard seed? It is rather a developing earthly community, beginning with a small band of brothers and sisters who understand and express in their lives the love of the Father in their relations to one another. Jesus liked this metaphor very much for he also compares faith to a mustard seed. Faith, or better, trust in the power of the spirit of love begins as something small, like a mustard seed, but it eventually grows into a great force of earthly transformation. The fellows of the Jesus Seminar argue that with multiple attestations as well as because of its striking nature, the mustard seed imagery probably expresses the authentic teaching of Jesus. They comment: "Jesus employs a surprising image with which to compare God's imperial rule."[38] The members of the Jesus Seminar speculate about the possible reason for this metaphor, but fail to consider the gematria of the term for mustard seed. It seems that Jesus would have been conscious of the equivalent of the Aramaic term in Greek, for that term in Greek, kokkos sinapeos (κοκκοσ σιναπεωσ), has powerful numerical significance. Its gematria is 1746, which is the sum of 666 and 1080.[39] This meaning perfectly completes the image of the seed of life that arises out of the unity of male and female, and expresses their harmony.

If we turn then to the number 153, the number of fishes in the final miracle of Jesus, we find that it contains a similarly potent numerology. In his treatise on circles, Archimedes uses the number 153 to refer to the mathematical proportions of the *vesica piscis*, literally the bladder of the fish. The *vesica piscis* is the figure formed by the intersection of two equal circles that pass through each other's centers. If the horizontal line between the two centers is 1, the vertical line is the square root of three. Lacking a symbol for the square root, the Greeks approximated this value by its approximate whole number equivalent, which is 265/153. The concept was then abbreviated simply as 153.[40] The *vesica piscis* represents the intersection of two equal circles, the male and female in deepest harmony, with the first creation of their union being the form created by their intersection. This form is indeed the seed of life, the mustard seed, which in its eventual growth will be capable of sheltering all life.

In view of these meanings the miracle of the fishes at the end of the Fourth Gospel, with its exact catch of 153, was bound to reverberate with profound significance for the educated reader of the time. Add to all of this the astrological significance of "the fishes" as the symbol of the age of Pisces, or the Age of the Fishes, whose beginning was underway during the life time of Jesus. A depiction of the symbol for the sign of Pisces shows its dependence on the *vesica piscis*. We can see also that the Christian symbol of the fish is the *vesica piscis* on its side. Early Christians, including Tertullian, Clement of Alexandria, and Augustine used the fish as the symbol of Christianity. At some point the astrological significance—with its more pagan, earth-centered connotations—drops out of the picture, and the early sources of the symbol are replaced by the acronym for orthodoxy of the Council of Nicea "Jesus Christ, Son of God, Savior," which is Ichthys (ΧΘΥΣ)—the Fish. This symbol of the single fish not only avoids the astrological connection, but truncates its potent symbolism: the relation of male and female of the two fishes that represent the Age of Pisces. It fails therefore to reflect the deeper meaning of the mustard seed, as the product of the union of male and female. Rather than focusing on the scene in the Fourth Gospel, where the tears of Mary Magdalene call forth the first appearance of the resurrected Jesus, Christianity is well on the way toward the patriarchal concept of the solitary savior, portrayed by Mel Gibson as alone in his tomb.

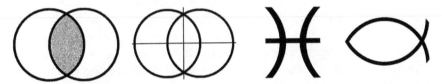

Vesica Piscis   **Astrological**   **Christian**
                           sign of Pisces **symbol of**
                                              the fish

There is one final value for the 153 fishes caught by Peter and the other disciples, as they are observed from the shore by Jesus and Mary. The gematria in Greek for "the Magdalene," η Μαγδληνη, is none other than 153! This gematria explains why she is called "Mary, the Magdalene" and not, as many assume the term means, "Mary of Magdala," supposedly derived from her birthplace in "Magdala." Calling this idea "a colossal error," Margaret Starbird explains that were the term a designation of her city of origin, her epithet would be Magdalaia (Μαγδαλαια).[41] Mary of Bethany does not have two homes, one in Bethany and another in a city called Magdala, which did not even exist at the time. She has one home, in Bethany, with her sister Martha, and her brother Lazarus. This is the one place that the itinerant Rabbi Yeshua can also call home. Rather than referring to a location, "the Magdalene" refers to a title or a status, which Mary achieved through her life with Jesus and through her teachings. "The Magdalene," Starbird argues, suggests a Hebrew term that means stronghold or tower. She cites the biblical book of Micah (or Michaeas) 4:8–10:

> As for you, O Magdal-eder, watchtower of the flock,
> O Stronghold of the Daughter of Zion
> The former dominion will be restored to you;
> Kingship will come to the Daughter of Jerusalem.[42]

Mary is "the Magdalene," the watchtower on the battlements of the holy city. She is the daughter of Jerusalem, to whom the king, the Messiah, has come. The establishment of the kingdom of God, the freedom and happiness of Zion, arises from a potent seed out of the marriage of Jesus and Mary. This is not about a physical bloodline, but a kingdom of the spirit of love.

The identity of the beloved of Jesus has been obscured by alterations of her gospel, perhaps necessarily, so that her words, and the teachings of Jesus, could enter the mainstream of what became the majority of orthodox Christians. The Latin translation of the Greek text has buried the evidence even further. But if we look deeply at the clues, the codes, the pregnant omissions throughout the texts of the gospel, we can see her absence, the evidence of her lost dominion and separation from her king, as symbolized by Micah's lament over Jerusalem at the time of Assyrian tyranny. As Marie Chauvel in *The Da Vinci Code* notes, however, "The pendulum is swinging. We are starting to sense the dangers of our history . . . and of our destructive paths. We are beginning to sense the need to restore the sacred feminine."[43]

A Tragic Romance Spoiled

Let us hazard a general reconstruction of the larger story, guided by an idea that puts dispersed pieces of a puzzle into an appealing and plausible pattern. At some point before the narrative of his public mission, Jesus has saved Mary from a threatened stoning. The story of the woman taken in adultery is absent in the earliest manuscripts of the Fourth Gospel, and in one it surprisingly appears at the very end.[44] Its very inclusion would have been an embarrassment for the community of the beloved disciple, especially during an early period closest to the lifetime of its founder. And yet the truth of the matter had to be somehow told, though without explicit connection to Mary Magdalene, for the story comes from Mary herself. The fact that in one version it could be placed at the very end of the text, in close proximity to the identification of its author as the beloved disciple, strongly underlines its connection to that person. It also suggests that the story is outside of the Gospel narrative altogether—and so possibly before the opening of the mission of Jesus by the testimony of John the Baptist.

With such an idea in mind, we see that Mary's first encounter with Jesus catalyzes her transformation from a highly successful and well-connected "sinner in the city," a courtesan to the rich and famous, to a follower of the austere John the Baptist. We noted above that when Jesus was accused of associating with prostitutes, he says that John the Baptist did the same. In fact, we suddenly see, it is the very same prostitute! Accused of associating in unseemly ways with the prostitute Mary Magdalene, Jesus replies that the undoubtedly austere John did the same.

Mary is indeed a repentant sinner, but one whose repentance was motivated by the unexpected intervention of a man who is different from ordinary men, from those hypocrites who see in her only one thing. As fate would have it, Mary recognizes her own personal savior once more when John points him out as the one who takes away the sins of the entire world. That is, he is the one who treats the outcasts and degraded of society with loving forgiveness rather than with damning judgment. She then becomes his first disciple, along with Andrew. She lavishly spends of her considerable wealth supporting Jesus and his group of followers. Soon she is not only a disciple, but his companion too, and partner in his mission. Her home in Bethany has become his home. In all the gospels, Jesus is said to love only three people: Mary, her sister Martha, and her brother Lazarus (John 11:5). This explicit statement of the Fourth Gospel has led at least one investigator to conclude that the unnamed beloved disciple must be Lazarus! He is after all the only *man* whom Jesus is said to have loved.

When Lazarus dies, Jesus is at first reluctant to step into the dangerous limelight to which a spectacular display of "the force" of spirit inevitably exposes him—although his teaching as recorded by his beloved is that others are capable of doing what he can do, and even more (John 14:12). But he is moved by Mary's tears to bring Lazarus back from the dead. In celebration of this miracle, she pours expensive oil on his body in the home of Simon, and provokes the anger of Simon's son, the traitor Judas. Mary has thus indirectly brought Jesus to his death. Through exposing Jesus to the adulation of the masses by his most awesome miracle, she has intensified the hostility of the threatened authorities. And she has provoked in Judas the jealous rage that sets up the betrayal. Linked inextricably to Jesus's death in this way, she stands alongside his mother at the cross, and is entrusted with her care, for Jesus's mother is of course also Mary's mother by marriage. She then comes first to the tomb as the person who has the clear right to care for the body of her spouse. Instead of finding the battered body of her lover, the tomb is empty, except for what she thinks is a gardener standing nearby. Who else could this man be? Until she hears her name pronounced in an unmistakable voice, "Mary."

Someone has spoiled what should have been the greatest tragic romance ever told by claiming that, despite the central dramatic importance of this woman, Jesus really loved someone else, and, as if it were a matter of insignificance, not telling us who that beloved person was.

Authenticity of the Fourth Gospel

With this new way of looking at the Fourth Gospel surprising features come into focus. The first miracle of Jesus takes place at a wedding feast. In the following chapter, John the Baptist compares Jesus with the bridegroom in love with his bride, while he, John, is like the friend of the groom who, without jealousy, is happy for his friend (John 3:27–30). Who would more readily record this description of Jesus as bridegroom but his own beloved bride? These are perceptions and recollections that would come naturally to a woman writer, one who secretly thrills at her own marriage with Jesus. John the Baptist is given exceptional space in the Fourth Gospel, as is befitting for the testimony of a former disciple. In a text that is generally dated from some sixty years after the death of John, there is precise detail about the places along the Jordan where John baptized, as these intersect with a carefully recorded itinerary of the movements of Jesus.

After this account of the Baptist's words comparing Jesus with a bridegroom, the author turns to Jesus's encounter with a Samaritan woman who had five husbands, and was presently living with a man who was not her legal husband. Here is another "sinner" by the standards of conventional morality. Jesus goes beyond turning water into wine by offering her "living water," the Life Force that comes from within—the Force of Spirit, which each person can find within herself. For as the Baptist says, while he himself baptizes with mere water, as a symbol of purification, the one who comes after him baptizes with spirit—that is, with the breath of life itself. But the (male) disciples, the author slyly recounts, could not understand what Jesus was doing talking with a (mere) woman. After giving his teaching to these generally despised foreigners, the Samaritans, Jesus next responds to the pleading of a father, a high ranking official, a Roman, whose son lay dying. The author no doubt also thought of the tragedy of the mother, standing by the bedside of her afflicted son, for she does not neglect to record the rejoicing of the household at the recovery of the boy.

These events are described in great detail, and situated precisely in time and space. When contemporary historians compare the historical accuracy of various gospel accounts regarding certain events of the life of Jesus, the Fourth Gospel stands out from the others. For example, while the Synoptic gospels describe the Last Supper as taking place during the Passover feast, the Fourth Gospel takes the more plausible position that it was not a Passover meal, but occurred before Passover—for the Jews would not have allowed a crucifixion during the seven days of the Passover festival.[45] There is a paradox here for those who admit this accuracy, but then claim that the lengthy teachings attributed to Jesus in this gospel must have been invented by a later author.

At the heart of this memorable last meal, the Synoptic gospels have Jesus implausibly ask his disciples to eat his body in the form of bread and drink his blood in the form of wine—the thought of ingesting blood being a central prohibition of the Jewish religion. Hence some historians suppose that this account was the invention of later Christian communities.[46] The Fourth Gospel completely omits this teaching about Jesus's body and blood from the account of the Last Supper. Instead, over protests against his supposed self-abasement, Jesus washes the feet of his disciples and then urges them to love each other as he has loved them and they him. Love is the authentic expression of the nature of God, whom Jesus calls Father. Seeing the love that Jesus has for them, the disciples see the Father. So Jesus prays: "that they may be one, as we are one, I with them and you with me, so they may be perfectly united." (John 17:22–23). It is this potential unity with each other, in the spirit of Jesus's love for them, that will empower them to surpass the works of Jesus himself. "Anyone who believes in me will perform the works I perform and will be able to perform even greater feats, because I'm on my way to the Father." This passage is explained at 14:28, where Jesus says: "If you loved me, you would be glad that I'm going to the Father, because the Father is greater than I am." The disciples will be able to perform greater feats than Jesus because the main teaching of Jesus is to become one with the love of the Father, the source of all Jesus's works.

In his lengthy and subtle teaching at the Last Supper as recorded in the Fourth Gospel, Jesus adopts a metaphor that would have special meaning for his beloved disciple. Preparing his followers for the horror that is soon to descend upon them, seemingly destroying all the hopes and aspirations, Jesus evokes the poignant image of a mother's labor in childbirth: "You will grieve, but your grief will turn to joy. A woman suffers pain when she gives birth because the time has come. When her child is born, in her joy she no longer remembers her labor because a human being has come into the world" (John 16:20–21). Life emerges out of the womb of the mother, no less than through the father's love. The happiness that will come to the followers of the message of love practiced by Mary and Jesus will obliterate all memory of suffering and persecution that the followers will face in the imminent the time of the crucifixion.

This washing of feet only occurs in this Gospel of the Beloved Disciple. With this alternative title in mind we recognize that this surprising and challenging performance occurs only a few days after Mary washes the feet of Jesus with precious oils. Jesus then reciprocates the gesture at the Last Supper. Jesus thus learns from the practice of Mary, who sets the example that Jesus extends to the others. This love for one another is the essence of the message of Jesus, and the true means of salvation of the Fourth Gospel. It is in another, more plausible context, the synagogue in Capernaum, that the Fourth Gospel places Jesus's teaching about eating his flesh and drinking his blood.[47] Jesus himself points out that his "grumbling disciples" must find this idea "shocking." Rather than being asserted without commentary as in the Synoptic gospels, the symbolism of the communion meal is explained as part of a larger theoretical context, a complex and subtle philosophical teaching about the oneness between Jesus and his followers. Jesus carefully explains that the communion practice symbolizes a spiritual, not a physical reality. For: "The spirit is life-giving; mortal flesh is good for nothing. The words I have used are 'spirit' and 'life.'"[48]

On the assumption that none of the canonical gospels are firsthand accounts, historians often regard the Fourth Gospel as less reliable than the others because its text, frequently recording events and ideas not found elsewhere, often fails the test of "multiple attestations"—that is, more than one appearance in the various gospels. So the Jesus Seminar regards the lengthy teachings of Jesus that are only recorded in the Fourth Gospel as largely a creation of the redactors of the "Johannine community," with most of these citations put in the lowest category of historical credibility.[49] What ranks highly instead are the short pithy sayings of Jesus in the Synoptic gospels that are found in more than one source, and are original and challenging in their expression and content.

Such brief sayings are said to characterize the true style of Jesus, and therefore the longer teachings recorded in the Fourth Gospel should be regarded as inventions of a later redactor. However, it is also recognized that the form of pithy sayings is one that is most likely to reflect the nature of an oral tradition that naturally tends to pass on shorter, more readily remembered sayings, losing in the process any lengthy, complicated ideas. Hence this form of narration, rather than being evidence of authenticity, may in fact indicate the contrary—that these sayings are truncated words of Jesus taken out of a larger theoretical context.

In terms of probable historical accuracy regarding the time and place of various events, the Fourth Gospel often excels the others. Why then not accept the teachings of Jesus recorded there as accurate accounts of the substance of Jesus's message to his disciples, his inner teachings, if not his popular parables for the general public? While some historians regard the Eucharistic meal as a later invention of the Christian communities because the notion of eating flesh and drinking blood would have been repulsive to earlier Jewish listeners, in the longer narration of the Fourth Gospel Jesus clearly recognizes this very problem.[50] So if the placing of the words at the Last Supper without any comment on its shocking nature seems implausible, the narration in the Fourth Gospel, in which Jesus frankly admits this impression and provides a complicated teaching to explain it, adds to the authenticity of this challenging idea and practice.

With multiple attestations from different sources, the Eucharistic practice gains authenticity, but with the direct admission of its surprising and even shocking character, the Fourth Gospel's presentation is doubly validated. And if we agree that the Eucharistic practice, so central to early Christianity, most likely stems from Jesus himself, it would seem probable that Jesus would have explained it in some detail, such as in the terms that we find in the Fourth Gospel. Jesus solves the evident problem by evoking the distinction between the higher spirit of love and the mundane physicalist interpretation of his words that indicates a general lack of comprehension of the spiritual or philosophical nature of his teachings. In doubting these teachings, in accusing their author of making them up, contemporary historians unconsciously line up with Andrew and Peter in the Gospel of Mary Magdalene.

Fundamental theological differences underlie the accounts of the different texts. While the Synoptics and Paul see the image of bread and wine as representing and reenacting the redeeming blood sacrifice of Jesus, the Fourth Gospel has a radically different orientation. The eating of bread and drinking of wine symbolize the unity in spirit of Jesus and his followers, a oneness of all in the life-giving spirit of love that expresses the true nature of the Father-Mother source of being. Robert Langdon considers these issues with special clarity in the film version of *The Da Vinci Code*. What does it mean that Sophie is the bearer of the bloodline of Jesus and Mary Magdalene? Maybe she is capable of greater feats than she has dreamed of, as he speculates on some of her recent accomplishments? And then he generalizes: "Why does it have to be human or divine? Perhaps the human is the divine."[51] Focusing narrowly on the bloodline of Jesus and Mary fails to grasp the spiritual meaning of the physical symbol. As Hegel explains, it is not Jesus himself who is central but the power of the Father, the power of Spirit, the Force of life and love that is found within every person.

NOTES

1. The Newton Project is publishing a collection of such writings at http://www.newtonproject.sussex.ac.uk/prism.php?id=1.

2. Dan Brown, *The Da Vinci Code* (New York: Doubleday, 2003), 444.

3. Dan Brown, *Da Vinci Code*, 444.

4. See Dan Brown, *Da Vinci Code*, 162 and 250. The *Shorter Oxford English Dictionary* implausibly traces "greal" to the Latin "gradalus" or dish.

5. Dan Brown, *Da Vinci Code*, 256.

6. Dan Brown, *Da Vinci Code*, 233.

7. Dan Brown, *Da Vinci Code*, 238–39.

8. Mark 1:31; from Ronald Knox's translation, *The Holy Bible* (New York: Sheed and Ward, 1956). All subsequent citations from the Bible are from this translation unless otherwise noted.

9. Dan Brown, *Da Vinci Code*, 246.

10. Karen L. King, *The Gospel of Mary of Magdala: Jesus and the First Woman Apostle* (Santa Rosa, CA: Polebridge Press, 2003), 15. The text including alternate readings from different sources takes up a mere six pages in this book. About half the original manuscript has been lost.

11. King, *Gospel of Mary*, 17.

12. King, *Gospel of Mary*, 145.

13. 1 Timothy 2:11–15. Thomas Cahill, *Desire of the Everlasting Hills* (New York: Doubleday, 1999), 156. See also King, *Gospel of Mary*, 56.

14. See the very detailed close-ups of the figure that is supposed to be that of the Apostle John, in "Images from Leonardo The Last Supper," Pinin Brambilla Barcilon and Pietro C. Marani, http://www.press.uchicago.edu/Misc/Chicago/504271.html (accessed 8-30-08) See also Dan Brown's website: http://www.dan-brown.com/secrets/davinci_code/last_supper.html (accessed 12/08/06).

15. Elaine Pagels, *Beyond Belief: The Secret Gospel of Thomas* (New York: Vintage Books, 2003).

16. Pagels, *Beyond Belief,* 174.

17. *The Gospel of Philip* 67:26–27; in *The Nag Hammadi Library,* James M. Robinson, gen. ed. (San Francisco: Harper Collins, 1990), 150.

18. The text of *The Gospel of Philip* does not say "on the mouth." The indication of where or how Jesus kissed Mary is a plausible interpretation of an obscure or missing part of the text.

19. King, *Gospel of Mary,* 152–53.

20. Dan Brown, *Da Vinci Code,* 261.

21. On this last film, see the article, "The 'Little Mermaid' and the Archetype of the Lost 'Bride'" by Margaret Starbird, written in 1999, http://ramon_k_jusino.tripod.com/littlemermaid.html. Starbird calls the de la Tour painting, "Magdalen with the Smoking Flame." In this film, revising the earlier Disney visions, it is the mermaid who saves the prince. Remarkable for anticipating (and perhaps improving on) the themes of *The Da Vinci Code,* the brief article by Starbird concludes with a copy of the logo for the high-end café giant Starbucks. The Starbucks logo shows a little mermaid whose tail fins connecting with her crown form the letters MM. Margaret Starbird is the author of *The Woman with the Alabaster Jar: Mary Magdalen and the Holy Grail* (1993) and *The Goddess in the Gospels: Reclaiming the Sacred Feminine* (1998). In testimony during a court trial on the charge of plagiarism, Dan Brown attributes much of his early interest in Mary Magdalene to these works of Starbird. Speaking of his research with his wife, Brown writes: "Margaret Starbird's books opened our eyes to the concept of the Church's subjugation of the sacred feminine." http://entertainment.timesonline.co.uk/tol/arts_and_entertainment/books/article741005.ece?token=null&offset=120&page=11 (accessed 8/30/08).

22. Dan Brown, *Da Vinci Code,* 245. A Wikipedia article on Mary Magdalene replies to the argument that in the context of Jewish law and practice the rabbi Jesus must have been married: "A counter-argument to this is that the Judaism of Jesus' time was very diverse and the role of the rabbi was not yet well defined. It was really not until after the Roman destruction of the Second Temple in A.D. 70 that Rabbinic Judaism became dominant and the role of the rabbi made uniform in Jewish communities. Before Jesus celibate teachers were known in the communities of the Essenes and John the Baptist also was celibate. Later, Paul of Tarsus was an example of an unmarried itinerant teacher among Christians. Jesus himself approved of voluntary celibacy for religious reasons and explicitly rejected a duty to marry: 'There are eunuchs, who have made themselves eunuchs for the kingdom of heaven. He that can take, let him take it' (Matthew 19:12)." http://en.wikipedia.org/wiki/Mary_Magdalene. But neither John the Baptist, the Essenes, nor Paul were popularly regarded as candidates for being the Messiah, which many followers of Jesus understood in the popular sense as a king in the royal Jewish bloodline who would reestablish an independent Jewish kingdom. Moreover, as noted below, Jesus distinguishes himself from ascetics like the Essenes and John the Baptist. He eats and drinks with tax collectors and prostitutes. As for the saying of Jesus regarding castrated eunuchs, who were forbidden by Jewish law from temple service as not being "full-

blooded male Judeans . . . capable of fathering children," the majority of the Fellows of the Jesus Seminar see this saying as an attack on "a male-dominated, patriarchal society in which male virility and parenthood were the exclusive norms," and a defense of another denigrated group together with "the poor, toll collectors, prostitutes, women generally, and children." As to Jesus's own marital status, "A majority of the Fellows doubted, in fact, that Jesus himself was celibate. They regard it is probable that he had a special relationship with at least one woman, Mary of Magdala." Robert W. Funk, Roy W. Hoover, and the Jesus Seminar, *The Five Gospels: What Did Jesus Really Say?* (New York: Harper Collins, 1993), 220–21.

23. King, *Gospel of Mary*, 149.

24. Genesis 38. This story is marvelously depicted by Thomas Mann in *Joseph and His Brothers*.

25. "So he left them, and went out of the city [Jerusalem] to Bethany, where he made his lodging" (Matthew 21:17),

26. Matthew 26:6, Mark 14:3.

27. See Thomas L. Brodie, *The Quest for the Origin of John's Gospel* (New York: Oxford University Press, 1993), 157–59.

28. Cf. Matthew 20:16.

29. Paul, 1 Corinthians 15:5–6. Paul provides a detailed list of those who have seen the resurrected Jesus, beginning with Peter and ending with himself. Mary is not mentioned. In Luke 24:12 Peter heeds the announcement of Mary and two other women that the tomb is empty, and later, in Luke 24:34, Peter, but not Mary, is said to have seen the resurrected Jesus.

30. Ramon K. Jusino, "Mary Magdalene: Author of *The Fourth Gospel?*" http://ramon_k_jusino.tripod.com/magdalene.html.

31. "By setting the Beloved Disciple over against Peter . . . , *The Fourth Gospel* gives the impression that he was an outsider to the group of best-known disciples, a group that would have included John son of Zebedee . . . . The external (late second-century) evidence identifying the Beloved Disciple as John is a further step in a direction . . . toward simplifying Christian origins by reduction to the Twelve Apostles." Raymond E. Brown, *The Community of the Beloved Disciple* (New York: Paulist Press, 1979), 34.

32. This is but one of various reconstructions of the history of the Fourth Gospel, leading to inter-scholarly accusations and assessments of the various positions as a work of "science fiction," an "exercise in creative imagination," an "invention of scholarly fancy," and "a genie which has been let out of the bottle." See Brodie, *Quest for the Origin*, 21.

33. Raymond E. Brown, *Community*, 154.

34. *The Gospel of Philip* 59:6–10; in Robinson, *Nag Hammadi Library*, 145.

35. Margaret Starbird, *Magdalene's Lost Legacy: Symbolic Numbers and the Sacred Union in Christianity* (Rochester, Vermont: Bear & Company, 2003), 46–47. Starbird bases her arguments primarily on two books which examine the gematria of ancient and biblical texts: John Michell, *The Dimensions of Paradise:*

The Proportions and Symbolic Numbers of Ancient Cosmology (San Franscisco: Harper & Row, 1990), and Tons Brunés, *The Secrets of Ancient Geometry—and Its Use*, trans. Charles M. Napier (Copenhagen: Rhodos, 1967).

36. See Starbird, *Magdalene's Lost Legacy*, 55.

37. Starbird, *Magdalene's Lost Legacy*, 56.

38. *The Five Gospels: What Did Jesus Really Say?*, trans. and commentary by Robert W. Funk, Roy W. Hoover, and the Jesus Seminar (HarperSanFrancisco, 1997), 60.

39. Starbird, *Magdalene's Lost Legacy*, 57–59.

40. Margaret Starbird, *The Goddess in the Gospels: Reclaiming the Sacred Feminine* (Rochester, VT: Bear & Company, 1998), 159–60. See Wikipedia, "Vesica Piscis," http://en.wikipedia.org/wiki/Vesica_piscis

41. Margaret Starbird, *Magdalene's Lost Legacy*, 128–29.

42. Margaret Starbird, *Magdalene's Lost Legacy*, 128–29.

43. Margaret Starbird, *Magdalene's Lost Legacy*, 128–29.

44. John 8:1–11. This "floating text" is also inserted in one manuscript at Luke 21:38. See Thomas L. Brodie, *The Quest for the Origin of John's Gospel* (New York: Oxford University Press, 1993), 157–59.

45. Jacques Baldet, *Jesus the Rabbi Prophet* (Rochester, VT: Inner Traditions, 2005), 171; trans. by Joseph Rowe from the French, *Histoire de Rabbi Jesus* (Paris: Éditions Imago, 2003).

46. Baldet, *Jesus the Rabbi Prophet*, 173.

47. John 6:53–56; citation from Funk, Hoover, and Jesus Seminar, *Five Gospels*.

48. John 6:61–63; citation from Funk, Hoover, and Jesus Seminar, *Five Gospels*.

49. E.g., see Funk, Hoover, and Jesus Seminar, *Five Gospels*, 411–12.

50. Baldet, who cites "Vermès and others" (Geza Vermès, *The Religion of Jesus the Jew* [Fortress Press, 1993]), dismisses the account in the Synoptics because "the taboos related to blood would have made this shocking to most Jews." (*Jesus the Rabbi Prophet*, 173). So low is his estimation of the general credibility of the Fourth Gospel that Baldet completely ignores the fact that it is the Fourth Gospel that originally makes this point.

51. Akiva Goldsman, *The Da Vinci Code: Illustrated Screenplay* (New York: Broadway Books, 2006), 203.

10

The Platonic Wisdom of the Gospel of Mary Magdalene

Fear is the path to the Dark Side. Fear leads to anger. Anger leads to hate. Hate leads to suffering.
—YODA

This is why you get sick and die: because you love what deceives you.
—THE GOSPEL OF MARY

The New Spirituality in Popular Culture

Philosophical reflection on the nature of Christianity in particular and religion in general runs through the popular culture explored in this book, from *The Simpsons*, with its critique of a Bible-based morality and religious hypocrisy, to major evocations and reworkings of the Christ figure in *The Matrix* and *Star Wars*. More generally, *Buffy the Vampire Slayer* and Woody Allen's *Crimes and Misdemeanors* address the larger metaphysical issues of the Judeo-Christian, and, we can add, the Islamic tradition as well—Judaism, Christianity, and Islam being the three "Abrahamic" religions with their doctrines of heaven and hell, human responsibility, and divine judgment. According to the philosophy of Kant, traditional religious concepts that go beyond the evidence of scientific reason are to be freely "postulated" and interpreted in the light of their impact on moral consciousness with its lofty ideal of creating the highest good. In matters that transcend scientific evidence, we remain free to think, speculate, and imagine in ways that promote human freedom and well-being.

For Hegel, however, we need not postulate a realm beyond scientific reason because dialectical science overcomes the limitations of a narrow scientism. Dialectical philosophical reason thereby complements religious doctrines that are expressed in the popular form of picture language appealing to the emotions rather than to reason. Religious consciousness is inherently a matter of feeling and imagination. But contrary to a narrow scientism, feeling and imagination are themselves vehicles for authentic experiences of reality. A developed philosophical reason should respect the authenticity of nonrational aspects of human experience while showing that they may contain truths that potentially have conceptual coherence and depth. Religion is therefore philosophy in the form of popular culture.

Hegel argues philosophically that there is an emotionally appealing and intellectually justifiable *religious* alternative to certain paradigms of external religious beliefs and practices—an alternative that does greater justice to the original teachings of the revolutionary founders of those religions. Opposing the traditional notion of an external deity linked to the Unhappy Consciousness of a self-denying humanity, Hegel provides theoretical justification for *Star Wars*'s notion of a universal Force or Spirit pervading all reality that is accessible through feeling while also constituting the rationally comprehensible core of the history of religions. A Hegelian exploration of the ideas that inspired Mel Gibson's *The Passion of the Christ* opens up an alternative vision of Christianity that avoids the disparagements and intimidations of external religious unhappy consciousness and joins with the alternative scenarios of the Christ figure already visited in *The Matrix* and *Star Wars*. In this exploration of culture and philosophy we therefore see how works of popular culture project imaginative new ways of looking at traditional ideas, give new life to congealed dogmas, and call forth certain too-often neglected aspects of the Western philosophical heritage.

The enormous success of Dan Brown's *The Da Vinci Code* demonstrates a tremendous interest in finding a new slant on the traditional religions. Brown's fictional adventure novel points to fundamental alternatives in the early years of Christianity before institutionalized religion, allied with the dark forces of Empire, imposed dogmatic beliefs while suppressing alternative "gnosis" or philosophical knowing. Such "Gnostic" religion was no abstract intellectualizing, but rather a further development of *philos-sophos*, or love of wisdom, the root of Western thought that was first expounded by Plato in imaginative allegories, in stories told by older teachers, and in theoretical formulations of the highest intellectual order.

The Search for the Holy Grail
in Contemporary Culture

Does *The Da Vinci Code*, while describing a fictional quest, rest on solid grounds of fact? A small library of books is now available to sort out truth from falsity in the claims supposedly made in the book. But as we have seen, the true interest of the book is in its presentation of alternative *ideas*. The Holy Grail is therefore more important as an idea than as a fact. San Greal is a misleading spelling for sounds that could be spelled otherwise: *sang real*, which means royal blood. Following out this clue, *The Da Vinci Code* explores the legend of the bloodline established by Jesus through the child born by his wife, Mary Magdalene. The child of Jesus and Mary, according to this legend, entered the bloodlines of the royal families of ancient Europe, in particular the Merovingian dynasty that preceded and gave rise to the Carolingians, famous for Charles the Great or Charlemagne.

This same story of hidden secrets in the history of Western civilization has parallels in some of the other popular sagas that we have been examining. It plays a key role in the *Matrix* trilogy, for the character known as "the Merovingian" is the keeper of the secrets of the Matrix. He controls "the Key Maker," whose keys will take Neo into the secret heart of the Matrix—back to "the Source" if he chooses to go there. But Neo makes a different choice from the allegedly rational one recommended by the Architect. He chooses the door that takes him to his Beloved, Trinity. Neo, the Christ figure of *The Matrix*, weds Trinity—whose name symbolizes the divine source of life in the form of a woman. She is the sacred feminine complement to Neo, the prophesied savior of the sacred city of Zion. Similarly, the Chosen One of *Star Wars*, Anakin Skywalker, secretly weds Padmé. The marriage, violating the norms of the Jedi order to which he adheres, in which Jedi knights are not allowed to leave the light of celibate priestliness and enter the darkness of marriage, does indeed lead Anakin to the Dark Side. But hope for a return is foreshadowed by the birth of the twin brother and sister, Luke and Leah. Their chaste love for one another embodies a return to a balance of masculine and feminine energies, of light and dark. Both the *Matrix* trilogy and the six episodes of *Star Wars* therefore complement the male action hero with a feminine partner. This displaces the required "love interest" from a sentimental sideline to the theoretical center of the action itself. In the end, both Neo and Luke reject the traditional masculine weapons of battle and thereby bring about the universalization of love that finally conquers the forces of evil.

If the prophesied saviors, Neo and Anakin, only achieve their goals through a kind of sacred marriage, they appear to deviate from the traditional religious model of the solitary male Savior, Jesus. But *The Da Vinci Code* tells us that this traditional model is a distortion: secret codes, works of art, and hidden documents take us to the concealed and banished beloved of Jesus, Mary Magdalene. *The Da Vinci Code* thereby proposes that the contemporary reworkings of the Christ figure in *The Matrix* and *Star Wars* reflect a repressed and buried historical fact. But genuine gnosis goes beyond mere belief in historical facts. The sacred marriage, or *hieros gamos*, of Jesus and Mary Magdalene is the embodiment of a personally inspiring and transfomative idea.

One idea leads to another, raising new questions in the quest—which is not primarily to discover the Grail as a physical entity but to understand the potential meaning of the Grail as an alternative idea and ideal. According to legends and cryptic evidences, precious documents have been handed down from generation to generation which provide a radically subversive reinterpretation of Christianity—so subversive that Popes and potentates have murdered to obtain and bury these parchments and scrolls: the idea that the Son of God, Jesus of Nazareth, had a wife who was none other than the woman taken in adultery and repentant prostitute of the New Testament, Mary Magdalene.

It is a fact that documents have been found such as those mentioned in the novel—the famous Dead Sea Scrolls, the scrolls found at Nag Hammadi, and other documents discovered in Egypt in the latter part of the nineteenth century. Several of these documents clearly establish that, going back at least to the first half of the second century, the Mary who was called the Magdalene was highly revered among certain groups of Christians. The most significant of the documents relating to Mary is the so-called Gospel of Mary, which was discovered in the late nineteenth century, and only published in the 1950s. *The Da Vinci Code* cites this manuscript as establishing Mary's special status for Christianity—both as the bride of Christ and as his primary Apostle. In the previous chapter we established as a fact that certain early Christians not only believed that Mary was the spouse of Jesus but that she was his first disciple and a teacher in her own right. A reexamination of textual evidence, moreover, gives credence to the notion that she was the beloved disciple of Jesus, the mysterious unnamed individual who, the Fourth Gospel explicitly says, is its author. To test this last idea, we will now compare the ideas of the buried and banned Gnostic Gospel of Mary with this central text of the orthodox Christian tradition.

The Gospel of Mary Magdalene

This fragmentary document, half of whose text has been lost, occupies about twenty manuscript pages and five pages in Karen King's translation.[1] After six missing manuscript pages, the extant text begins with a discussion of sin and the true nature of the human being. Peter asks the risen Jesus: "What is the sin of the world?" Jesus replies: "There is no such thing as sin."[2] He explains that no particular actions are in themselves sinful. Sin consists in "adultery" or illicit mixing of matter and spirit. When the soul, which is the true person, mistakenly identifies itself with its body, it causes for itself sickness, suffering, and death. "This is why you get sick and die: because you love what deceives you."[3] It is the soul, not matter, not the body, that contains the Image of God.

In this understanding, the Savior does not suffer the agony of crucifixion in order to redeem humanity, but shows human beings how they can redeem themselves from their own self-inflicted suffering: by setting off on a quest to find the root nature of the self, which Jesus calls the Son of Man, and the translator modernizes in gender-free language as "the child of true Humanity." Within each person is his true nature as the child of humanity. Not the child of this or that father and mother, or this or that family or nation, but the child of all humanity. The individual is thus the human species becoming self-conscious. This is precisely Hegel's concept that we examined in chapter 6. It is to bring mankind to such an understanding of itself, the Gospel of Mary goes on to say, "that the Good came among you, pursuing (the good) which belongs to every nature. It will set it within its root."[4] In other words, in the person of Jesus, "the Good," which every being naturally pursues, enters our world in order to show each of us this root nature within ourselves. Consciously embodying this goodness himself, Jesus teaches us to find the goodness that is within each of us, the goodness by which we are linked to all of humanity, and which we have lost or abandoned by committing metaphysical adultery—by identifying with our separate bodies and pursuing a matter-based agenda that divides us from one another.

Liberation from suffering lies within, by discovering the true self, the Son of Man or child of humanity, that exists within each of us. The title of Son of Man, not Son of God, was the favored term by which Jesus refers to himself in the canonical gospels and writings of the New Testament—those writings officially recognized by the Catholic Church at the Council of Nicea in 325 AD. Adopting "Son of Man" as his preferred title, Jesus asserts his unity with all of humanity, subverting thereby the limited identities with family, nation, or religion that keep human beings from identifying with their common humanity. Thus Jesus implicitly sets up a model for all: we are all sons or daughters of humanity.

We recognize these ideas from our reading of Kant. The "Holy One of the Gospels," according to Kant, is the model for each of us to follow only because he recognized more fully than any the fact that the humanity within each of us is sacred. If in the canonical gospels the title Son of Man has this implicit meaning, recognized there by Kant, it is explicitly stated in the Gospel of Mary, as Jesus here directly teaches that each of us is a "Son of Man." By identifying this true inner nature by which each of us is linked to all of us, the Savior shows the way by which each person can save herself. This way is not something outside of us—an external Savior or a mediating Church. Nor is it a set of rules that we are obliged to follow and a sin to violate—a law imposed on us by an external authority, State, or Church. The true salvation is only found within each of us. It is the inner goodness of soul by which each of us is linked to every one of us. It is necessary to engage in a quest to find this secret source of human redemption, for it is only available to the seeker. But the persistent seeker is guaranteed success. Hence Jesus exhorts, Seek and ye shall find. The quest will be successful because the mystery is not a hidden object that is far from us or a particular institution that is outside of us, but a knowledge or wisdom that is already contained within each of us. So in the Gospel of Mary the Savior exhorts:

> Acquire my peace within yourselves! Be on your guard so that no one deceives you by saying, 'Look over here! Or 'Look over there! For the child of true Humanity [literally, the Son of Man] exists within you. Follow it! Those who search for it will find it. Go then, preach the good news about the Realm [literally, the Kingdom]. Do not lay down any rule beyond what I determined for you, nor promulgate law like the lawgiver, or else you might be dominated by it.[5]

Enslavement to the Powers of Darkness

When Jesus departs from the scene for the final time, Mary, upsetting Peter and Andrew, steps readily into his place. Peter asks her, as the woman Jesus loved most, to provide them with some consoling words about the Master. But she is more than just a wife who reveals homely details of her private life with Jesus. She is a teacher in her own right. Mary recounts a vision that she once had of Jesus, and that she afterwards discussed with him. She asks him how such visions are possible. Are such visions seen with the soul or with the spirit? Jesus replies that it is the mind, existing between the soul and the spirit, that sees the vision. The manuscript then breaks off for four pages, and when it resumes Jesus is describing the ascent of the soul through four stages, each one of which is dominated by a "power" of the material world that tries to entrap the soul. The manuscript picks up with the second power, Desire, and then discusses the succeeding powers of Ignorance and Wrath. Wrath itself has seven forms—the first three of which are the forms of darkness, desire, and ignorance. Since ignorance and desire are here repeated, this suggests that the first power is that of darkness. In confronting the power of Wrath, the Savior evokes the Platonic theory of remembrance. In overcoming the powers of the world, he says, the soul has been "set loose . . . from the chain of forgetfulness."[6]

Mary's account is a further elaboration of the teaching that Jesus had given to the entire group before his departure. The adultery or illicit marriage of soul and body, in which the soul identifies itself with the body, inevitably gives rise to, and produces a dependency on, the worldly powers that dominate the lives of individuals. Only a correct understanding or knowledge—gnosis—can prevent this entrapment and free the soul from its dependence and suffering, including its domination by enslaving laws. Such gnosis is a remembrance of something the soul has once known but has forgotten because of its descent into the world of matter. The power of Desire interrogates the soul from this perspective: "I did not see you go down, yet now I see you go up. So why did you lie since you belong to me?" The soul replies, "I saw *you*. You did not see me nor did you know me. You (mis)took the garment (I wore) for my (true) self. And you did not recognize me."[7] Desire mistakes the garb of the body for the soul itself, and so fails to see the descent of the soul into the body. Desire is therefore now surprised to see the soul's ascent beyond the ensnaring power of bodily desires. How indeed can the soul ascend beyond bodily life if it hadn't descended into the body in the first place? The evolution of spirit presupposes its original involution in matter, as Hegel argues, following the Platonic and neo-Platonic ideas that are also sources for the Gospel of Mary. The soul undergoes repeated incarnations in physical embodiments, Plato says, on its way to achieving as full an embodiment of spiritual truth in this world as is possible.

The Savior teaches that it is the inner understanding of the *mind* that links the individual "soul" to the higher reality of the universal "spirit." It is by such gnosis of the mind or higher philosophical understanding that we overcome the isolation of egotistical, body-centered awareness—and the resultant enslavement to the powers of darkness, desire, ignorance, and wrath. This inner understanding goes beyond simple faith in words received from others and formulated in laws that are enforced by external authority or fear of punishment. Jesus warns his followers to be careful that they too, behaving like the powers of the world, do not set up new enslaving laws, but stick to this essential teaching of inner freedom and the spirit of universal love.

This saving knowledge consists in finding the true nature of the self by freeing oneself from the fetters of the worldly powers. This teaching is consistent with what Socrates learns from the Apollo at Delphi and Neo finds in the kitchen of the Oracle—know thyself. It adds two elements to this Greek heritage: the dimension of the Book of Genesis according to which the soul is made in the image of God, and the idea that the Good, which all things naturally pursue in Plato's philosophy, itself descends into the material world in a special way through the person of Jesus.

In the Platonizing context in which this document was written,[8] the implication is that if the soul fails to avoid the snares set by the confining powers of the world, it must return once more to the material world where it lives out the form of servitude to the powers to which it has abandoned itself. Enslavement in this material world, not punishment in an afterlife, is the outcome of "the sin of the world." As in Plato, Hinduism, and Buddhism, the choices we make in our previous lives can return us to the darkness and illusions of the cave or *maya* in which we are prisoners of worldly powers. In their version of these ideas the Gnostic Christians, instead of setting up a separate cult of a particular God-man, link the teachings of Jesus with the ancient philosophical wisdom of both the West and the East.

The Gospel of Mary sets forth the metaphysical premises of reincarnation. For if the person is essentially a unity of soul and body, reincarnation in another body is impossible. Then there is only one lifetime before the final judgment, and it matters above all that one's body be capable of resurrection. Separation of soul and body in death becomes highly problematic for the Aristotelian theory of hylomorphism—the philosophical doctrine of the intrinsic unity of soul and body—that was adopted by the medieval Church, and which the Gospel of Mary condemns as a kind of metaphysical adultery. If the soul is intrinsically linked to the body, how can the soul continue to exist after the death of the body? On the other hand, if, as Plato teaches, we keep returning to this world as a result of our previous choices, if, in other words, we keep getting second chances to get it right, what role is there for a Church as keeper of the keys of salvation?

If our fate through all eternity depends on our behavior in a single lifetime, fear of damnation is a powerful motivation to sacrifice personal freedom and to follow the laws promulgated by authorities that promise eternal reward for compliance and eternal damnation for disobedience. So, despite the obvious problem that hylomorphism creates for the doctrine of personal immortality, the doctrine of only one lifetime in this world facilitates enslavement to the powers of darkness that rule the earth. Knowledge of the descent of the soul into the body, recognition of the body as the clothing but not the substance of the soul, is essential to conquering the powers that control worldly existence—powers to which we give ourselves through failure to understand our true nature. The teaching of the Gospel of Mary, which follows Plato in identifying the true person with the soul, can therefore propound the Platonic version of judgment, karma, and reincarnation: that beginning from the very circumstances of our birth we are the architects of our own lives.[9]

Descent of the Word of God

According to *The Da Vinci Code*, the powers of Church and State collaborated, in the Council of Nicea in 325 CE, in condemning the views of such texts as the Gospel of Mary and in attempting to destroy them. Hence defenders of an alternative understanding of the teachings of Jesus concealed these documents in the deserts and caves of the Middle East. The Gospel of Mary and other recently recovered documents from the times of early Christianity regard Jesus's special love of Mary as unproblematic. It is her status as a teacher that is in dispute in the texts. But even the mere notion that Jesus had a wife was anathema to the power of a patriarchal order that puts women in a subordinate place to men, and bolsters its own prestige by claiming its role as the earthly representative of the Son of God, co-equal to the Father. According to Leigh Teabing,[10] Jesus's marriage to Mary Magdalene undermines the assertion of his divinity, the doctrine of the Council of Nicea that Jesus is "true God of true God." Marriage to Mary Magdalene speaks more of a man than of a god. And yet it is precisely the divinity of Jesus that enhances the significance of Mary as the incarnation of the sacred feminine. Overall, *The Da Vinci Code* is more interested in pursuing this idea of the sacred feminine represented by Mary than it is in downgrading the status of Jesus as the incarnation of the divine masculine.

If we turn to the documents on which *The Da Vinci Code* claims to rest, such as the Gospel of Mary, we see that Jesus is clearly no ordinary mortal man. He comes to his disciples after his death, and then departs from them to go to the heavenly sphere. He is the incarnation of "the Good." But that Jesus is the incarnation or manifestation of the Good does not mean that he is *the same as* the Good. The alternative, either God or man, was not characteristic of much early Christian thinking. Elaine Pagels argues[11] that had we only the gospels of Mathew, Mark, and Luke, there would be no serious grounds for asserting the divinity of Jesus as the Council of Nicea defines this. So Irenaeus at the end of the second century, fighting for a Christian orthodoxy of beliefs, insists that in addition to these "synoptic" gospels, the Fourth Gospel was of crucial importance because, according to him, *only* the Fourth Gospel clearly asserts the divinity of Jesus. Thus the Fourth Gospel opens with the words: "At the beginning of time the Word already was; and God had the Word abiding with him, and the Word was God. . . . And the Word was made flesh, and came to dwell among us."[12]

Thanks to later habits of associating the four gospels as one consistent teaching, Christians today read into the various titles given to Jesus in the gospels of Mathew, Mark, and Luke, including "Son of God," the assertion of Jesus's divinity, and so the position of the Nicene Creed that Jesus is "true God of true God." However, in 2 Samuel, the Lord God so designates King David: "I will prolong for ever his royal dynasty; he shall find in me a father, and I in him a son."[13] Such a title by no means indicates equality with Yahweh. The title "Son of God" is therefore an appropriate designation for the Messiah who is to become a king in the bloodline of David. So Nathanael, at the beginning of the Fourth Gospel, links the two titles, with special emphasis not on the first but on the second: "Thou, Master," he says to Jesus, "art the Son of God, thou art the King of Israel." But in his reply to Nathanael, Jesus refers to himself as "Son of Man."[14] This title that Jesus himself favored reflects the essential continuity between the Fourth Gospel, or the Gospel of the Beloved Disciple, and the Gospel of Mary.

As for the opening words of the Fourth Gospel, "At the beginning of time the Word already was; and God had the Word abiding with him, and the Word was God. . .", both biblical and philosophical readings are suggested. In the Greek text, the term for "Word" is "Logos," from which the term "logic" is derived. It evokes the meaning of science, understanding, or "gnosis." In the Hebrew Bible, we find similar expressions referring to God's Wisdom. Thus, Ecclesiasticus 1:1, 4 states that "All wisdom has one source; it dwelt with the Lord God before ever time began. . . . First she is of all created things; time never was when the riddle of thought went unread." We will come back to the fact that Wisdom here, which dwelt with God from before the beginning of time, is personified as a feminine figure. The early "Gnostic" writers clearly appreciated the Fourth Gospel well before its canonization as "gospel truth" by a church that had come under the power of the Roman Empire. But these writers understood it differently from Irenaeus and the later orthodoxy. Reflecting a Platonic philosophical heritage and anticipating Plotinus's later conception of emanation, the Gnostic Christian writer Ptolemy interprets the Fourth Gospel's teaching of the Word of God descending into the form of the flesh-and-blood Jesus as a kind of succession of waves of energy. The original Source is not to be *equated with* the manifested form. Here is the same essential idea of descent that we find in the Gospel of Mary in which Jesus is said to embody the descent of the Good. But in both texts, Jesus affirms his own title as Son of Man, as Child of True Humanity. We have seen in earlier chapters how Hegel defends such a theory of emanation or involution, leading to a forgetfulness or oblivion of being in the abandonment or separation from its divine nature experienced by the ego, and through the abandonment of the abandonment, a "return to the Source" in the human community bound together in the Holy Spirit of love.

As in the Gospel of Mary, the Fourth Gospel depicts a struggle with the powers of darkness. The Word of God that enters a human body is life and light: "And the light shines in darkness, a darkness which was not able to master it" (John 1:5). The world is governed by the powers of darkness and their dark lord, whom Jesus in the Fourth Gospel repeatedly calls, "the prince of this world" (John 12:3, 14:30, 16:11). But those who follow the teachings of Jesus "he empowered to become the children of God." Jesus does not exclaim exclusivity as the "Son of God." So he tells Mary Magdalene in their meeting by the tomb not to cling to him, for "I am going up to him who is my Father and your Father, who is my God and your God" (John 20:17). Their true unity is one of spirit, not a clinging of bodies. Those claiming exclusivity for Jesus as the unique Son of God may point to the text in this same gospel which says of the Word become flesh: "we had sight of his glory, glory such as belongs to the Father's only-begotten Son, full of grace and truth." However, the translator Ronald Knox notes: "Some of the best manuscripts here read 'God, the only-begotten' instead of 'the only-begotten Son.'"[15] The former reading accords with the overall thrust of the teaching of this gospel that each human being, by recognizing her or his oneness with all of humanity, is as much a daughter or son of God as is Jesus.

Thus the kind of identity relation to God that Jesus claims is not unique to himself but the title of every human being, who is made, as the Book of Genesis states, in the image of God. So, later on in the same gospel, Jesus says to his followers, "The man who has learned to believe in me will be able to do what I do; nay, he will be able to do greater things yet" (John 12:14). Here "belief" is not a matter of assent to an intellectual doctrine, but *trust* that one is a child of God and so has the power that comes from this status. It is not a matter of blind faith in a dogma that saves, but trust in the validity of a teaching that can turn the follower to an inner, transformative truth—resulting in an empowerment, a liberation from the dark powers that normally govern the world. In relating oneself to the power of the Father, the individual would do well to follow the advice that Obi-Wan gives to Luke as the means of connecting to the Force: "let go your conscious self and act on instinct. . . . Your eyes can deceive you. Don't trust them. . . . Stretch out with your feelings." Or, as Morpheus advises Neo: "You have to let it all go, Neo. Fear, doubt, and disbelief. Free your mind."

Rather than seeing the Fourth Gospel's theology as involving a process of emanation and transformation, of identity and difference, Irenaeus, like the majority at the Council of Nicea, adopted the simplified formula of a strict equation. The Word of God comes from God and therefore *is* God. The Word of God becomes the person of Jesus and therefore Jesus *is* the Word of God and so *is* God. No special spiritual insight or "gnosis" is required for comprehending this item of faith, however troublesome it may be for a theology that declares that there is only one God. The minority who opposed the Council's final position wondered how the position that Jesus is equal to the Father, which in this formulation is found in none of the four canonical gospels, could be regarded as the orthodox one. They also wondered how this differs from the polytheism of the pagans. But Emperor Constantine, who called the council, was anxious to get on with the more practical matters of ruling a precariously united empire and opted for this formula. Thereafter, it became dangerous for anyone to oppose it. And so in such a political context the first great heresy was established—Arius's position that Jesus was a great spirit in the angelic hierarchy, but still under God the Father.[16]

Where the text of the Gospel of Mary creates difficulties, aside from what it says about Mary, is not so much in its linking of Jesus to the Good, which an Irenaeus could interpret as a formula of identity, but in its clear insistence that the human soul as the image of God shares with Jesus this relation to the Good, so that each person is capable of finding the Good within oneself through right knowledge and self-transformation. This is what it means to be a true human being, a child of true humanity, or Son of Man. So Mary asserts that Jesus "has made us true human beings."[17] The Good enters the world in the flesh to break the stranglehold on human beings of the powers of darkness and to show the way out of illusion. It is then up to each individual to seek and then find the truth about the self, the image and likeness of God within us, and with this understanding to free ourselves from the self-deceptions in which we are entangled. The primary self-deception and ultimate source of darkness is the identification of oneself with one's body. This misidentification is the original darkness which leaves the individual a prey to desires, and a victim of ignorance. Ignorance of our true nature leaves us vulnerable and fearful, and so also, in self-defense, we become aggressive, wrathful beings. The Son of Man is therefore not a special individual set apart from the rest of us who comes to save us, but the inner truth and potentiality of each human being as a soul that enters a material body from out of the imperishable realm of Spirit. When we fully understand this, we can ourselves take up the enlightening mission of Jesus, as Mary does when, at the departure of the Savior, she comforts the dismayed disciples and teaches them. Mary is thus the Platonic philosopher who, like Jesus, brings light into the darkness of the cave of human bondage.

The metaphysical dualism of the Gospel of Mary does not imply a Stoical indifference to the body and the physical world, which the Stoics regarded as outside the control of the mind. True knowledge of the self gives power to heal the body, and even to prevent death. The Gospel of Mary recalls Socrates rather than Epictetus. In chapter 5 we examined Socrates' teaching that the pursuit of virtue, which consists in maintaining the *primacy* of the good of the soul to that of the body, is the foundation of a flourishing human society.[18]

Andrew, Peter's brother, finds Mary's teaching about enslavement to the four powers of the world very "strange."[19] Andrew and Peter fail to recognize how the discourse on the soul's ascent through the powers of darkness consistently fills out the teaching Jesus had just given them about the nature of "the sin of the world." Peter all but accuses Mary of lying: "Did he, then, speak with a woman in private without our knowing about it? Are we to turn around and listen to her? Did he choose her over us?" Mary is in tears at this accusation. "My brother Peter, what are you imagining? Do you think that I have thought up these things by myself in my heart or that I am telling lies about the savior?"[20]

The fourth disciple in this gospel is Levi, who is described in the gospels of Mark and Luke as a tax collector who became a disciple of Jesus but was not one of the twelve apostles. Levi criticizes Peter: "Peter, you have always been a wrathful person. Now I see you contending against the woman like the Adversaries." The Adversaries are the Satanic powers that rule the world. Levi accuses Peter, in his disdain of a woman teacher, of falling under the power of the Lord of Darkness, the prince of this world. Levi defends Mary by saying that the Savior "knew her completely and loved her steadfastly." An alternative text reads, "Assuredly the Savior's knowledge of her is completely reliable. That is why he loved her more than us."[21] Levi links this love to Mary's capacity for wisdom. Levi concludes the extant dialog: "We should clothe ourselves with the perfect Human"—Levi repeats Mary's account of the teaching of Jesus—"acquire it for ourselves as he commanded us, and announce the good news, not laying down any other rule or law that differs from what the Savior said."[22]

Theoretical Quest for the Meaning of Mary

The excluded, condemned, and hidden texts found in the deserts of Egypt show that the early Christians were engaged in a quest centering on the meaning of the relation between Jesus and Mary Magdalene. That there was a special relationship is merely the starting point. The question is—what is the deep meaning of this relationship for the communities of Christians? What is its meaning for spiritual transformation? With the aid of rediscovered documents, three interpretations, in ascending order of complexity, can be distinguished: that of the Gospel of Thomas, that of the Gospel of Mary, and that of the Gospel of Philip.

The Gospel of Thomas gives an account of this relationship that is least disturbing to the tradition of male hierarchy. In its final saying, logion 114, we read: "Simon Peter said to them, 'Make Mary leave us, for females are not worthy of life.' Jesus said: 'Look, I shall guide her to make her male, so that she too may become a living spirit resembling you males. For every female who makes herself male will enter the kingdom of heaven.'"[23]

Here again we see the conflict between Peter and Mary, with Peter taking an aggressive stance. What is Mary doing with us? How can a mere woman be worthy of spiritual truth and teaching? Jesus's reply that he personally will guide her affirms a special relation and commitment to Mary, but understood through the lens of traditional patriarchy. Women can become male, in the sense of developing the higher faculties of mind that are required of the spiritual life and that are presumed to be natural for men but difficult for women to acquire. Women are not inexorably subordinate to the imperatives of their physical bodies as women, but by special effort they can have the capacity of spiritual understanding that males readily have by the fact of being male. Women therefore have the capacity to become like men, and if they do this they will be able to enter the kingdom of the spiritual life.

The Gospel of Mary constitutes a major advance beyond this position. The true human being, the Son of Man or Child of True Humanity, is a nongendered soul that enters a gendered body. To make special laws based on gender differences is to commit "the sin of the world." It is Peter who is put to task here, not Mary. He has claimed that prerogatives based on mere physicality have meaning for the spiritual life and the teaching of the Gospel, and therefore it is he, not Mary, who is the one taken in spiritual adultery, the "sin" of illicitly confusing soul and body. The background assumption that Mary is the prostitute who was taken in adultery, as recounted in John 8:1–11, clarifies the unusual understanding of the nature of sin as metaphysical "adultery."Implicitly, the Gospel of Mary tells its readers, who identify Mary with the woman taken in adultery and the "sinner in the city" who washes the feet of Jesus with her tears and precious ointment, that her alleged sin is not as serious as that of Peter—if hers is a sin at all. It is a sin only if she subordinates soul to body and so becomes subject to the powers of darkness, desire, ignorance, and wrath. Peter here is clearly guilty of such sin. The deep meaning of spiritual adultery is not so much exemplified by a woman who has sex with married men who pay for her services, as by the claim that women cannot teach because of the nature of their bodies. The peculiar interpretation of sin in the Gospel of Mary as metaphysical "adultery" can therefore be read as an exoneration of Mary's past and of Jesus's choice of her as his beloved companion—not merely as a wife in the traditional sense, but as an esteemed companion on the spiritual plane.

The Gospel of Mary suggests that Jesus's special love of Mary is unique—and goes beyond the ordinary love of a husband for a wife. Critics who say that both prostitute and wife are equally degrading designations for Mary find support in this text. For Jesus she is more than a mere wife. She is the most apt student of Jesus's teachings. She is the one most capable of receiving and then teaching his wisdom. But why this is so is left unclear.

Hieros Gamos

There is a third theory of the meaning of Mary in the hidden documents that have resurfaced in the twentieth century. In the Gospel of Philip, in a passage that is partly quoted in *The Da Vinci Code*, we read the following:

> As for Wisdom who is called "the barren," she is the mother of the angels and the companion of the Savior. Maria, the Magdalene—she is the one the Savior loved more than all the disciples and he used to kiss her on

her mouth often. The rest of the disciples. . . . They said to him, "Why do you love her more than us?" The Savior replied; he said to them, "Why do I not love you like her? If a blind man and one who sees are both in the dark, they do not differ from each other. When the light comes, then the one who sees will see the light, and the one who is blind will remain in the dark."[24]

In this text, Mary is mysteriously connected with Wisdom. King explains that an alternative possible reading directly identifies Wisdom and Mary Magdalene. "Wisdom . . . is the mother of the angels and the companion of the savior, Maria the Magdalene."[25] To understand this meaning we need to turn from Greek philosophical presuppositions to Judaic ones. The Judaic religion has its roots in the rejection of pagan, earth-centered, goddess-related religions of early agricultural societies. In the Book of Exodus, Moses follows the explicit commands of God to rid "the people" of their defilement: "First they must wash their clothes; then he bade them hold themselves in readiness for the third day, and have no commerce with their wives."[26] Thus the encounter with God requires purification of the men from sexual defilement with their wives. At that same period of time, pagan priestesses in the surrounding early agricultural societies were engaging in ritual sexual intercourse under the open sky in order to promote the fertility of the earth and the joy of existence.[27] This is the holy marriage or *Hieros Gamos* of *The Da Vinci Code* that appalled young Sophie when she stumbled on its enactment in the cellars of her grandfather's mansion. Her visceral reaction was in the spirit of the religion of the Hebrews and subsequent Christian and Muslim derivatives, with their banishment of sexual intercourse, as a form of defilement, from religious ritual. The Hebrews, expressing a male-centered, nomadic, herding way of life, rejected a form of worship, widespread in early agricultural communities, that was intimately dependent on the power and bodies of women.

And yet, as an expression of one of the ancient peoples at a time of the great goddess religions, the Hebrew Bible contains important traces of the sacred feminine. We cited the mention in the Book of Job of God's maternal womb: "Was it thou or I shut in the sea behind bars? No sooner had it broken forth from the womb than I dressed it in swaddling-clothes of dark mist, set it within bounds of my own choosing, made fast with bolt and bar; thus far thou shalt come, said I, and no further; here let thy swelling waves spend their force." Is the sea created by the male God Yahweh or Jehovah, or is there also a female source of creation? Wisdom—in Greek, *Sophia*—is presented in some texts as the feminine companion to the masculine Creator. She, like the Word in the beginning of the Fourth Gospel, is with God from the beginning of creation. According to Proverbs, in words that complement those of Job, she is the partner of the male Lord of creation and his true Beloved:

> What am I, the wisdom that speaks to you? . . . Love me, and thou shalt earn my love; wait early at my doors, and thou shalt gain access to me. . . . The Lord made me his when first he went about his work, at the birth of time, before his creation began. . . . I was there when he built the heavens, when he fenced in the waters with a vault overhead, when he fixed the sky overhead, and leveled the fountain-springs of the deep. . . . I was at his side, a master-workman, my delight increasing with each day, as I made play before him all the while; made play in this world of dust, with the sons of Adam for my play-fellows. (Proverbs 8:12, 17, 22, 27–28, 30–31)

The author of the Book of Wisdom writes of Wisdom that she is the Spirit that descends on those who love her: "Whence, then, did the prudence spring that endowed me? Prayer brought it; to God I prayed, and the spirit of wisdom came upon me. . . . She, from my youth up has been my heart's true love, my heart's true quest; she was the bride I longed for, enamoured of her beauty" (Wisdom 7:7, 8:2).

The writer's quest for Wisdom is a quest for the sacred feminine. The Jewish mystical tradition of the Kabbalah, reflecting these and other Biblical sources, elaborates a scheme of reciprocal and interdependent masculine/feminine energies as the fundamental pattern of creation and of hidden human wisdom. In the secretive and subversive wisdom of the Kabbalists,

> The rabbinic concept of *Shekhinah*, divine immanence, blossoms into the feminine half of God, balancing the patriarchal conception that dominates the Bible and the Talmud. . . . According to Kabbalah, every human action here on earth affects the divine realm, either promoting or hindering the union of Shekhinah and her partner—the Holy One, blessed be he. God is not a static being, but dynamic becoming. Without human participation, God remains incomplete, unrealized. It is up to us to actualize the divine potential in the world. God needs us.[28]

The rediscovered Gnostic texts, destroyed or hidden with the consolidation of the orthodox male-centered Christian Church, reflect just such an orientation. The early proponent of a Christian orthodoxy of uniformly defined beliefs, Irenaeus, at the end of the second century, denounces the Gnostic Christian teacher Marcus as the agent of Satan. According to Pagels: "As Irenaeus tells it—perhaps adding details for the sake of sensation—Marcus claimed that divine truth had revealed itself to him naked, 'in feminine form, having descended upon him from invisible and ineffable space, for the world could not have borne [the truth] coming in masculine form.'"[29]

The association of the Spirit of God with a female Wisdom that descends on those who profess love for her is central to the Gnostic Gospel of Philip, which highlights three women in the life of Jesus: "Mary his mother and her sister and (the) Magdalene, the one who was called his companion." Again, as in the other examples, it is taken for granted that Mary was the special companion of Jesus. This is not stated as something to be marveled over or to be shocked by, but is presented simply as a well-known, unremarkable fact. What is important in these banished and buried documents is the meaning that is attributed to this relationship—a meaning that goes far beyond that of ordinary husband-wife relationships. As we have seen, the text identifies Mary Magdalene with Wisdom. The same three women of the Gospel of Philip stand around the cross of Jesus in the Fourth Gospel, but there they are overshadowed by a mysterious fourth person, an unnamed man. It is he, we read, who is the beloved of Jesus, and *not* Mary the Magdalene. What should be a straightforward identification of the beloved of Jesus is awkwardly transformed into an insoluble puzzle.

As in the biblical books of Proverbs and Wisdom, the newly recovered documents depict the Holy Spirit of God as a feminine principle of creation. In its examination of the spiritual meaning of the virgin birth of Jesus, the Gospel of Philip relates that while physically Jesus was the son of Mary and Joseph, his spiritual birth came when the Holy Spirit descended upon him at his baptism by John. Writing of the doctrine according to which Mary conceived Jesus by the Holy Spirit, the Gospel of Philip argues, "Some said, 'Mary conceived by the holy spirit.' They are in error. They do not know what they are saying. When did a woman ever conceive by a woman? . . . And the lord would not have said 'My father who is in heaven' (Matthew 16:17) unless he had had another father, but he would have said simply 'My father.'"[30] Pagels elaborates the Gospel of Philip's understanding of the spiritual meaning of this descent of the Holy Spirit: "so we too, first born physically can be 'born again through the holy spirit' in baptism, so that 'when we become Christians we came to have both a father and a mother,' that is, both the heavenly Father and the holy spirit."[31] Far from being inventions of Satan, as Irenaeus claimed, such ideas stem directly from sources in the Hebrew Bible.

In the Gospel of Philip, as in the Gospel of Mary, the love of Jesus for Mary Magdalene has special spiritual significance. But whereas in the

Gospel of Mary Jesus loves Mary because he sees in her the capacity to receive wisdom from him, the Gospel of Philip takes the meaning of the love-relationship to a deeper level. If Jesus is the incarnation of the Father, Mary is the incarnation of the divine Mother, the Holy Spirit, or Wisdom herself. Jesus therefore comes to Mary, not to teach her, but to acquire from her a sacred Wisdom. As described by the author of the book of Wisdom, she is "my heart's true love, my heart's true quest; she was the bride I longed for, enamoured of her beauty."

In the Fourth Gospel, John the Baptist relates his vision of the Spirit descending on Jesus in the form of a dove. He tells two of his disciples what he has witnessed and points out Jesus to them. One of the disciples is Andrew, the brother of Peter. The other is not identified. Who is this unidentified follower of John the Baptist if not the Beloved Disciple who mysteriously appears throughout the gospel mistakenly named after the apostle John, son of Zebedee? For those who have found this key to the mysteries of the gospels, reading them along with the texts buried in the deserts of Egypt, the various dials of a complexly constructed cryptex line up perfectly.[32] When her name is restored to the unnamed first disciple of Jesus, the Fourth Gospel tells us that Jesus has been blessed with the descent of the divine feminine, Wisdom, drawing to him at that very moment his beloved in the flesh, Mary Magdalene.

By connecting Mary Magdalene with Sophia or Wisdom in the books of the Hebrew Bible, the Gospel of Philip takes the quest for the meaning of the Holy Grail to the next level. Here we finally see the emergence of the sacred feminine, which, according to *The Da Vinci Code*, is what this quest is really all about. Jesus is the lover who is in quest of the sacred bride, the embodiment of the feminine Spirit of God, who will fill him with Wisdom. This is how he can love her above all human beings, because he sees in her the image of the divine Mother, the complement to his own relation to the Father. Only through the marriage of Father and Mother, symbolized by the *vesica piscis* and the mustard seed, does real creativity occur.

The Gospel of Philip replies to a problem implicit in the metaphysics of the Gospel of Mary. This, we saw, is no teaching of Stoical indifference to the body. The proper understanding or gnosis of the relation between soul and body is the condition for attaining physical wholeness and health as well as social well-being. The goal is the overcoming of suffering in bodily existence, a happy life as an embodied soul—that is, as Mary says, a true human life. A flourishing physical life is esteemed, even if our existence in a physical body is only temporary. But when it comes to gendered differences and sexual attraction the standpoint of the

Gospel of Mary inconsistently suggests indifference. Jesus loves Mary because of her soul, not her body. Mary's love for Jesus is essentially a spiritual, not a physical one. Their special, personal relationship, as a couple sharing sexual intimacy, is a matter of indifference or insignificance, philosophically speaking.

Thanks to its closer connection with the mystical undercurrent of Hebrew spirituality, the Gospel of Philip, by equating Mary with Wisdom, evokes the mystical sexuality, the *Hieros Gamos*, implicit in the biblical accounts of Proverbs, Wisdom, and the Song of Songs. In the Gospel of Mary, the Good enters the world not to lead us out of it, but to show us how to pursue the good in all of nature. What we are to overcome is not the world in its physicality, but the dark powers that presently rule the world. We are made in the image of God, the Gospel of Mary repeats from the Hebrew Bible. But as a number of the recovered texts point out, the full Biblical source says: "So God made man in his own image, made him in the image of God. Man and woman both, he created them."[33] If the image of God is gendered, both man and woman, then God must be a dyad of male and female—Father God and Mother God. Thus Genesis also states "Let *us* make man, wearing our own image and likeness."[34] The Gospel of Philip completes this idea by telling us that the physical love of a man for a woman and a woman for a man, the physical union of masculine and feminine attributes in any sexual union,[35] is itself an image and embodiment of the divine union of the Father and the Mother that is responsible for all creation.

Making a Man Out of Mary

From this perspective we can return to the Gospel of Thomas and correct the natural mistake of the author—natural in the context of the patriarchal chauvinism against which Jesus, through his encounter with Mary, revolted. We have seen that according to this gospel Jesus said of Mary: "Look, I shall guide her to make her male, so that she too may become a living spirit resembling you males. For every female who makes herself male will enter the kingdom of heaven."[36] From the vantage point of the Gospel of Mary supplemented by the Gospel of Philip Jesus would have said something quite different, something like the following: "Look, she has guided me to see that the female is the presence in the flesh of the living Spirit of God. For only if the male recognizes the Spirit of Wisdom that lives in women will he be able to enter the kingdom of heaven on earth, which consists in enjoying the divine play of a true human life." Thomas and Peter no doubt thought that Jesus must have made a Freudian slip, and so Thomas duly corrected what he heard to make it come out as he honestly thought Jesus must have meant it. Still subject to the powers of darkness, they failed to see to whom Jesus was directing his remark, "When the light comes, then the one who sees will see the light, and the one who is blind will remain in the dark."

The etymological meaning of "Philosophy" is love (*philos*) of wisdom (*sophos*). The philosopher is therefore the lover of divine Sophia or Wisdom. The Platonizing teachings of the Gospel of Mary linked to the Judaic elements of the Gospel of Philip combine through their inquiry into the meaning of Mary Magdalene in a unique vision of the philosopher's quest for Wisdom. But orthodox Christianity, dogmatized and made obligatory through the power of Constantine's empire, has canonized an interpretation of the Fourth Gospel according to which the *Logos*, who is in the beginning with God, is embodied in a solitary male Savior. This doctrine displaces the divine feminine Sophia who, according to the earlier Hebrew tradition that is further elaborated in the buried Gnostic Christian texts, accompanies and cooperates with the Father God in their joint acts of creation. The result of this victory of patriarchal orthodoxy, backed as it was by the terrorizing power of the Roman state, is the submergence of the alternative view. In response to this suppression, secret societies and master keepers of keys must maintain the vigil for an alterative vision, whose truth they try to hide in the open for those who have eyes to see. Thus, according to *The Da Vinci Code*, one of these master keepers of the secret wisdom, Leonardo Da Vinci, in his "Last Supper," clearly depicts a woman at the side of Jesus, giving his own interpretation to the text of the Fourth Gospel that reads: "Jesus had one disciple, whom he loved, who was sitting with his head at Jesus' breast." But without eyes to see, we instead suppose in accordance with the imposed tradition that this is only a very feminized portrait of the Apostle John. The secret of this portrait, then, is reduced to Leonardo's sexual orientation, rather than seen as a product of his revolutionary philosophical understanding.

Our study of the references to Mary and other seemingly related women in the canonical Gospels reveals a cryptic "Gospel Code" leading through various strands to the powerful presence and central significance of Mary Magdalene as the beloved of Jesus. Ironically, the very text that was adopted as the bulwark of an orthodoxy of dogmatic belief against Gnostic heresy and pagan feminization of divinity, when deciphered with certain keys, turns out to enshrine the banished Idea. The Gnostic teaching of unity of all humanity in the divine is therefore laid out before the Christian community in a text that is supposed to say the opposite. So when Jesus says in the Fourth Gospel, "My Father and I are one" (John 10:30), instead of seeing this unity as the special privilege of the unique Son of God, second person of the Trinity, the medieval mystic Meister Eckhart recognizes a universal truth for all human beings, together with the rejection the Unhappy Consciousness and all ideas of God as an all-powerful overlord. In his commentary on this text of the Fourth Gospel, Hegel approvingly cites Meister Eckhart's saying, "The eye with which God sees me is the eye with which I see him: my eye and his eye are the same."[37] In this same Gospel of the Beloved Disciple, Jesus prays for his followers: "that they may all be one, as we are one; that while thou art in me, I may be in them, and so they may be perfectly made one" (John 17:22–23). In line with these texts, Kant affirms the sacredness of human-ity itself. And Hegel, reading in this gospel of the Soul Mate unity of Jesus and his Beloved the binding Force of Life and the oneness of all human-ity in the Spirit of love, prepares the philosophical terrain for George Lucas's distillation of religion in *Star Wars*.

No new documents need therefore be uncovered, because everything is hidden in the open for those who have eyes to see. Texts had to be hidden, not only in the deserts of Egypt, but in out in the open thanks to subtle alterations whose purpose was not to destroy the truth but to blind the narrowly focused eyes of the censors. In this way the greatest of all the Gnostic sources survived the repression as the central text of the orthodox Christian religion, which then could be read in two opposed ways depending on the guiding Idea of the reader. The chief method of this concealment was a simple disguise by which the editor of the Fourth Gospel cunningly clothed its author in the garb of a man, knowing that a shrewd reader with eyes to see, a Leonardo Da Vinci, would recognize the trick. And so we suddenly see a new meaning con-cealed in the text of the Gospel of Thomas where Jesus says of Mary Magdalene: "I shall guide her to make her male."

Forgotten Founder of Western Philosophy

On the surface, the canon of Western philosophy seems to support mas-culine privilege in the realm of knowledge. Proponents of an alternative vision must have learned the lesson of the gruesome death of Hypatia, the great woman neo-Platonic philosopher of the early fifth century who was torn apart by a mob fueled from denunciations of her alleged pagan-ism by the Christian Patriarch Cyril of Alexandria. Traditionally, philoso-phy has appeared to be the all-but-exclusive enterprise of men in quest of rational ideas. The classical canon of Western philosophy takes us

from Socrates to Plato to Aristotle to the Stoics and so on. Most male figures were bachelors, and if a few were married, as was Socrates, they
were known for not being very complimentary to their spouses. All but
forgotten in this emphasis on male philosophers is the very evident, but
still generally overlooked, fact that a central teacher of the young
Socrates, and hence a true initiator of Western philosophy, was a certain
wise woman, Diotema of Manteneia. Socrates recounts her initiation of
him into the mysteries of philosophy in his discourse in *The Symposium*.
The true beginning of philosophy, Diotema teaches Socrates, is love—
physical, sexual love. If philosophy is about truth and ideas, these come
naturally to those who are in love. Diotema therefore says: "For he who
would proceed aright in this matter should begin in youth to visit beautiful forms; and first, if he be guided by his instructor aright, to love one
such form only—out of that he should create fair thoughts. . . ."[38]

We begin with the love of one fair form, one beautiful person. We fall
under the spell of the beautiful, as this is incarnated in one beautiful person. In this experience of love everything is transformed, magically permeated by a higher significance, while all externally motivated pragmatic
pursuits lose their interest. Others, who do not know the secret of this
magic, call it madness. Thus it is desire or sexual passion for a beautiful
person that, according to the Gospel of Mary, first liberates the individual
from the power of darkness. The next step consists in freeing oneself from
the exclusivity of such a potent force, which the Gospel of Mary calls the
power of desire. For the Gospel of Mary, the soul, rising beyond the
power of darkness, must next liberate itself *from* the power of desire. The
soul must nevertheless first take its path *through* this power. It is the
power of desire that initially breaks the hold on us of the power of darkness. For Socrates, if we recognize the underlying teaching of Diotema in
his famous allegory of the cave, it is desire of a beautiful person that first
frees the individual from the darkness of the cave. The soul thus rises to
higher and higher forms of consciousness until it recognizes the sun of
Beauty shining everywhere. For the Gospel of Mary, the next stage in the
ascent of the soul, liberation from ignorance, parallels and elaborates the
idea of Socratic ignorance. If ignorance keeps us from rising to our true
human nature, recognition of this ignorance is the key to liberation. But
for many of those whose ignorance has been thus exposed, but who
refuse to recognize their ignorance, the culminating power of wrath finds
its outlet in the murder of the bearers of loving light. Socrates thus kin-
dled the murderous wrath of the religious and political leaders of Athens
whose ignorance his probing questions brought to light. Exposing the
ignorance or nullity of the ego ignites the life-or-death struggle. The only

option for the ego, armed with its abstract knowledge and related technologies of power, is to kill or be killed. Likewise Jesus was crucified for having exposed the ultimate emptiness of the dark powers of Judea, and so for having enraged these masters of an external religion of blind obedience, fear and damnation:

> Woe to . . . you hypocrites that shut the door of the kingdom of heaven in men's faces . . . you hypocrites that swallow up the property of widows, under cover of your long prayers . . . blind leaders, who say, if a man swears by the temple, it goes for nothing; if he swears by the gold in the temple, his oath stands . . . blind leaders that have a strainer for the gnat, and then swallow the camel! . . . you hypocrites that are like whitened sepulchres, fair in outward show, when they are full of dead men's bones and corruption within. . . . (Matthew 23:13–28)

Thus the ultimate key to overcoming the powers of the world consists both in recognizing one's ignorance and in rising above the desperate anger of the ego whose essential nullity has been thus exposed.

If erotic love liberates us from the darkness of ordinary life where we mistake the shadow for the reality, the outer garb of the body for the real self, the power of such awakened desire may also shackle us to one person or one object exclusively. Finding beauty in one person, we fear to lose it, and this fear leads to anger and violence—the dark powers of evil that disrupt the natural harmony of a truly human life. Exaggerating the relative truth of this phenomenon, the Jedi knights in their Stoic rejection of attachment effectively outlaw love. As Yoda says in *The Phantom Menace*, evoking a cascading series of forms that parallels those mentioned in the Gospel of Mary: "Fear is the path to the Dark Side. Fear leads to anger. Anger leads to hate. Hate leads to suffering." But for the Gospel of Mary, as for its Platonic source, this sequence of experiences cannot be short-circuited by an intellectualized, Stoic compassion. Knowledge or gnosis only comes through the process, the succession of forms of life and death which Hegel calls the crucifixion of Spirit.

Diotema refers to the madness of exclusive love as "the violent love of the one." But her solution to this problem is not to recommend Stoicism or the counterweight of intellectual pursuits. It is not by sublimating passion into reason that we free ourselves, Diotema teaches, but by universalizing passion—by recognizing that beauty is everywhere. The philosophical lover of wisdom is the person who sees the True, the Good, and the Beautiful—Plato's Trinity of the fundamental forms of the Oneness of being—embodied in every person and every form of human life. This is the true role of rationality—not to form a counterweight to the disruptive force of beauty, but to recognize the presence of goodness and beauty in more than one person, in more than one project, in more than one pursuit. The true Platonic lover does not necessarily leave sexuality behind but expands the scope of love. Reason universalizes, and in the service of love of Wisdom this means to uncover the universality of the encounter with beauty and goodness that first arises in the sexual love of one person for another and so wrests individuals from their caves of conventional consciousness. The Gnostic gospels of Mary and Philip combine in the understanding that the True—knowledge, reason, or gnosis—consists in the loving recognition of the embodiment of the masculine aspect of the Good and the feminine aspect of the Beautiful, God and Goddess, throughout all reality.

The Fourth Gospel, which we now recognize to be the *first* Gospel of Mary Magdalene, puts forward this Platonic Idea: The masculine *Logos* of Reason that descends into a world of darkness awakens to its true nature and mission only with the descent of the feminine Spirit of Wisdom. The Gospel of Mary, together with other texts in the Gnostic tradition, further develop seminal themes of this Gospel of the Beloved Disciple. The world of ordinary experience is in truth the shadow world of the Platonic cave. But more ominously, it is a world given over to the powers of darkness and their evil prince. In such a world, sin is essentially ignorance. The Greek word translated "sin" is *hamartia*, which means missing the mark, making a mistake, being in error.[39] But such error has serious, deadly consequences, as it produces enslavement to dark powers that rule the earth. Jesus, an emissary of the divine fullness or "pleroma" within which all real being exists, brings the light of his teachings into this shadow world, and consequently provokes the wrath of the dark powers, bringing about his death. It is not the death of Jesus that frees souls from enslavement, but the light of the truth that he teaches. It is the truth of the inherent deathlessness of the human spirit. This is the truth that challenges all hierarchies of power in the name of an authentic human existence governed not by laws that separate people from one another but by the love that unites them.

The Gospel of Truth, another Gnostic text attributed to the early Christian philosopher Valentinus (100–153 CE), develops the opening of the Fourth Gospel as well as the themes of the Gospel of Mary by vividly depicting the journey of the totality of souls from the Father, who is also the Mother. This journey is an emanation that takes place within the divine substance of all the expressions of Spirit which subsequently fall into the darkness of oblivion—the forgetfulness of Being! Originally free beings with godlike power, we become preoccupied with a pseudo-reality, in which our own ignorance takes on the form of independent beings that fetishistically rule over us, false idols of our own creation that we worship in fear and trembling. The truth of our real nature that the one who is called the Savior teaches therefore brings forth both liberation and joy. The real truth of the journey is that we always remain within the divine reality that is our source. We remain always within the Kingdom of the Father/Mother's love even as we build mesmerizing creations based on fear and death. The Gospel of Truth begins by clearly echoing the Fourth Gospel:

> The gospel of truth is joy for those who have received from the Father of truth the grace of knowing him, through the power of the Word that came forth from the pleroma [the divine fullness], the one who is in the thoughts and the mind of the Father, that is, the one who is addressed as the Savior, that being the name of the work he is to perform for the redemption of those who were ignorant of the Father... [I]gnorance of the Father brought about anguish and terror; and the anguish grew solid like a fog, so that no one was able to see. For this reason error became powerful; it worked on its own matter foolishly, not having known the truth. It set about with a creation, preparing with power and beauty the substitute for the truth. This was not then a humiliation for [the Father], the incomprehensible, inconceivable one, for they were nothing, the anguish and the oblivion and the creature of deceit, while the established truth is immutable, imperturble, perfect in beauty. [40]

The Gnostic Gospel of Truth continues the Platonic teaching according to which the false beauty of terrifying, exclusive, and transitory loves can be replaced by the recognition of universal and imperishable beauty. Finding beauty everywhere does not mean ceasing to find it in the one whose love first awakens us to reality. The beloved who first teaches this real wisdom can be the soul's companion throughout its ascent. In the same *Symposium* where he places the teachings of Diotema, Plato puts in the mouth of the comic playwright Aristophanes an account of sexual love as the attempt of individuals to reconstitute the human being's fundamental god- or goddesslike wholeness. In the beginning, Aristophanes humorously relates, human beings were a marvel to behold, moving rapidly and powerfully through four-legged, four-armed majesty. With such power these entire human beings contended with the gods themselves. Zeus therefore split the original human beings in half, and ever since we have been trying to reconstitute our primordial unity by bonding to one another in sexual union. Here is the true meaning of love: "[H]uman nature was originally one and we were a whole, and the desire and pursuit of the whole is called love." [41] This pursuit of wholeness proceeds through our many incarnations as we perfect ourselves to the point at which we can be restored once more to the original wholeness of our being by finding that very "other half," the true Soul Mate, with whom we were united in the beginning: "Wherefore, if we would praise him who has given to us the benefit, we must praise the god Love, who is our greatest benefactor, both leading us in this life back to our own nature, and giving us high hopes for the future, for he promises that if we are pious, he will restore us to our original state, and heal us and make us happy and blessed."[42]

* * * * *

The outlawed and buried texts of the hidden gospels turn to this and other Platonic sources, to buried passages of the Hebrew Bible, and to the mystery of the mutual love of Jesus and Mary Magdalene that is present throughout the Gospels, for those with eyes to see, to illuminate the meaning of the divine feminine. In the process, overlooked and hidden female sources of Western wisdom come into the forefront of our awareness, from Diotema to Mary Magdalene to the Gnostic and neo-Platonic tradition espoused by Hypatia. Professionally immersed in such literature, symbologist Robert Langdon finds the end of his quest in the very place from which he began. He stands near what on the surface is a miniature pyramid in the Louvre. But for the heightened imagination of the lover of wisdom, this is only the tip of buried depths, the tomb perhaps of Mary Magdalene herself. "With a sudden upwelling of reverence, Robert Langdon fell to his knees. For a moment, he thought he heard a woman's voice . . . the wisdom of the ages . . . whispering up from the chasms of the earth."[43]

NOTES

1. Karen L. King, *The Gospel of Mary of Magdala: Jesus and the First Woman Apostle* (Santa Rosa, CA: Polebridge Press, 2003), 13–18.

2. King, *Gospel of Mary*, 13.

3. King, *Gospel of Mary*, 14. This is a reconstruction of a defective text. King actually translates: "This is why you get si[c]k and die: because [you love] what de[c]ei[v]s you."

4. King, *Gospel of Mary*, 13.

5. King, *Gospel of Mary*, 14.

6. King, *Gospel of Mary*, 16. In Mary's sophisticated teaching on liberation from the seven powers of wrath we see a distant source of Luke's demeaning

and simplistic report that Jesus had once freed Mary from seven devils.

7. King, *Gospel of Mary*, 16.

8. So argues Karen King, *Gospel of Mary*, 41–42.

9. Consider also the implications for abortion. In the framework of reincarnation, abortion may temporarily upset the specific plans of the soul, but it does not destroy the soul's chance at living a human life. However, if the individual soul is intrinsically linked to a specific human body, abortion renders irremediable damage to the person.

10. Dan Brown, *The Da Vinci Code* (New York: Doubleday, 2003), 233.

11. Elaine Pagels, *Beyond Belief: The Secret Gospel of Thomas* (New York: Vintage Books, 2003), 150–51.

12. John 1:1, 1:14. Ronald Knox, trans., *The Holy Bible* (New York: Sheed and Ward, 1956). All subsequent citations from the Bible are from this translation.

13. 2 Samuel 7:13–14. The book of the Bible 2 Samuel is also known as 2 Kings.

14. John 1:49–51. Based on my own search of the Bible texts, Jesus refers to himself as "Son of Man" eighty-five times in the four gospels. Old Testament uses of this designation, with similar connotations, are particularly found in the book of the prophet Ezekiel as the term by which God addresses his prophet (ninety-four times). By contrast, while the term "Son of God" is used in the four gospels twenty-seven times, it is only in the Fourth Gospel that Jesus himself adopts this title, together with that of "Son of Man."

15. John 1:14–18. Knox's comment is on p. 86 of the New Testament. Footnote 4 apparently refers to both instances of this expression.

16. Pagels, *Beyond Belief*, 175.

17. King, *Gospel of Mary*, 15.

18. "For I do nothing but go about persuading you all, old and young alike, not to take thought for your persons and your properties, but first and chiefly to care about the greatest improvement of the soul. I tell you that virtue is not given by money, but that from virtue come money and every other good of man, public as well as private." Plato, *Apology*, in *The Dialogues of Plato*, vol. 7 of *Great Books of the Western World* (Chicago: Encyclopaedia Britannica, Inc., 1952), 206; 30.

19. King, *Gospel of Mary*, 17.

20. King, *Gospel of Mary*, 17.

21. King, *Gospel of Mary*, 17.

22. King, *Gospel of Mary*, 18.

23. The Gospel of Thomas, logion 114. Robert W. Funk, Roy W. Hoover, and the Jesus Seminar, translation and commentary, *The Five Gospels* (San Francisco: HarperSanFrancisco, 1993), 532.

24. Gospel of Philip 63:30–34. Cited from King, *Gospel of Mary*, 145. I have omitted brackets used to indicate reconstructed parts of this text.

25. King, *Gospel of Mary*, 204.

26. Exodus 19:14–15.

27. See Thomas Cahill, *The Gifts of the Jews: How a Tribe of Desert Nomads Changed the Way Everyone Thinks and Feels* (New York: Doubleday, 1998), 42–44.

28. Daniel C. Matt, introduction to *The Essential Kabbalah* (Edison, NJ: Castle Books, 1997), 1–2.

29. Pagels, *Beyond Belief,* 94.

30. Gospel of Philip 55:24:36. In James M. Robinson, general editor, *The Nag Hammadi Library* (San Francisco: HarperSanFrancisco: 1990), 143. I have removed brackets indicating reconstruction.

31. Pagels, *Beyond Belief,* 131.

32. See Brown, *Da Vinci Code,* 322. The cryptex is a small box which opens when its numerous dials line up correctly.

33. Genesis 1:27. In her seminal work, *The Gnostic Gospels*, Elaine Pagels devotes a detailed chapter to this topic, "God the Father/God the Mother." Elaine Pagels, *The Gnostic Gospels* (New York: Vintage books, 1981), 57–83.

34. Genesis 1:26. That the creation is the result of the union of the male god Jehovah and a female goddess is the teaching of the Mormons, the Church of Jesus Christ of Latter Day Saints. Mormons also suggest that Mary Magdalene was the wife of Jesus. See "Mary Magdalene's modern makeover," by James Patrick Holding, at http://www.equip.org/atf/cf/%7B9C4EE03A-F988-4091-84BD-F8E70A3B0215%7D/JAM015.pdf.

35. That is, whether heterosexual or homosexual. Rejection of homophobia is implicit in these texts. It is the spiritual meaning, not the biological, of male and female principles, like yang and yin, that counts for the Gospel of Philip, just as for the Gospel of Mary to discriminate based on the attributes of the body by itself is to commit "the sin of the world." Nevertheless, these spiritual meanings must be physically embodied in some form or other.

36. The Gospel of Thomas, logion 114, from Funk, Hoover, and Jesus Seminar, *Five Gospels,* 532.

37. Hegel, *Lectures on the Philosophy of Religion,* 1:347.

38. Plato, *Symposium,* vol. 7 of *Great Books of the Western World* (Chicago: Encyclopaedia Britannica, 1952), 167; 210.

39. Jacques Baldet, *Jesus the Rabbi Prophet* (Rochester, VT: Inner Traditions, 2005), 138–39.

40. The Gospel of Truth, in Robinson, *Nag Hammadi Library,* 40.

41. Plato, *Symposium,* 158; 192–93.

42. Plato, *Symposium,* 159; 193.

43. Brown, *Da Vinci Code,* 454.

Epilogue

John Dominic Crossan, the historian of the historical Jesus,[1] said in a recorded question and answer period after a Chautauqua lecture:

> I think the next century's debate is not going to be between science and religion, both of which are losing out to fantasy. The next debate really is religion and fantasy, and whether religion will become a small but important subsection of fantasy. . . . My undergraduates said they have no problem with the resurrection of Jesus as bodily because Elvis Presley was back too. . . . I realized: I'm back in the first century. I have to hustle for my resurrection against your resurrection. They had no problem with miracles. They had seen all the funny stuff. . . . [Crossan mentions the film *The Sixth Sense*.] It's all weird out there—*The X-Files*. This [i.e., Christianity] is just one more subsection of the weirdness. All right then, we have to go out and fight for *our* weirdness.[2]

In his books and lectures Crossan is not arguing against the competing and prevailing fantasies of contemporary film and TV, but with profound misinterpretations of the Christian religion. The God of Jesus, he argues with historical cogency, was a God of distributive justice, not a God of power and retribution, a God of radical egalitarianism, not a God of hierarchies and exclusions. But since the Roman emperor Constantine called the Council of Nicea in 325 CE to establish and impose a creed of orthodox Christian beliefs, he argues, dominant currents of Christianity have defended just such a God of power and hierarchy. The only way to restore authentic Christianity, he concludes, is to return to the teaching of the historical Jesus and challenge the inequalities of our own time as

Jesus would have done. Young people, he says, will respond to that idea just as courageous early Christians, opposing the heartlessness and injustice of the Roman Empire, had done.

If such is the core idea of Christianity, why not look more closely at some of the fantasy, at some of the surrounding weirdness that is overwhelming both established religions and science, and recognize that here too can be found messages of radical egalitarianism and social empowerment similar to the teachings of Jesus? As such they evoke alternative traditions in the history of philosophy, as in the works of Kant and Hegel, that have sought to rethink this tradition in ways that reinforce human freedom and equality, while challenging stultifying conceptions of external religion. Such fantasies that seek to challenge the inequalities of our time, while deepening our understanding of what constitutes a true human life, are in fact a potential complement to, and in many ways a rediscovery of, the gospel of the historical Jesus.

NOTES

[1] John Dominic Crossan, *The Historical Jesus: Life of a Mediterranean Peasant* (San Franscisco: HarperSanFrancisco, 1991); *The Birth of Christianity: Discovering What Happened in the Years Immediately after the Execution of Jesus* (San Franscisco: HarperSanFrancisco, 1998).

[2] John Dominic Crossan, Chautauqua Lecture Series 2000, week 4, lecture 3, "How? The Methods for Historical Jesus Research," at 1 hour, 02:33–04:08. The lecture series can be ordered at www.ciweb.org.

Index

REMOVE

CPSIA information can be obtained
at www.ICGtesting.com
Printed in the USA
BVHW03s1701220718
522313BV00001B/44/P